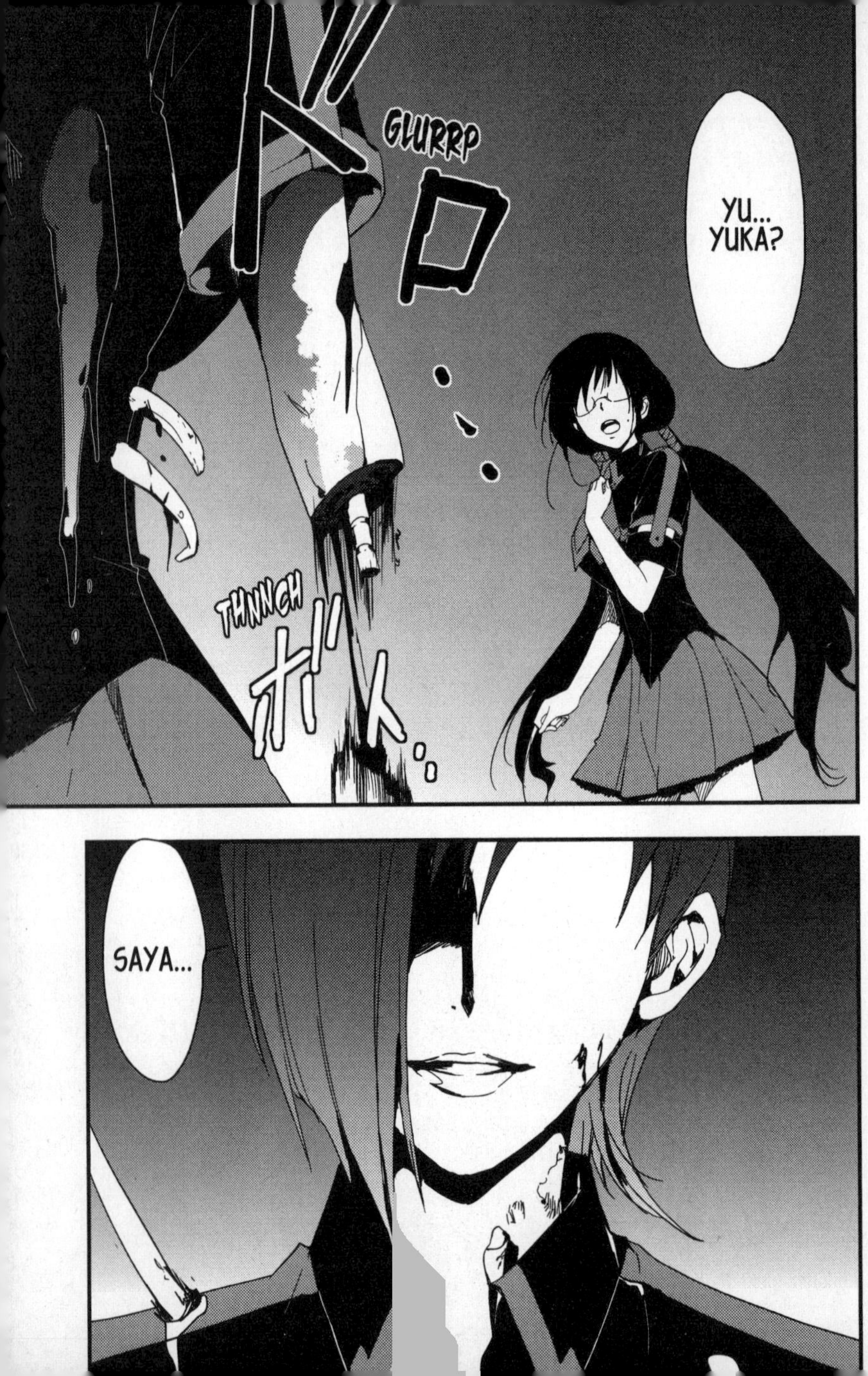
YU... YUKA?
GLURRP
ドロ
THNNCH
SAYA...

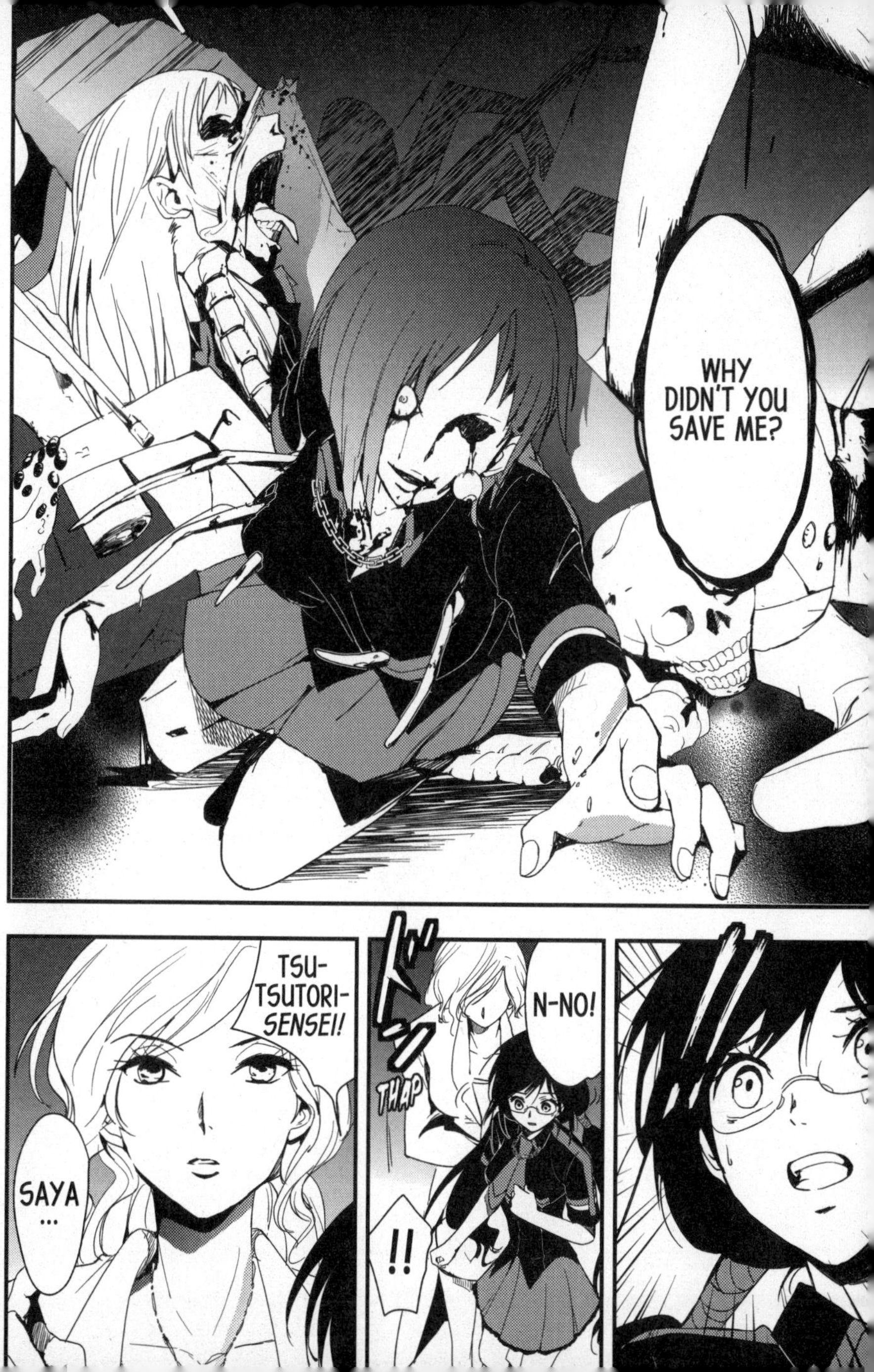
WHY DIDN'T YOU SAVE ME?
N-NO!
THAP
!!
TSU-TSUTORI-SENSEI!
SAYA ...

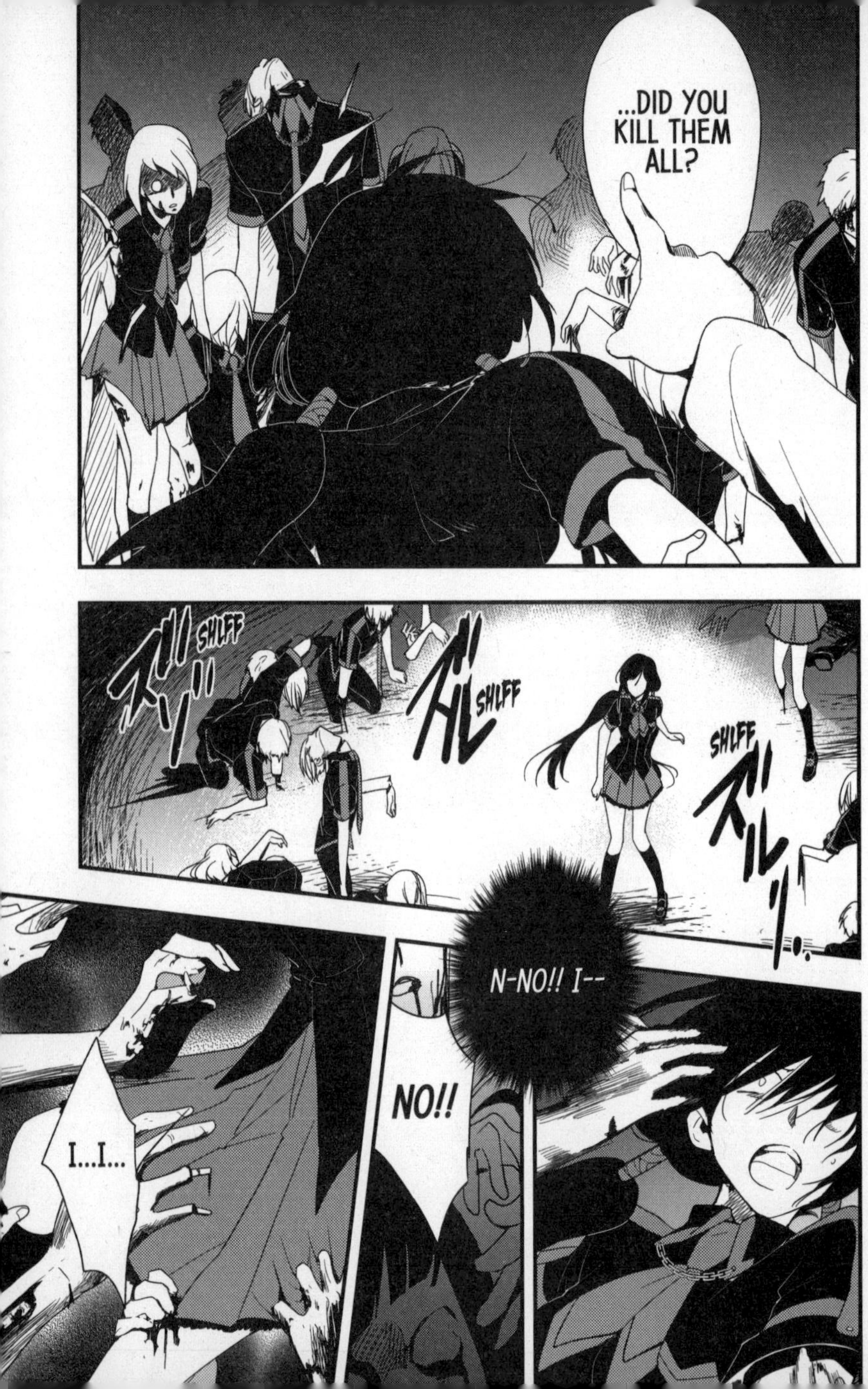
...DID YOU KILL THEM ALL?
SHLFF
SHLFF
SHLFF
N-NO!! I--
NO!!
I...I...

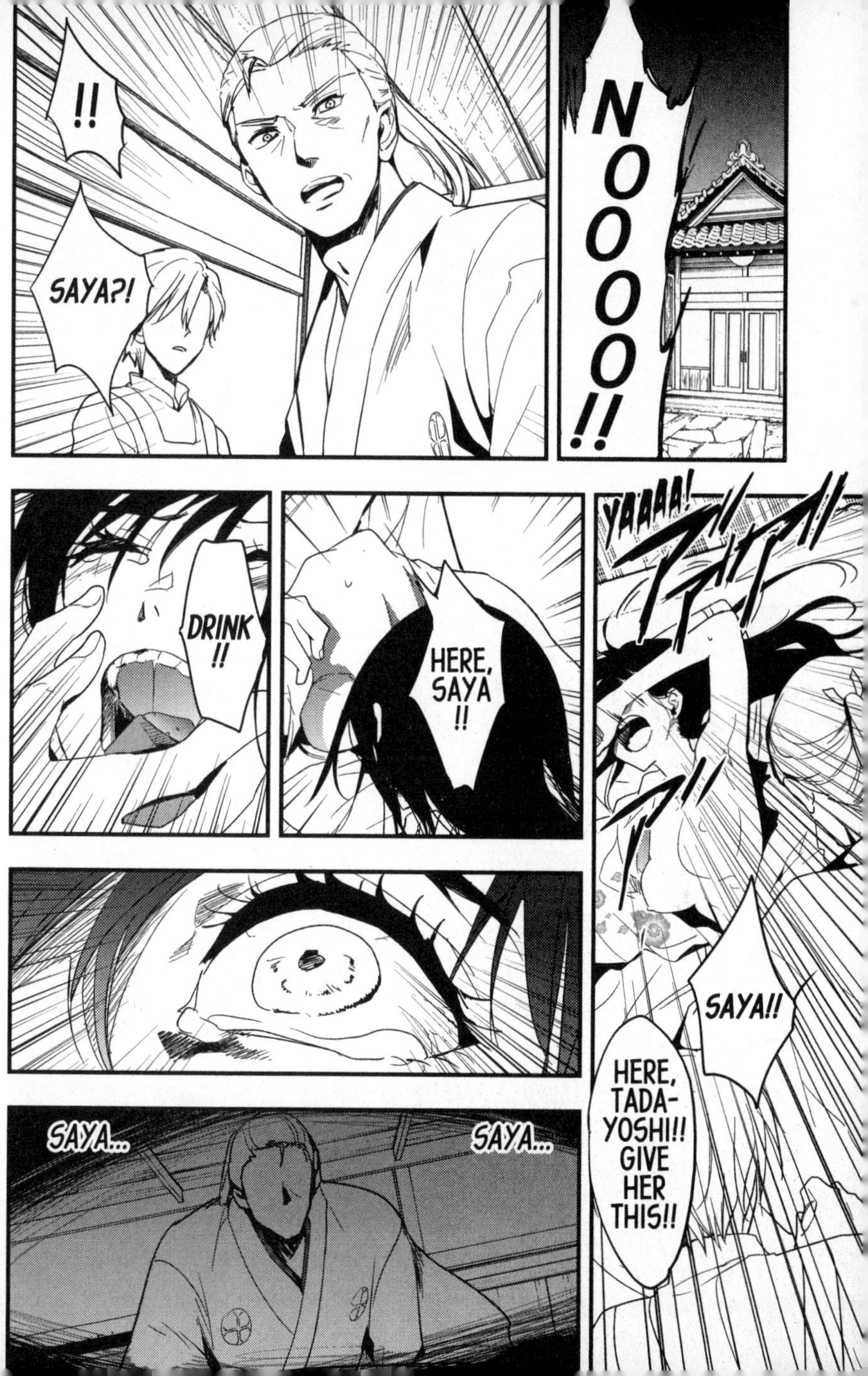

NOOOO!!
!!
SAYA?!
YAAAA!
SAYA!!
HERE, TADA-YOSHI!!! GIVE HER THIS!!
HERE, SAYA!!
DRINK!!
SAYA...
SAYA...

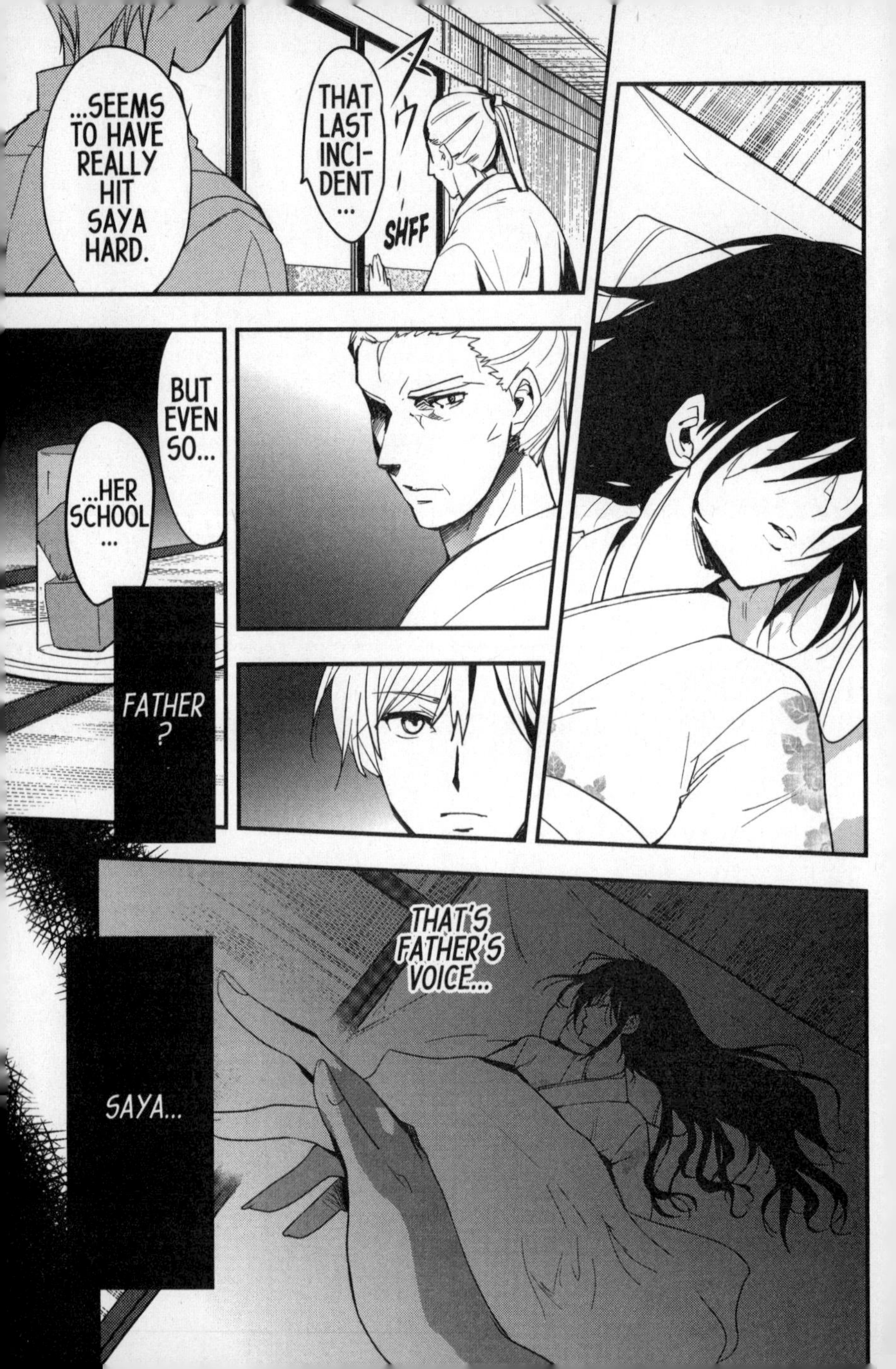
THAT LAST INCIDENT...
SHFF
...SEEMS TO HAVE REALLY HIT SAYA HARD.
BUT EVEN SO...
...HER SCHOOL...
FATHER?
THAT'S FATHER'S VOICE...
SAYA...

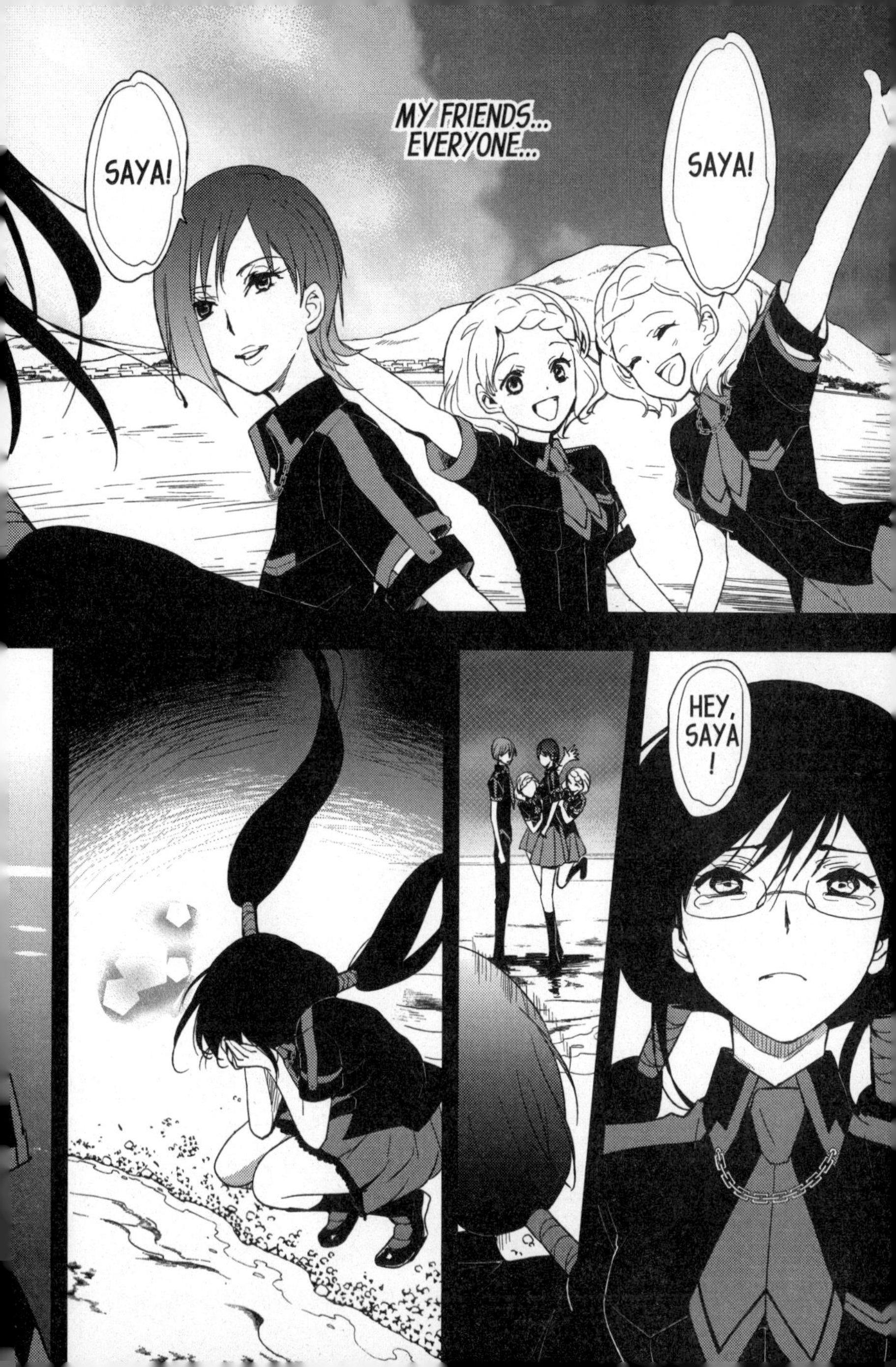
SAYA!
MY FRIENDS... EVERYONE...
SAYA!
HEY, SAYA!

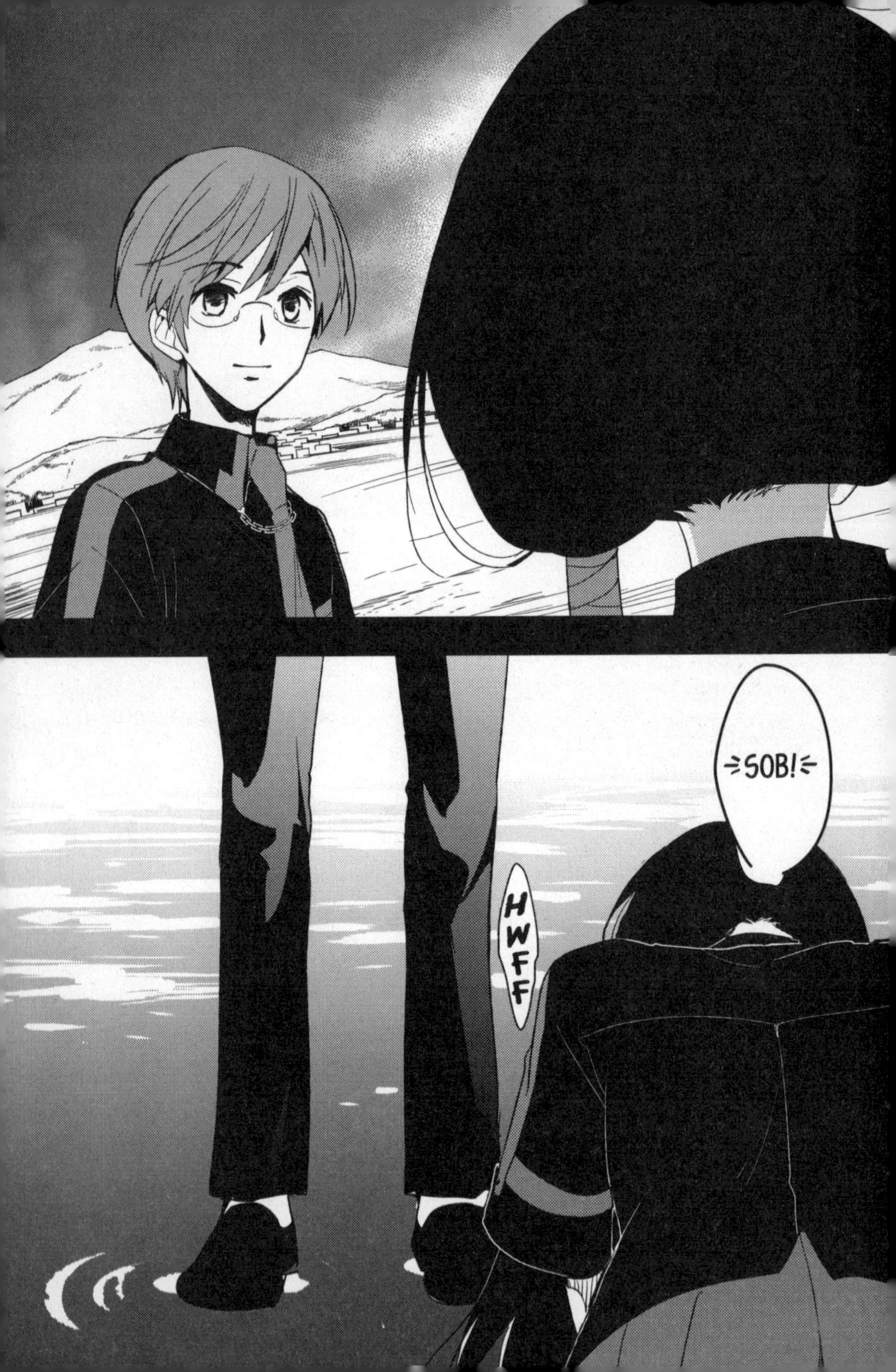
SOB!
HWFF

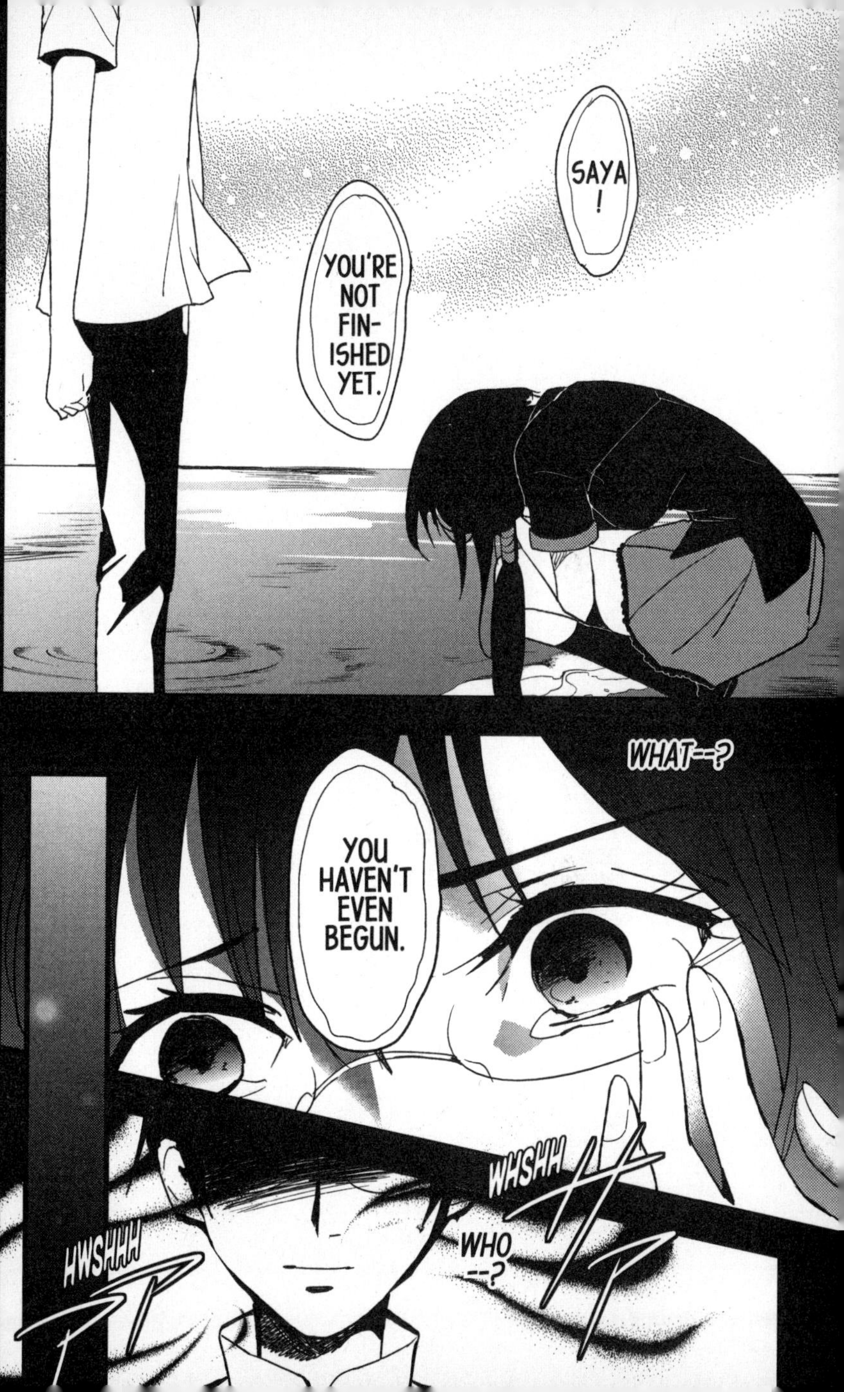
SAYA!
YOU'RE NOT FIN-ISHED YET.
WHAT--?
YOU HAVEN'T EVEN BEGUN.
WHSHH
WHO --?
HWSHHH

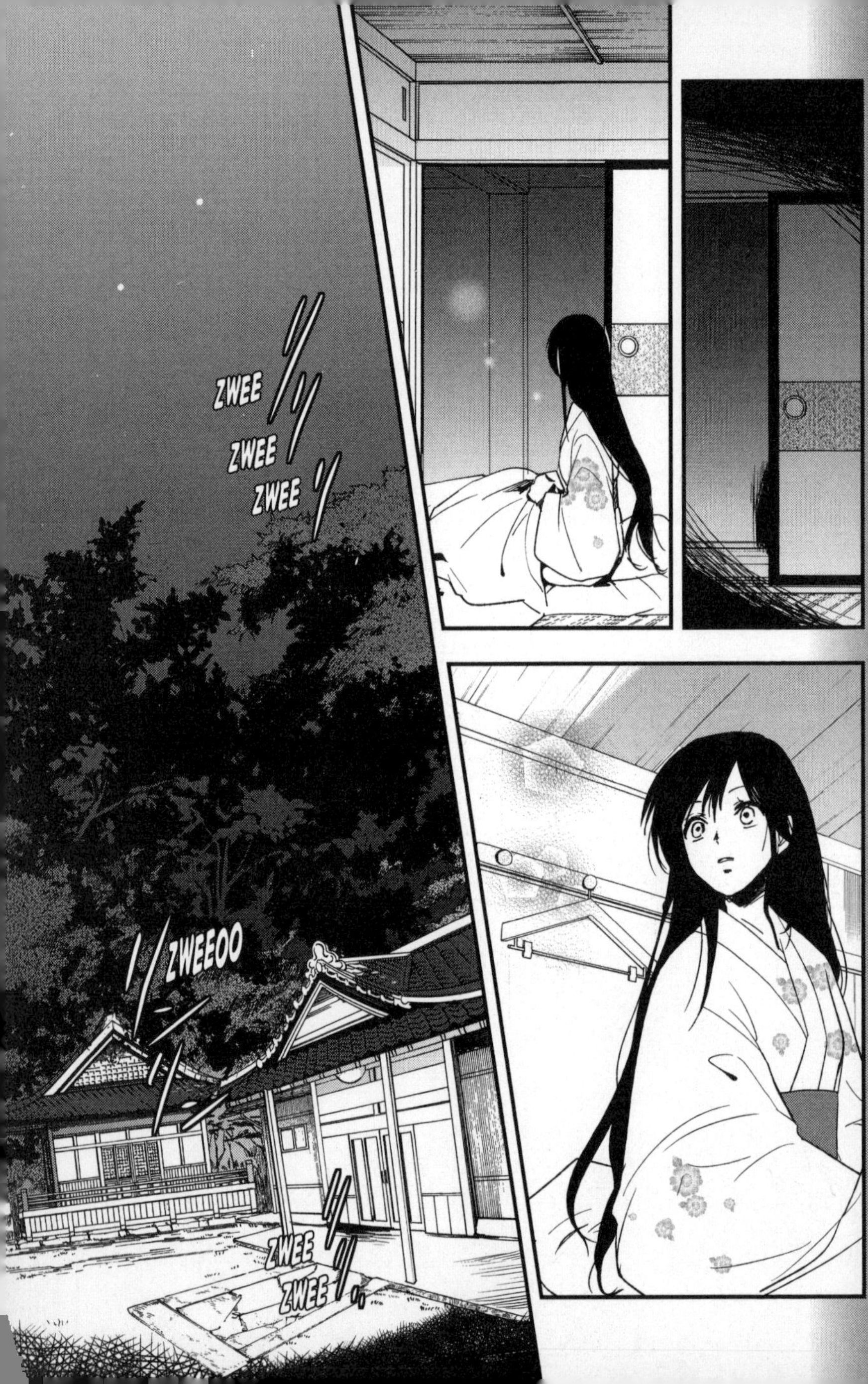
ZWEE
ZWEE
ZWEE
ZWEEOO
ZWEE
ZWEE

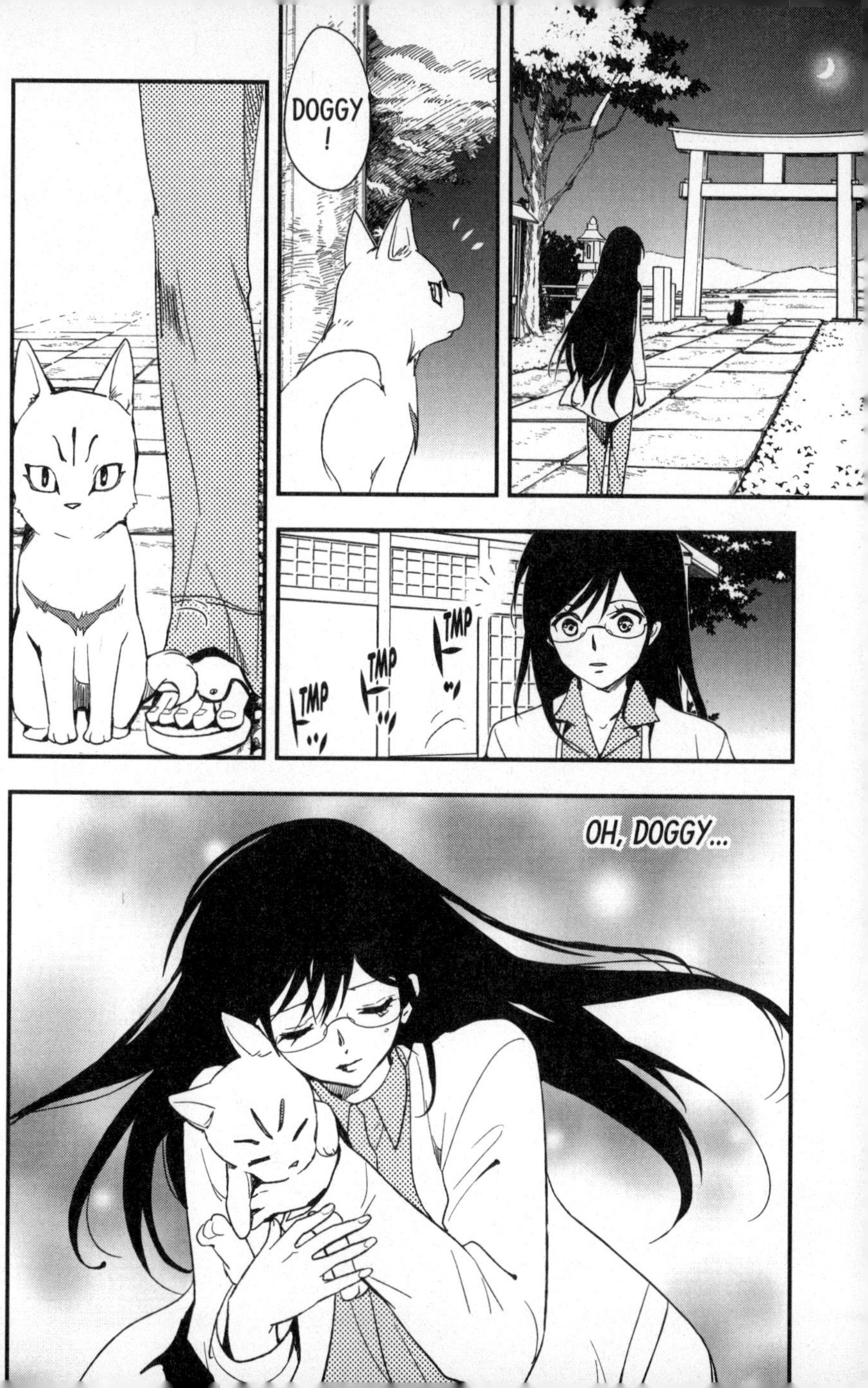
DOGGY
!
TMP
TMP
TMP
OH, DOGGY...

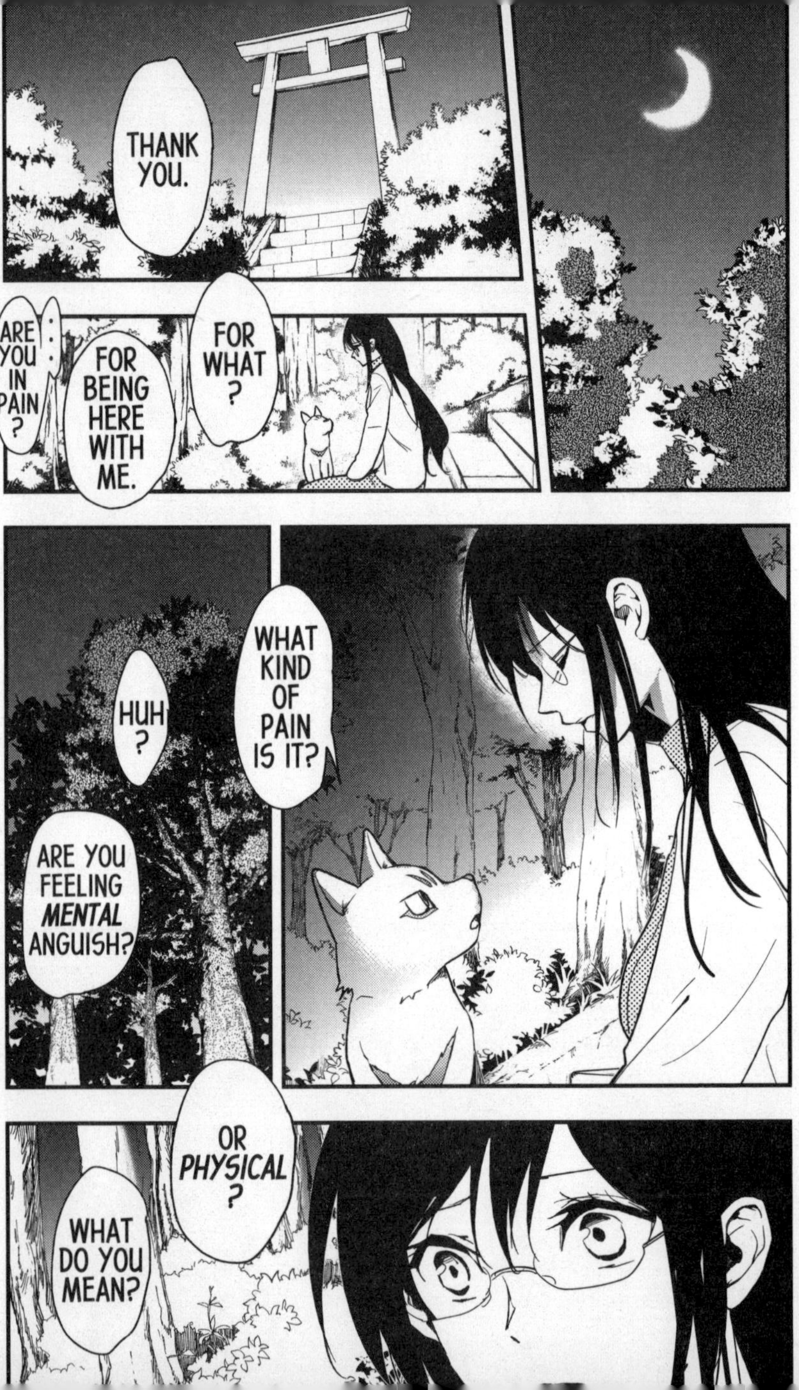
THANK YOU.
FOR WHAT?
FOR BEING HERE WITH ME.
...
ARE YOU IN PAIN?
WHAT KIND OF PAIN IS IT?
HUH?
ARE YOU FEELING MENTAL ANGUISH?
OR PHYSICAL?
WHAT DO YOU MEAN?

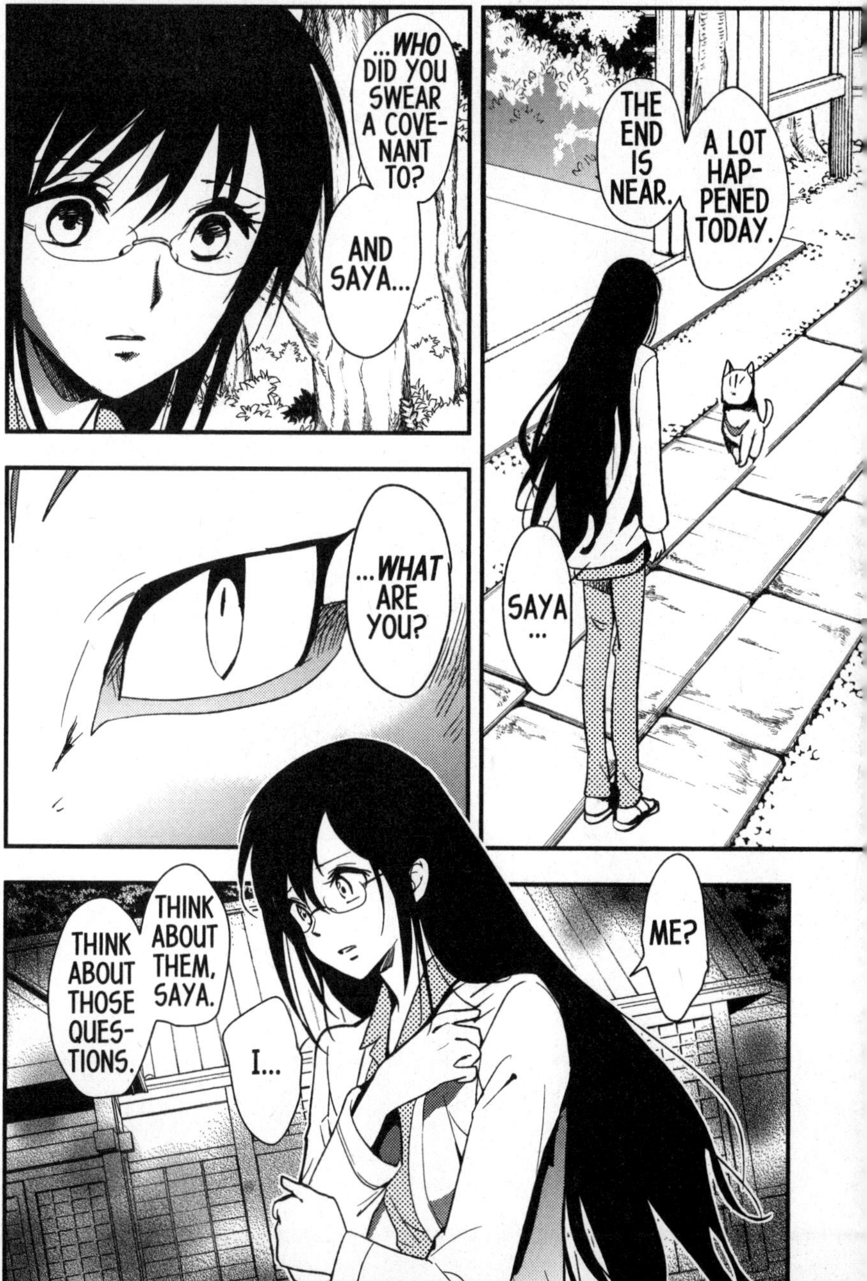
A LOT HAPPENED TODAY.
THE END IS NEAR.
SAYA...
...WHO DID YOU SWEAR A COVENANT TO?
AND SAYA...
...WHAT ARE YOU?
ME?
THINK ABOUT THEM, SAYA.
THINK ABOUT THOSE QUESTIONS.
I...

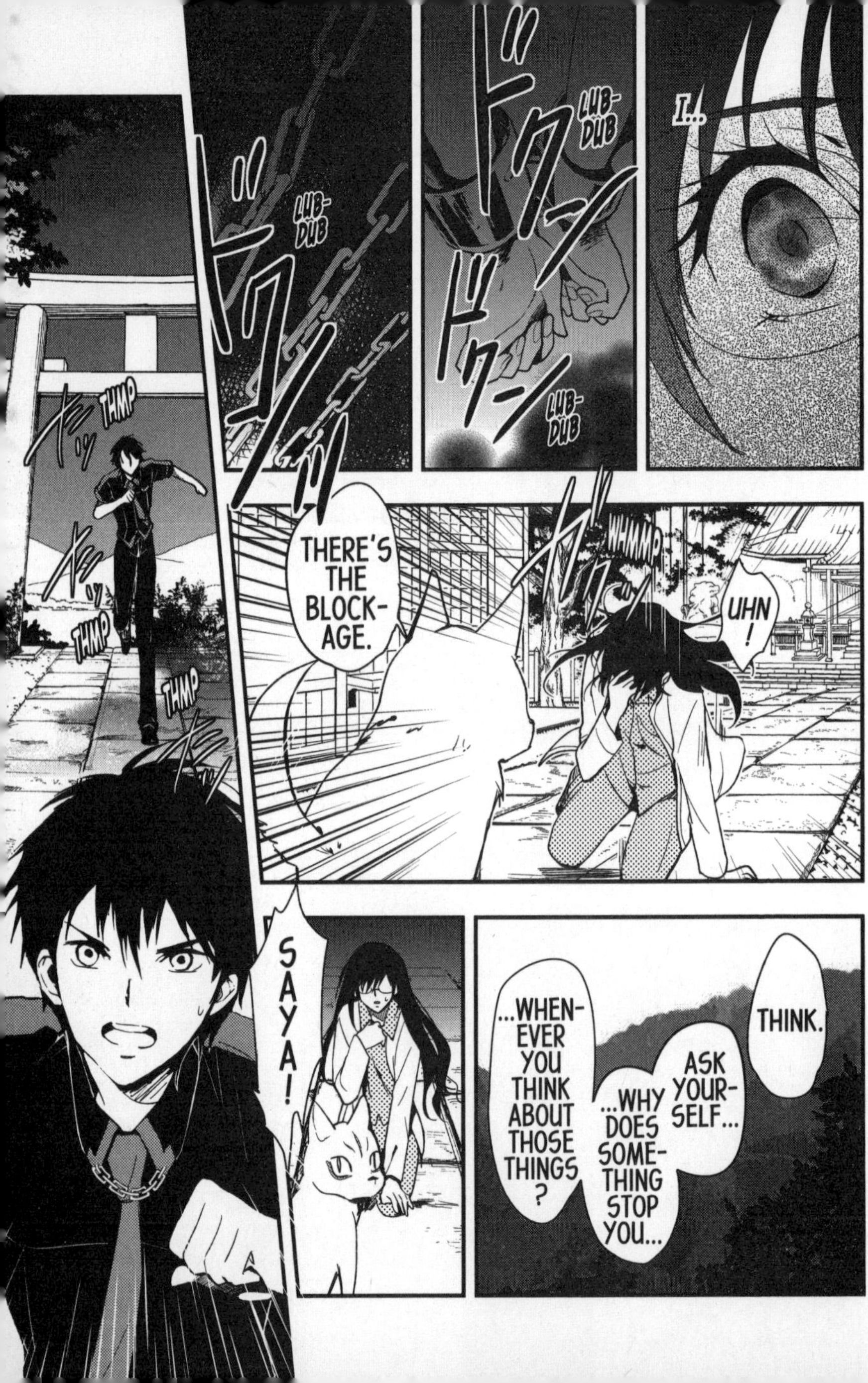

I...
ドクン
LUB-DUB
ドクン
LUB-DUB
ドクン
LUB-DUB
UHN!
WHMMP
THERE'S THE BLOCK-AGE.
THMP
THMP
THMP
THINK.
ASK YOUR-SELF...
...WHY DOES SOME-THING STOP YOU...
...WHEN-EVER YOU THINK ABOUT THOSE THINGS?
SAYA!

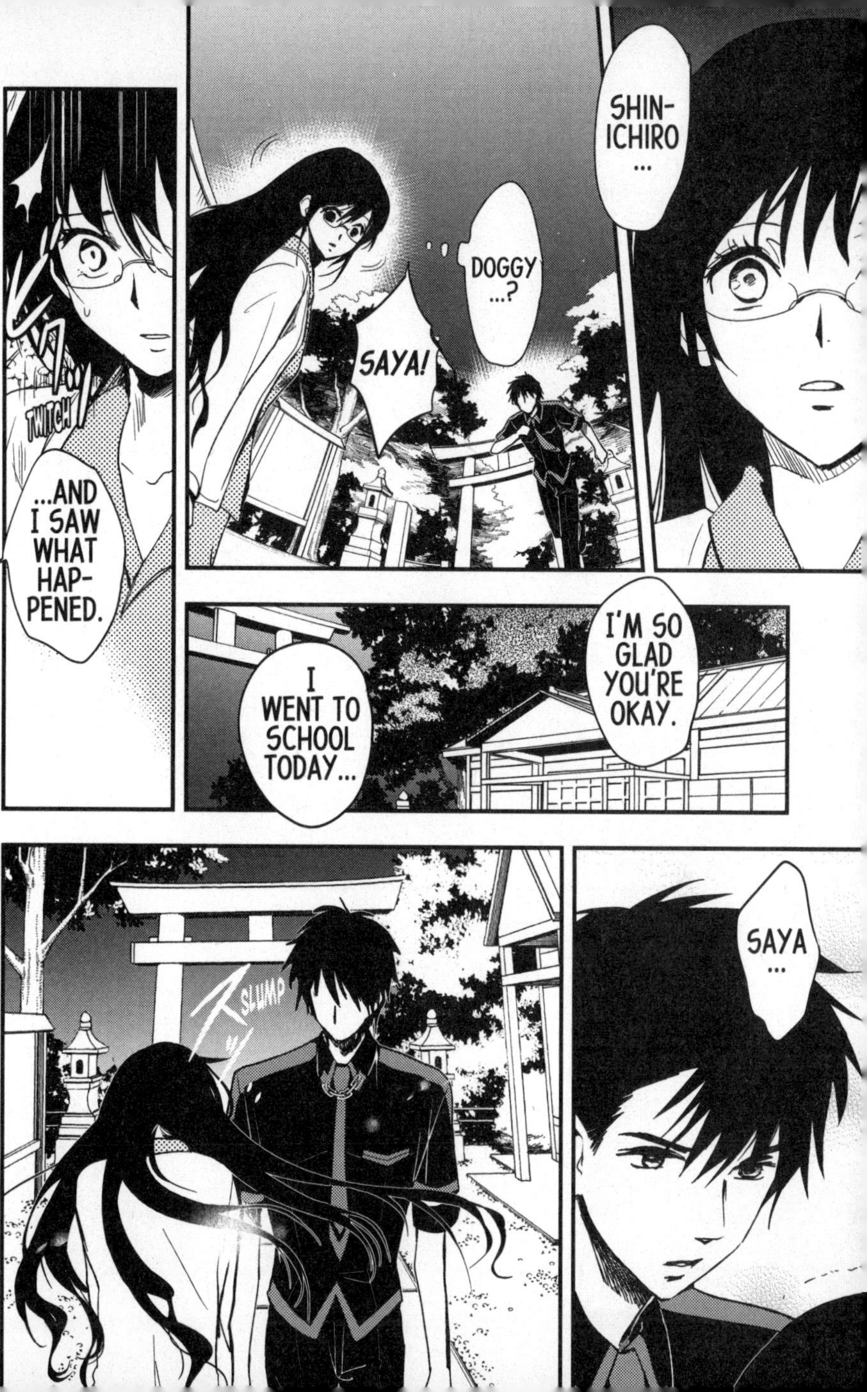
SHIN-ICHIRO...
DOGGY...?
SAYA!
I'M SO GLAD YOU'RE OKAY.
I WENT TO SCHOOL TODAY...
TWITCH
...AND I SAW WHAT HAPPENED.
SAYA...
SLUMP

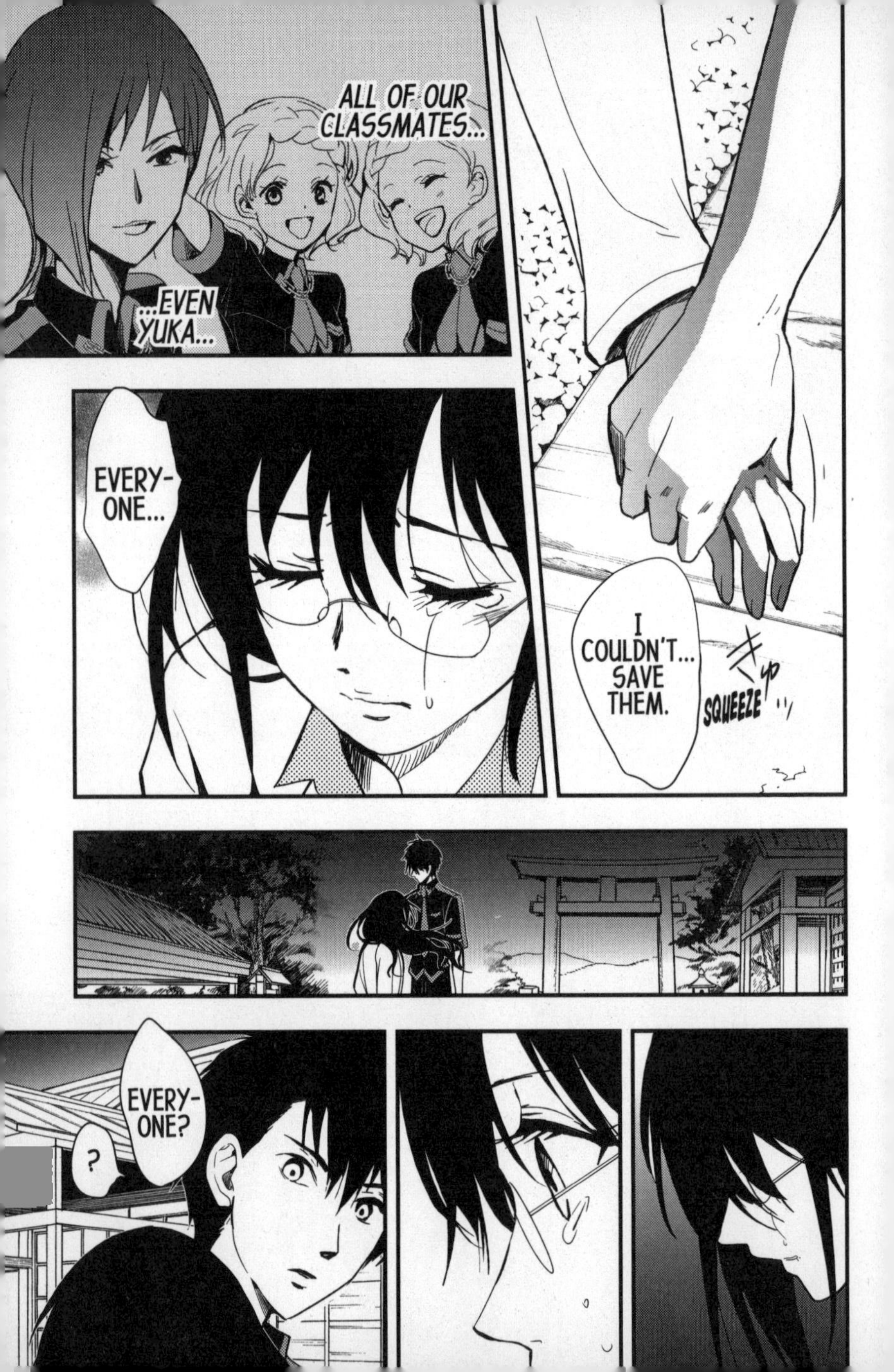
I COULDN'T... SAVE THEM.
SQUEEZE
ALL OF OUR CLASSMATES...
...EVEN YUKA...
EVERY-ONE...
EVERY-ONE?
?

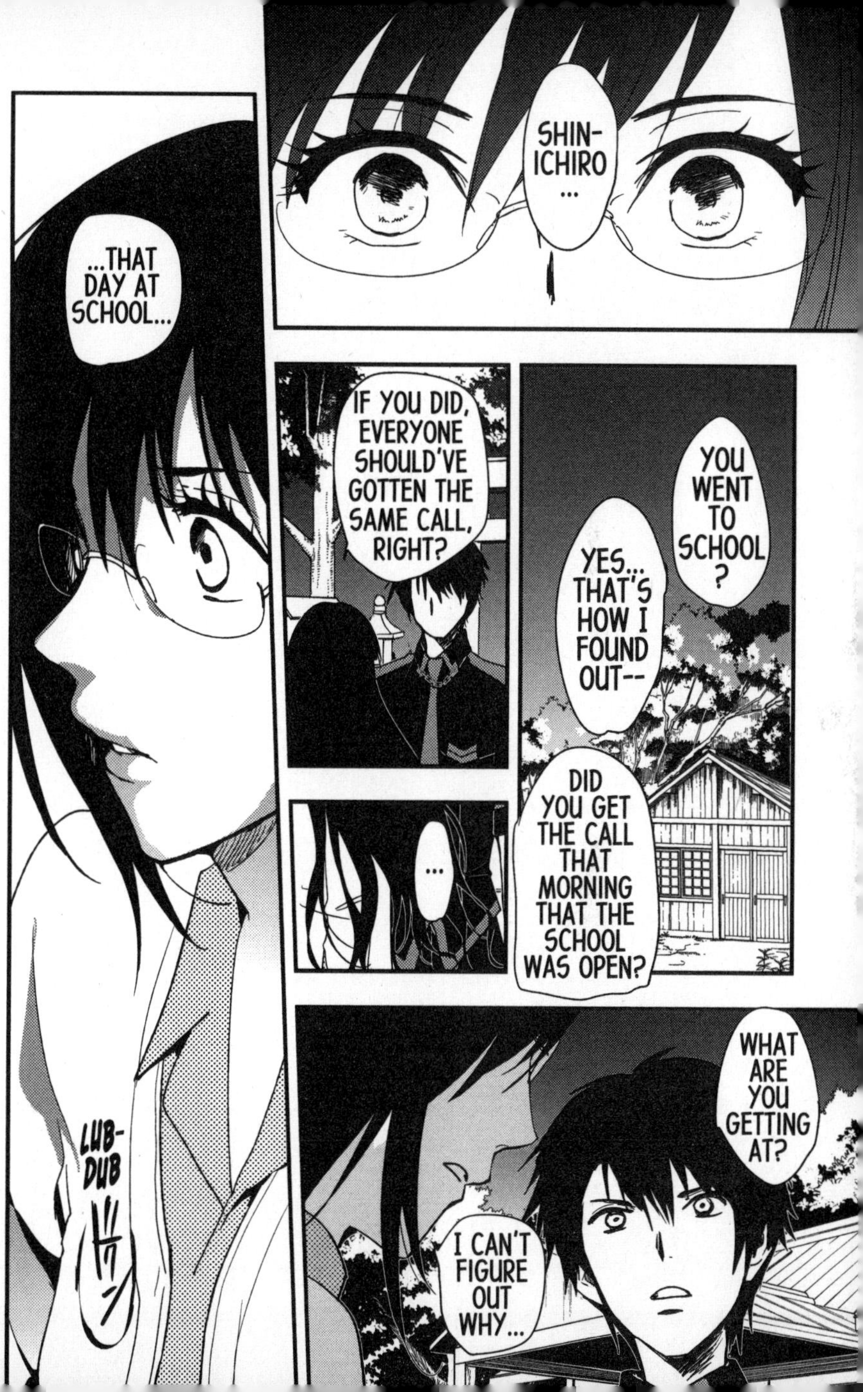
SHIN-ICHIRO ...
YOU WENT TO SCHOOL ?
YES... THAT'S HOW I FOUND OUT--
DID YOU GET THE CALL THAT MORNING THAT THE SCHOOL WAS OPEN?
IF YOU DID, EVERYONE SHOULD'VE GOTTEN THE SAME CALL, RIGHT?
...
WHAT ARE YOU GETTING AT?
I CAN'T FIGURE OUT WHY...
...THAT DAY AT SCHOOL...
LUB-DUB

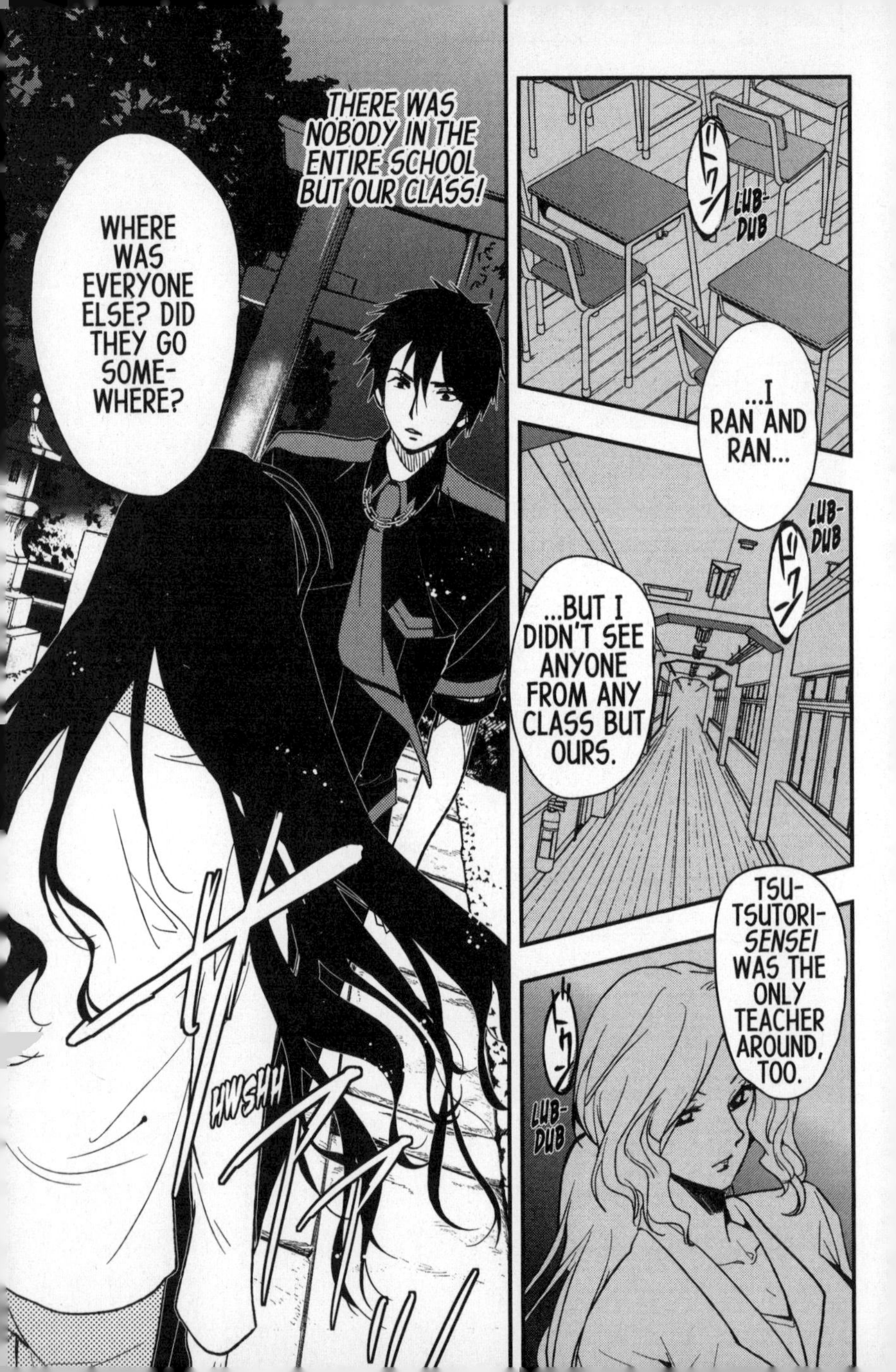
LUB-DUB
...I RAN AND RAN...
LUB-DUB
...BUT I DIDN'T SEE ANYONE FROM ANY CLASS BUT OURS.
TSU-TSUTORI-SENSEI WAS THE ONLY TEACHER AROUND, TOO.
LUB-DUB
THERE WAS NOBODY IN THE ENTIRE SCHOOL BUT OUR CLASS!
WHERE WAS EVERYONE ELSE? DID THEY GO SOME-WHERE?
HWSHH

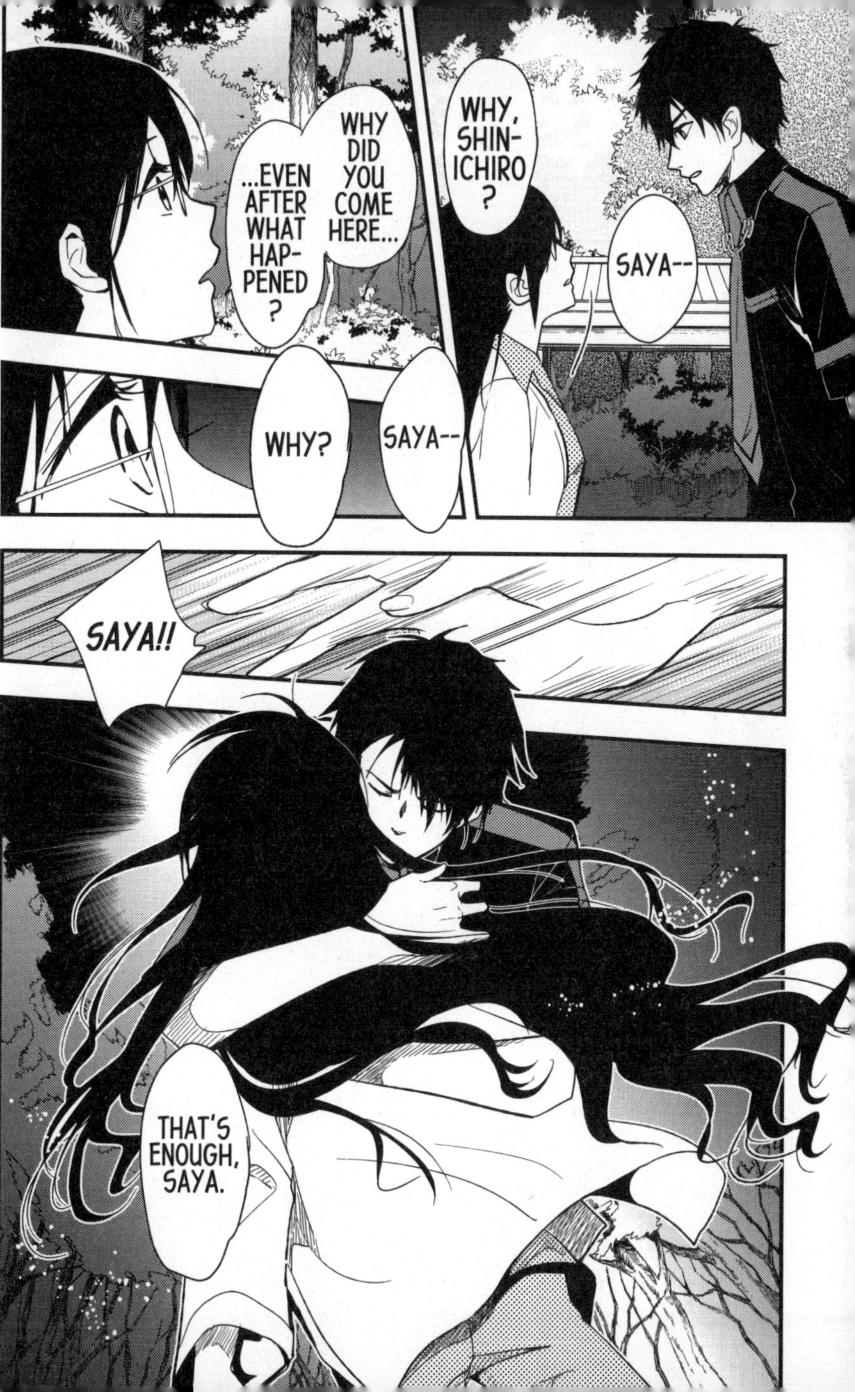
SAYA--
WHY, SHIN-ICHIRO?
WHY DID YOU COME HERE...
...EVEN AFTER WHAT HAP-PENED?
SAYA--
WHY?
SAYA!!
THAT'S ENOUGH, SAYA.

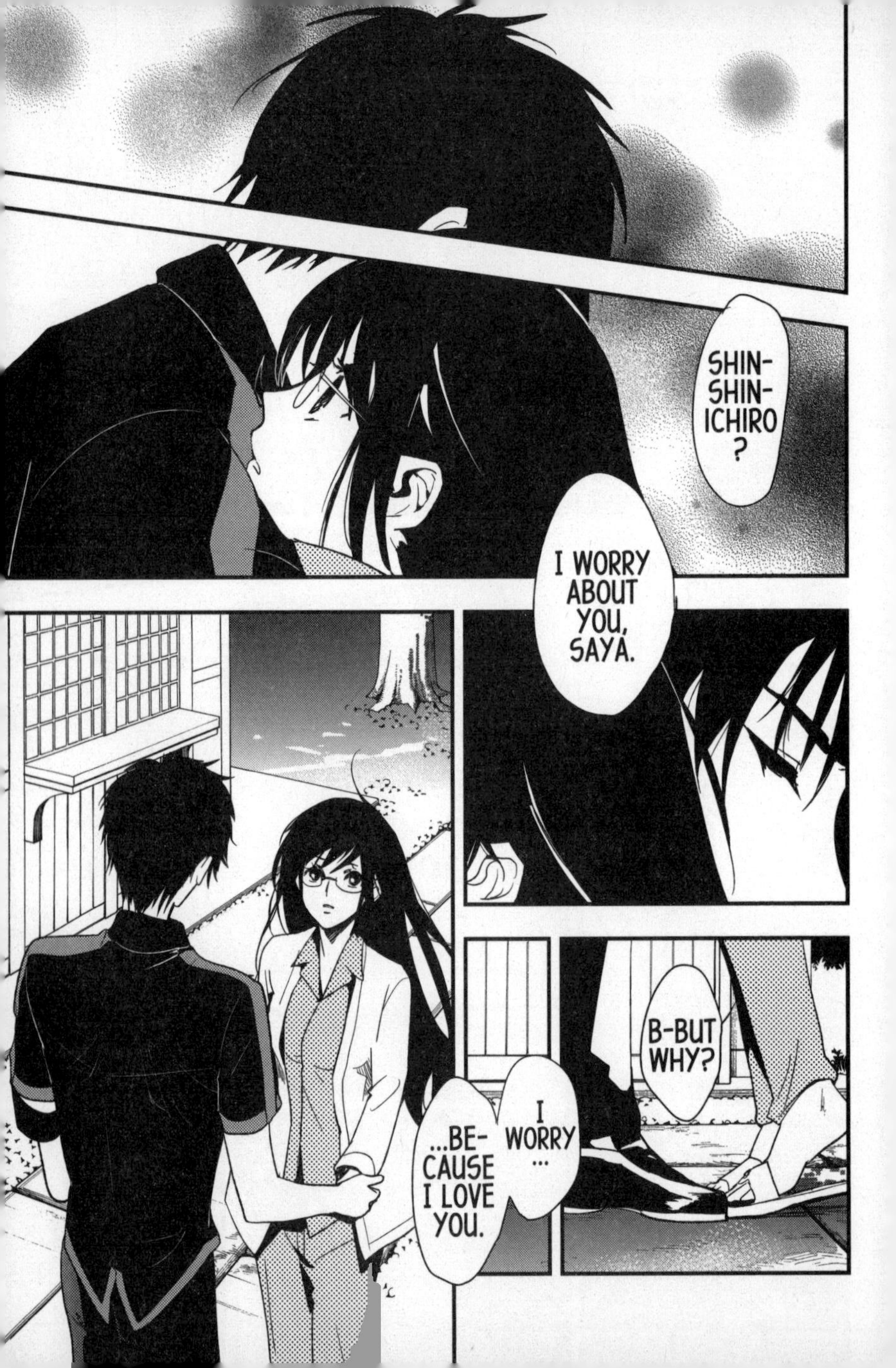
SHIN-SHIN-ICHIRO?
I WORRY ABOUT YOU, SAYA.
B-BUT WHY?
I WORRY...
...BE-CAUSE I LOVE YOU.

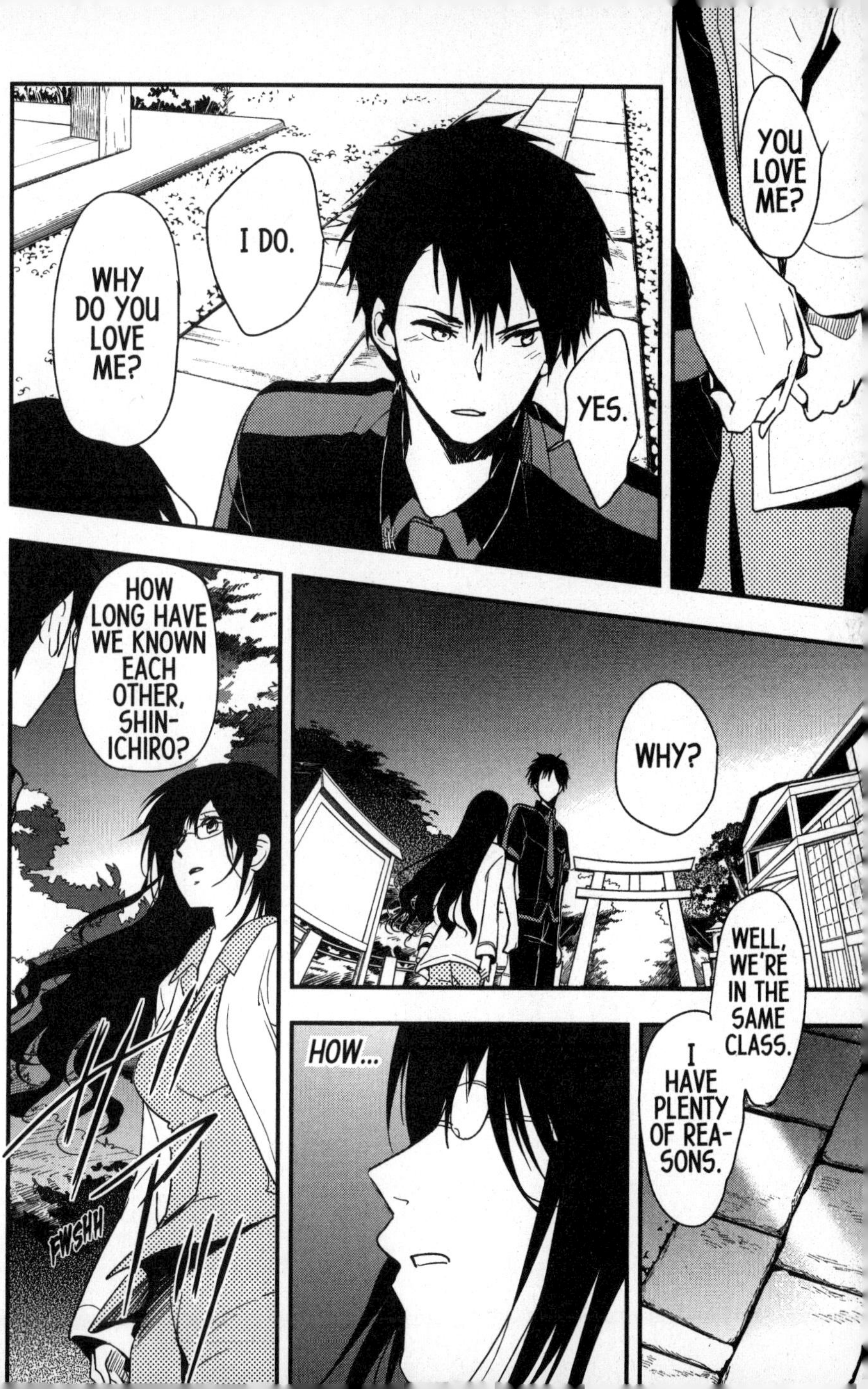
YOU LOVE ME?
YES.
I DO.
WHY DO YOU LOVE ME?
WHY?
WELL, WE'RE IN THE SAME CLASS.
I HAVE PLENTY OF REA-SONS.
HOW...
HOW LONG HAVE WE KNOWN EACH OTHER, SHIN-ICHIRO?
FWSHH

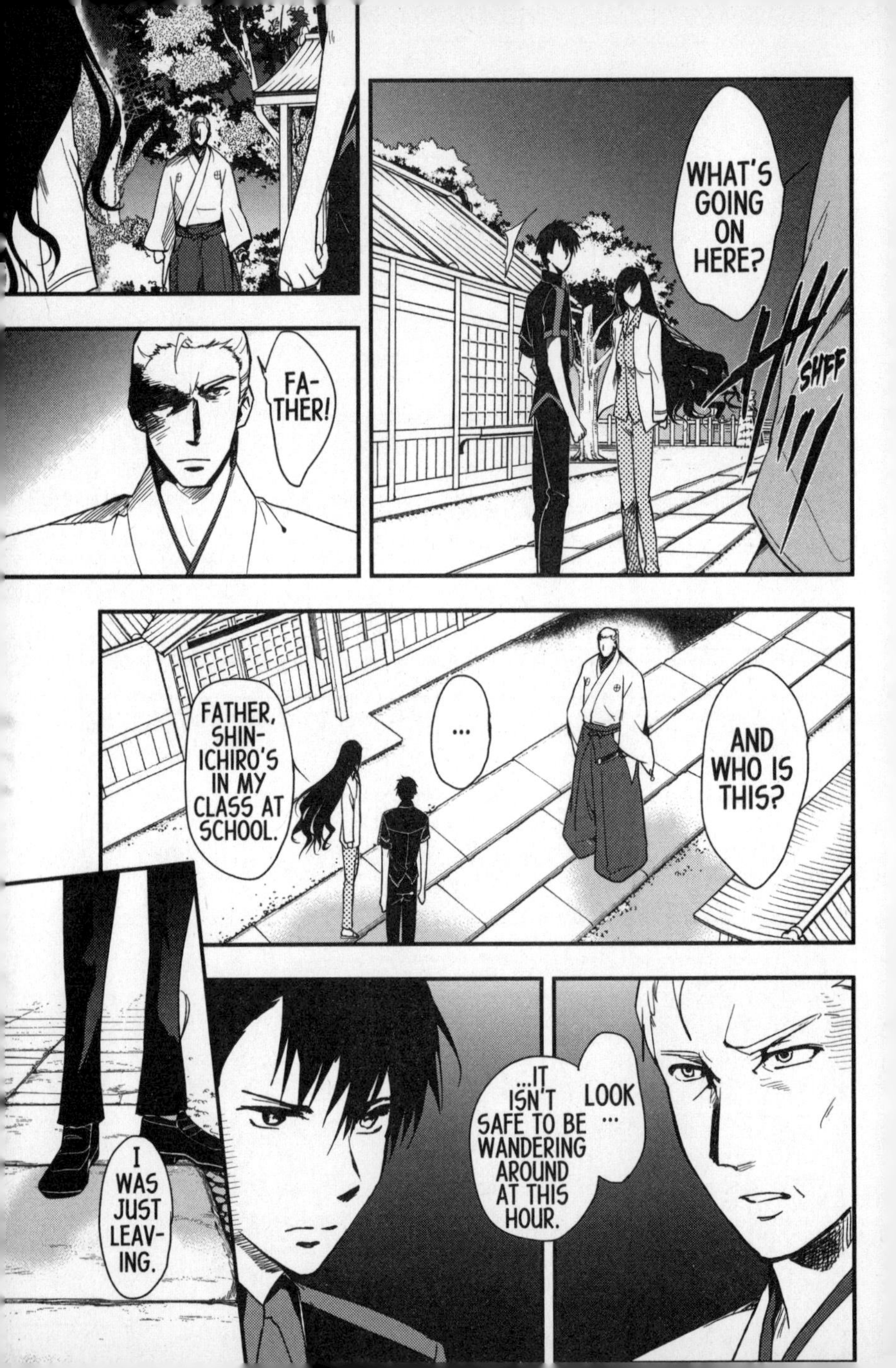
WHAT'S GOING ON HERE?
SHFF
FA-THER!
AND WHO IS THIS?
...
FATHER, SHIN-ICHIRO'S IN MY CLASS AT SCHOOL.
LOOK...
...IT ISN'T SAFE TO BE WANDERING AROUND AT THIS HOUR.
I WAS JUST LEAV-ING.

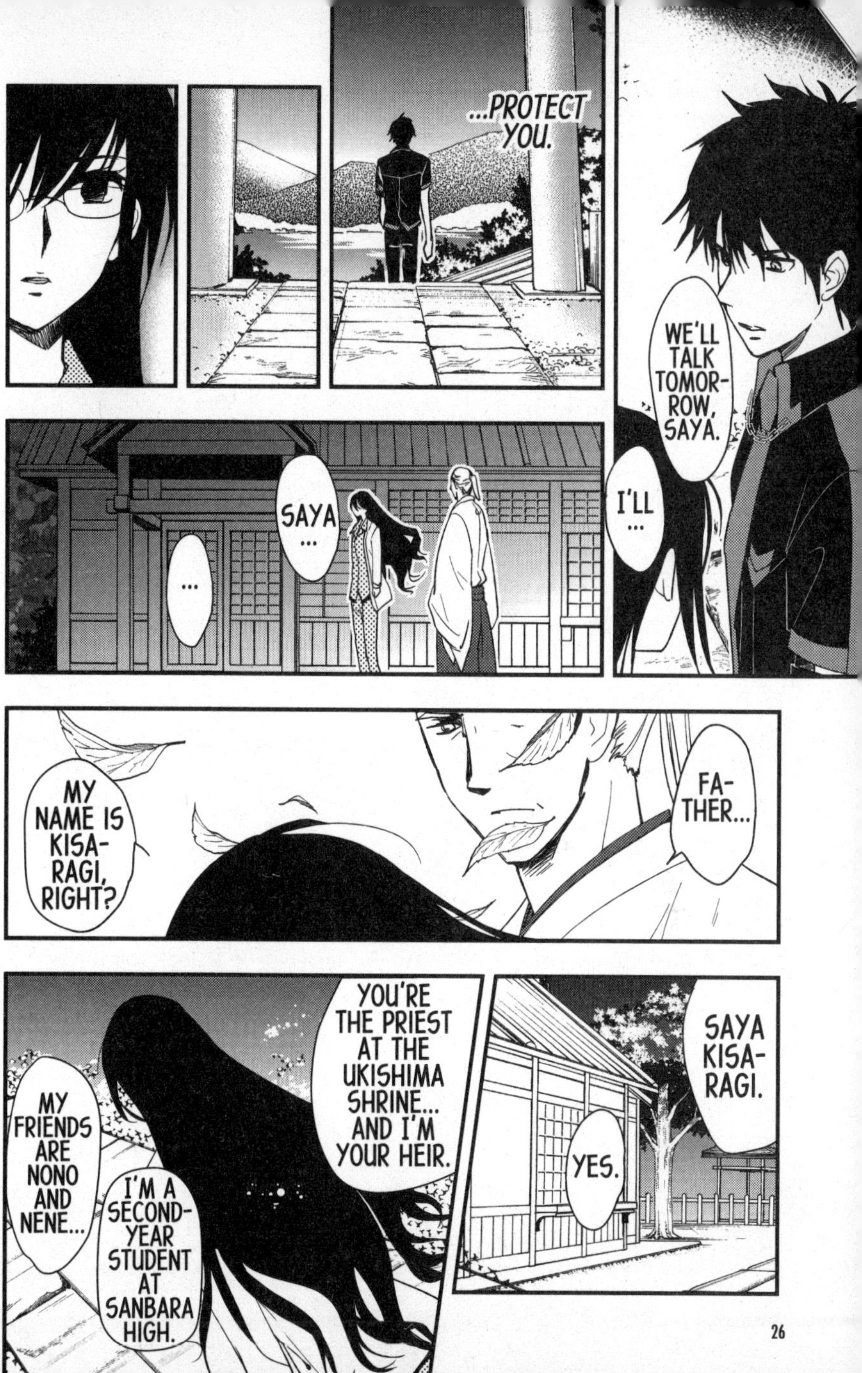
WE'LL TALK TOMORROW, SAYA.
I'LL ...
...PROTECT YOU.
SAYA ...
...
FATHER...
MY NAME IS KISARAGI, RIGHT?
SAYA KISARAGI.
YES.
YOU'RE THE PRIEST AT THE UKISHIMA SHRINE... AND I'M YOUR HEIR.
MY FRIENDS ARE NONO AND NENE...
I'M A SECOND-YEAR STUDENT AT SANBARA HIGH.

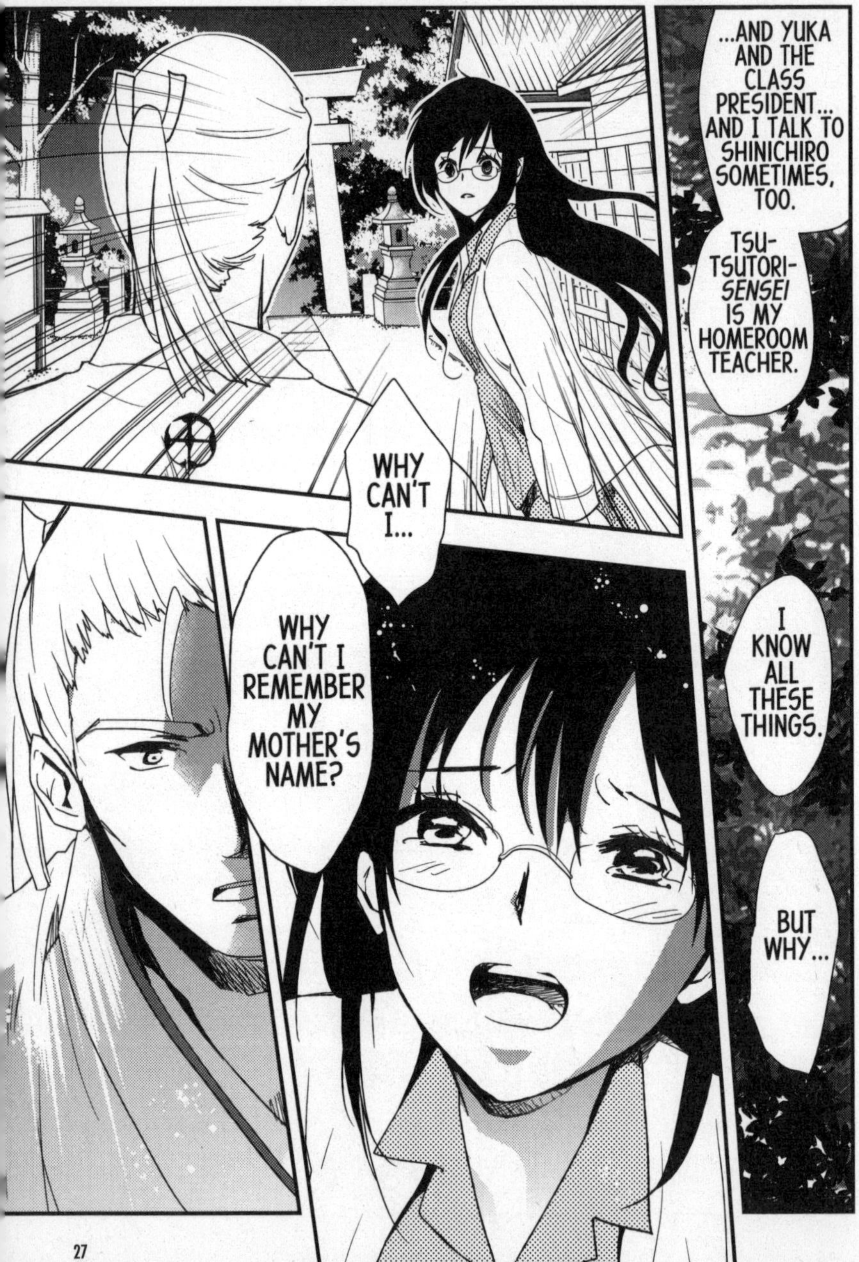
...AND YUKA AND THE CLASS PRESIDENT... AND I TALK TO SHINICHIRO SOMETIMES, TOO.
TSU-TSUTORI-*SENSEI* IS MY HOMEROOM TEACHER.
I KNOW ALL THESE THINGS.
BUT WHY...
WHY CAN'T I...
WHY CAN'T I REMEMBER MY MOTHER'S NAME?

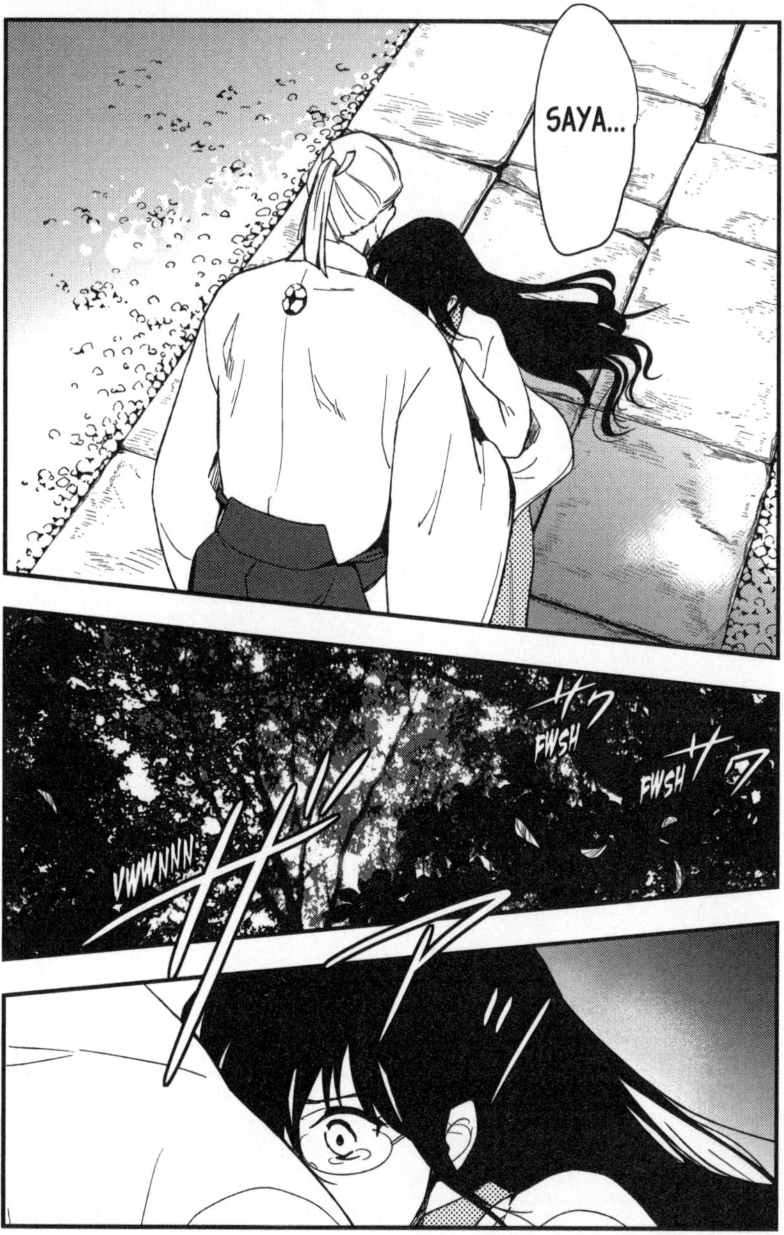
SAYA...
FWSH
FWSH
VWWNNN

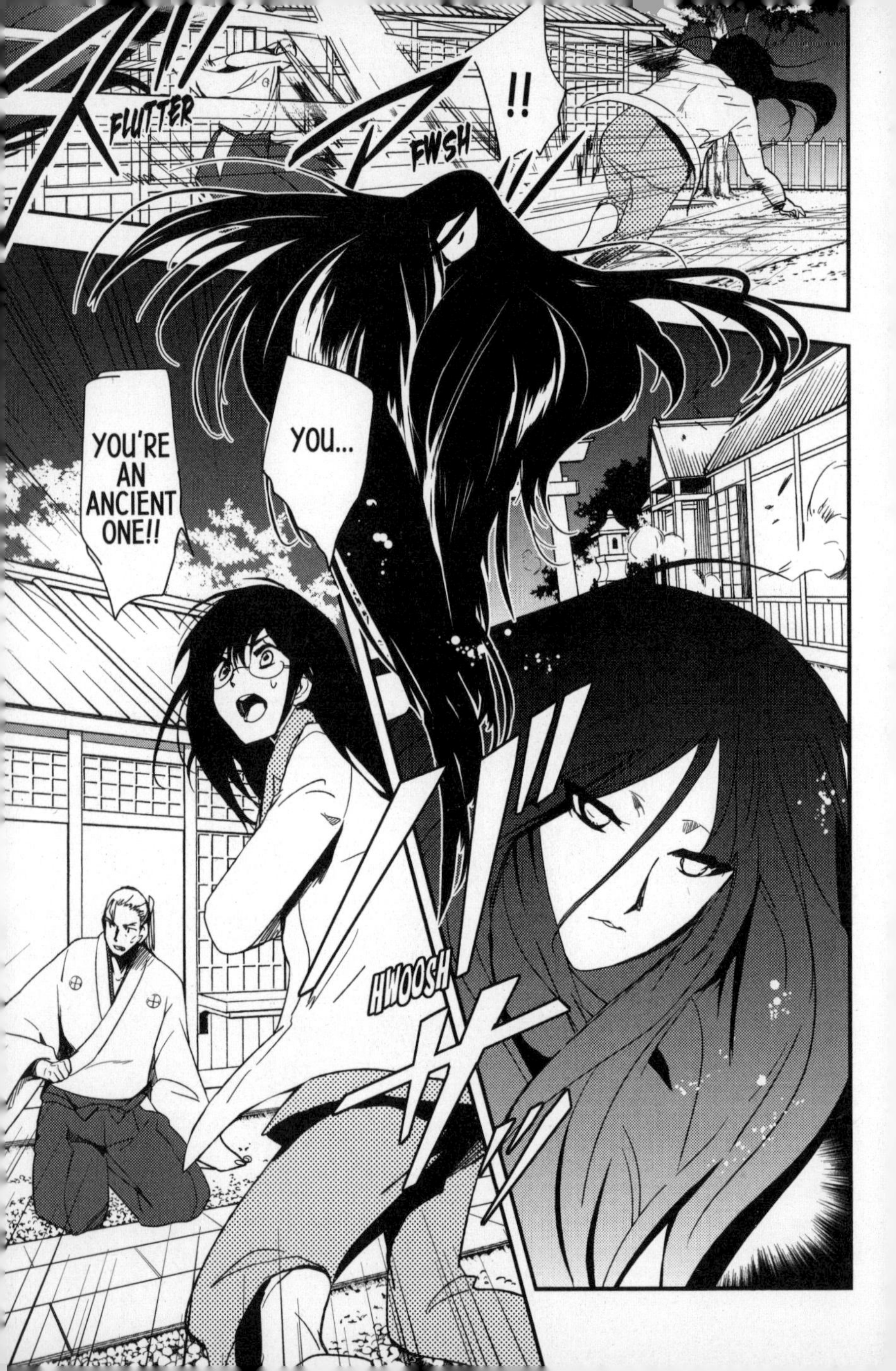
!!
FWSH
FLUTTER
YOU...
YOU'RE AN ANCIENT ONE!!
HWOOSH

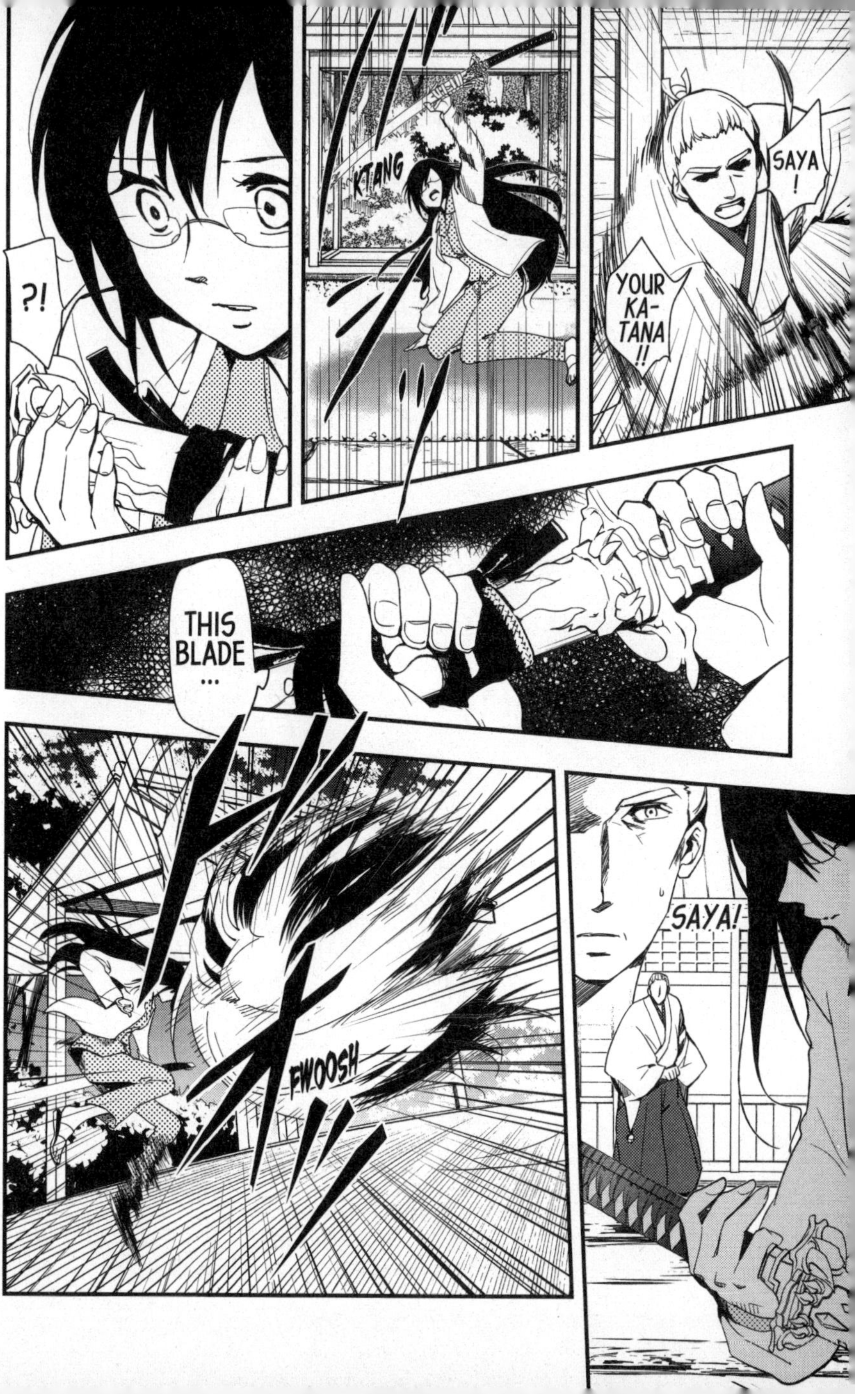
SAYA!
YOUR KATANA!!
KTANG
?!
THIS BLADE...
SAYA!
FWOOSH

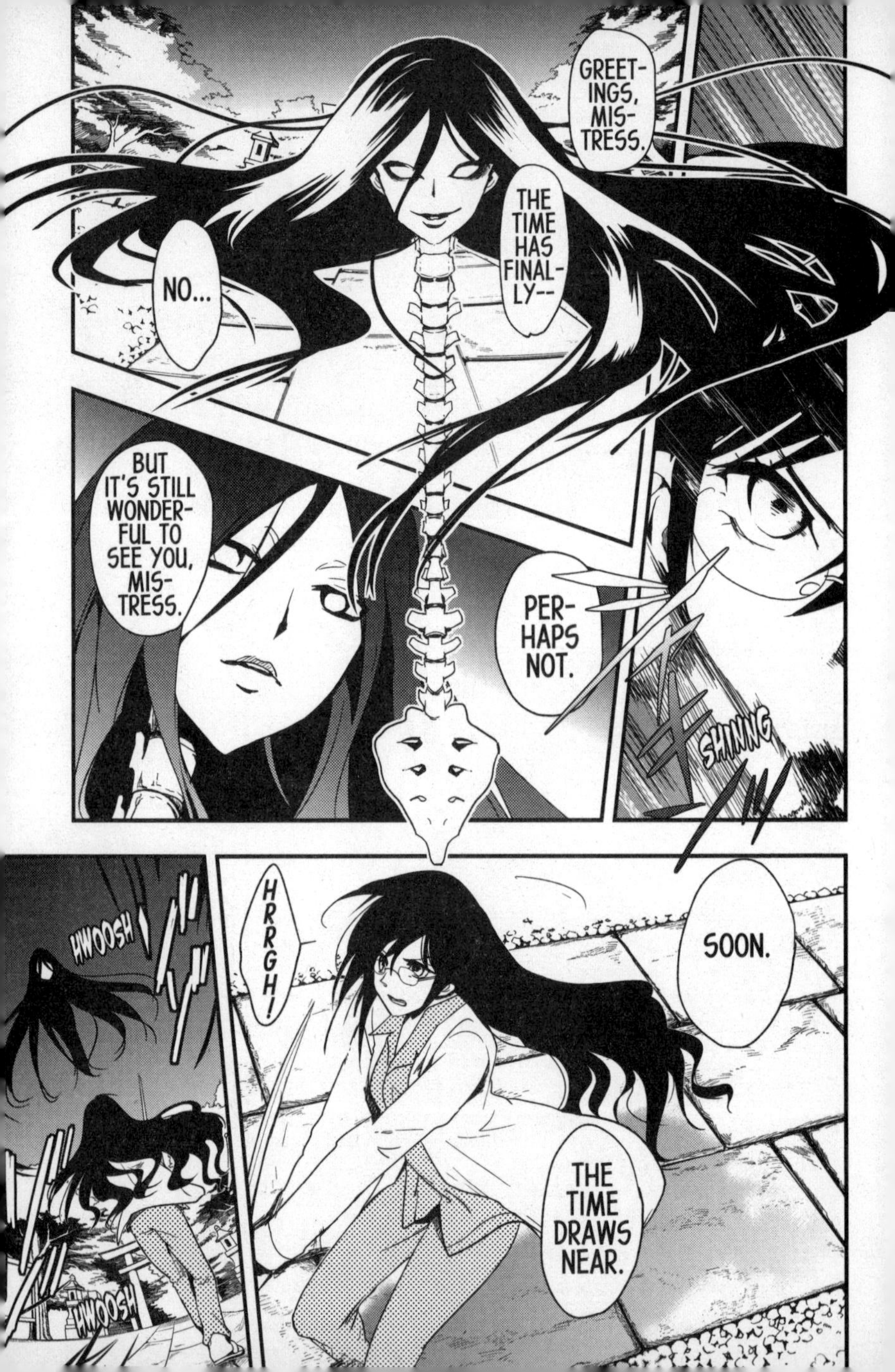
GREETINGS, MISTRESS.
THE TIME HAS FINALLY--
NO...
PERHAPS NOT.
SHINNG
BUT IT'S STILL WONDERFUL TO SEE YOU, MISTRESS.
SOON.
HRRGH!
THE TIME DRAWS NEAR.
HWOOSH
HWOOSH

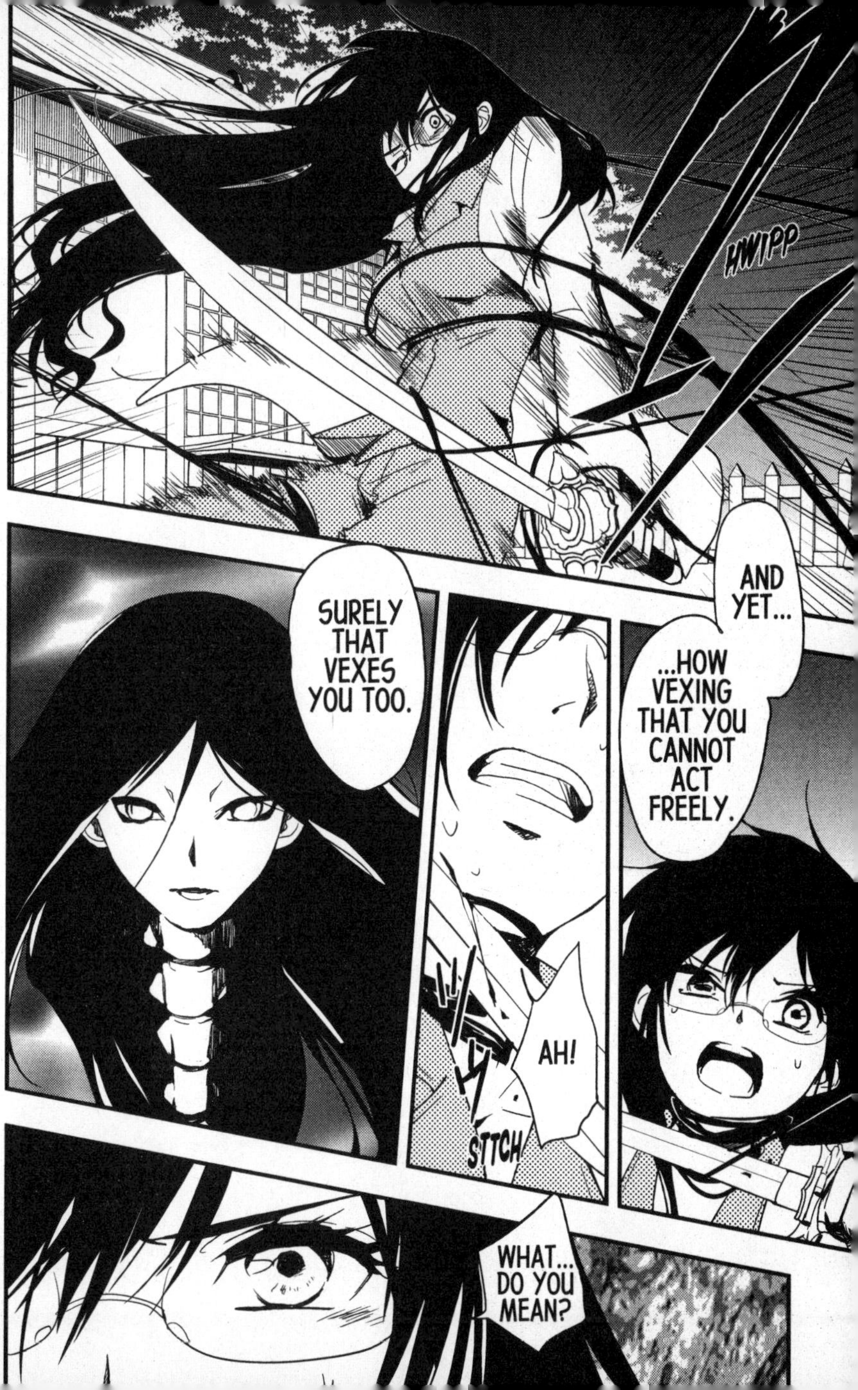
HWIPP
AND YET...
...HOW VEXING THAT YOU CANNOT ACT FREELY.
AH!
STTCH
SURELY THAT VEXES YOU TOO.
WHAT... DO YOU MEAN?

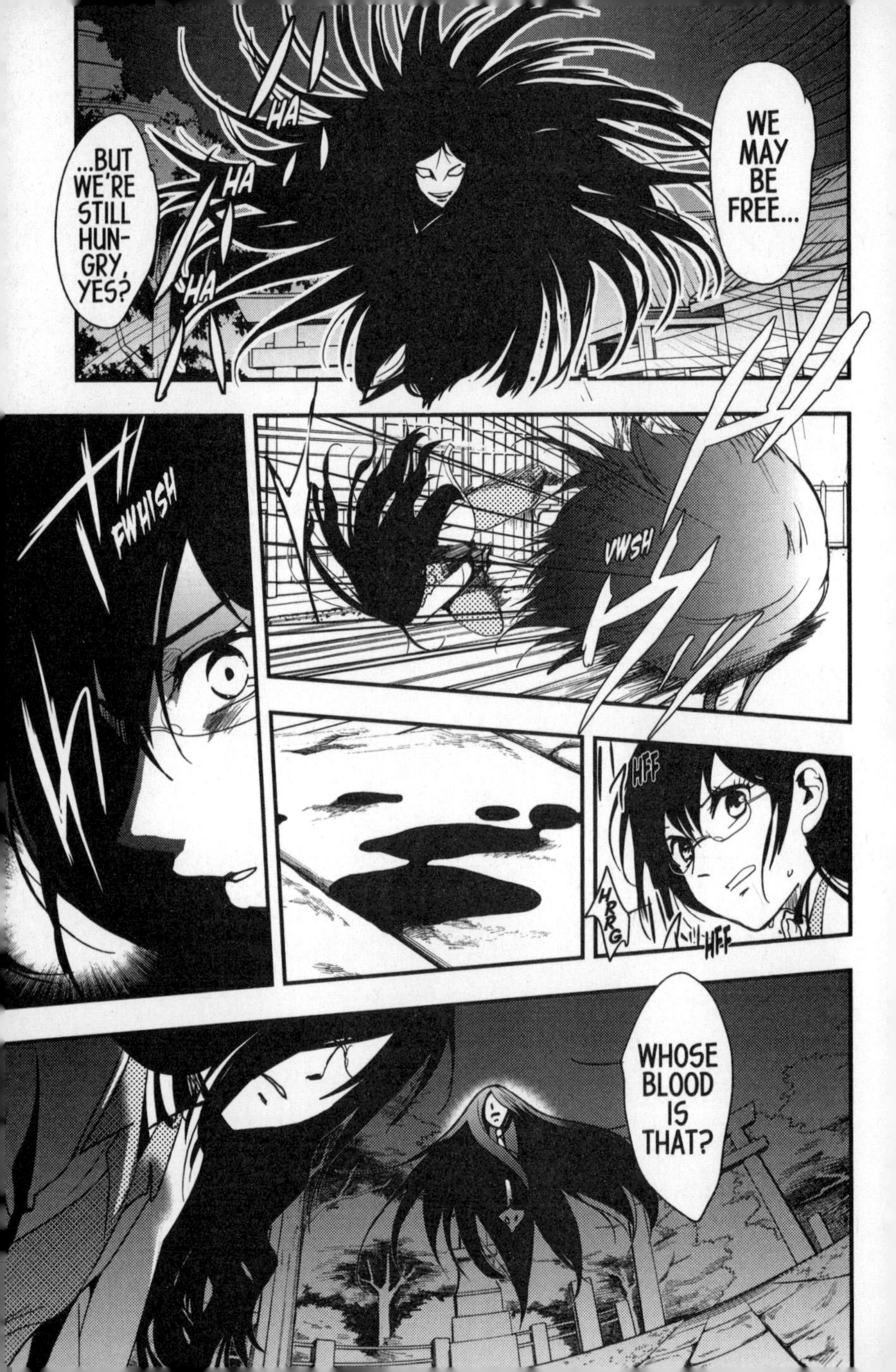
WE MAY BE FREE...
HA
HA
HA
HA
...BUT WE'RE STILL HUNGRY, YES?
VWSH
HFF
HRRG
HFF
FWHISH
WHOSE BLOOD IS THAT?

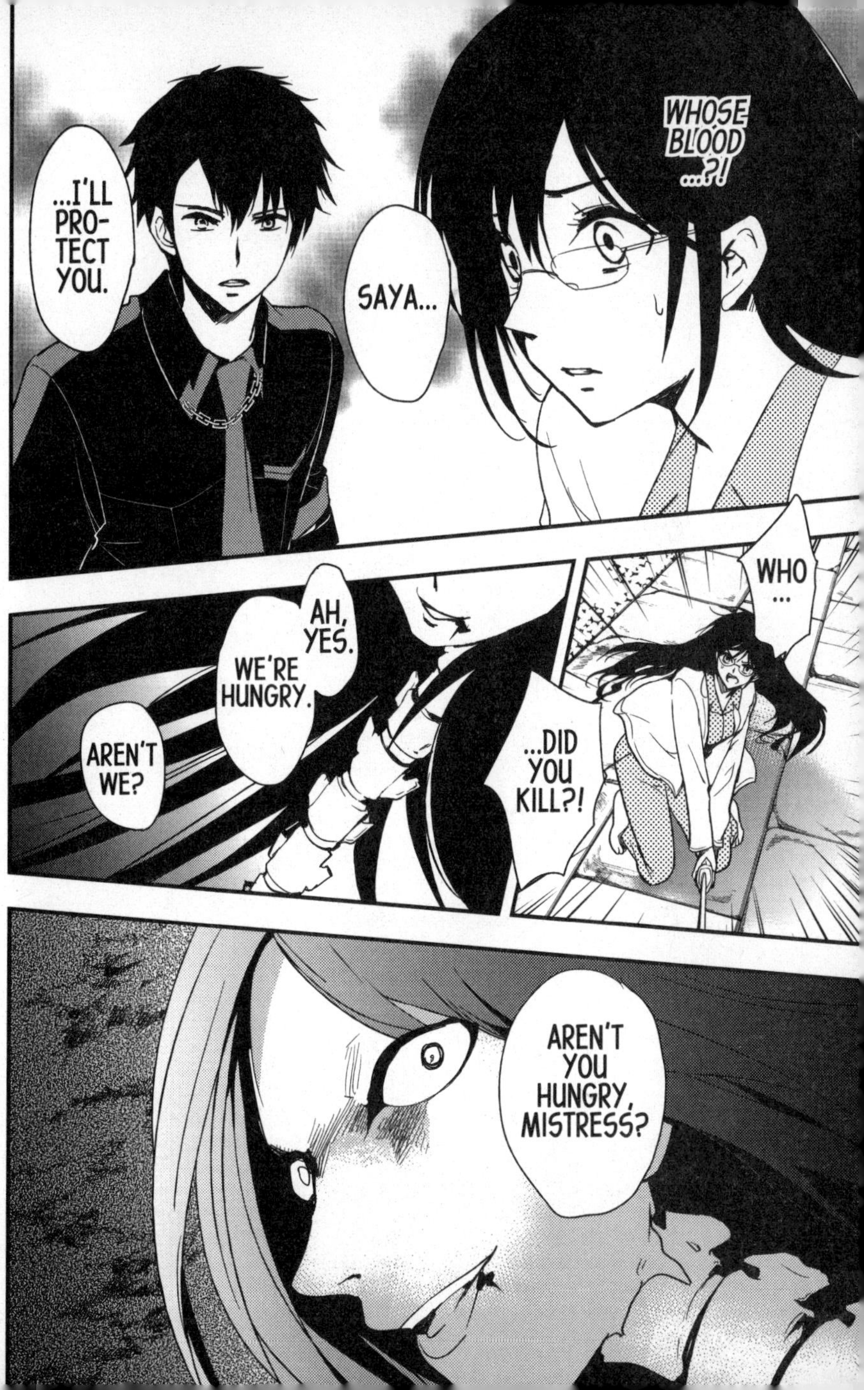
WHOSE BLOOD ...?!
SAYA...
...I'LL PRO-TECT YOU.
WHO ...
...DID YOU KILL?!
AH, YES. WE'RE HUNGRY.
AREN'T WE?
AREN'T YOU HUNGRY, MISTRESS?

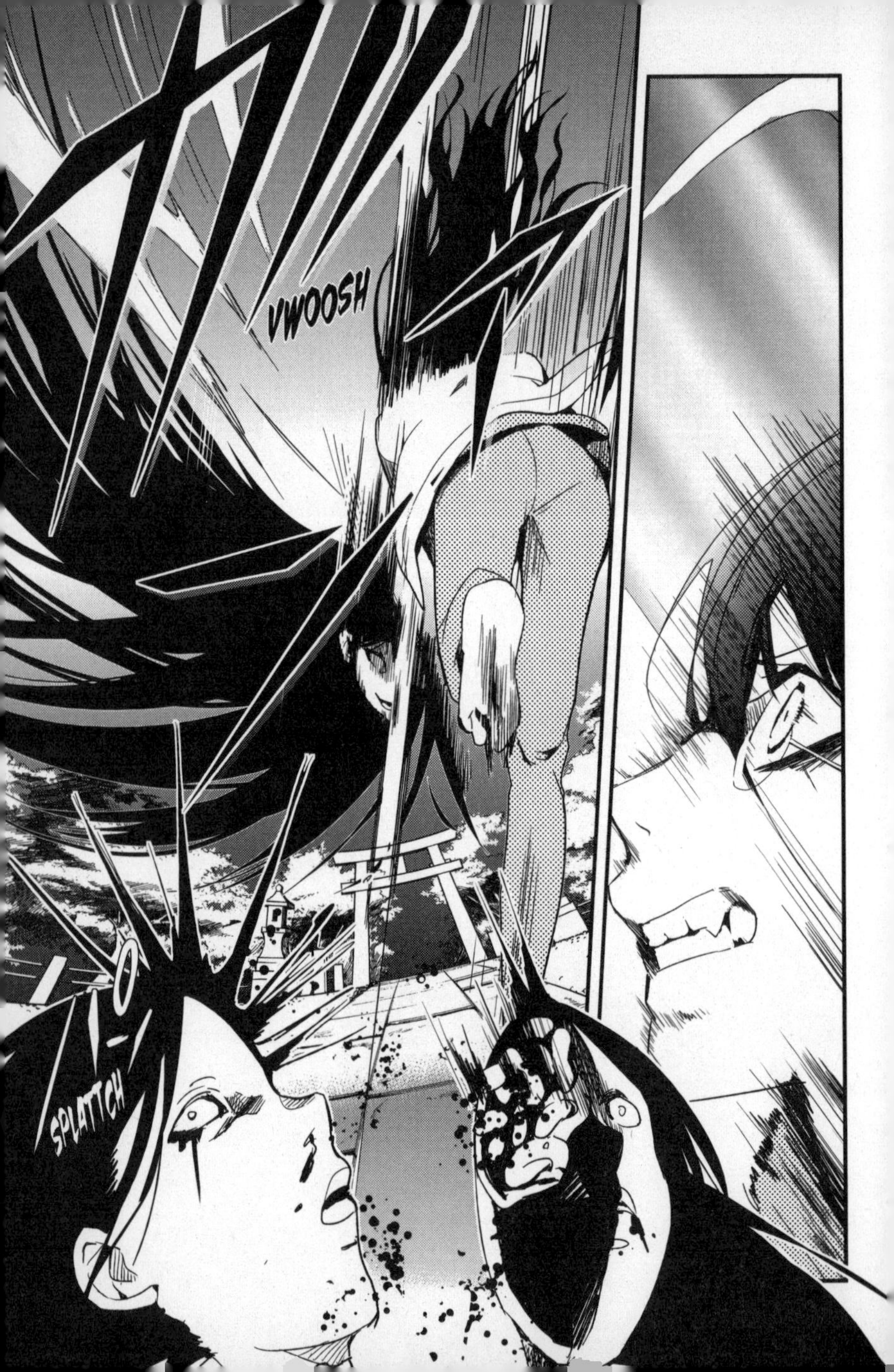
VWOOSH
SPLATTCH

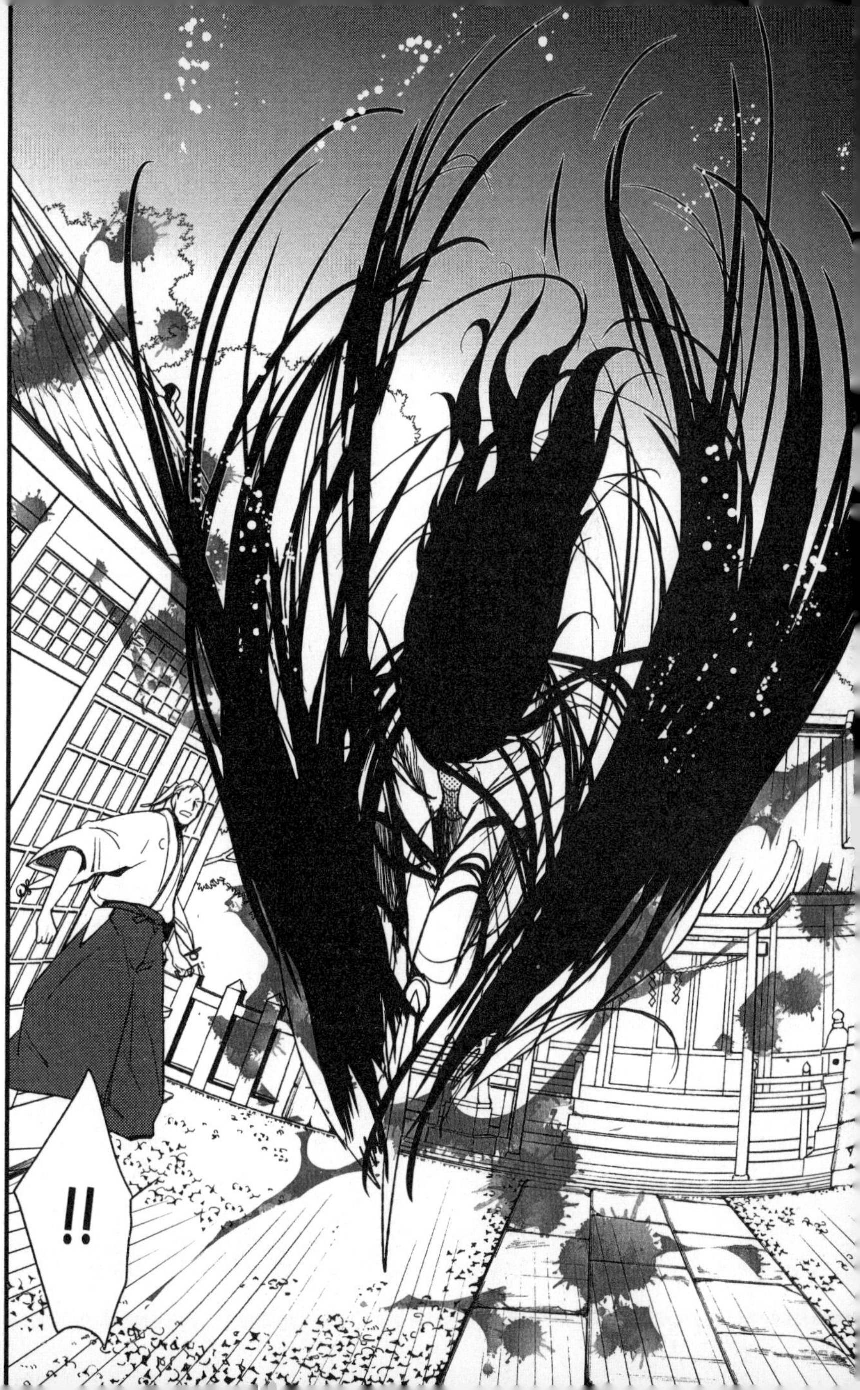
!!

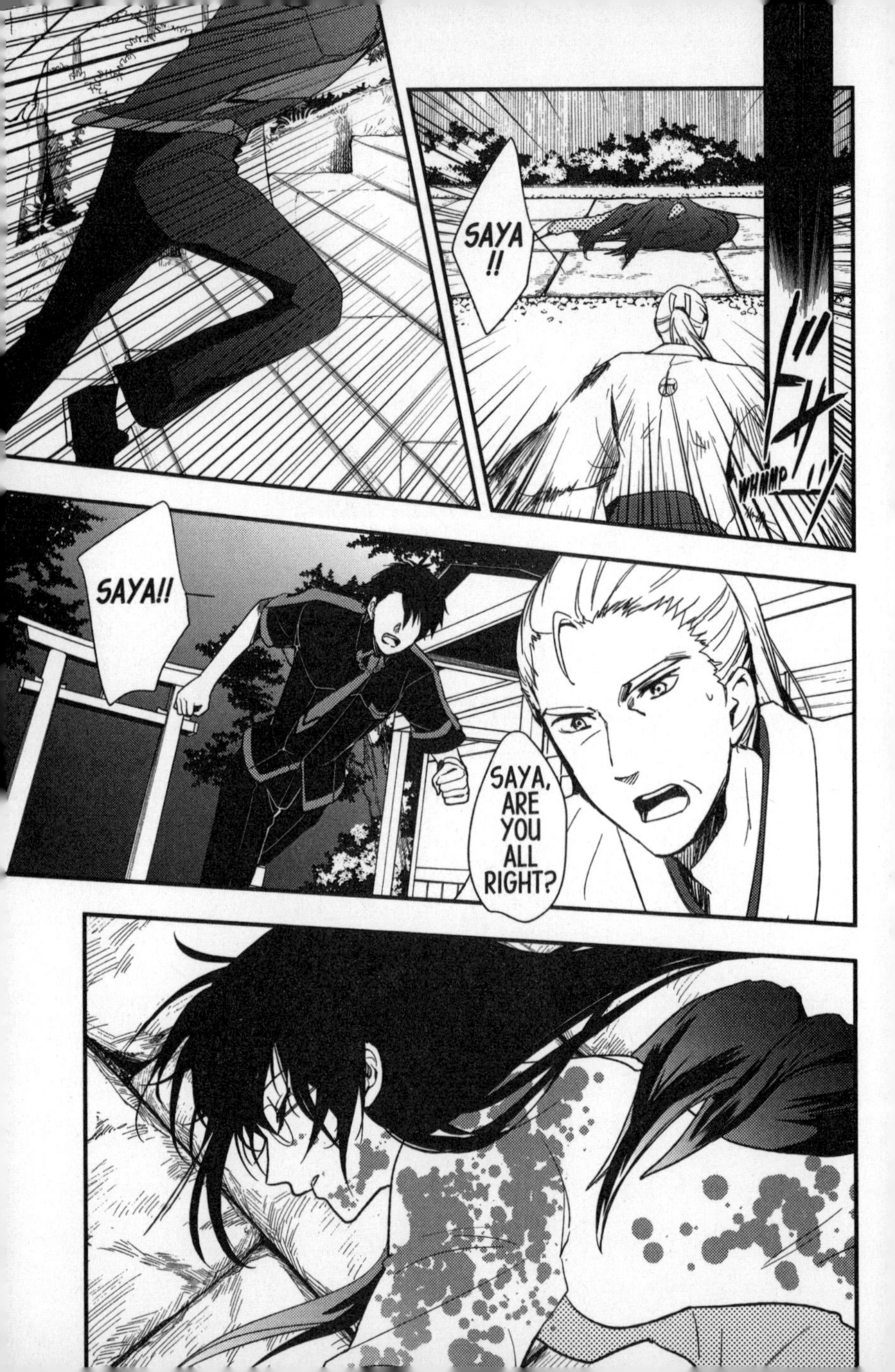
SAYA !!
WHMMP
SAYA, ARE YOU ALL RIGHT?
SAYA!!

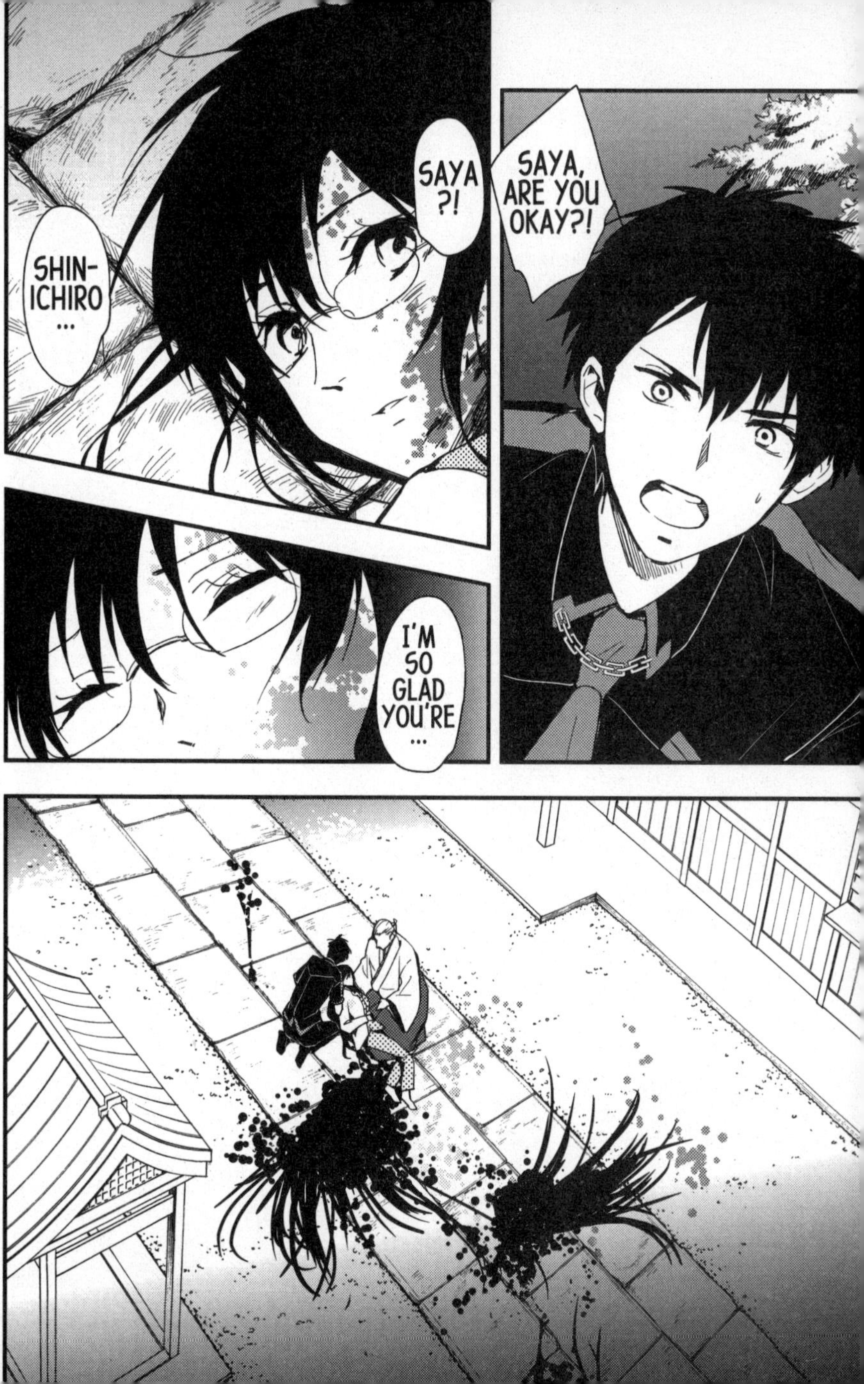
SAYA, ARE YOU OKAY?!
SAYA ?!
SHIN-ICHIRO ...
I'M SO GLAD YOU'RE ...

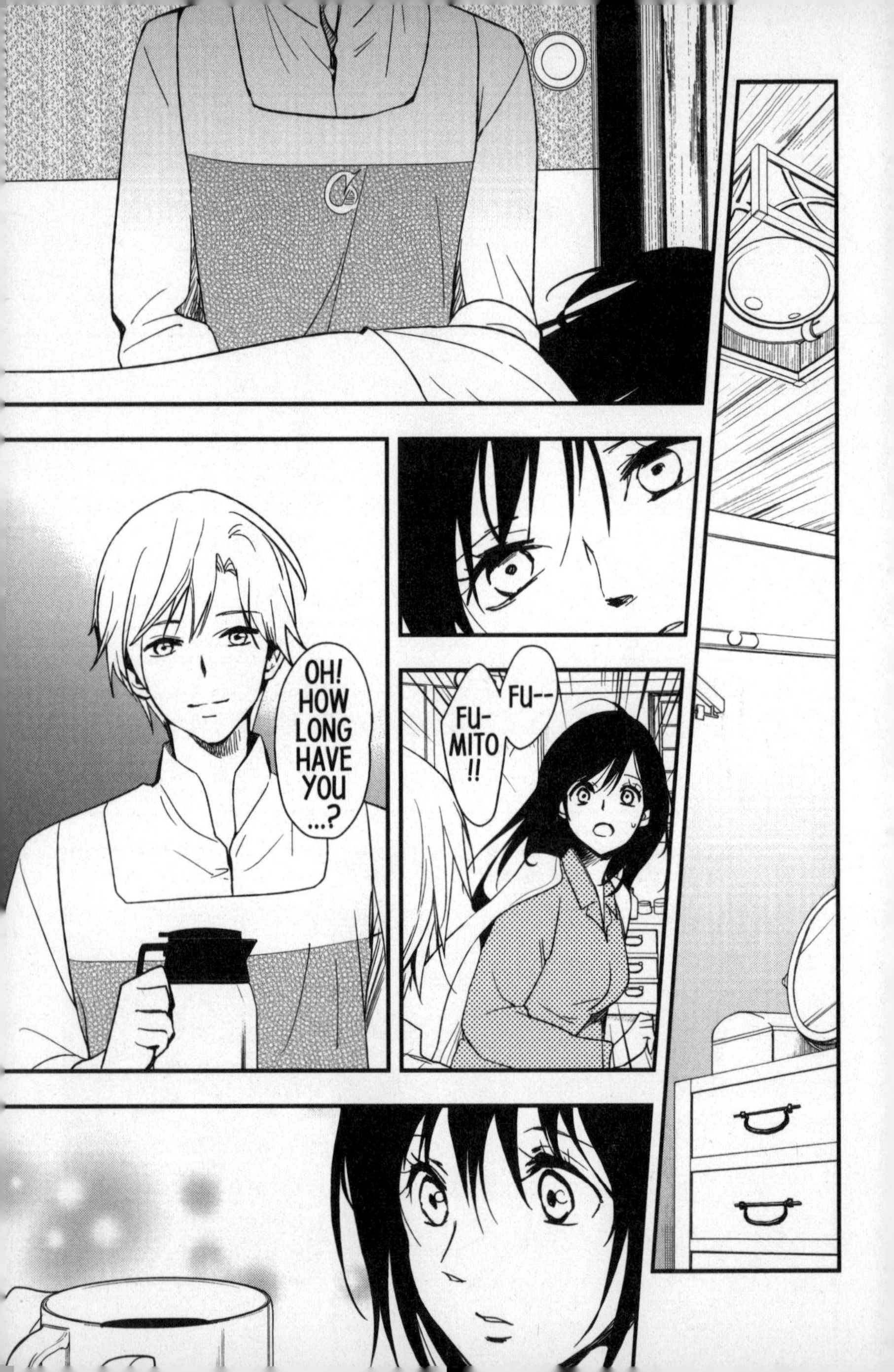
FU--
FU-MITO!!
OH! HOW LONG HAVE YOU ...?

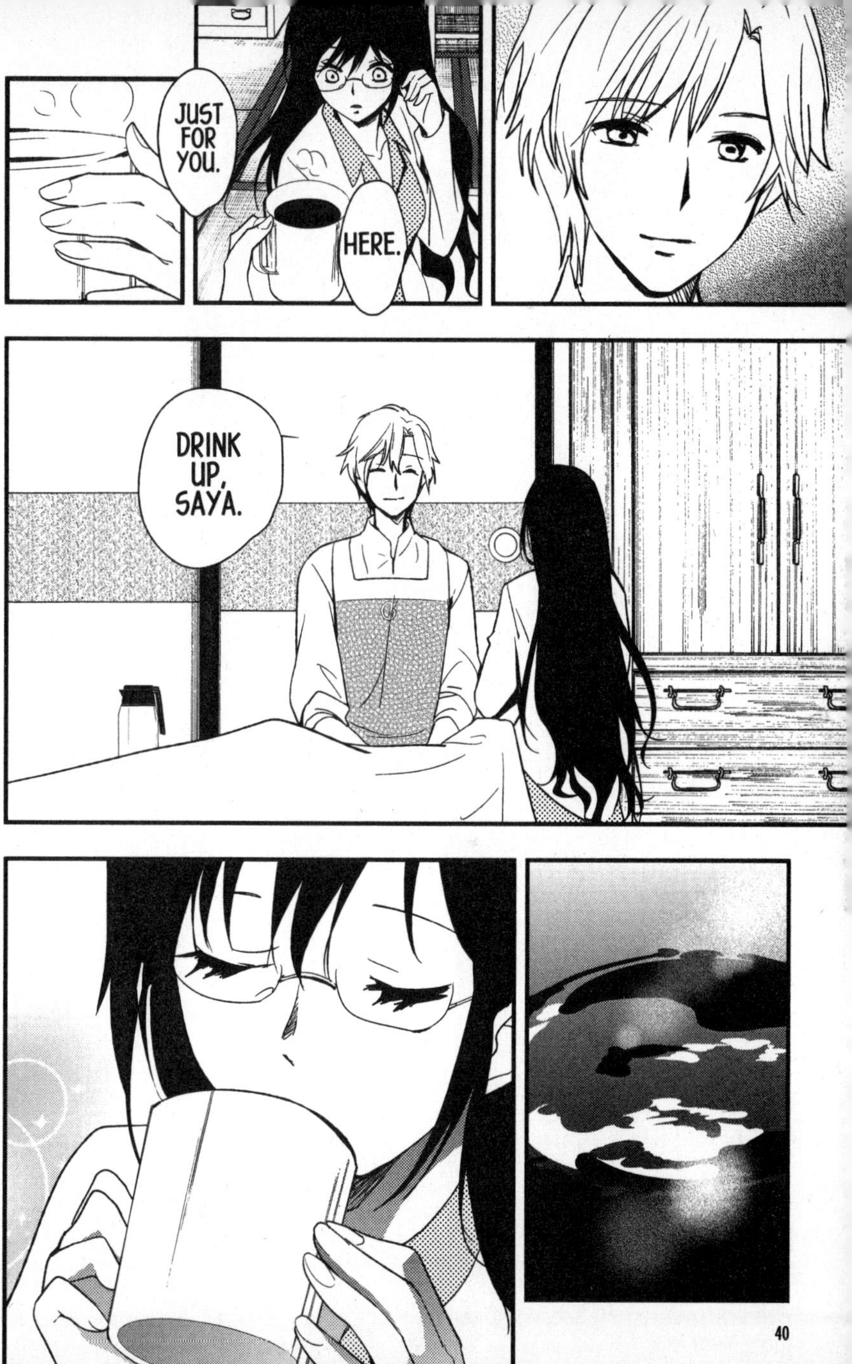
HERE.
JUST FOR YOU.
DRINK UP, SAYA.

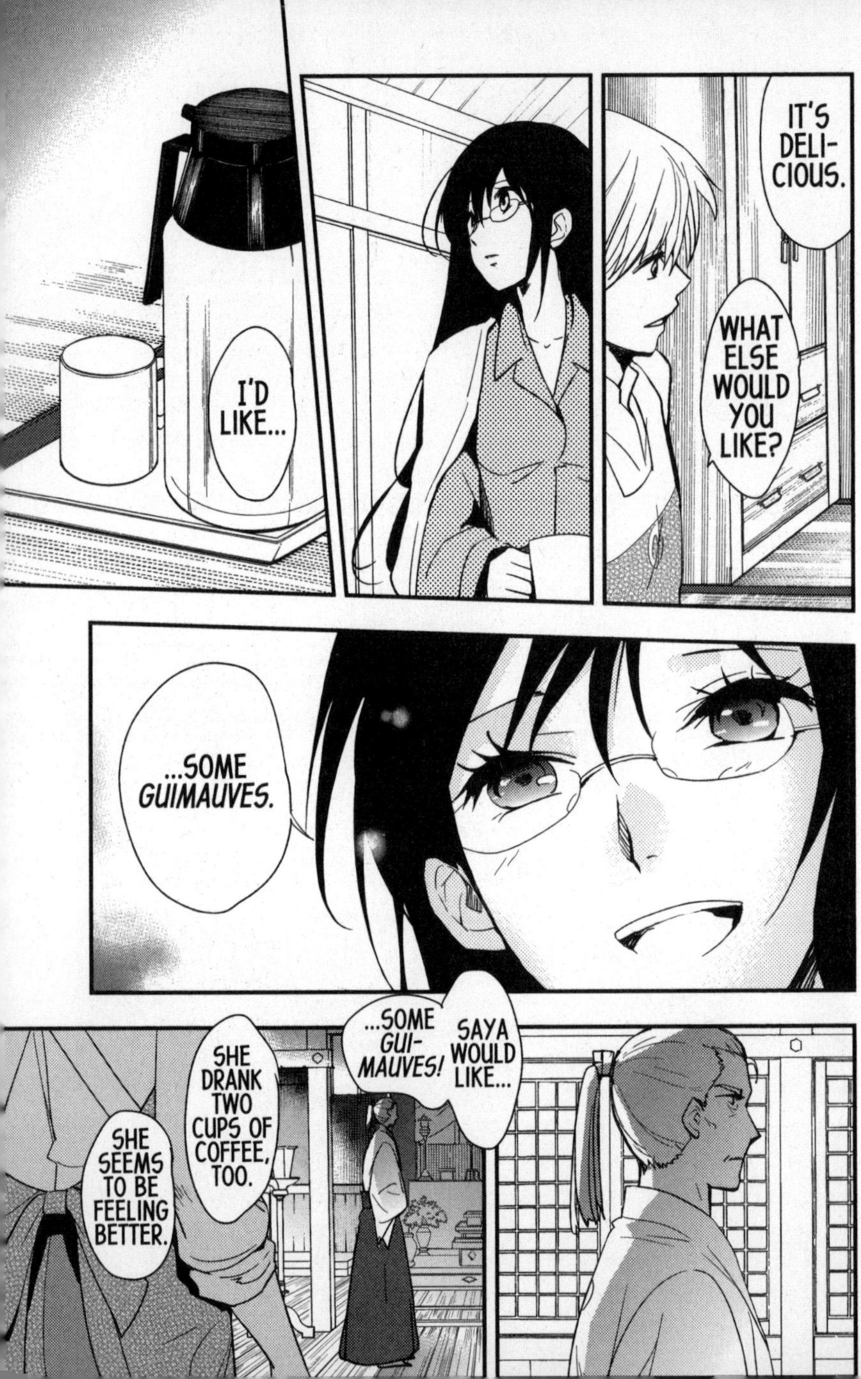
IT'S DELICIOUS.
WHAT ELSE WOULD YOU LIKE?
I'D LIKE...
...SOME *GUIMAUVES.*
SAYA WOULD LIKE...
...SOME *GUIMAUVES!*
SHE DRANK TWO CUPS OF COFFEE, TOO.
SHE SEEMS TO BE FEELING BETTER.

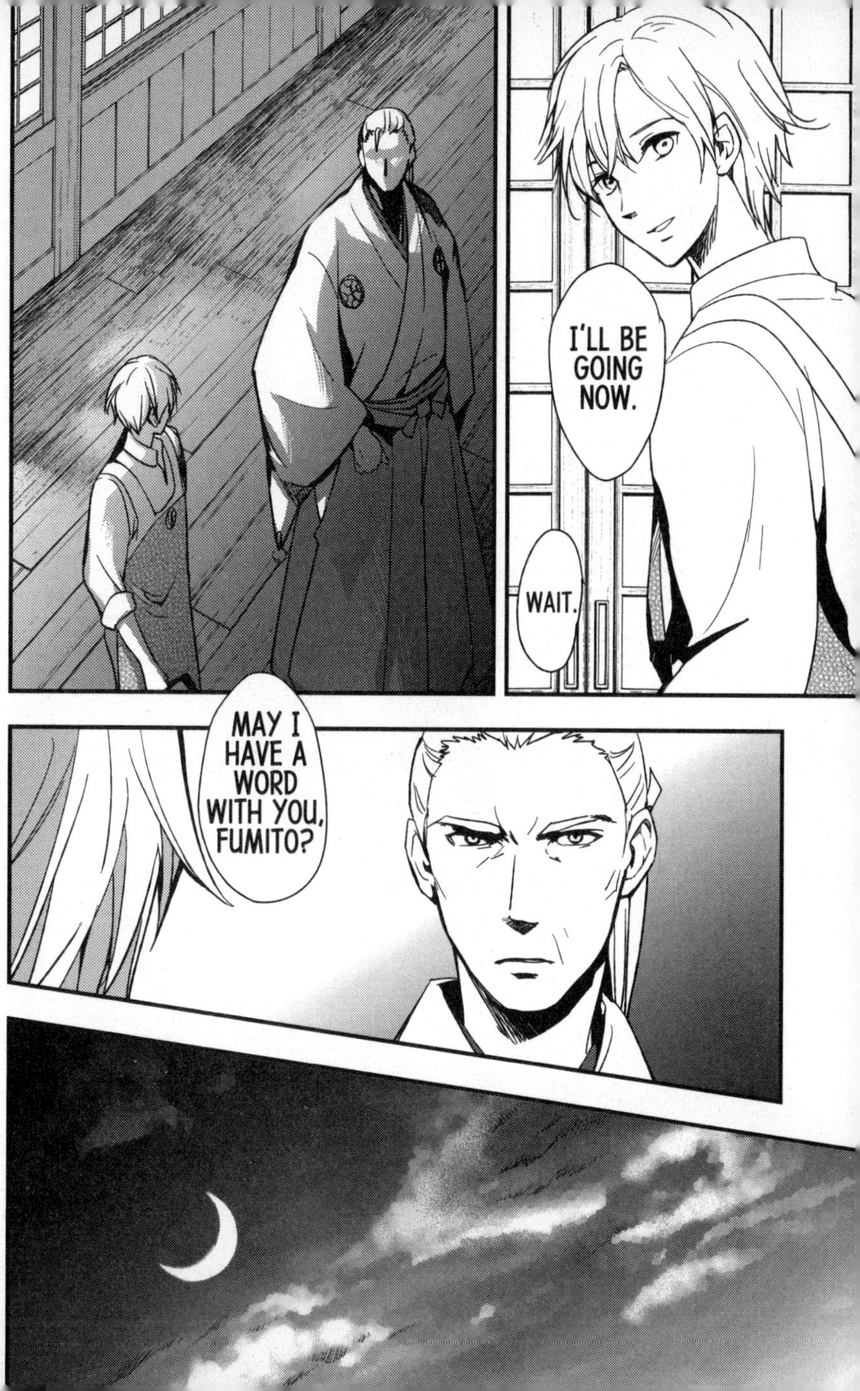
I'LL BE GOING NOW.
WAIT.
MAY I HAVE A WORD WITH YOU, FUMITO?

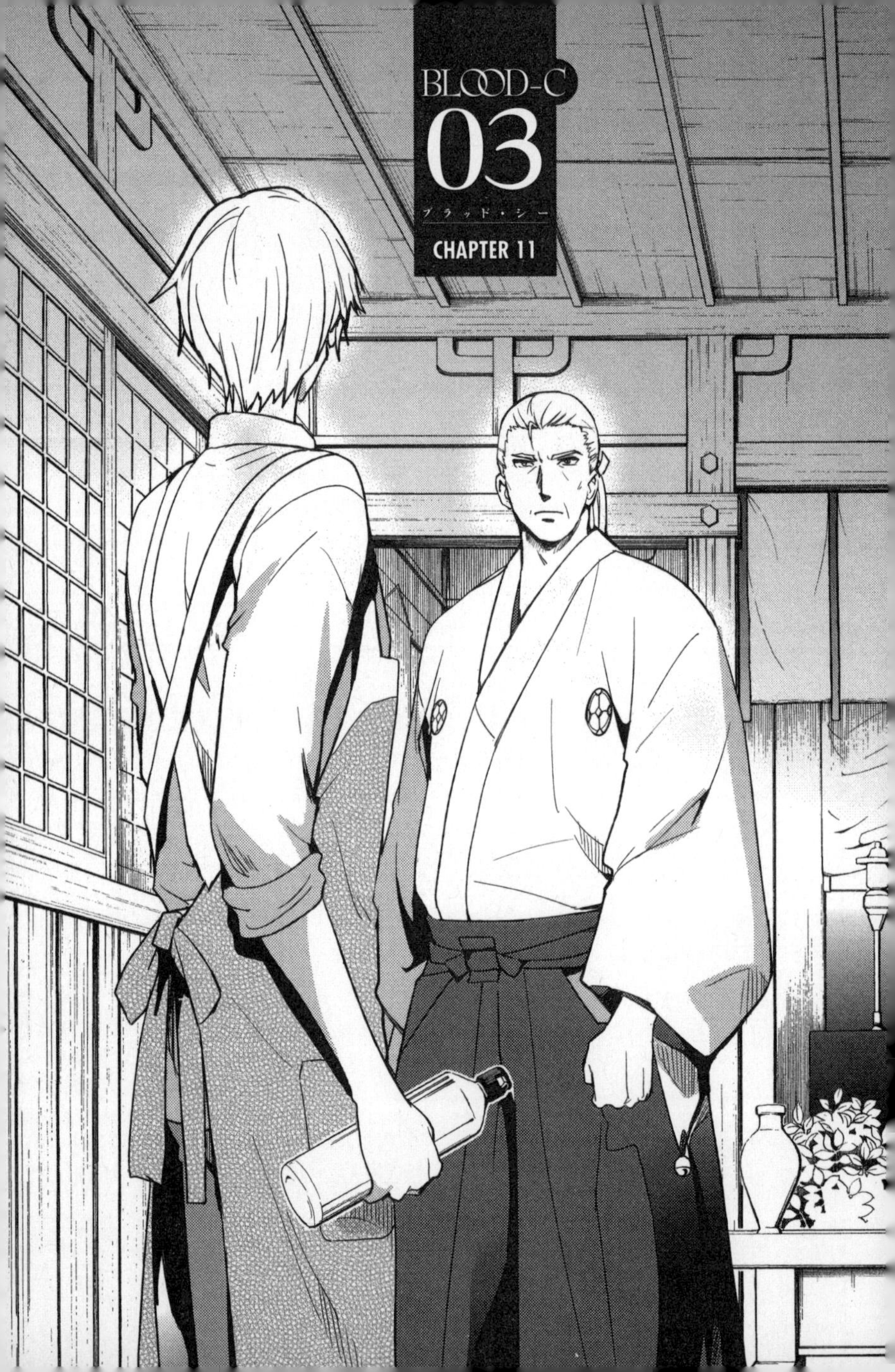
BLOOD-C
03
ブラッド・シー
CHAPTER 11

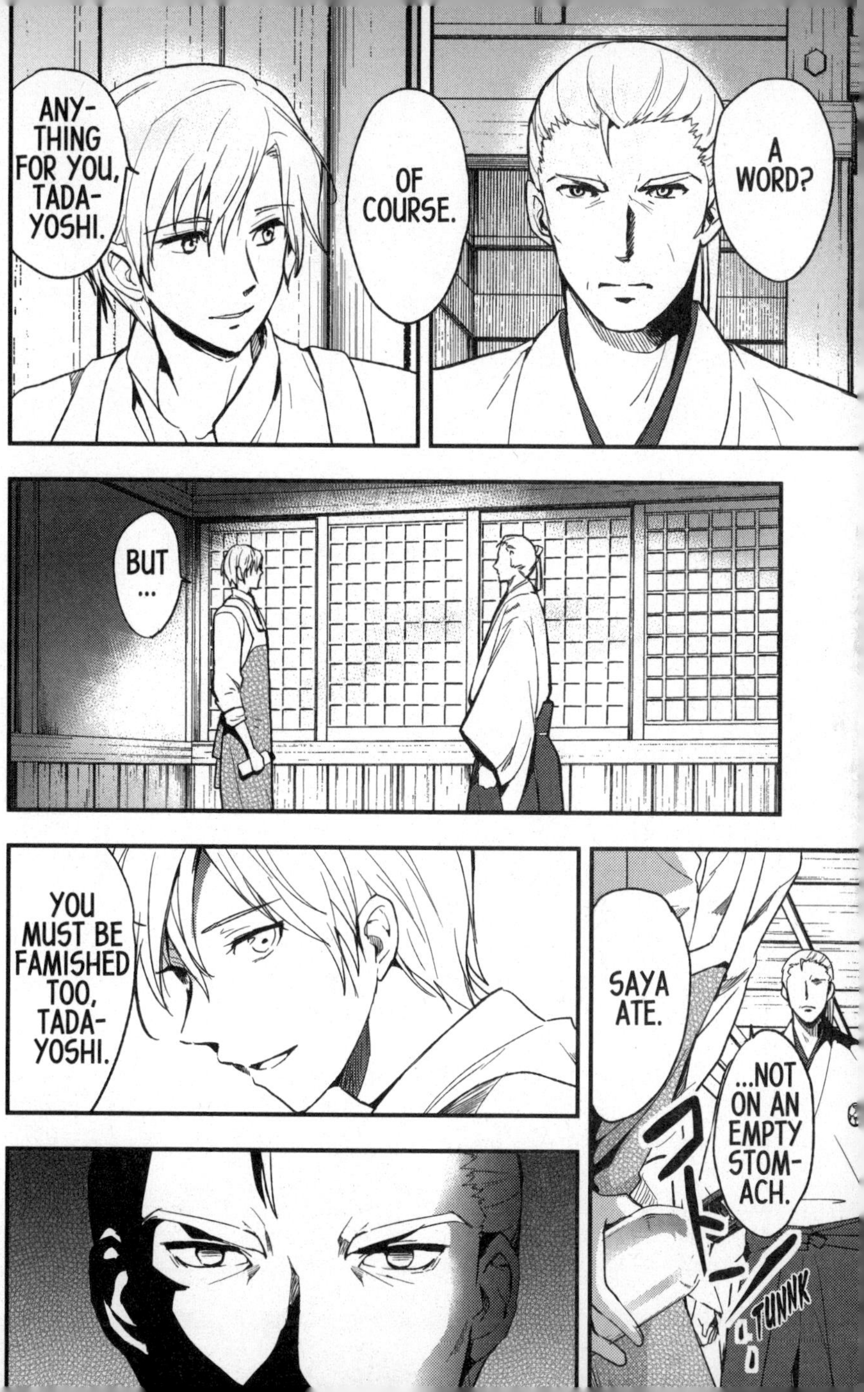
A WORD?
OF COURSE.
ANY-THING FOR YOU, TADA-YOSHI.
BUT ...
SAYA ATE.
...NOT ON AN EMPTY STOMACH.
TUNNK
YOU MUST BE FAMISHED TOO, TADA-YOSHI.

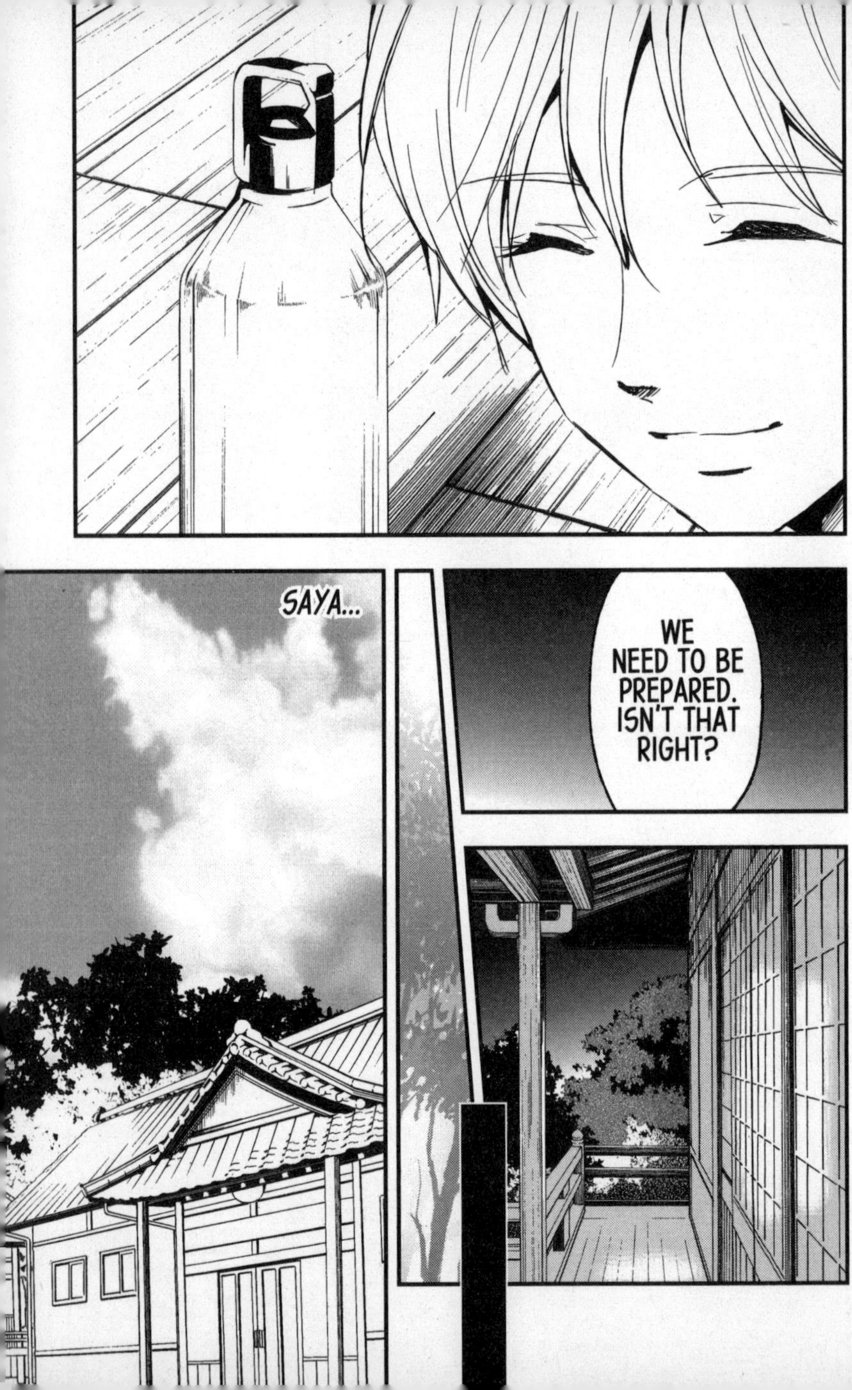
WE NEED TO BE PREPARED. ISN'T THAT RIGHT?
SAYA...

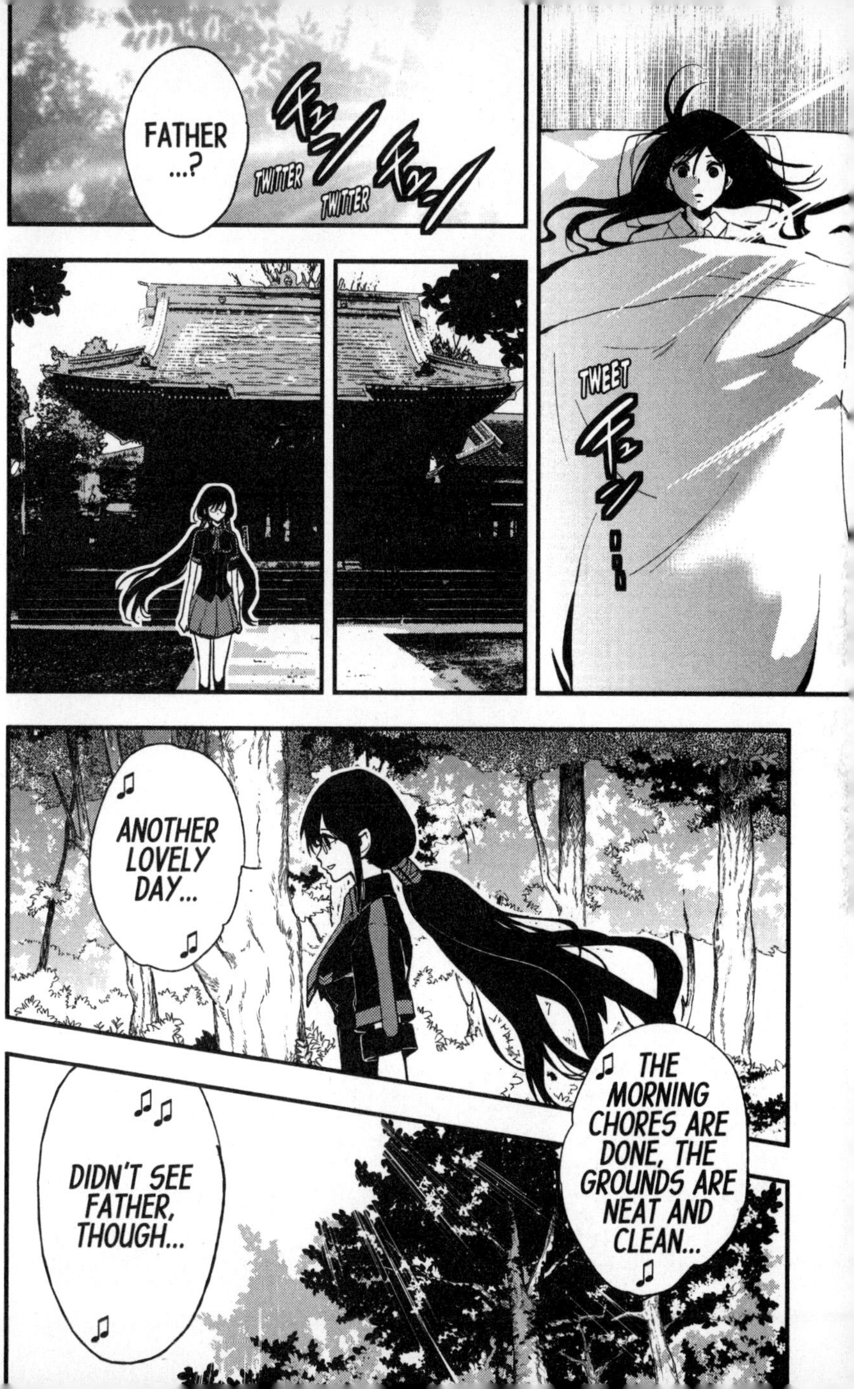
TWEET
FATHER ...?
TWITTER
TWITTER
ANOTHER LOVELY DAY...
THE MORNING CHORES ARE DONE, THE GROUNDS ARE NEAT AND CLEAN...
DIDN'T SEE FATHER, THOUGH...

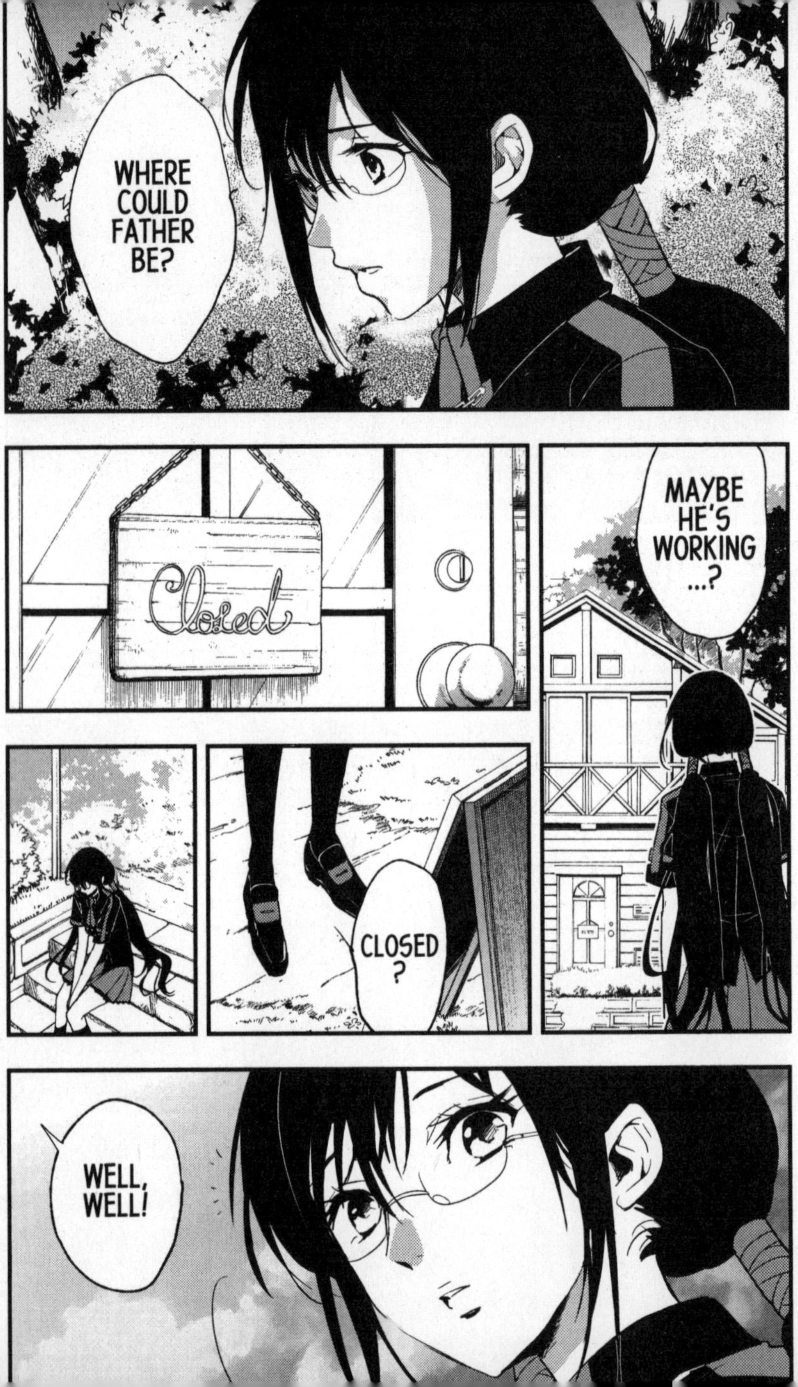
WHERE COULD FATHER BE?
MAYBE HE'S WORKING ...?
Closed
CLOSED ?
WELL, WELL!

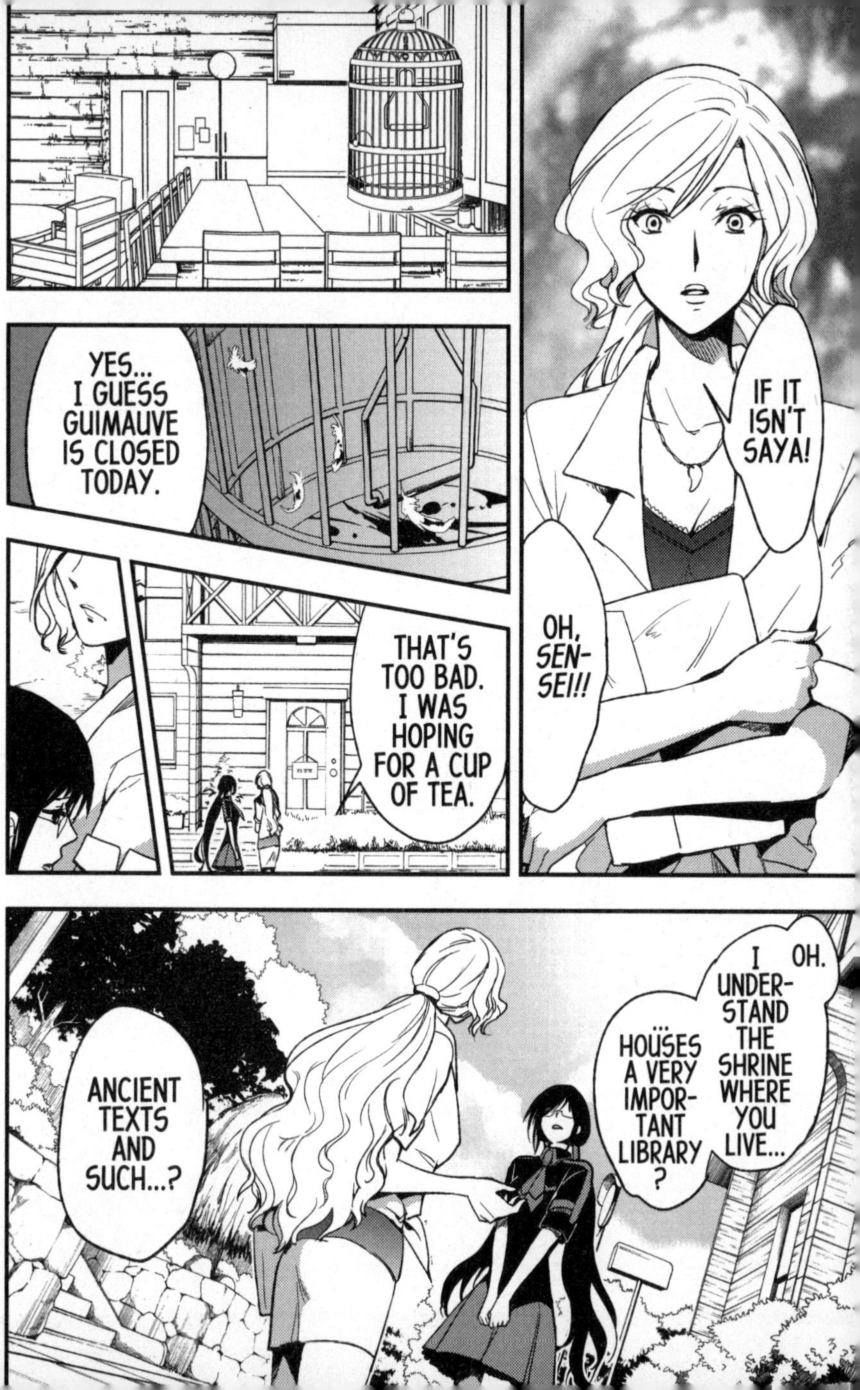
IF IT ISN'T SAYA!
OH, SENSEI!!
YES... I GUESS GUIMAUVE IS CLOSED TODAY.
THAT'S TOO BAD. I WAS HOPING FOR A CUP OF TEA.
OH.
I UNDERSTAND THE SHRINE WHERE YOU LIVE...
...HOUSES A VERY IMPORTANT LIBRARY?
ANCIENT TEXTS AND SUCH...?

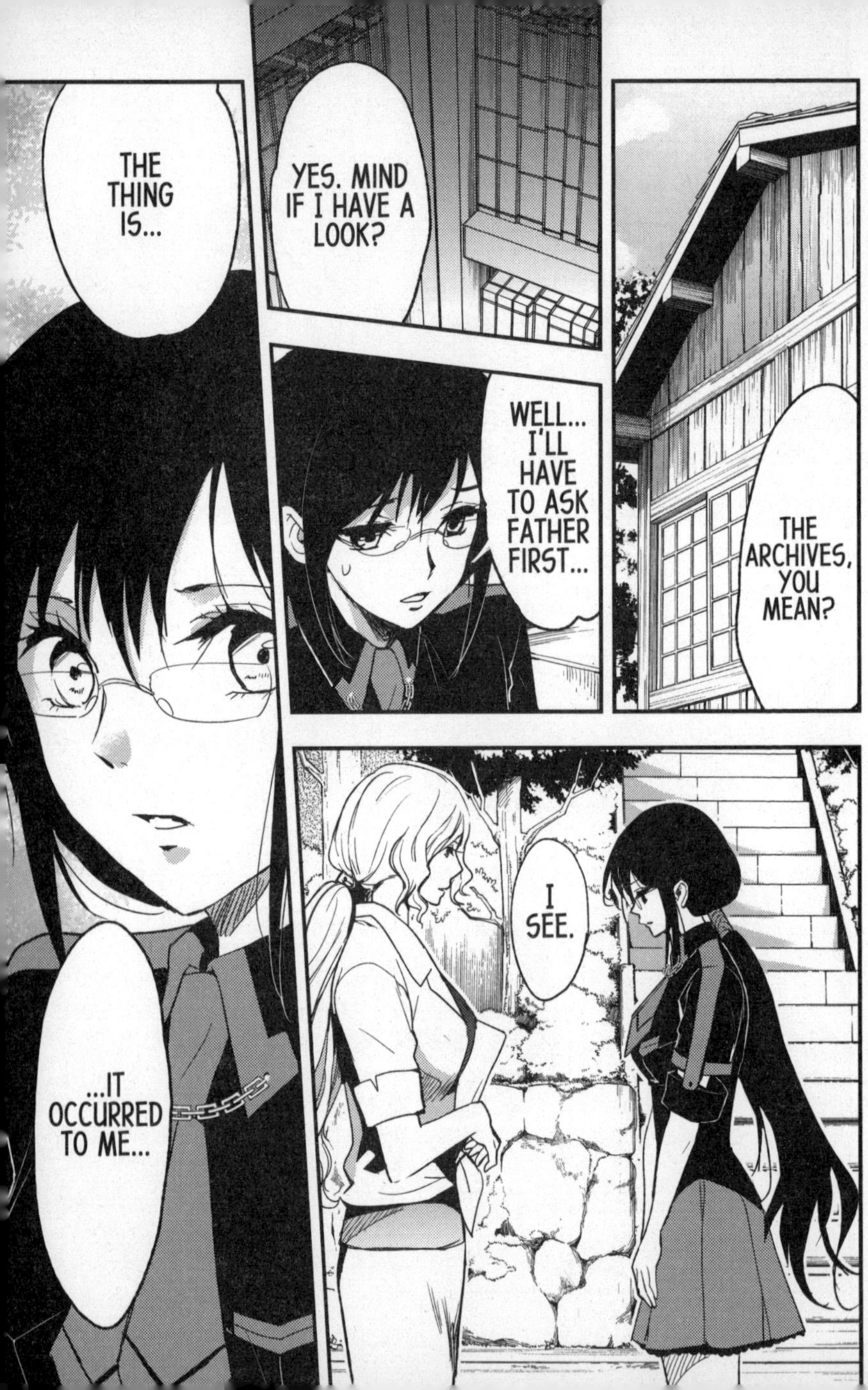
THE ARCHIVES, YOU MEAN?
YES. MIND IF I HAVE A LOOK?
WELL... I'LL HAVE TO ASK FATHER FIRST...
I SEE.
THE THING IS...
...IT OCCURRED TO ME...

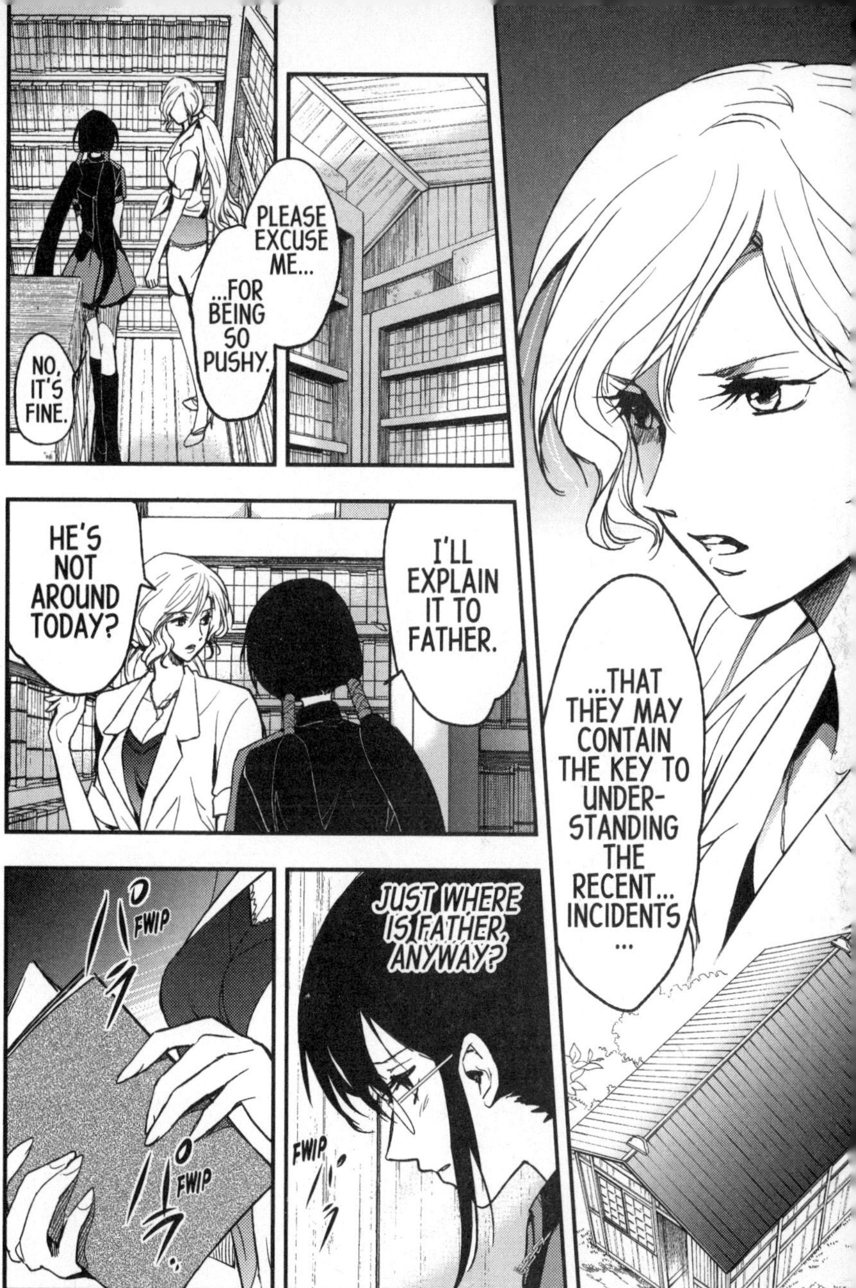
...THAT THEY MAY CONTAIN THE KEY TO UNDER-STANDING THE RECENT... INCIDENTS ...
PLEASE EXCUSE ME...
...FOR BEING SO PUSHY.
NO, IT'S FINE.
I'LL EXPLAIN IT TO FATHER.
HE'S NOT AROUND TODAY?
JUST WHERE IS FATHER, ANYWAY?
FWIP
FWIP
FWIP

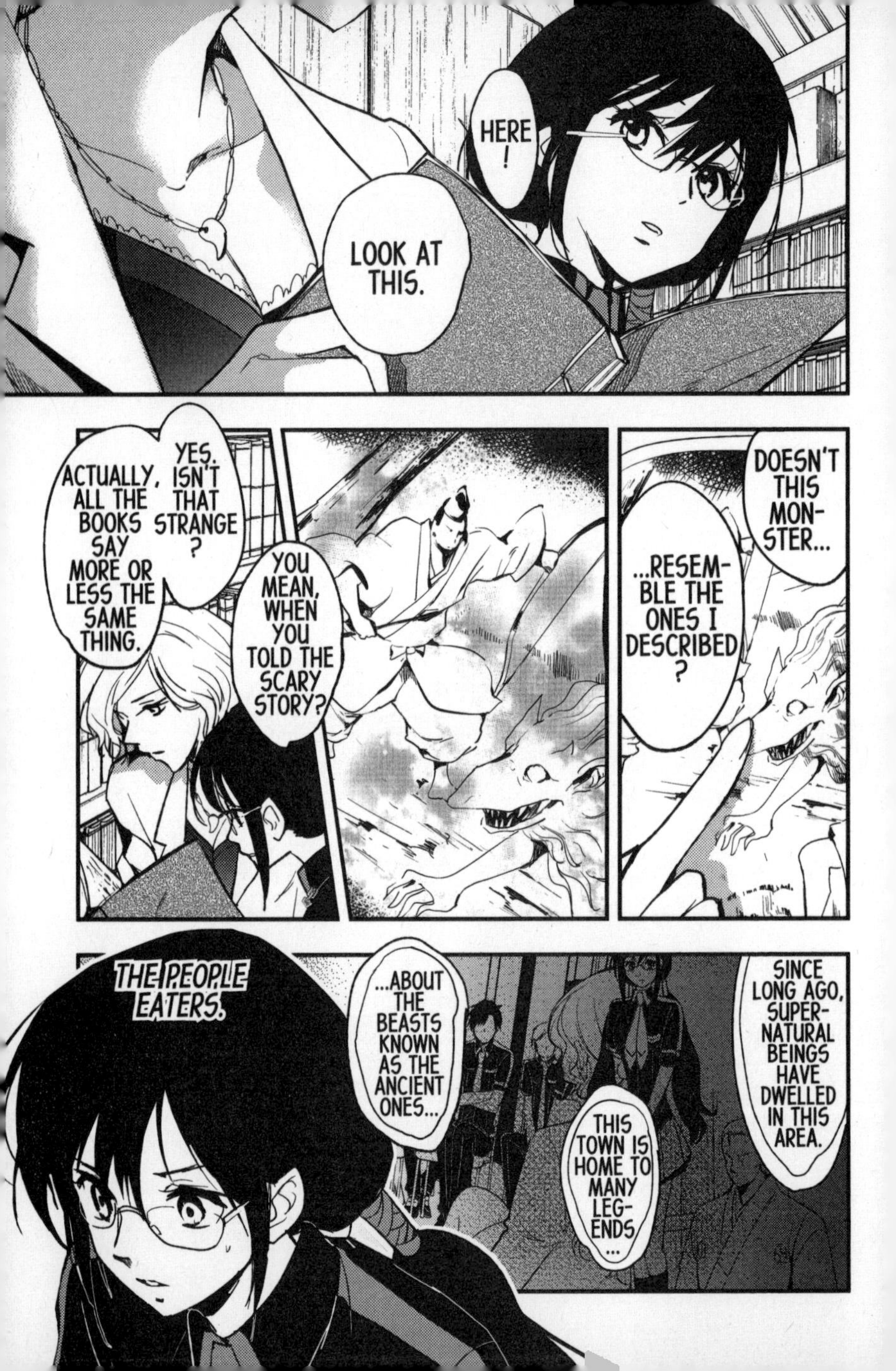
HERE!
LOOK AT THIS.
DOESN'T THIS MONSTER...
...RESEMBLE THE ONES I DESCRIBED?
YOU MEAN, WHEN YOU TOLD THE SCARY STORY?
YES. ISN'T THAT STRANGE?
ACTUALLY, ALL THE BOOKS SAY MORE OR LESS THE SAME THING.
SINCE LONG AGO, SUPERNATURAL BEINGS HAVE DWELLED IN THIS AREA.
THIS TOWN IS HOME TO MANY LEGENDS...
...ABOUT THE BEASTS KNOWN AS THE ANCIENT ONES...
THE PEOPLE EATERS.

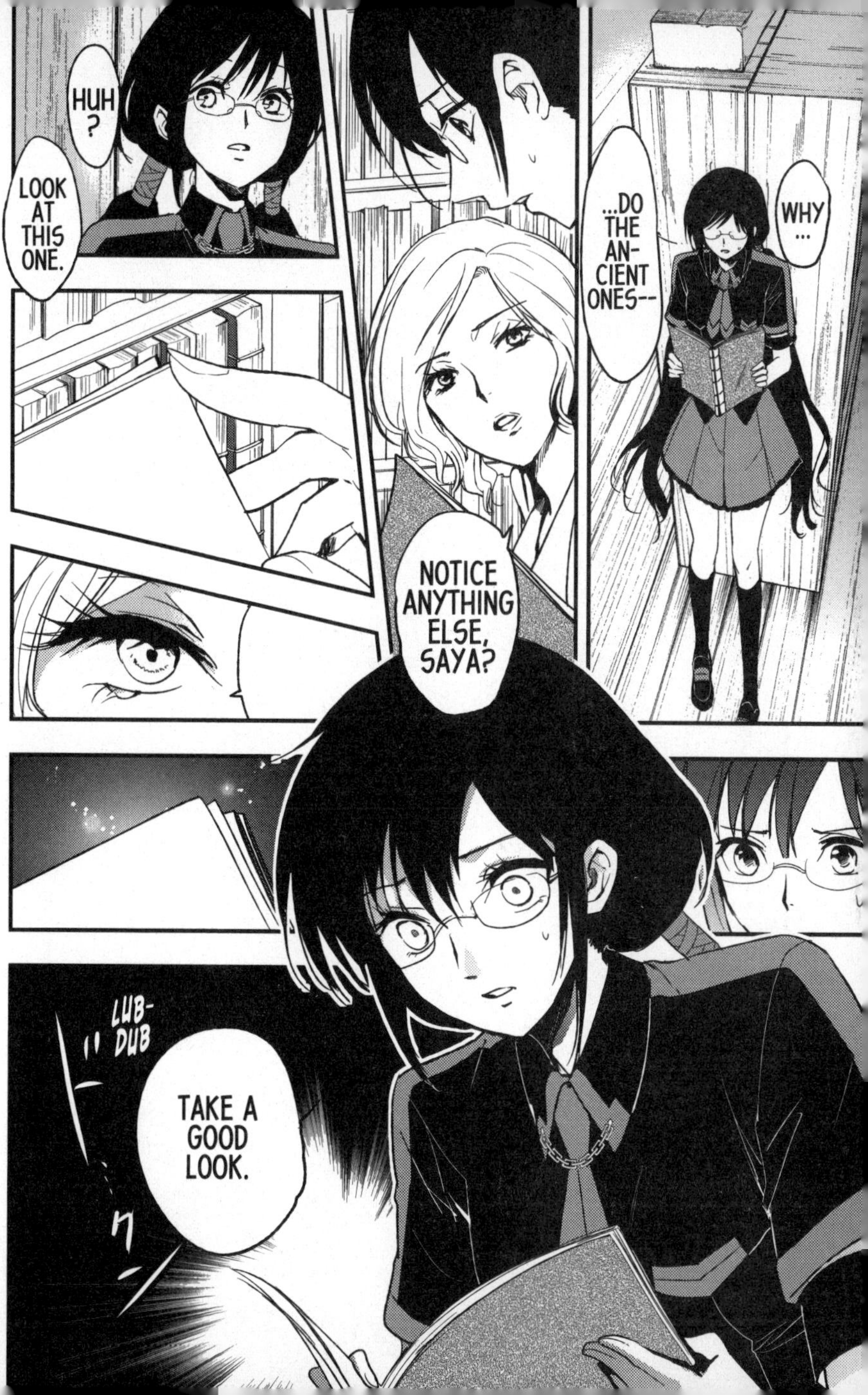
WHY ...
...DO THE AN-CIENT ONES--
NOTICE ANYTHING ELSE, SAYA?
HUH ?
LOOK AT THIS ONE.
LUB-DUB
TAKE A GOOD LOOK.

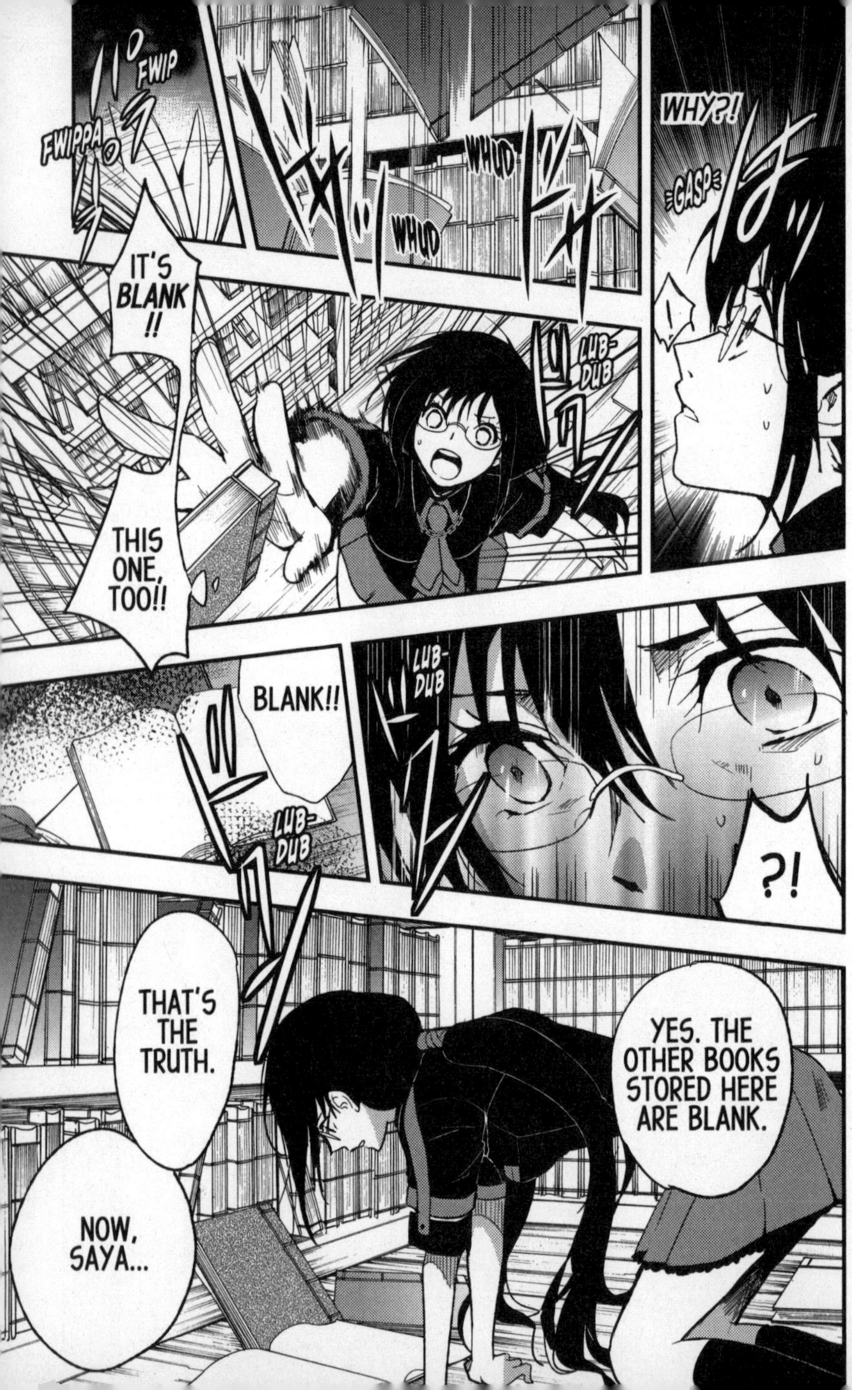

WHY?!
GASP
WHUD
WHUD
FWIP
FWIPPA
LUB-DUB
IT'S BLANK!!
THIS ONE, TOO!!
?!
LUB-DUB
BLANK!!
LUB-DUB
YES. THE OTHER BOOKS STORED HERE ARE BLANK.
THAT'S THE TRUTH.
NOW, SAYA...

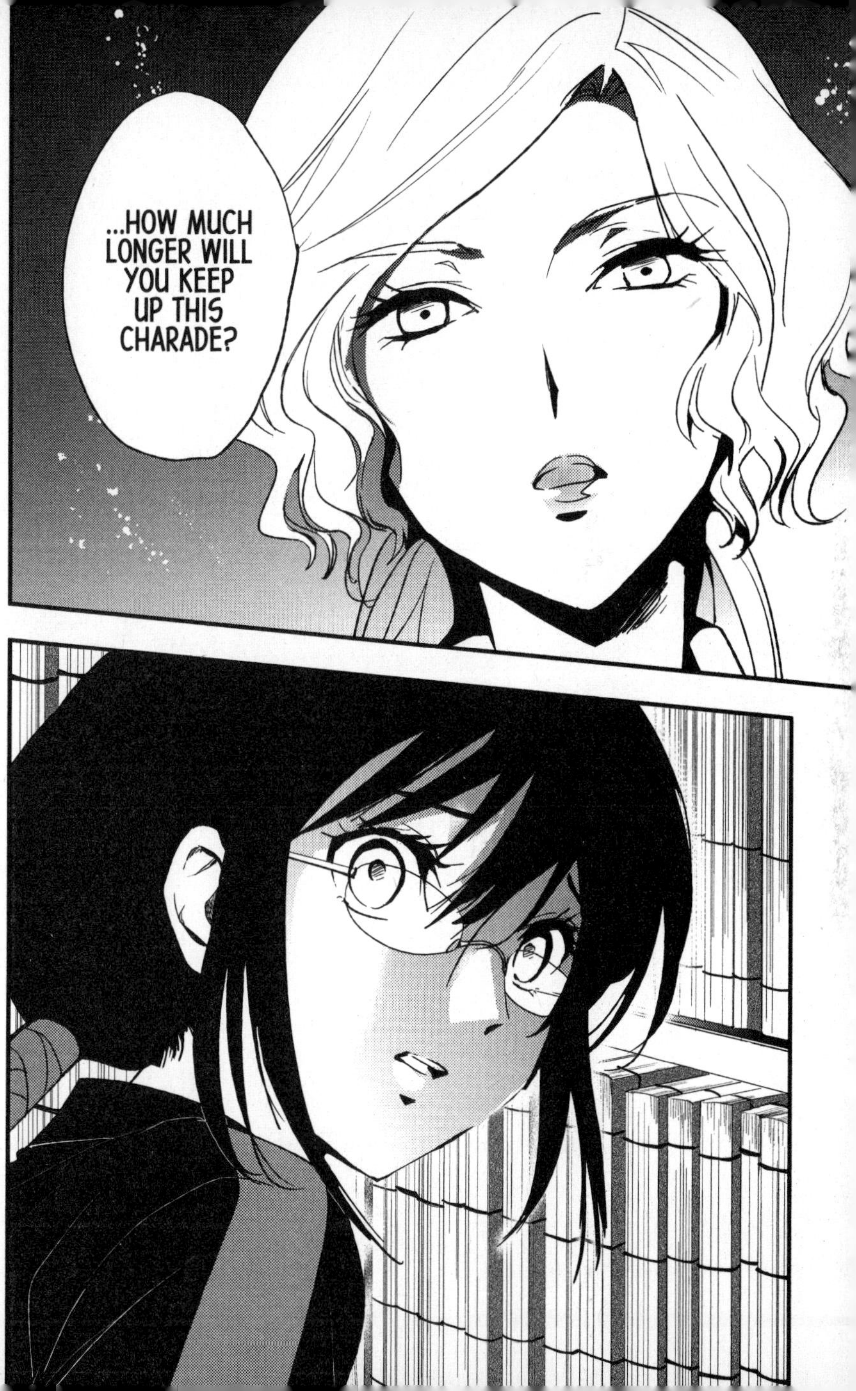
...HOW MUCH LONGER WILL YOU KEEP UP THIS CHARADE?

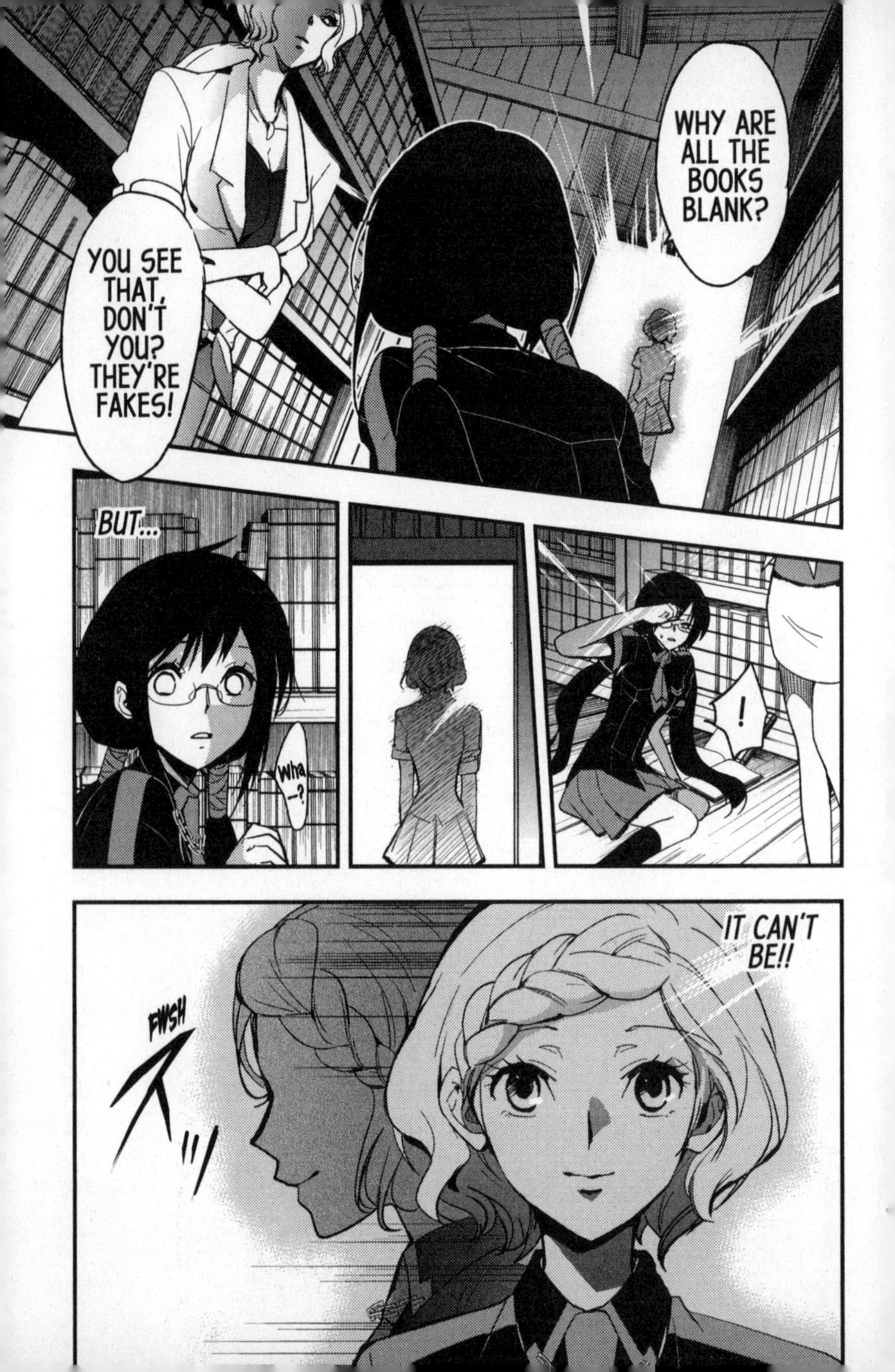
WHY ARE ALL THE BOOKS BLANK?
YOU SEE THAT, DON'T YOU? THEY'RE FAKES!
!
BUT...
Wha—?
IT CAN'T BE!!
FWSH

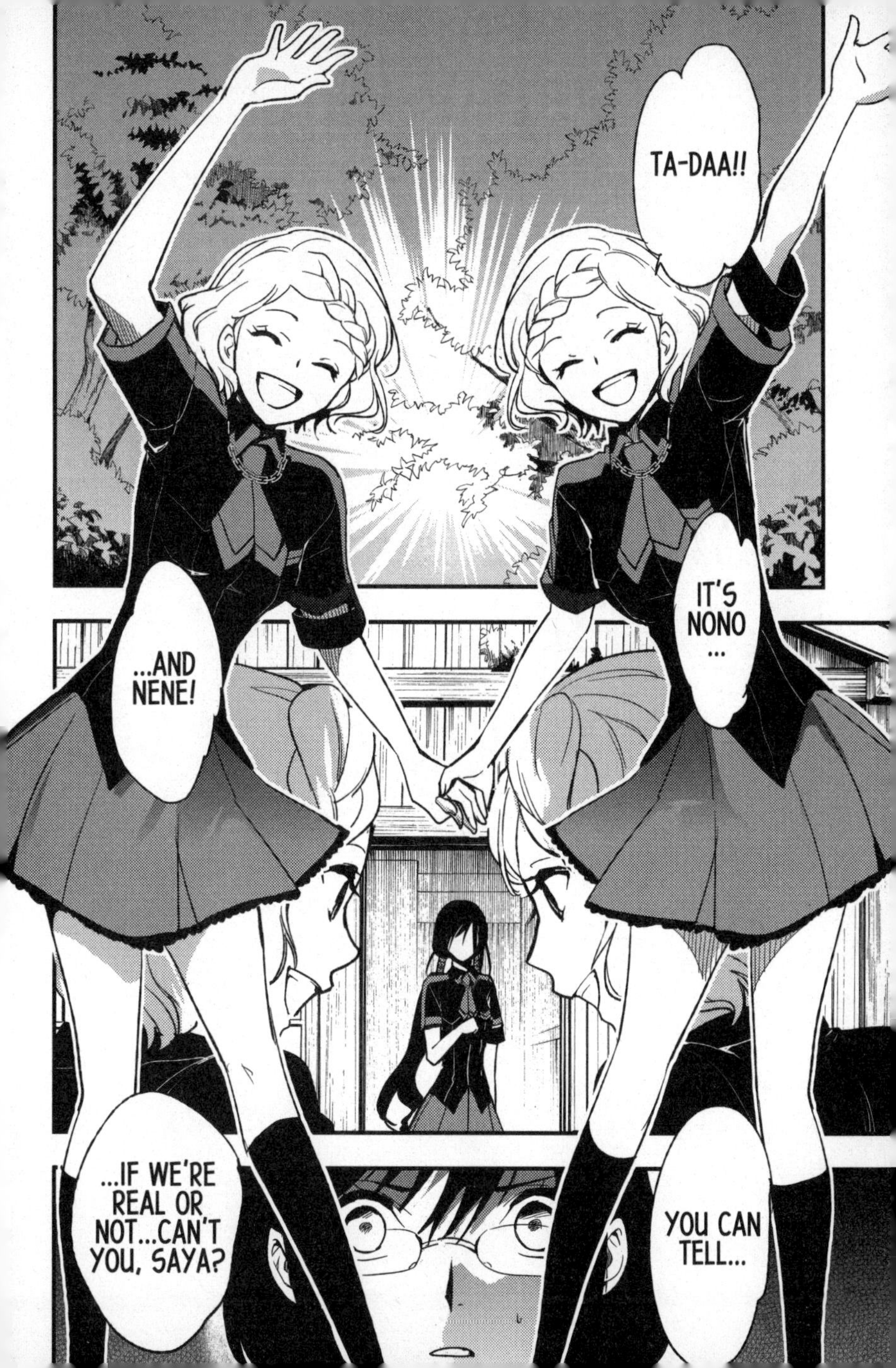
TA-DAA!!
IT'S NONO ...
...AND NENE!
YOU CAN TELL...
...IF WE'RE REAL OR NOT...CAN'T YOU, SAYA?

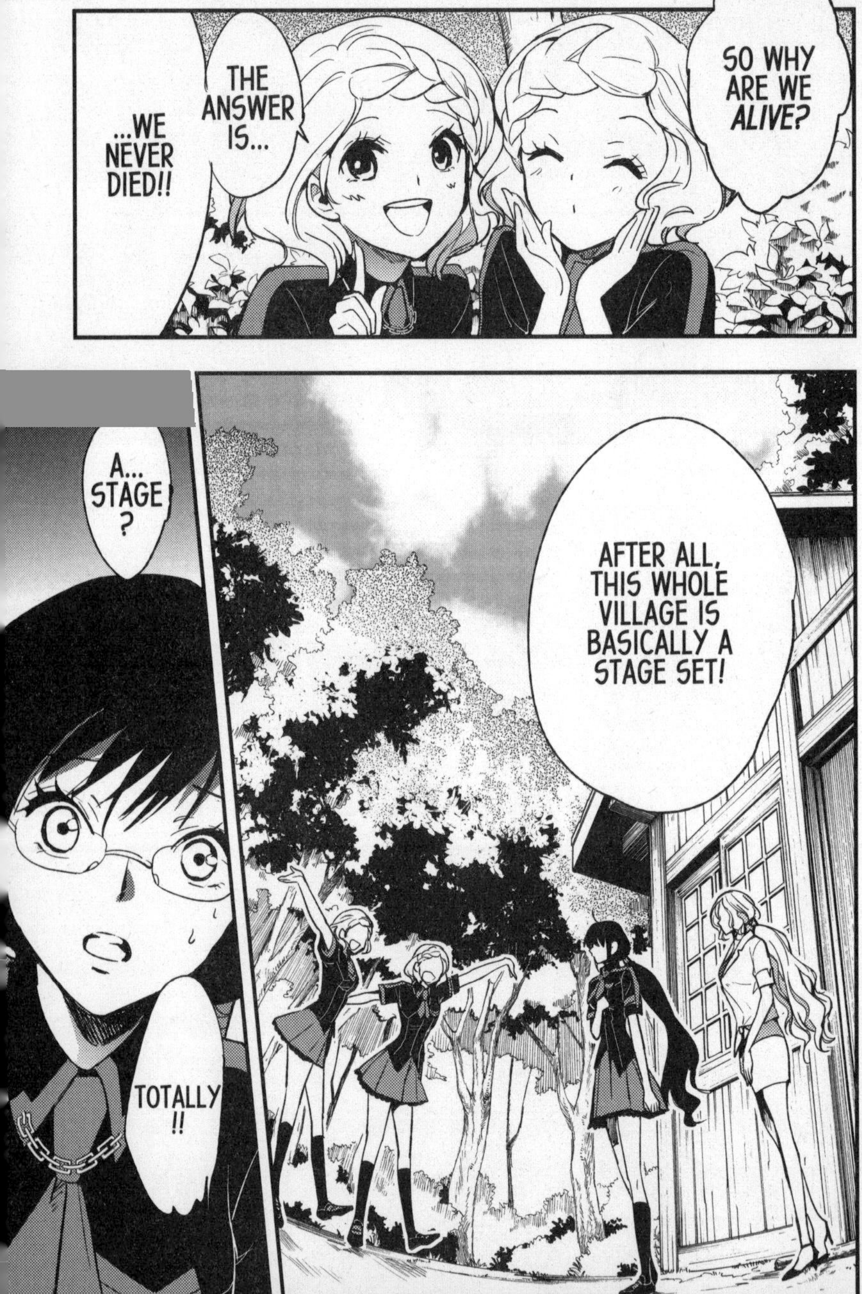
SO WHY ARE WE *ALIVE*?
THE ANSWER IS...
...WE NEVER DIED!!
AFTER ALL, THIS WHOLE VILLAGE IS BASICALLY A STAGE SET!
A... STAGE?
TOTALLY!!

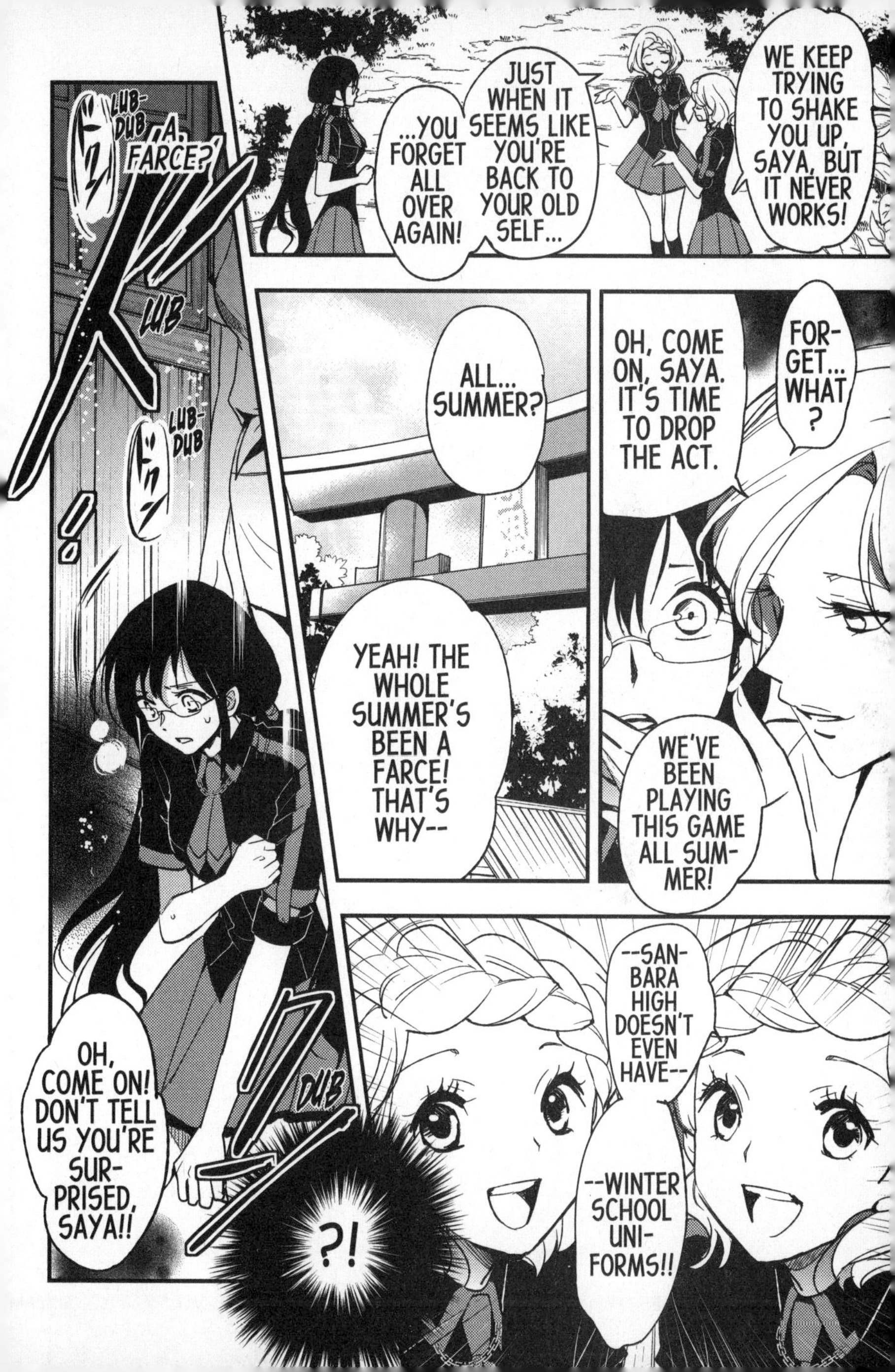
WE KEEP TRYING TO SHAKE YOU UP, SAYA, BUT IT NEVER WORKS!
JUST WHEN IT SEEMS LIKE YOU'RE BACK TO YOUR OLD SELF...
...YOU FORGET ALL OVER AGAIN!
FOR-GET... WHAT?
OH, COME ON, SAYA. IT'S TIME TO DROP THE ACT.
WE'VE BEEN PLAYING THIS GAME ALL SUM-MER!
ALL... SUMMER?
YEAH! THE WHOLE SUMMER'S BEEN A FARCE! THAT'S WHY--
--SAN-BARA HIGH DOESN'T EVEN HAVE--
--WINTER SCHOOL UNI-FORMS!!
LUB-DUB
A, FARCE?
LUB
LUB-DUB
!
OH, COME ON! DON'T TELL US YOU'RE SUR-PRISED, SAYA!!
DUB
?!

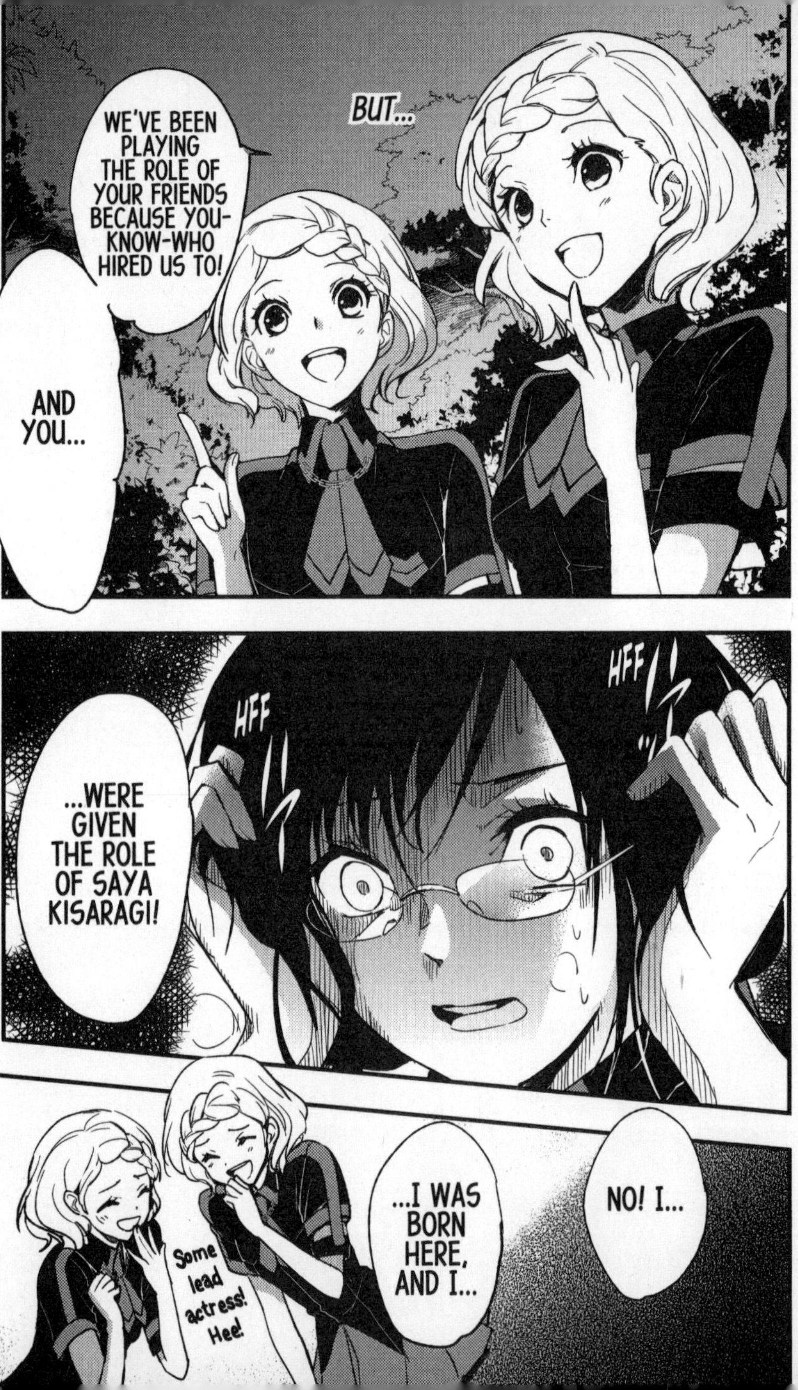
BUT...
WE'VE BEEN PLAYING THE ROLE OF YOUR FRIENDS BECAUSE YOU-KNOW-WHO HIRED US TO!
AND YOU...
HFF
HFF
...WERE GIVEN THE ROLE OF SAYA KISARAGI!
NO! I...
...I WAS BORN HERE, AND I...
Some lead actress! Hee!

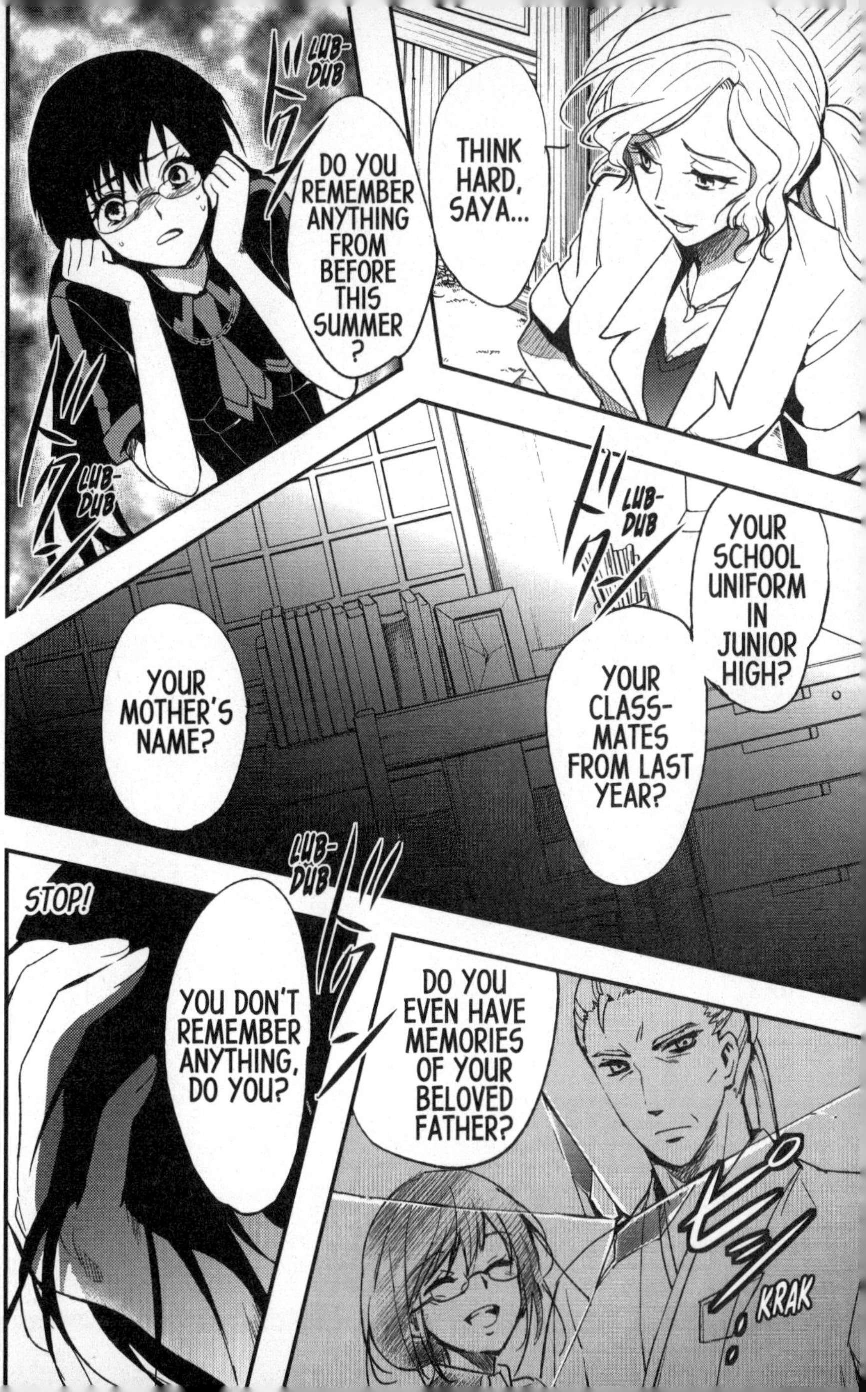
THINK HARD, SAYA...
DO YOU REMEMBER ANYTHING FROM BEFORE THIS SUMMER?
LUB-DUB
LUB-DUB
LUB-DUB
YOUR SCHOOL UNIFORM IN JUNIOR HIGH?
YOUR CLASS-MATES FROM LAST YEAR?
YOUR MOTHER'S NAME?
KRAK
DO YOU EVEN HAVE MEMORIES OF YOUR BELOVED FATHER?
LUB-DUB
YOU DON'T REMEMBER ANYTHING, DO YOU?
STOP!

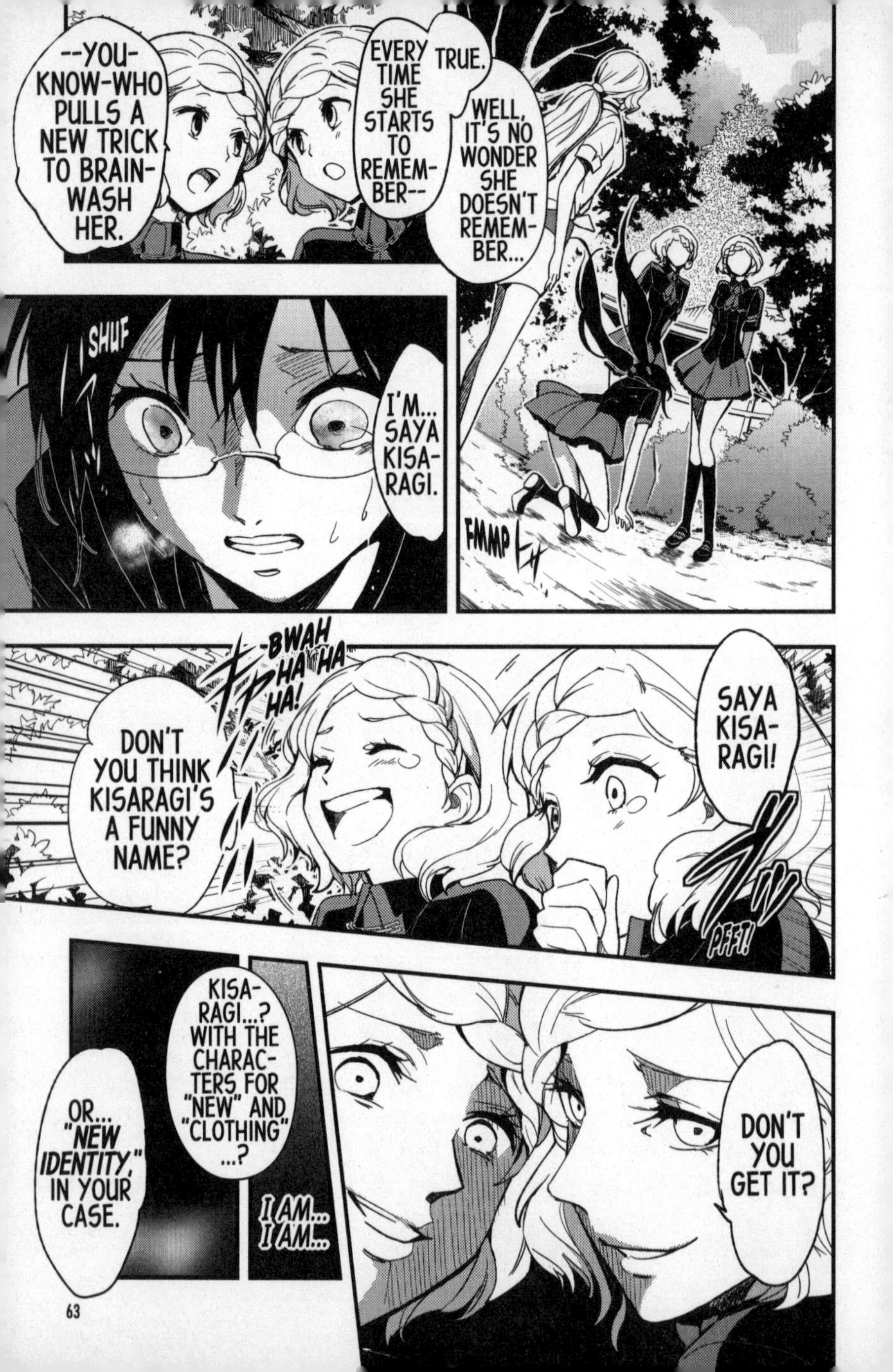
TRUE.
WELL, IT'S NO WONDER SHE DOESN'T REMEMBER...
FMMP
EVERY TIME SHE STARTS TO REMEMBER--
--YOU-KNOW-WHO PULLS A NEW TRICK TO BRAIN-WASH HER.
SHUF
I'M... SAYA KISARAGI.
SAYA KISARAGI!
PFFT!
BWAH HA HA HA!
DON'T YOU THINK KISARAGI'S A FUNNY NAME?
DON'T YOU GET IT?
KISARAGI...? WITH THE CHARACTERS FOR "NEW" AND "CLOTHING" ...?
OR... "*NEW IDENTITY*," IN YOUR CASE.
I AM... I AM...

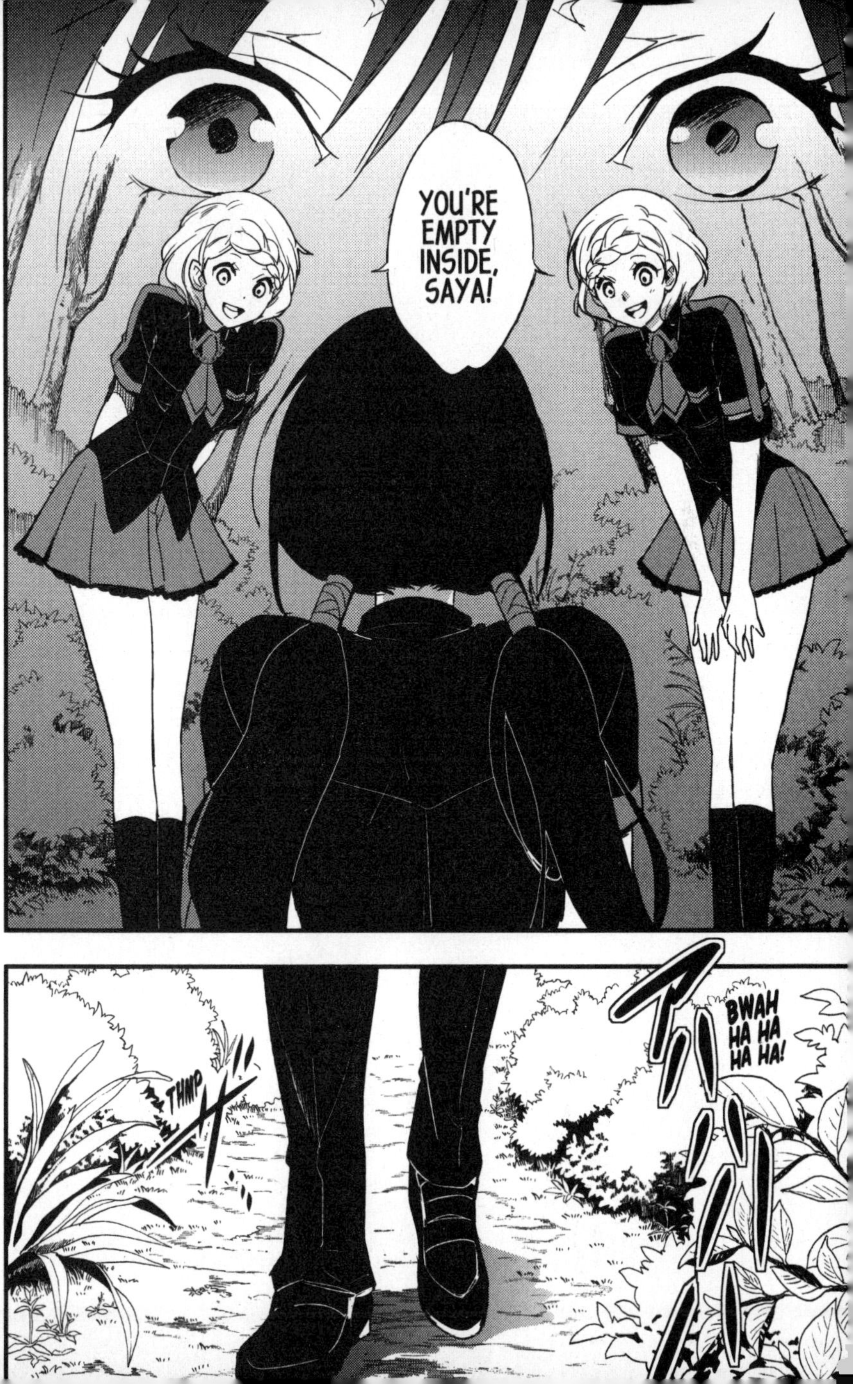
YOU'RE EMPTY INSIDE, SAYA!
BWAH HA HA HA HA!
THMP

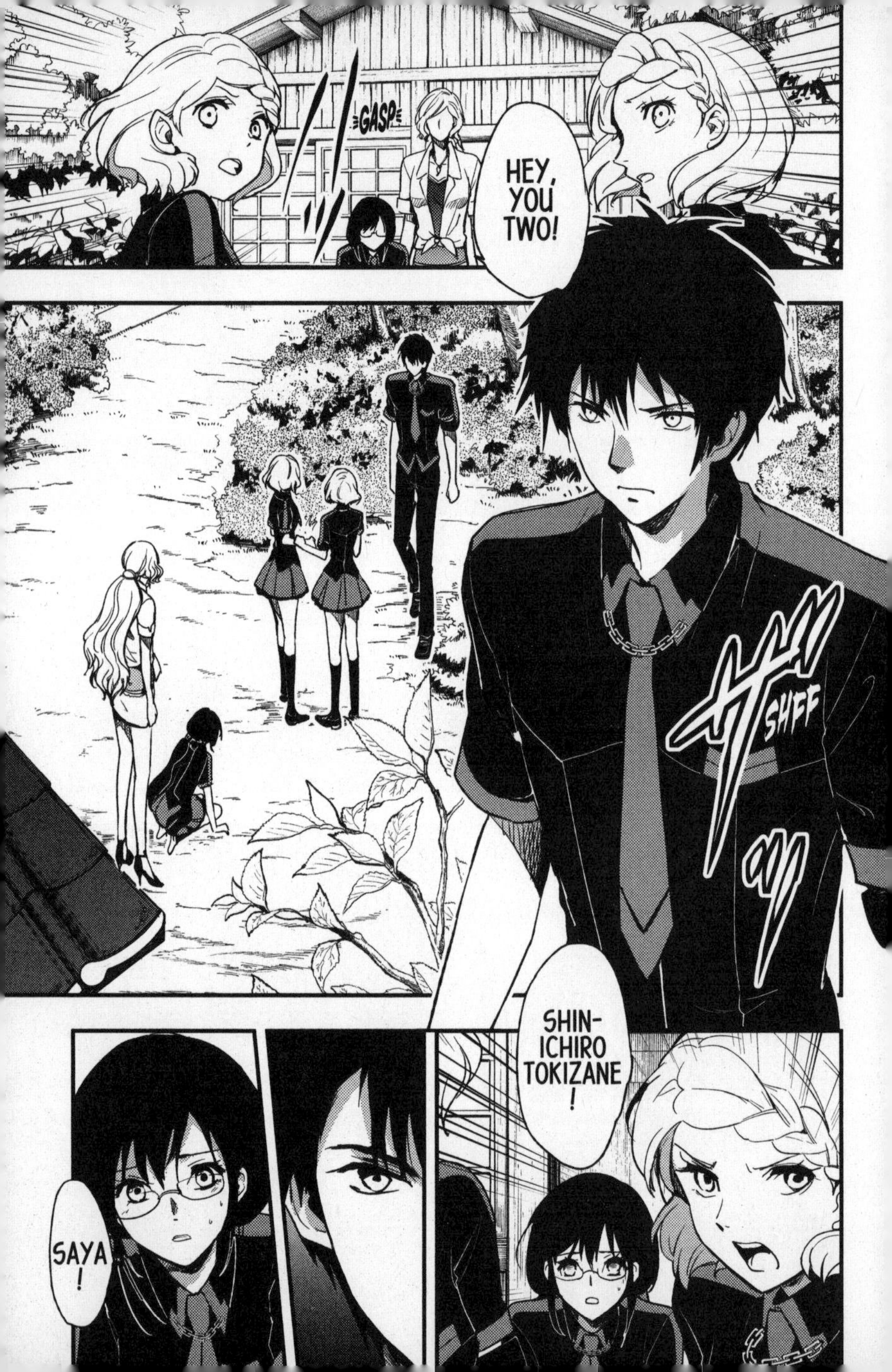
HEY, YOU TWO!
GASP
SHFF
SHIN-ICHIRO TOKIZANE!
SAYA!

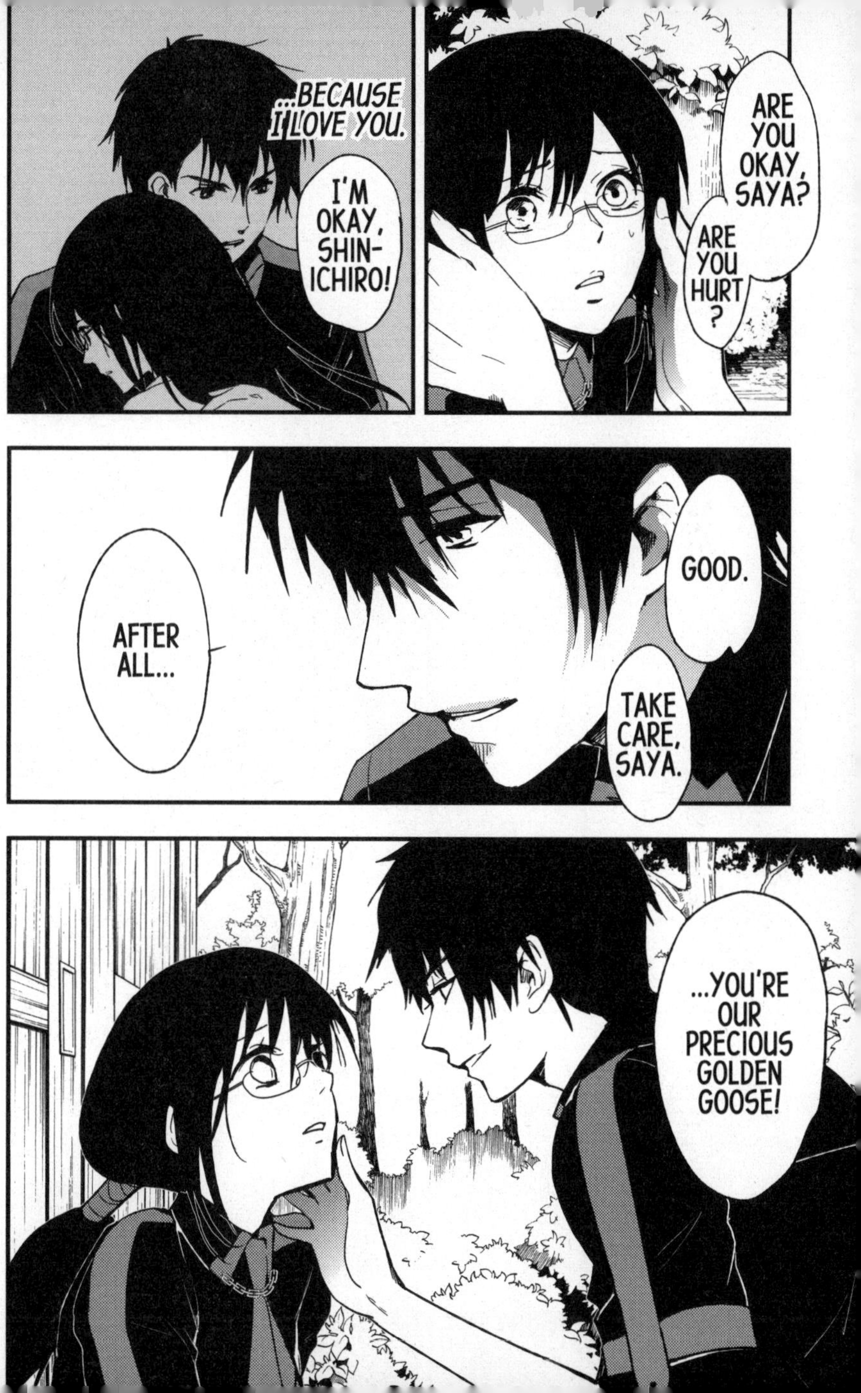
ARE YOU OKAY, SAYA?
ARE YOU HURT?
...BECAUSE I LOVE YOU.
I'M OKAY, SHIN-ICHIRO!
GOOD.
TAKE CARE, SAYA.
AFTER ALL...
...YOU'RE OUR PRECIOUS GOLDEN GOOSE!

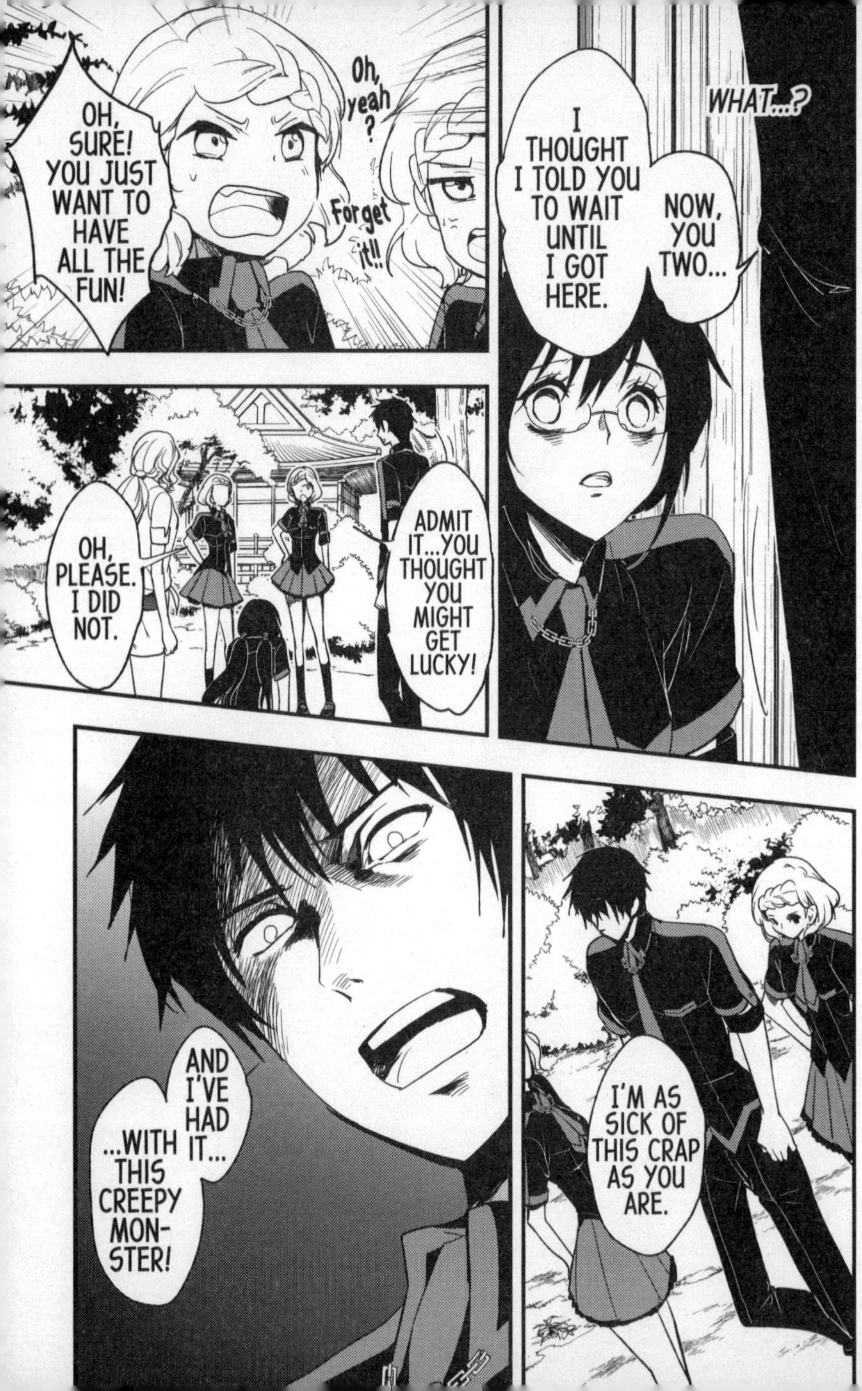
WHAT...?
NOW, YOU TWO...
I THOUGHT I TOLD YOU TO WAIT UNTIL I GOT HERE.
Oh, yeah?
Forget it!!
OH, SURE! YOU JUST WANT TO HAVE ALL THE FUN!
ADMIT IT...YOU THOUGHT YOU MIGHT GET LUCKY!
OH, PLEASE. I DID NOT.
I'M AS SICK OF THIS CRAP AS YOU ARE.
AND I'VE HAD IT...
...WITH THIS CREEPY MON-STER!

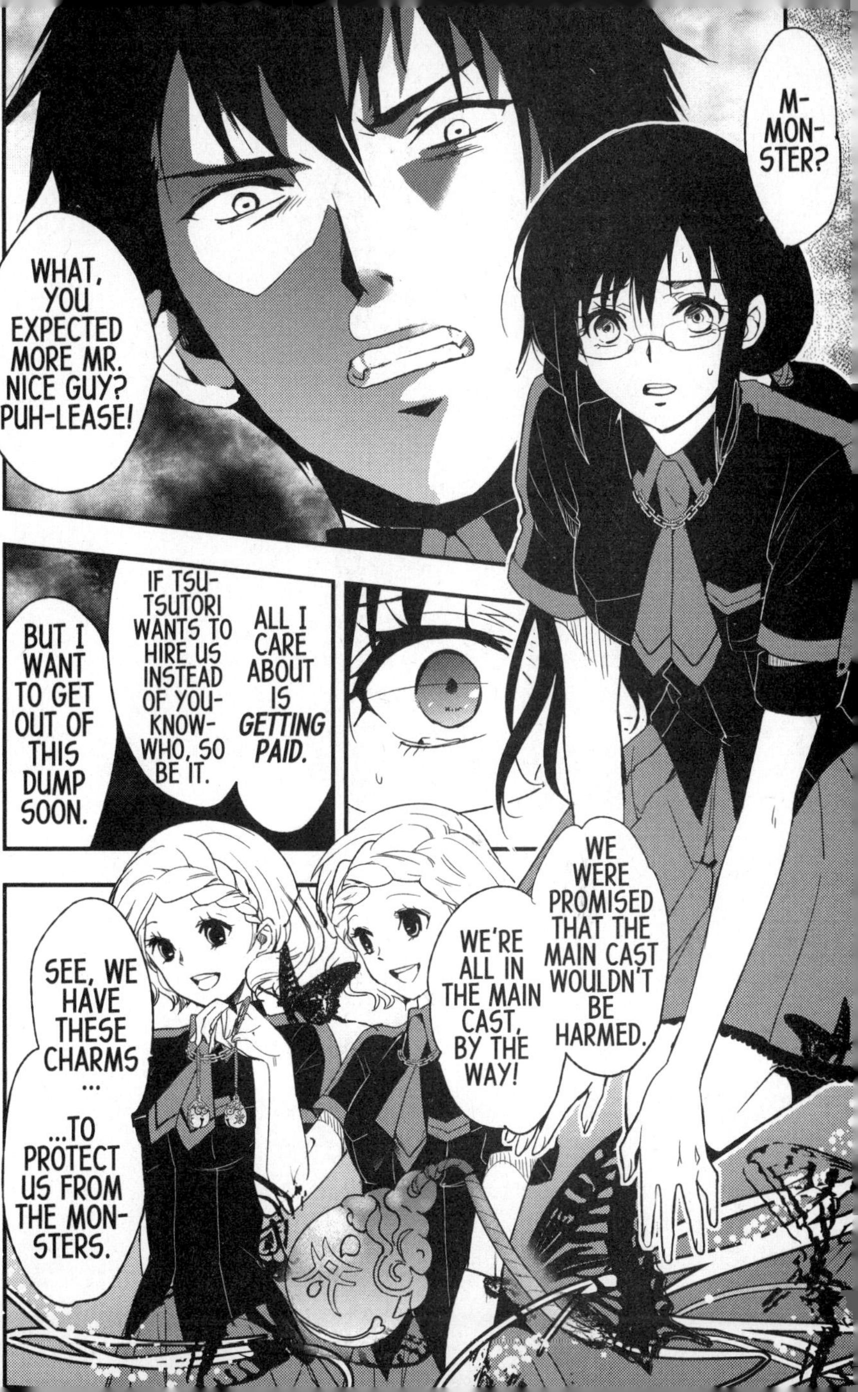
M-MONSTER?
WHAT, YOU EXPECTED MORE MR. NICE GUY? PUH-LEASE!
ALL I CARE ABOUT IS *GETTING PAID.*
IF TSUTSUTORI WANTS TO HIRE US INSTEAD OF YOU-KNOW-WHO, SO BE IT.
BUT I WANT TO GET OUT OF THIS DUMP SOON.
WE WERE PROMISED THAT THE MAIN CAST WOULDN'T BE HARMED.
WE'RE ALL IN THE MAIN CAST, BY THE WAY!
SEE, WE HAVE THESE CHARMS...
...TO PROTECT US FROM THE MONSTERS.

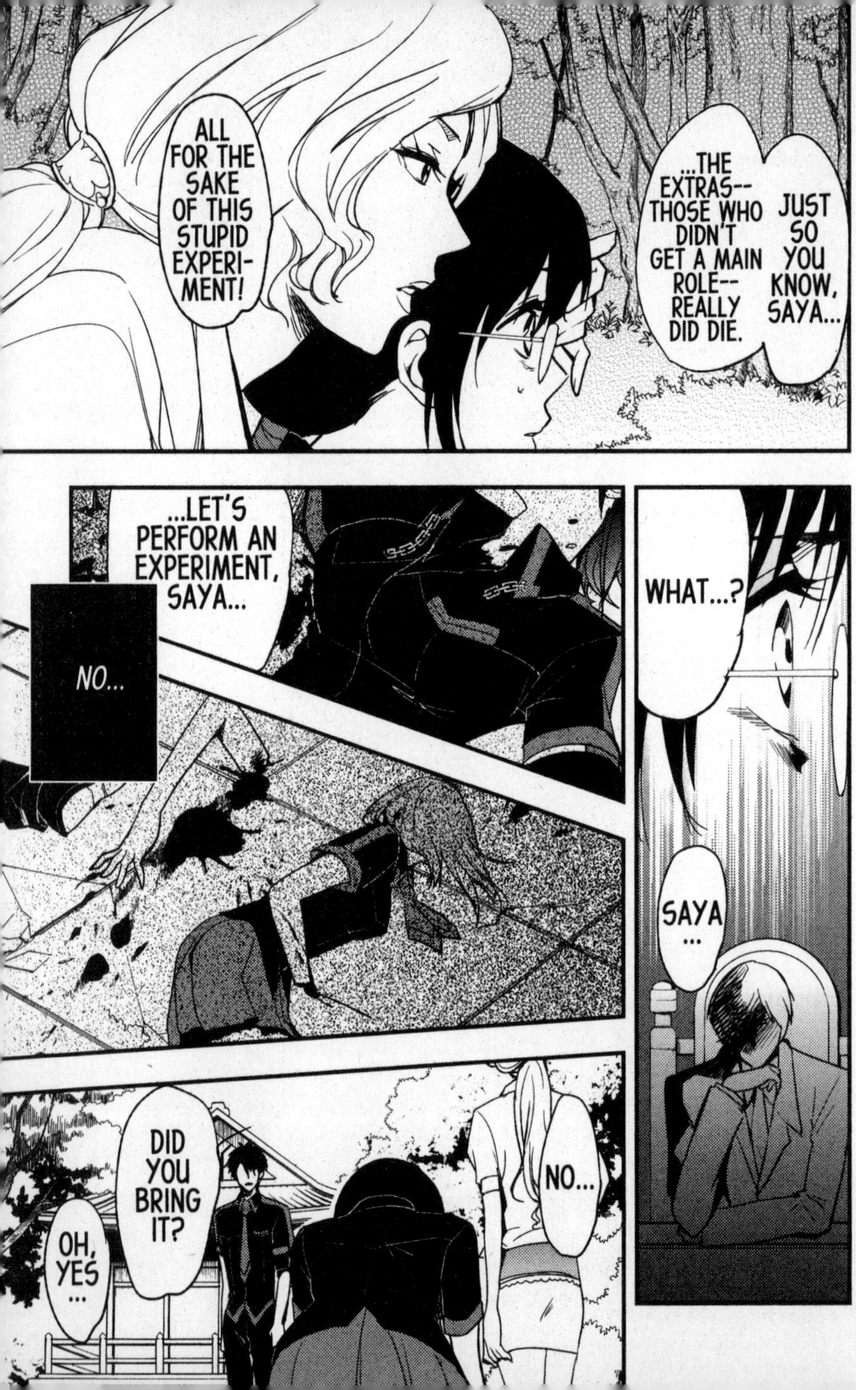
JUST SO YOU KNOW, SAYA...
...THE EXTRAS-- THOSE WHO DIDN'T GET A MAIN ROLE-- REALLY DID DIE.
ALL FOR THE SAKE OF THIS STUPID EXPERIMENT!
WHAT...?
SAYA...
...LET'S PERFORM AN EXPERIMENT, SAYA...
NO...
NO...
DID YOU BRING IT?
OH, YES...

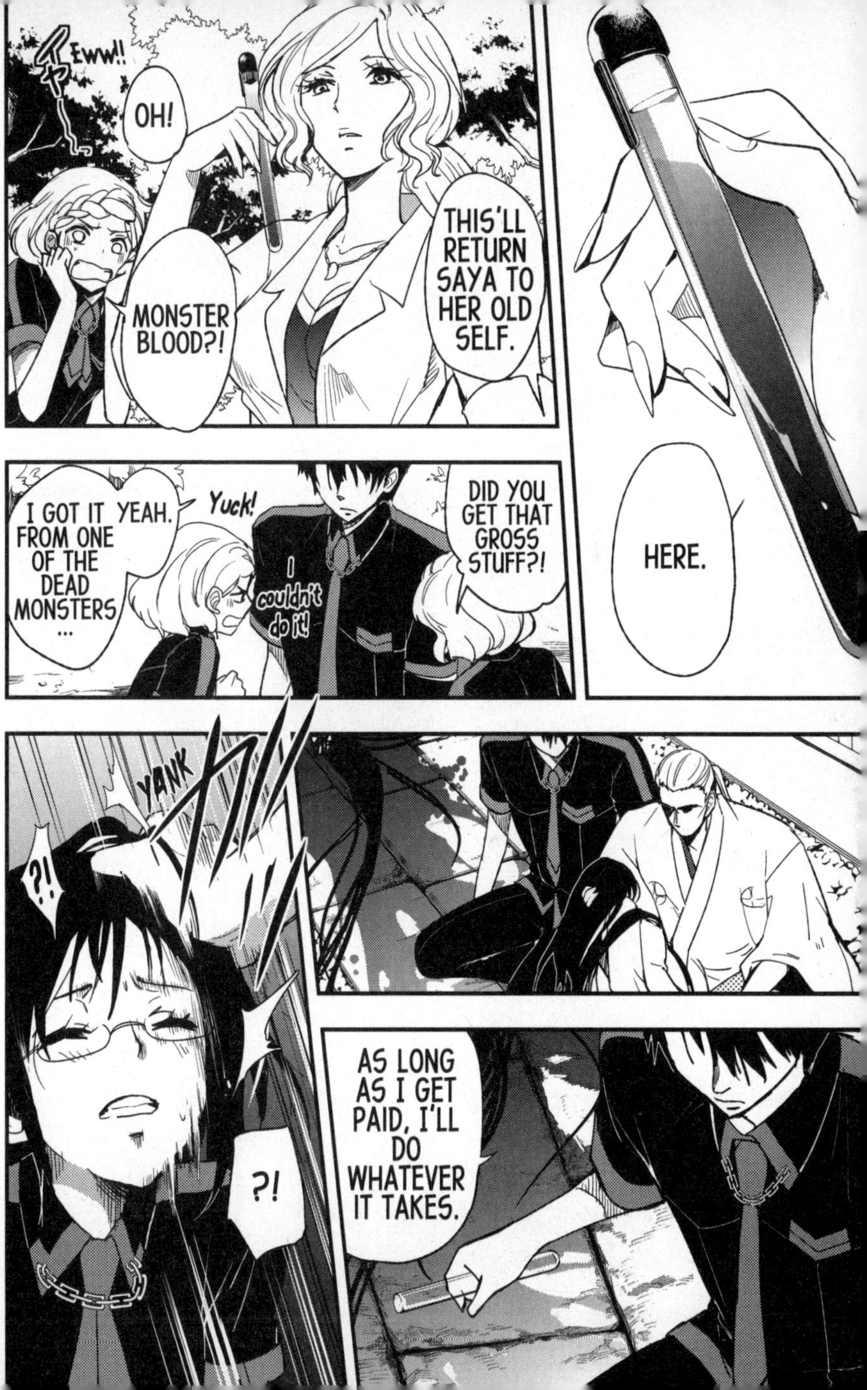
HERE.
THIS'LL RETURN SAYA TO HER OLD SELF.
Eww!!
OH!
MONSTER BLOOD?!
DID YOU GET THAT GROSS STUFF?!
I couldn't do it!
Yuck!
YEAH. I GOT IT FROM ONE OF THE DEAD MONSTERS ...
AS LONG AS I GET PAID, I'LL DO WHATEVER IT TAKES.
?!
YANK
?!

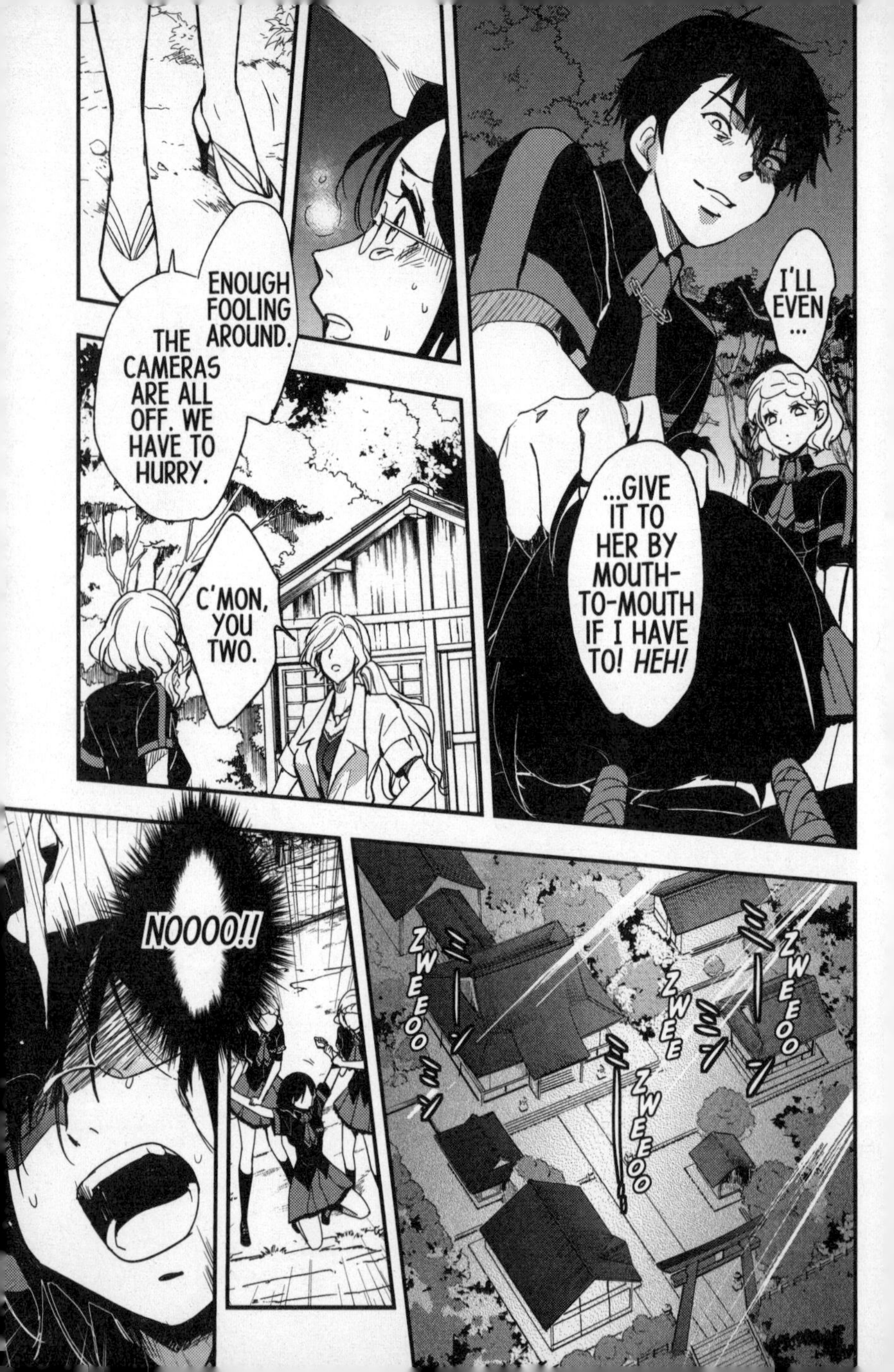
I'LL EVEN...
...GIVE IT TO HER BY MOUTH-TO-MOUTH IF I HAVE TO! HEH!
ENOUGH FOOLING AROUND. THE CAMERAS ARE ALL OFF. WE HAVE TO HURRY.
C'MON, YOU TWO.
ZWEEOO
ZWEE
ZWEEOO
ZWEEOO
NOOOO!!

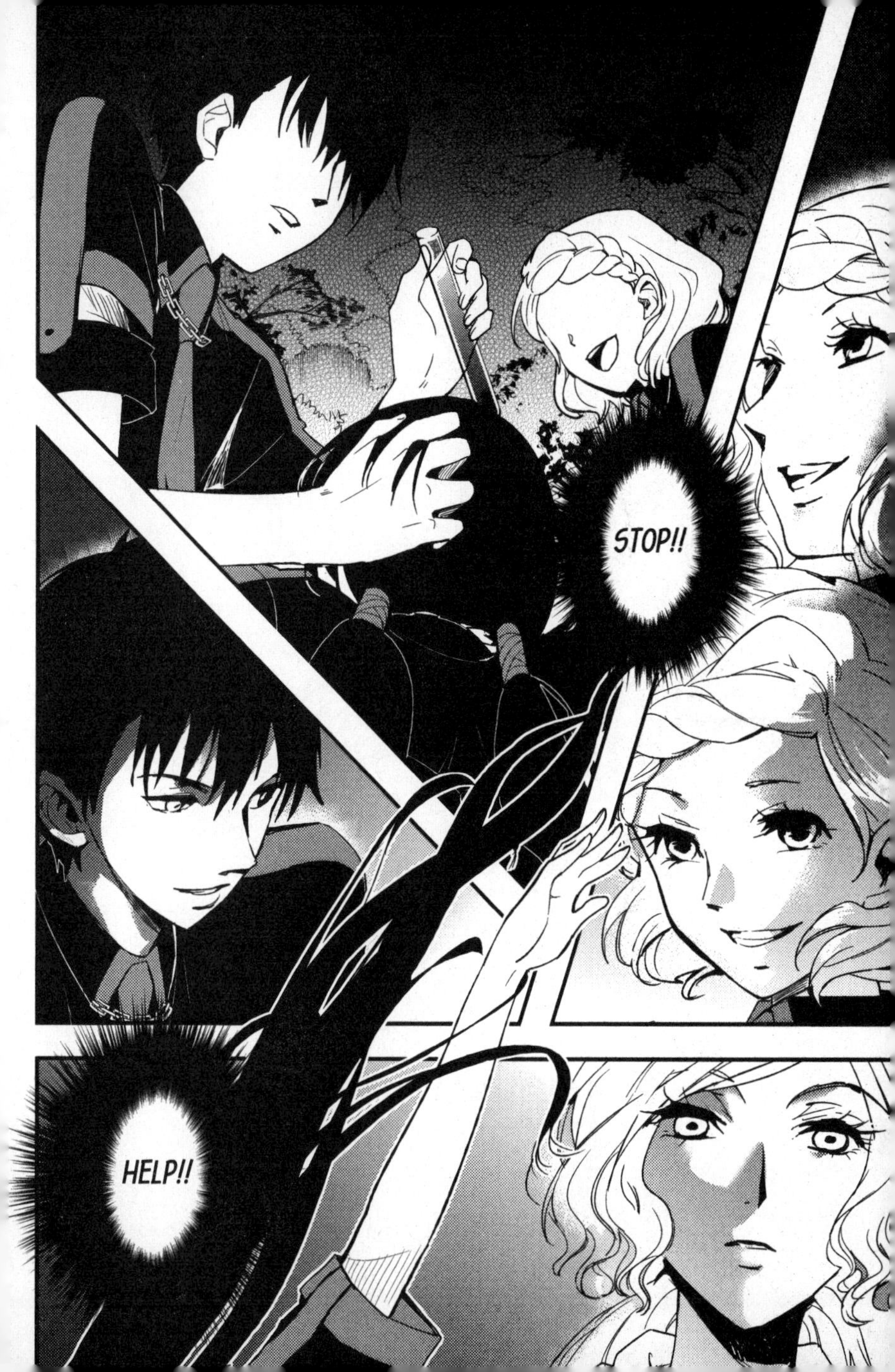
STOP!!
HELP!!

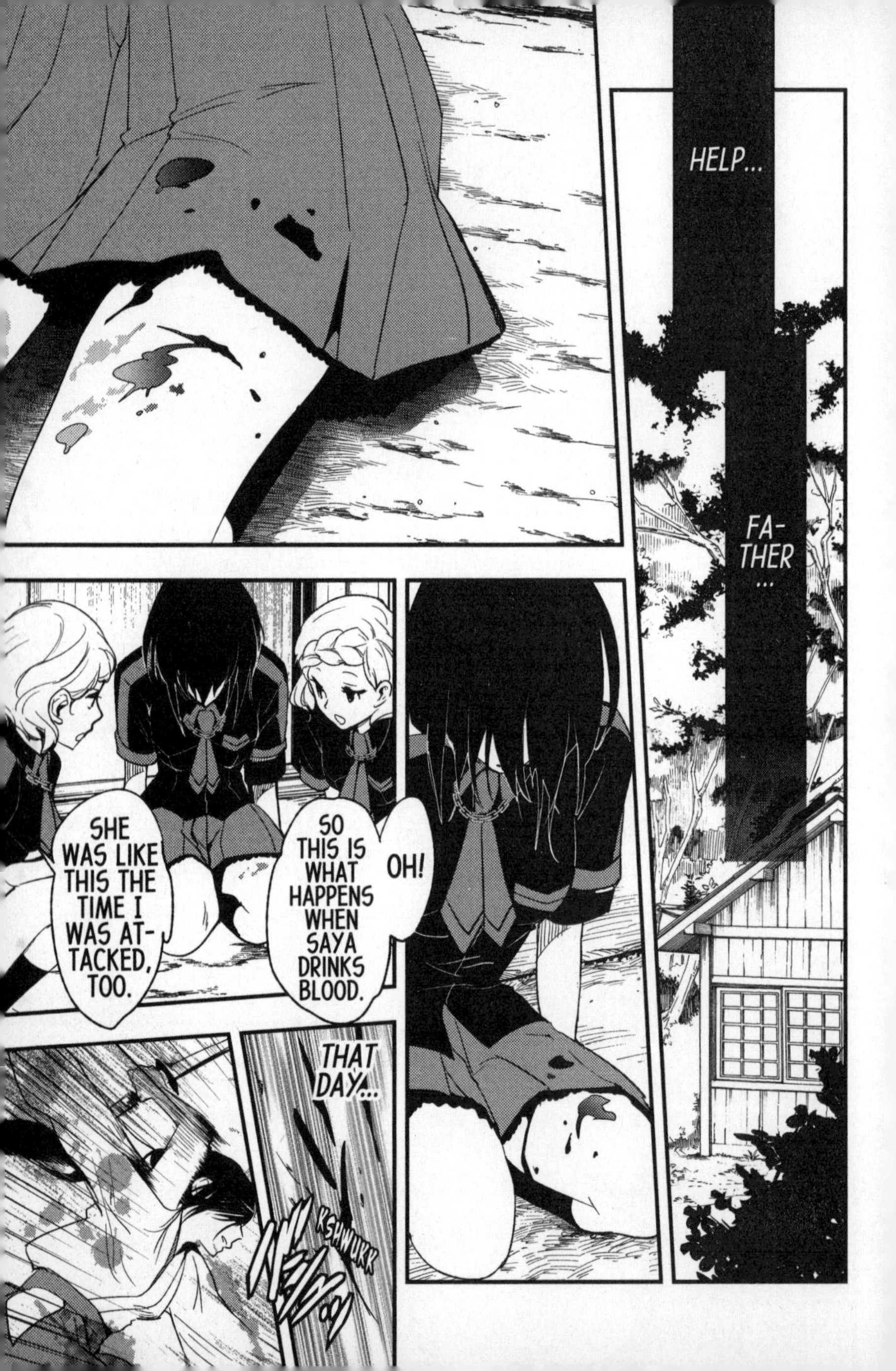
HELP...
FA-THER...
OH!
SO THIS IS WHAT HAPPENS WHEN SAYA DRINKS BLOOD.
SHE WAS LIKE THIS THE TIME I WAS AT-TACKED, TOO.
THAT DAY...
KSHWUKK

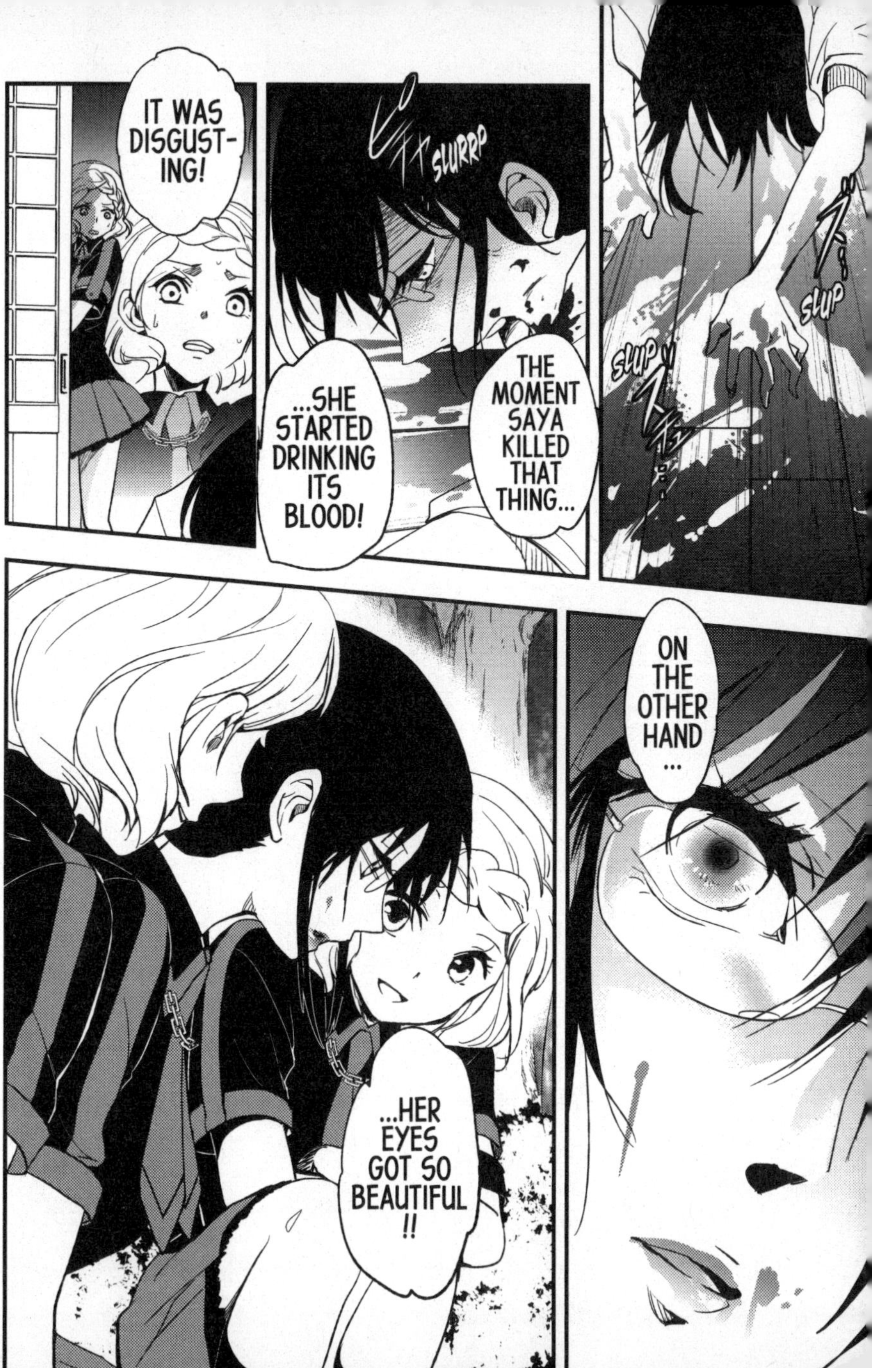
SLUP
SLUP
SLURRP
THE MOMENT SAYA KILLED THAT THING...
...SHE STARTED DRINKING ITS BLOOD!
IT WAS DISGUST-ING!
ON THE OTHER HAND...
...HER EYES GOT SO BEAUTIFUL!!

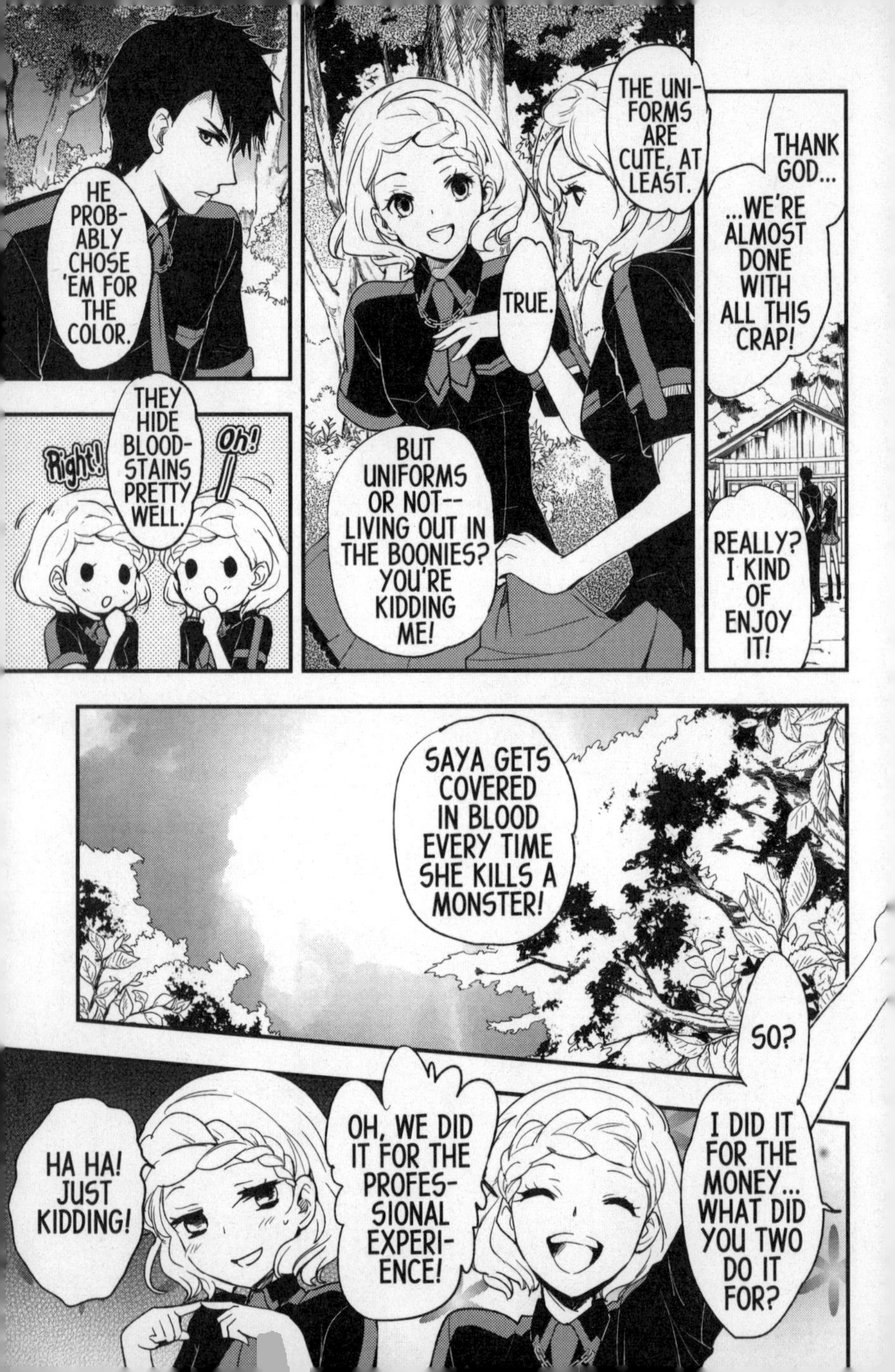
THANK GOD...
...WE'RE ALMOST DONE WITH ALL THIS CRAP!
REALLY? I KIND OF ENJOY IT!
THE UNI-FORMS ARE CUTE, AT LEAST.
TRUE.
BUT UNIFORMS OR NOT-- LIVING OUT IN THE BOONIES? YOU'RE KIDDING ME!
HE PROB-ABLY CHOSE 'EM FOR THE COLOR.
THEY HIDE BLOOD-STAINS PRETTY WELL.
Oh!
Right!
SAYA GETS COVERED IN BLOOD EVERY TIME SHE KILLS A MONSTER!
SO?
I DID IT FOR THE MONEY... WHAT DID YOU TWO DO IT FOR?
OH, WE DID IT FOR THE PROFES-SIONAL EXPERI-ENCE!
HA HA! JUST KIDDING!

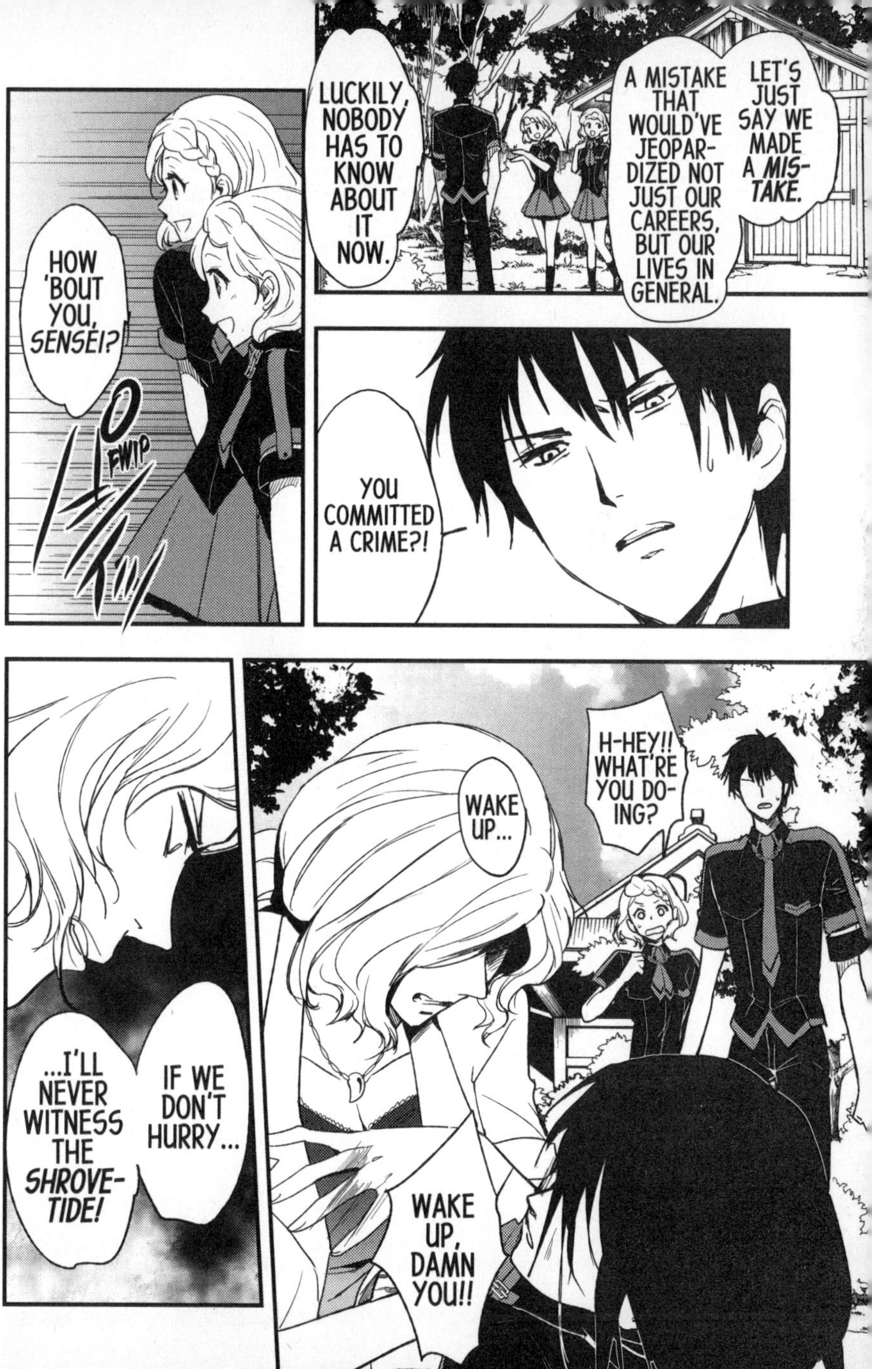
LET'S JUST SAY WE MADE A MISTAKE.
A MISTAKE THAT WOULD'VE JEOPARDIZED NOT JUST OUR CAREERS, BUT OUR LIVES IN GENERAL.
LUCKILY, NOBODY HAS TO KNOW ABOUT IT NOW.
YOU COMMITTED A CRIME?!
HOW 'BOUT YOU, SENSEI?
FWIP
H-HEY!! WHAT'RE YOU DOING?
WAKE UP...
WAKE UP, DAMN YOU!!
IF WE DON'T HURRY...
...I'LL NEVER WITNESS THE SHROVETIDE!

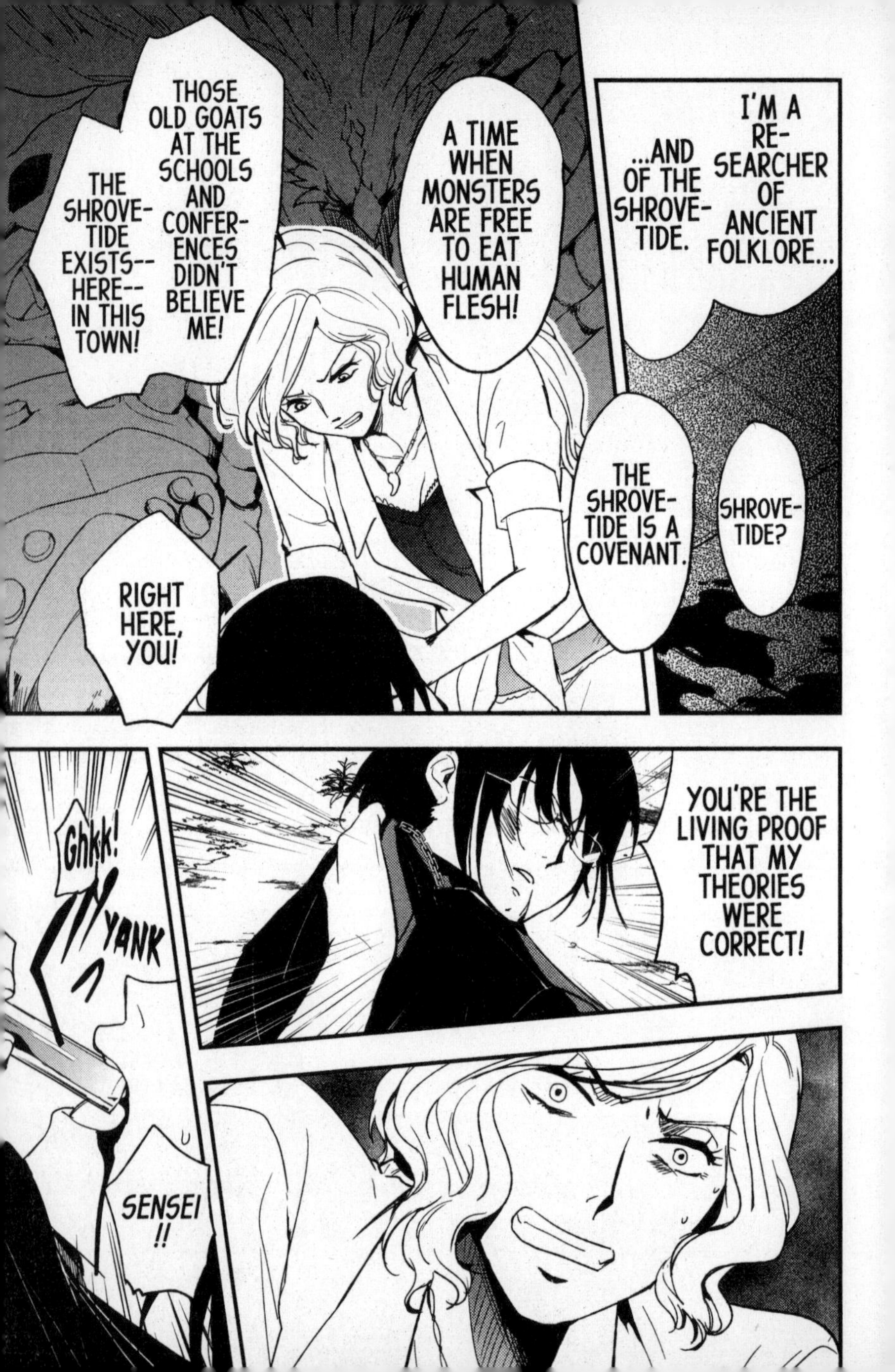
I'M A RESEARCHER OF ANCIENT FOLKLORE...
...AND OF THE SHROVETIDE.
SHROVETIDE?
THE SHROVETIDE IS A COVENANT.
A TIME WHEN MONSTERS ARE FREE TO EAT HUMAN FLESH!
THOSE OLD GOATS AT THE SCHOOLS AND CONFERENCES DIDN'T BELIEVE ME!
THE SHROVETIDE EXISTS--HERE--IN THIS TOWN!
RIGHT HERE, YOU!
YOU'RE THE LIVING PROOF THAT MY THEORIES WERE CORRECT!
Ghkk!
YANK
SENSEI!!

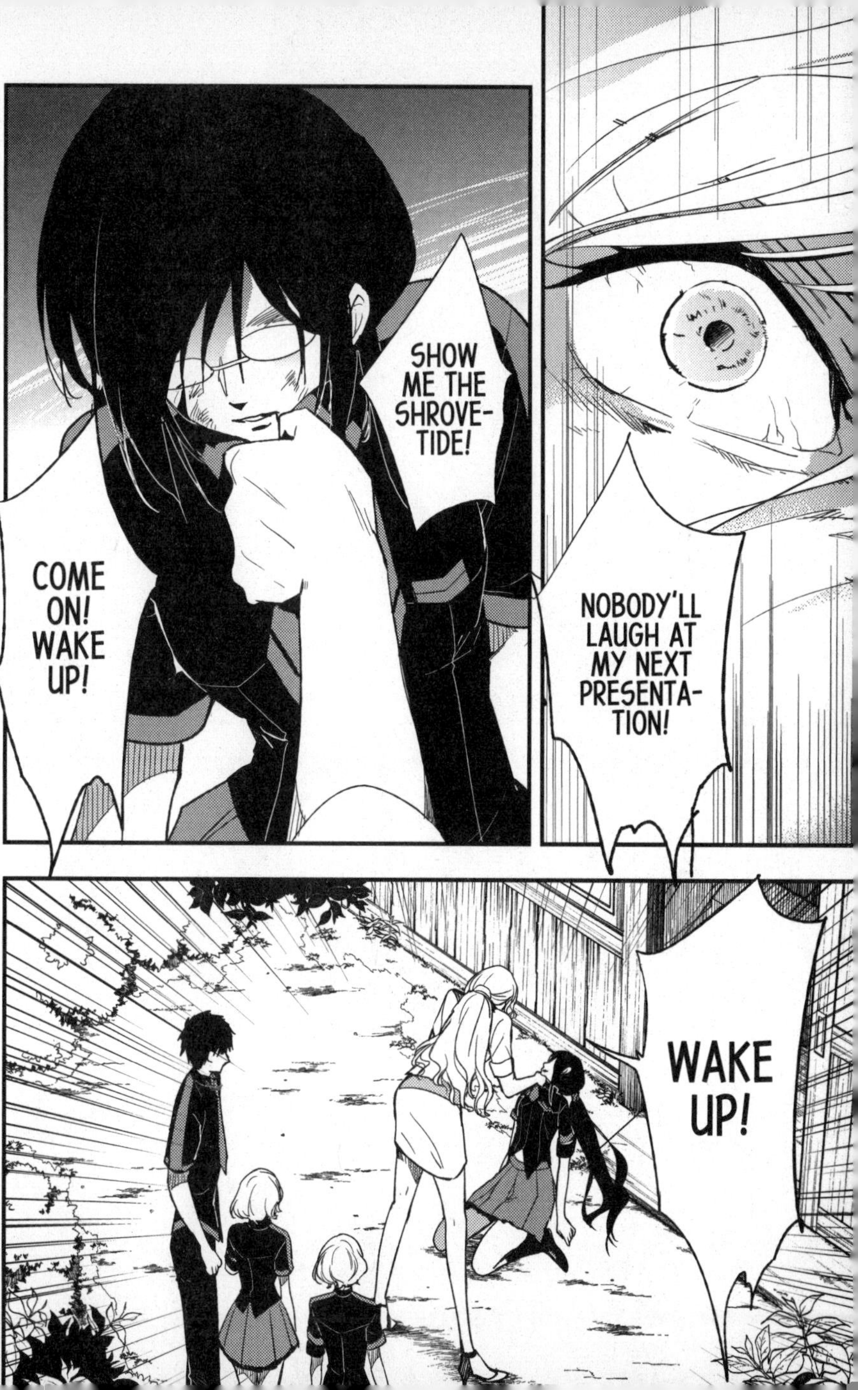
NOBODY'LL LAUGH AT MY NEXT PRESENTA-TION!
SHOW ME THE SHROVE-TIDE!
COME ON! WAKE UP!
WAKE UP!

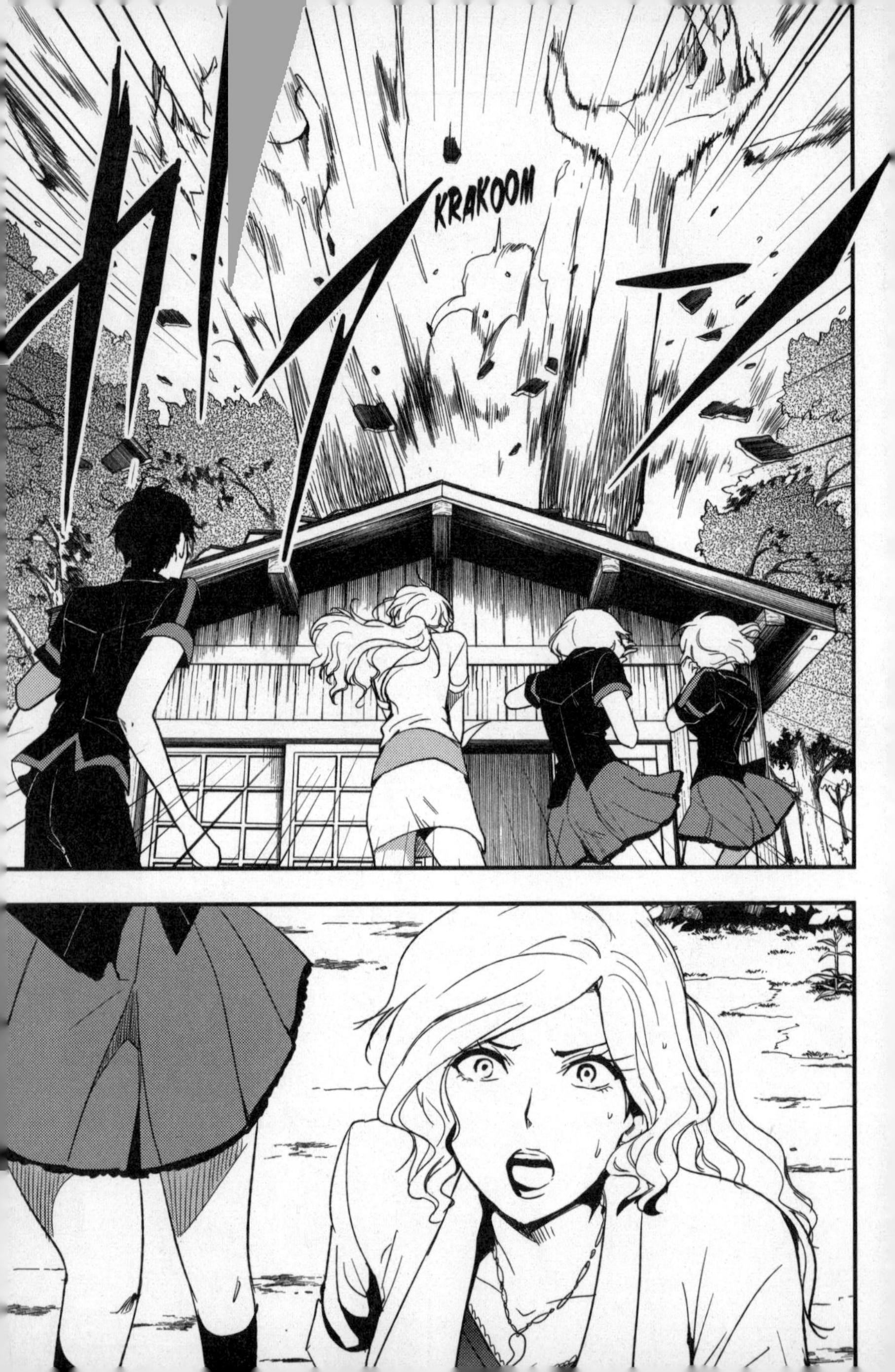
KRAKOOM

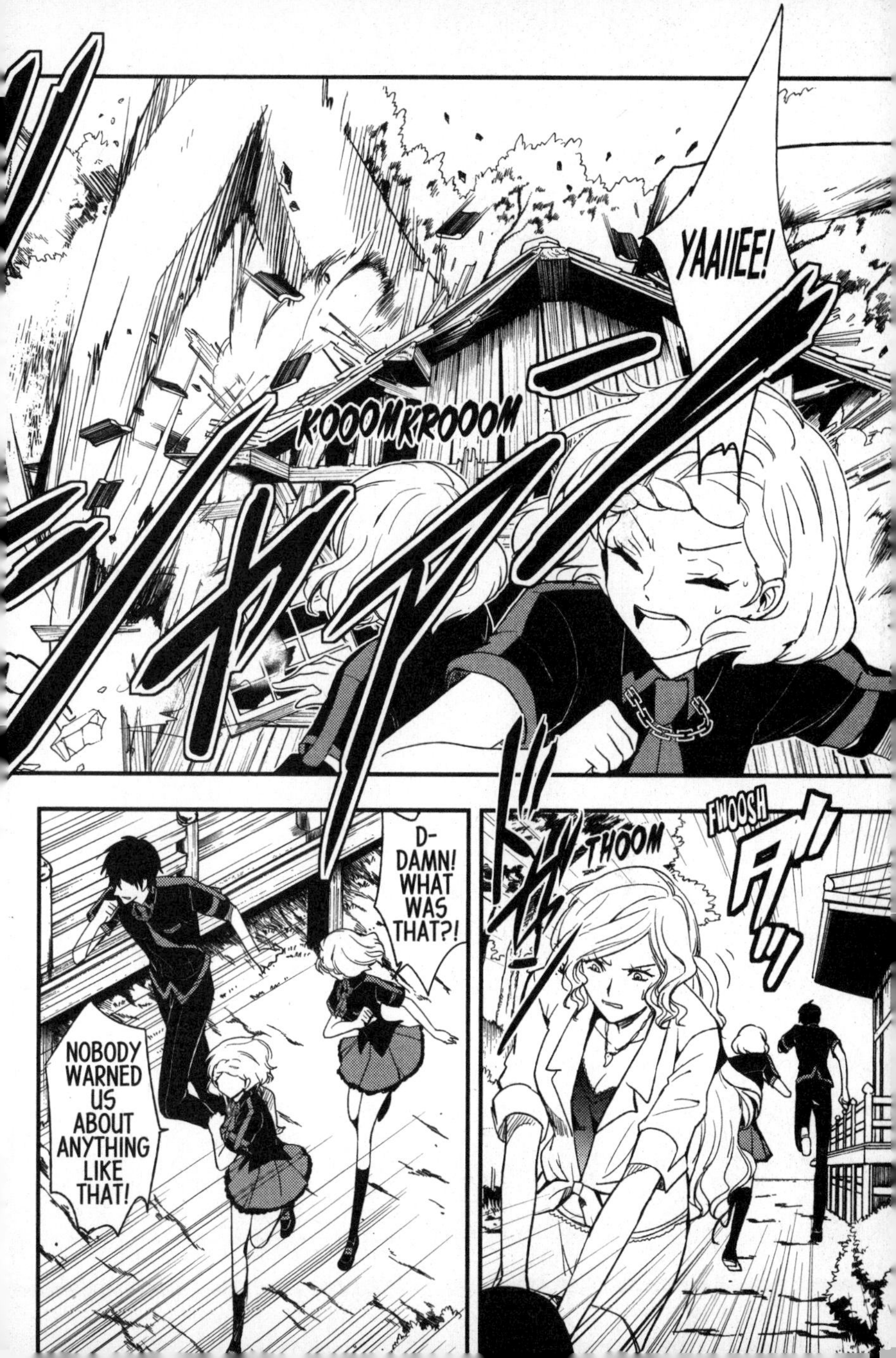
YAAIIEE!
KOOOMKROOOM
FWOOSH
THOOM
D-DAMN! WHAT WAS THAT?!
NOBODY WARNED US ABOUT ANYTHING LIKE THAT!

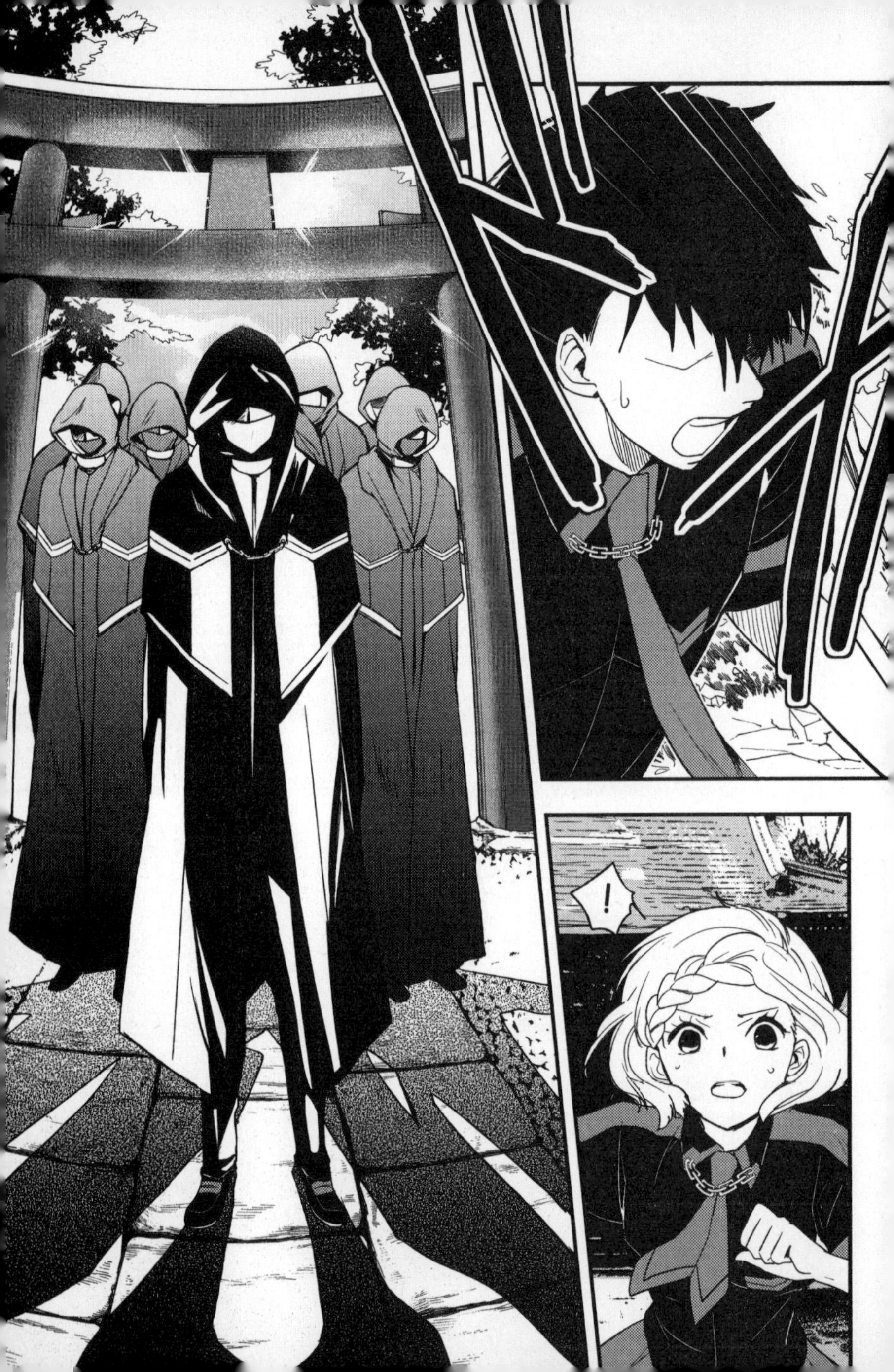
!

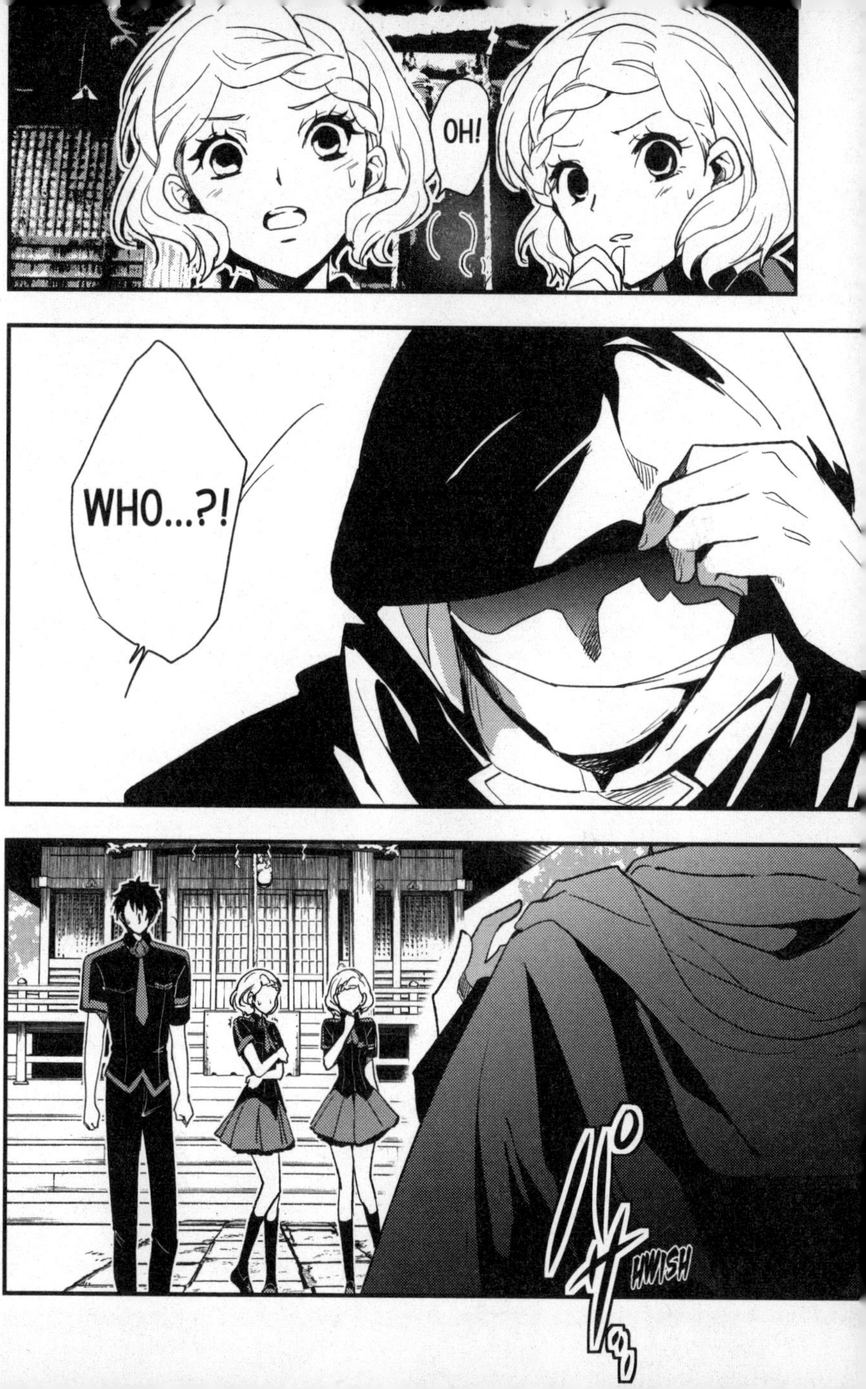
OH!
WHO...?!
HWISH

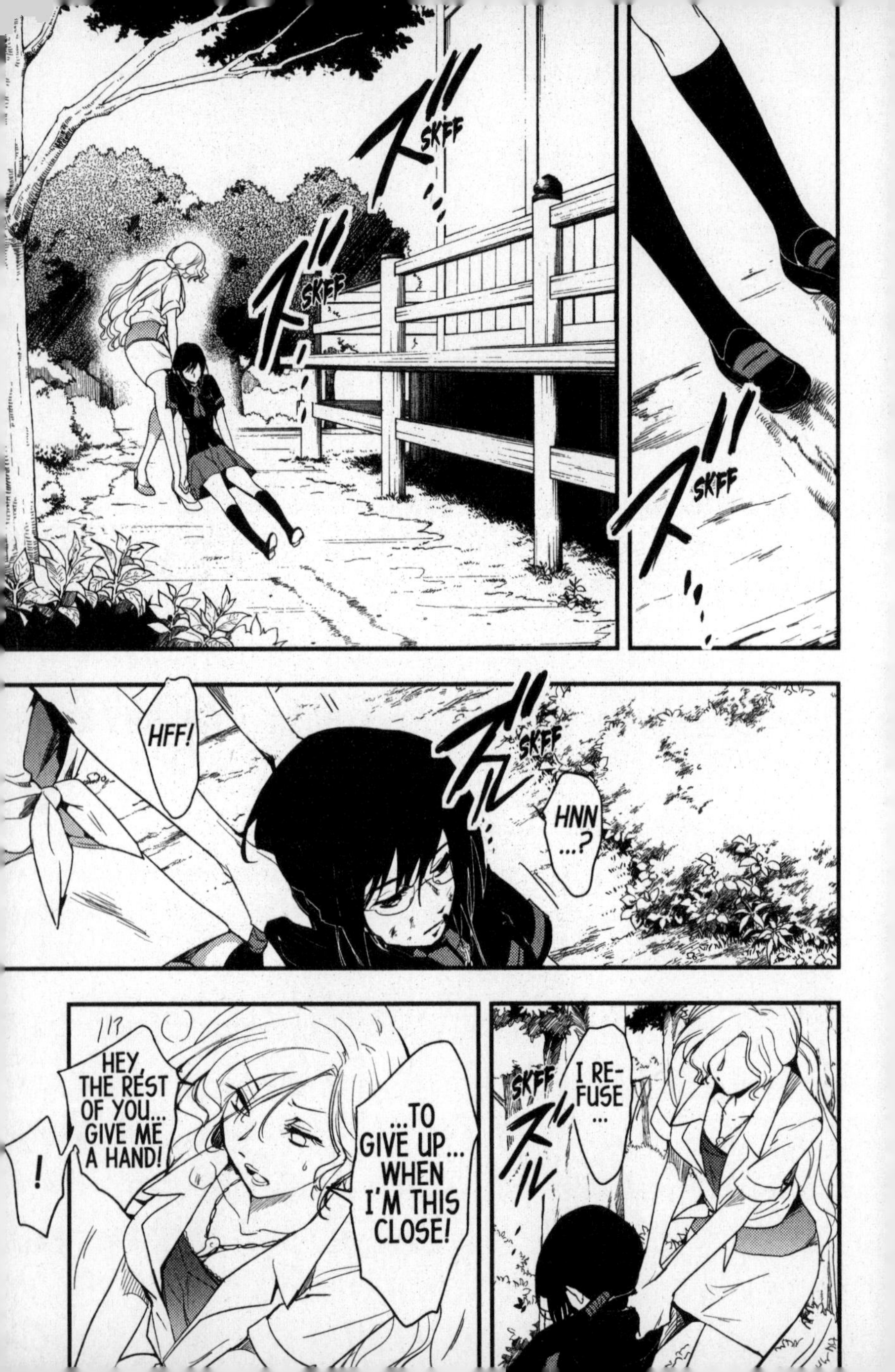
SKFF
SKFF
SKFF
SKFF
HNN ...?
HFF!
I RE-FUSE ...
SKFF
...TO GIVE UP... WHEN I'M THIS CLOSE!
HEY, THE REST OF YOU... GIVE ME A HAND!
!

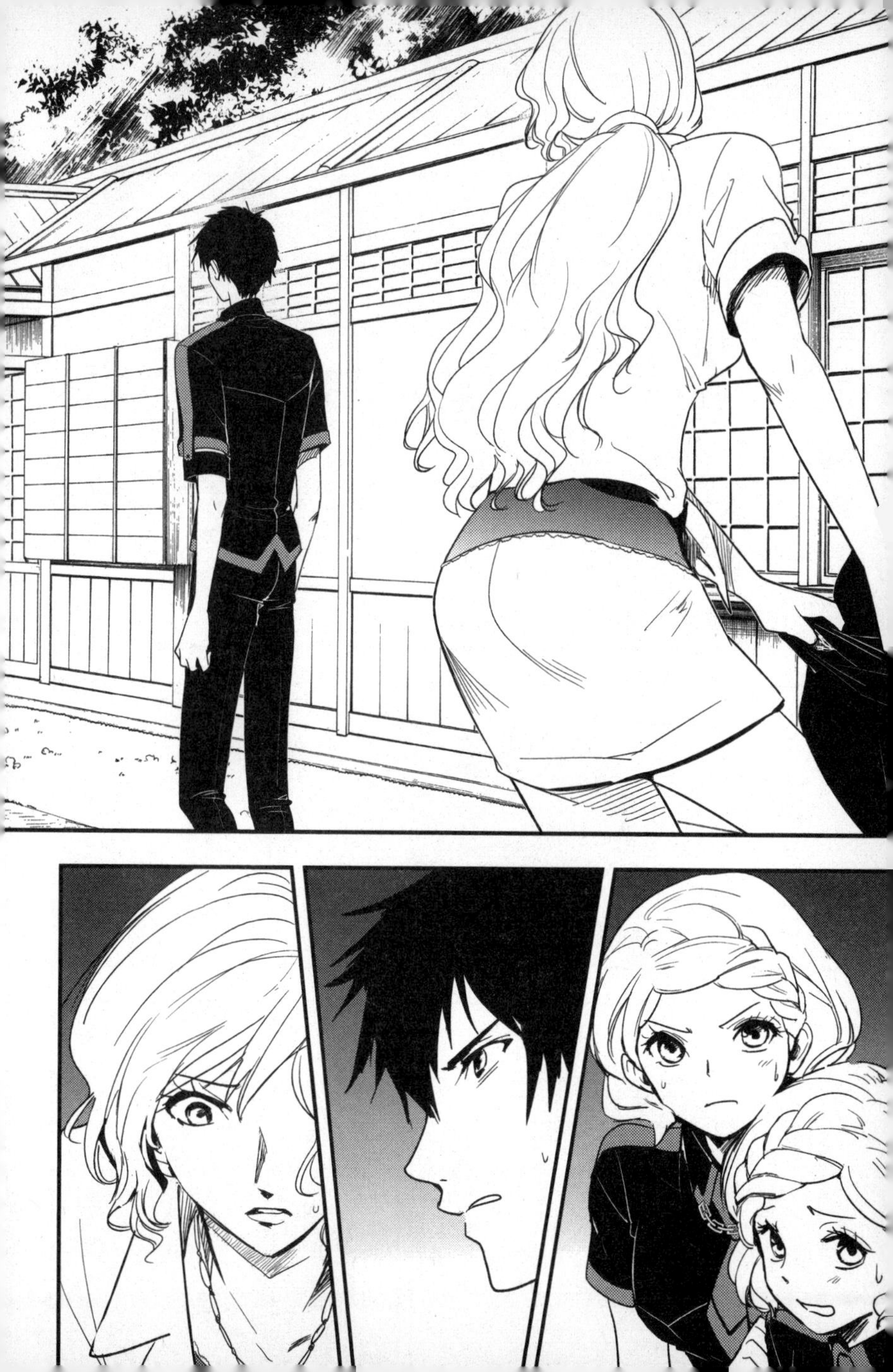

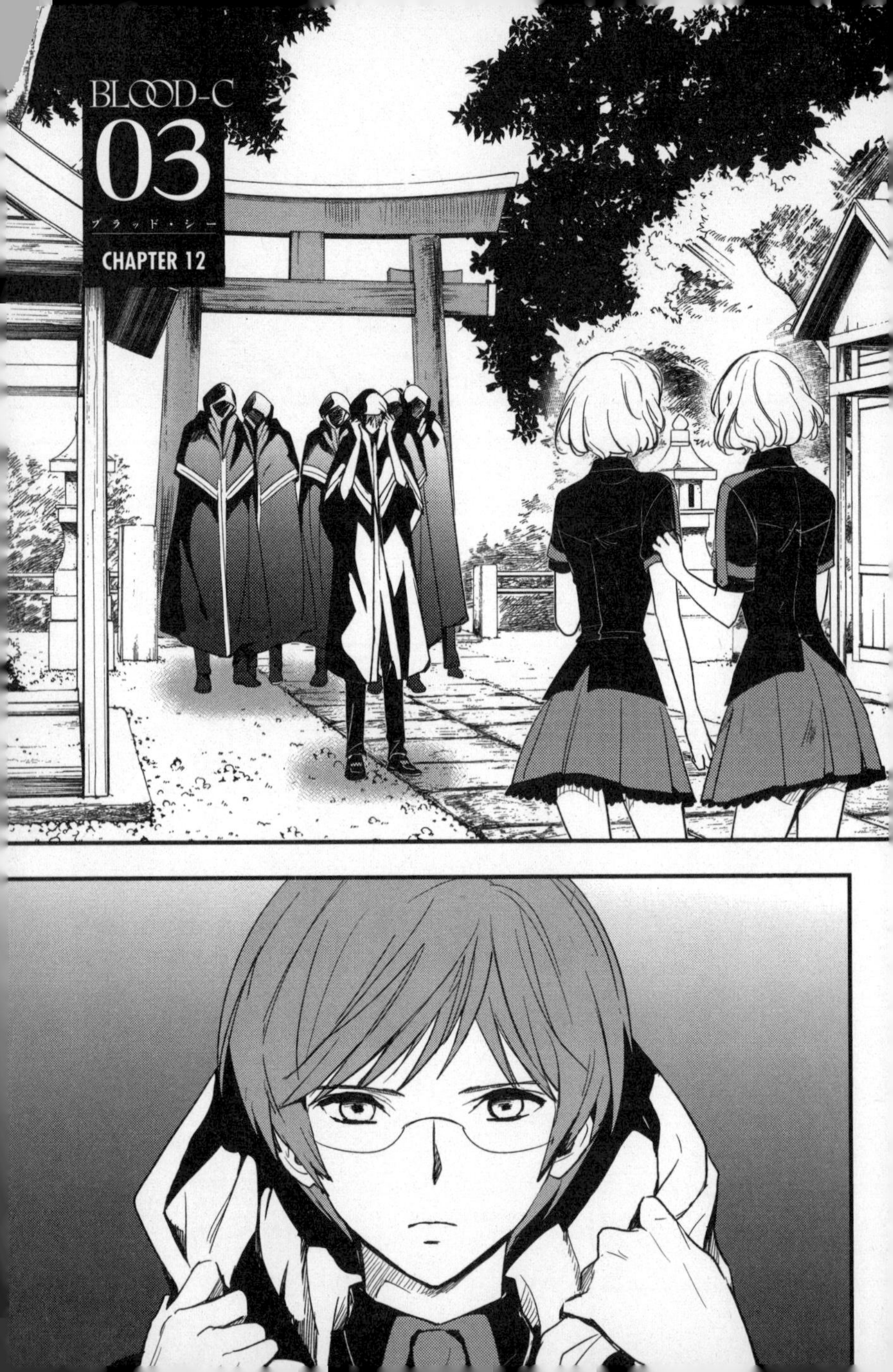
BLOOD-C
03
ブラッド・シー
CHAPTER 12

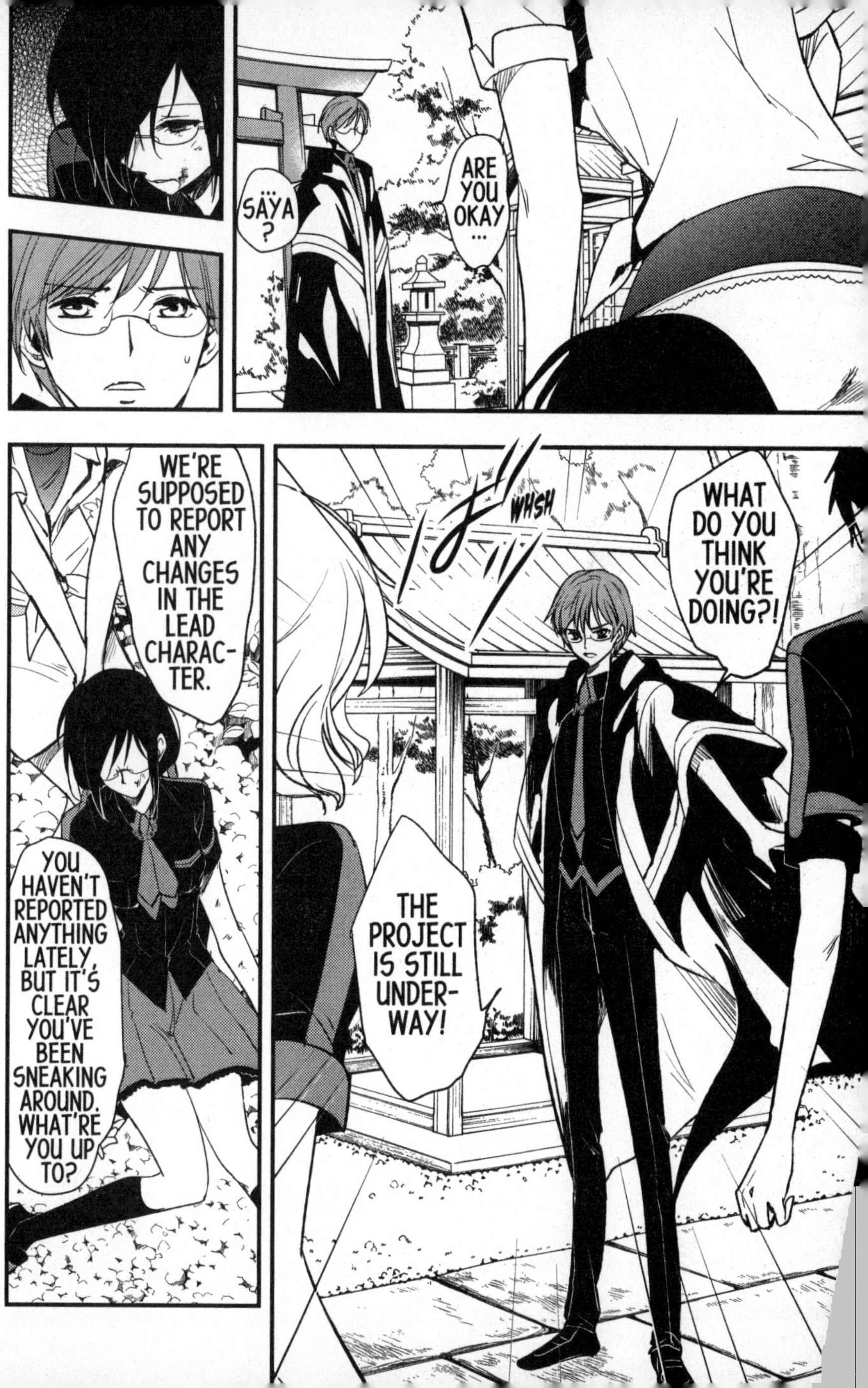
ARE YOU OKAY...
...SAYA?
WHAT DO YOU THINK YOU'RE DOING?!
WHSH
THE PROJECT IS STILL UNDERWAY!
WE'RE SUPPOSED TO REPORT ANY CHANGES IN THE LEAD CHARACTER.
YOU HAVEN'T REPORTED ANYTHING LATELY, BUT IT'S CLEAR YOU'VE BEEN SNEAKING AROUND. WHAT'RE YOU UP TO?

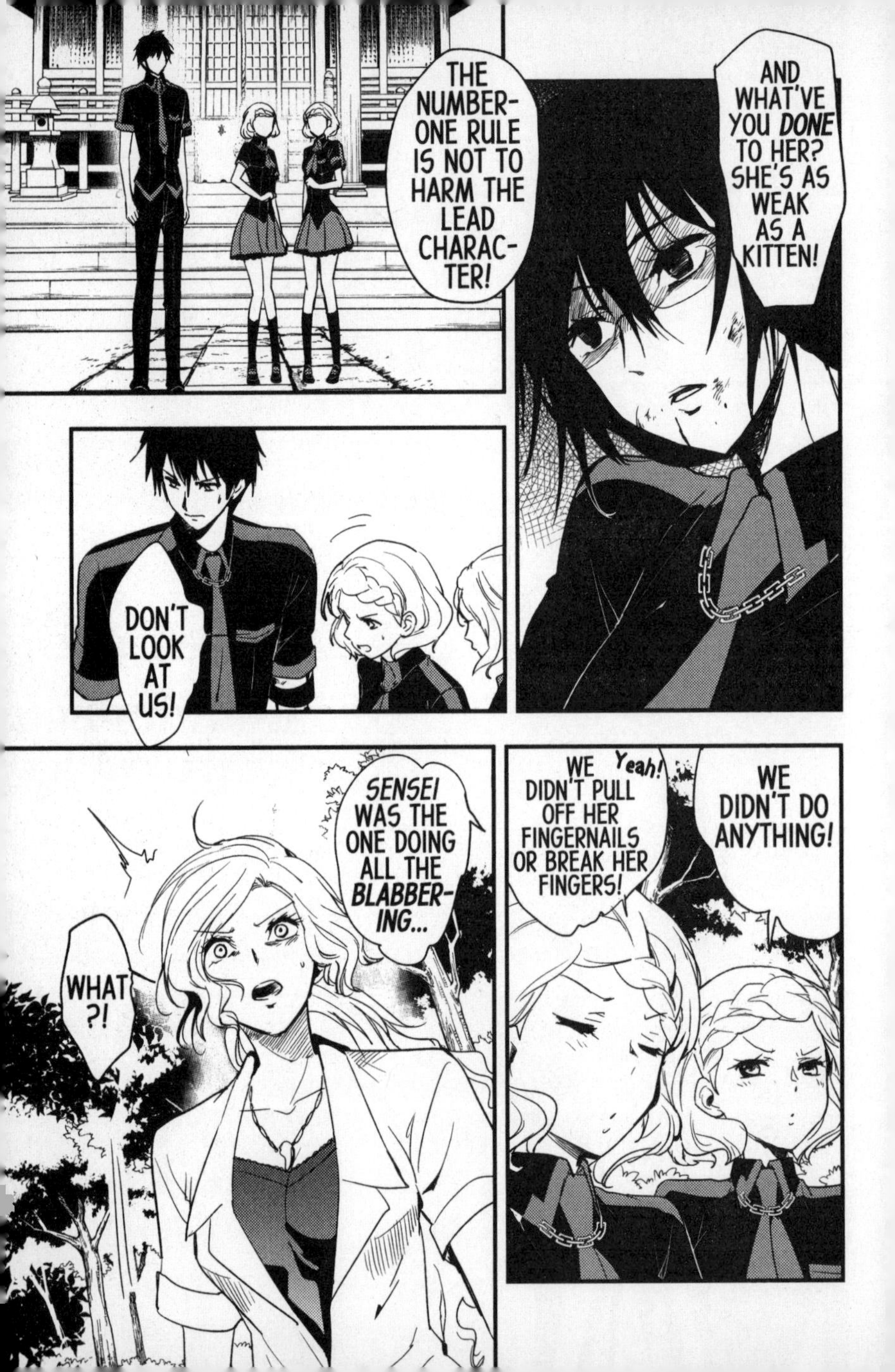
AND WHAT'VE YOU *DONE* TO HER? SHE'S AS WEAK AS A KITTEN!
THE NUMBER-ONE RULE IS NOT TO HARM THE LEAD CHARACTER!
DON'T LOOK AT US!
WE DIDN'T DO ANYTHING!
WE DIDN'T PULL OFF HER FINGERNAILS OR BREAK HER FINGERS!
Yeah!
SENSEI WAS THE ONE DOING ALL THE *BLABBERING*...
WHAT?!

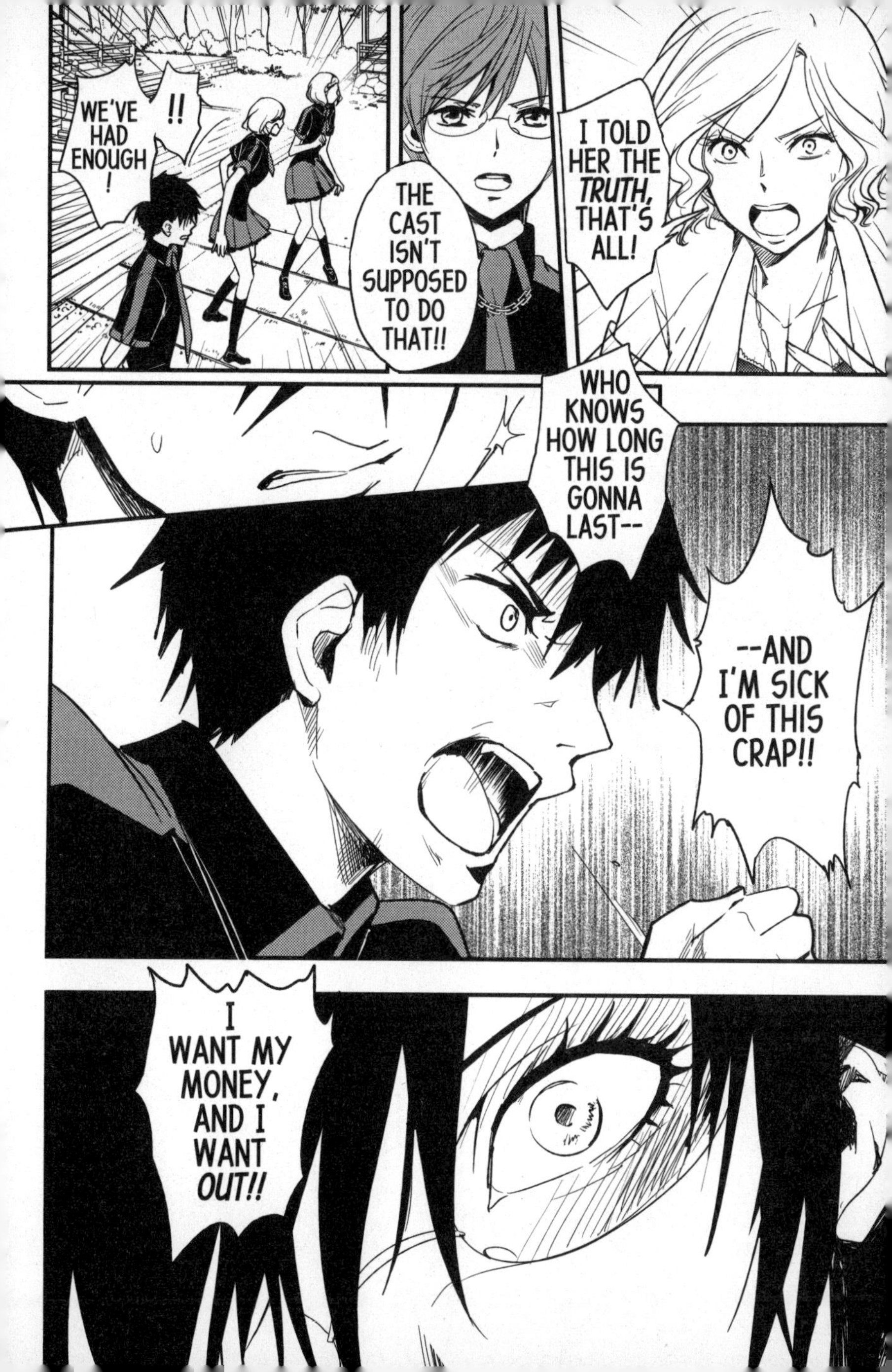
I TOLD HER THE *TRUTH*, THAT'S ALL!
THE CAST ISN'T SUPPOSED TO DO THAT!!
!!
WE'VE HAD ENOUGH!
WHO KNOWS HOW LONG THIS IS GONNA LAST--
--AND I'M SICK OF THIS CRAP!!
I WANT MY MONEY, AND I WANT *OUT*!!

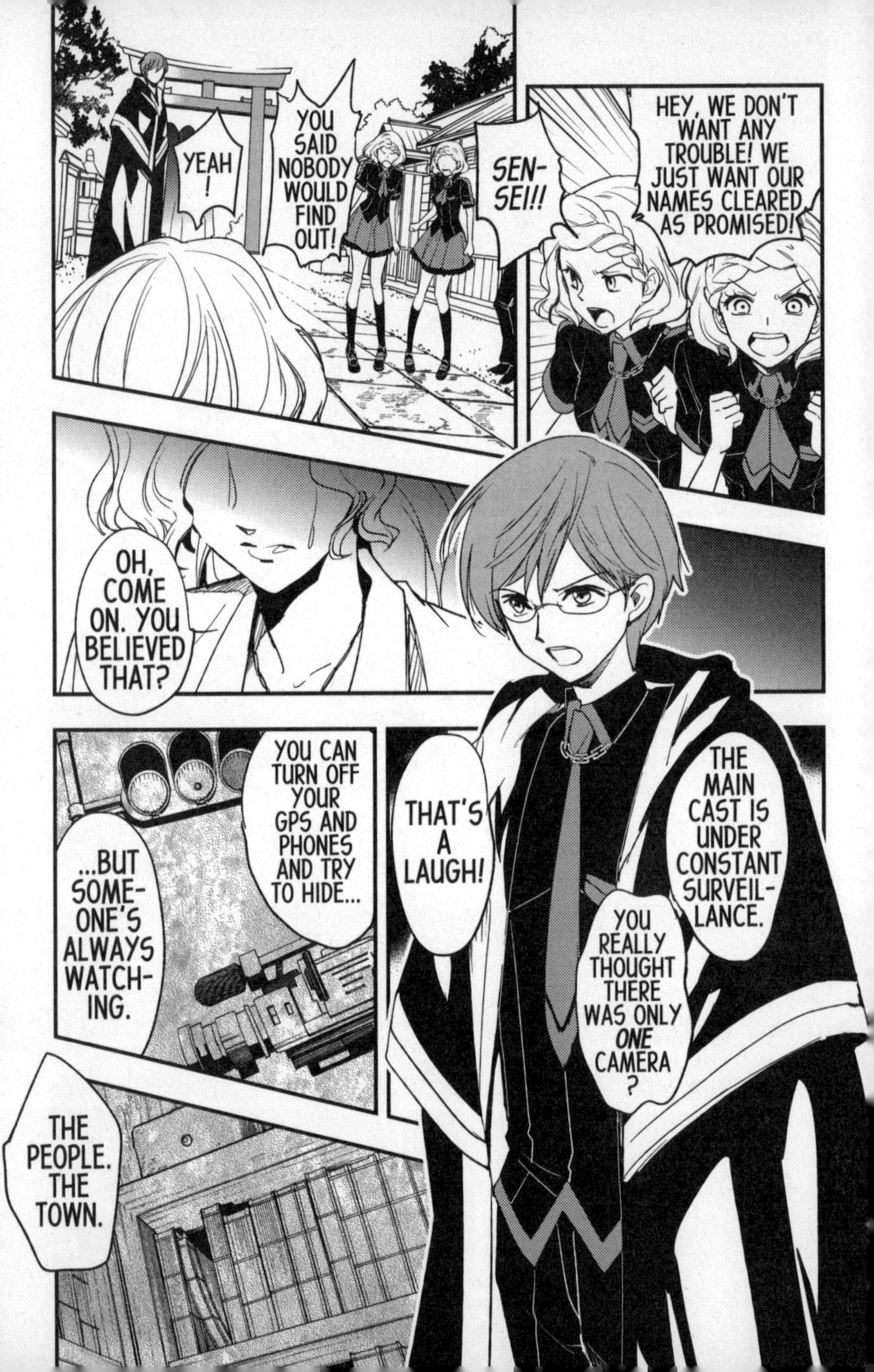
SEN-SEI!!
HEY, WE DON'T WANT ANY TROUBLE! WE JUST WANT OUR NAMES CLEARED AS PROMISED!
YOU SAID NOBODY WOULD FIND OUT!
YEAH!
OH, COME ON. YOU BELIEVED THAT?
THAT'S A LAUGH!
THE MAIN CAST IS UNDER CONSTANT SURVEIL-LANCE.
YOU REALLY THOUGHT THERE WAS ONLY *ONE* CAMERA?
YOU CAN TURN OFF YOUR GPS AND PHONES AND TRY TO HIDE...
...BUT SOME-ONE'S ALWAYS WATCH-ING.
THE PEOPLE. THE TOWN.

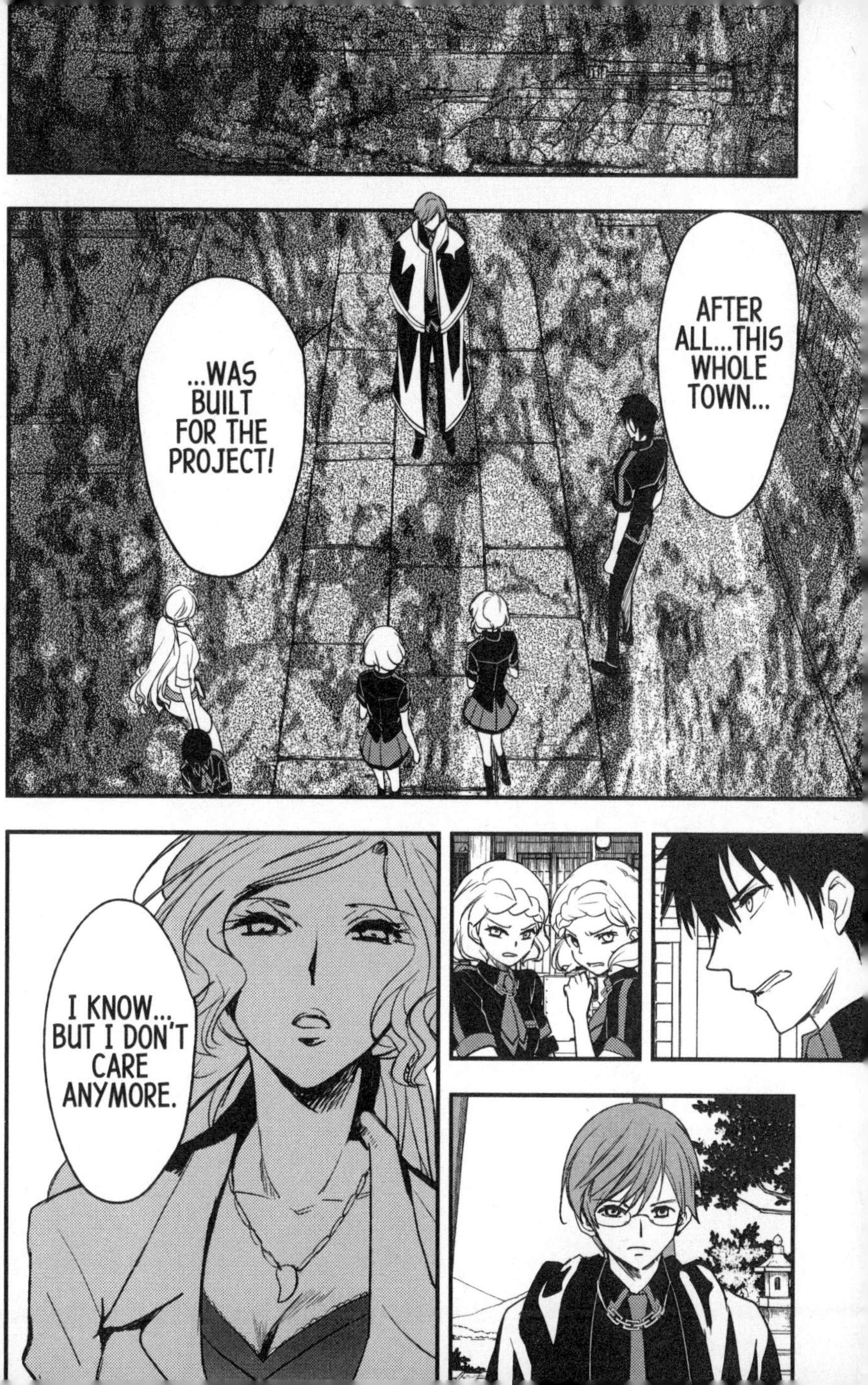
AFTER ALL...THIS WHOLE TOWN...
...WAS BUILT FOR THE PROJECT!
I KNOW... BUT I DON'T CARE ANYMORE.

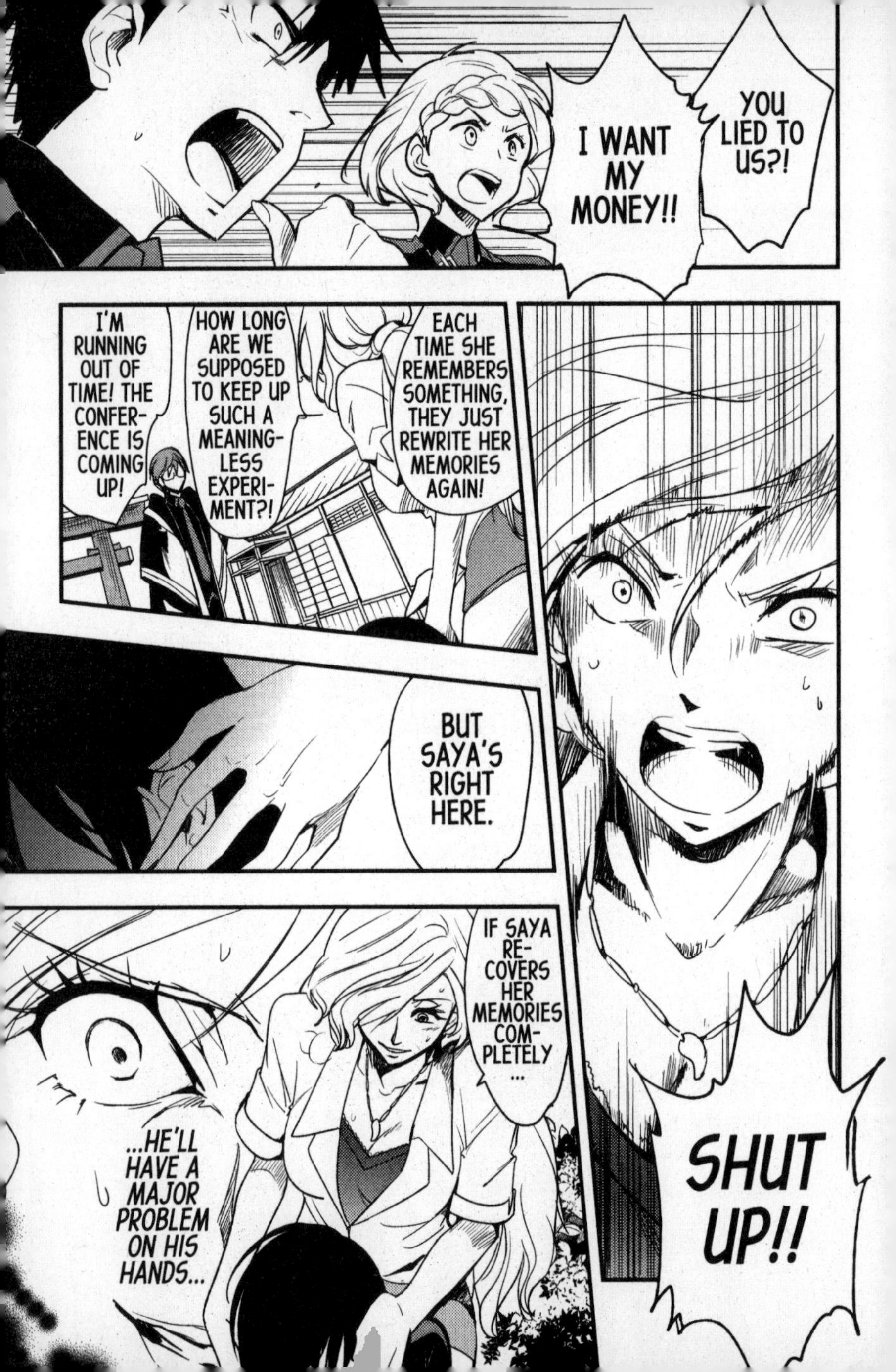

YOU LIED TO US?!
I WANT MY MONEY!!
SHUT UP!!
EACH TIME SHE REMEMBERS SOMETHING, THEY JUST REWRITE HER MEMORIES AGAIN!
HOW LONG ARE WE SUPPOSED TO KEEP UP SUCH A MEANING-LESS EXPERI-MENT?!
I'M RUNNING OUT OF TIME! THE CONFER-ENCE IS COMING UP!
BUT SAYA'S RIGHT HERE.
IF SAYA RE-COVERS HER MEMORIES COM-PLETELY ...
...HE'LL HAVE A MAJOR PROBLEM ON HIS HANDS...

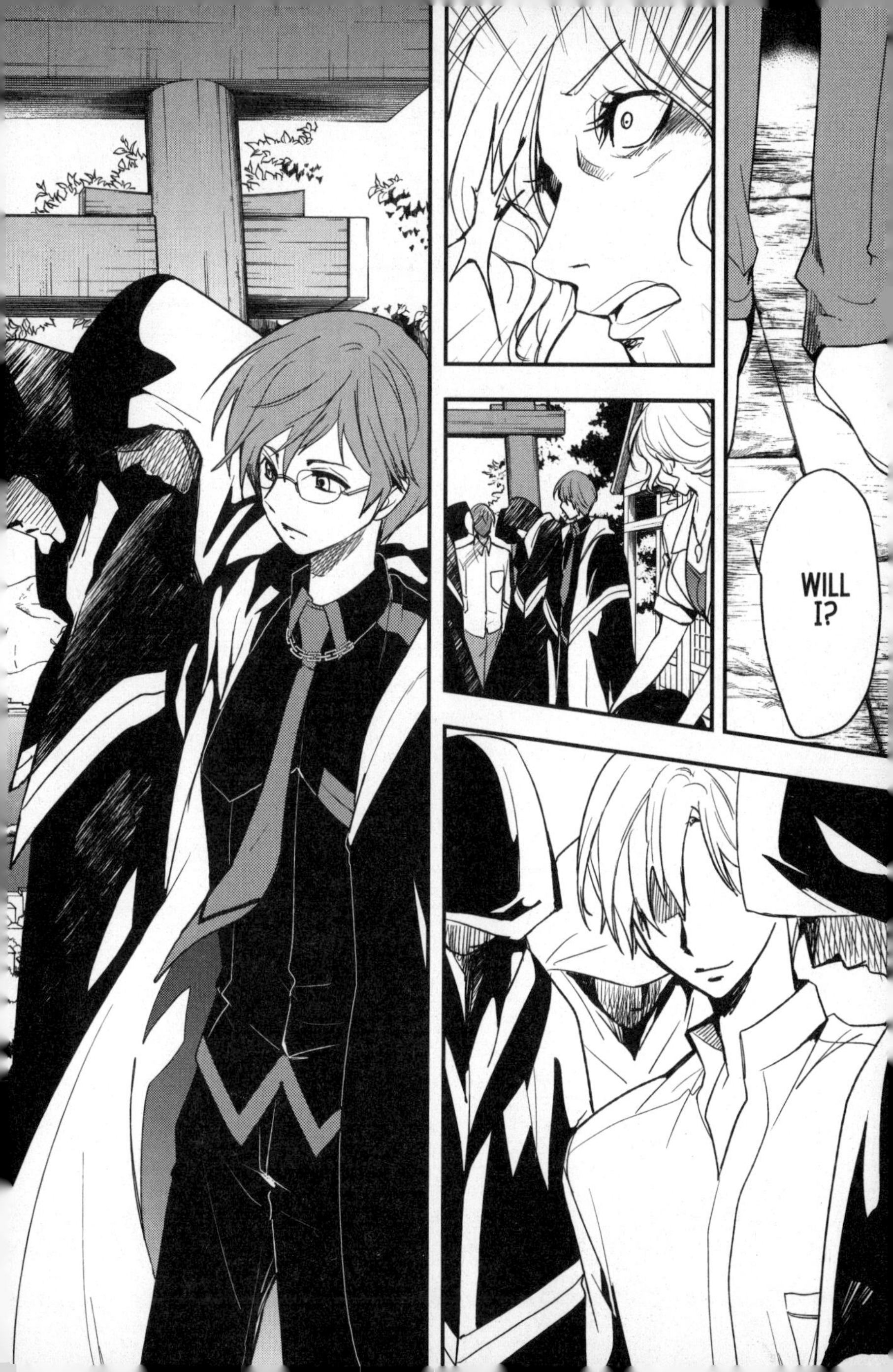
WILL I?

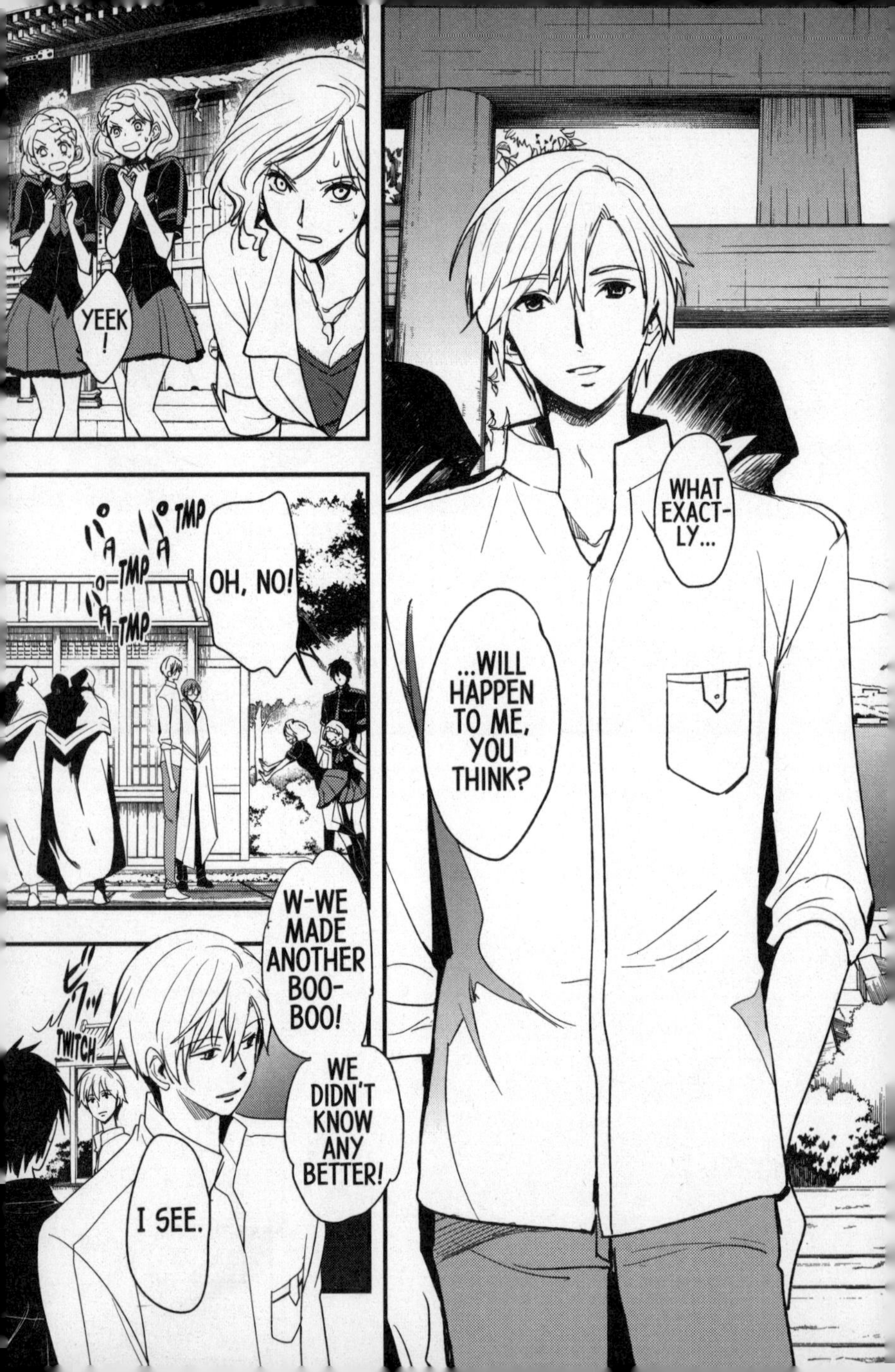
WHAT EXACT-LY...
...WILL HAPPEN TO ME, YOU THINK?
YEEK!
パ TMP
パ TMP
パ TMP
パ TMP
OH, NO!
W-WE MADE ANOTHER BOO-BOO!
WE DIDN'T KNOW ANY BETTER!
ビクッ TWITCH
I SEE.

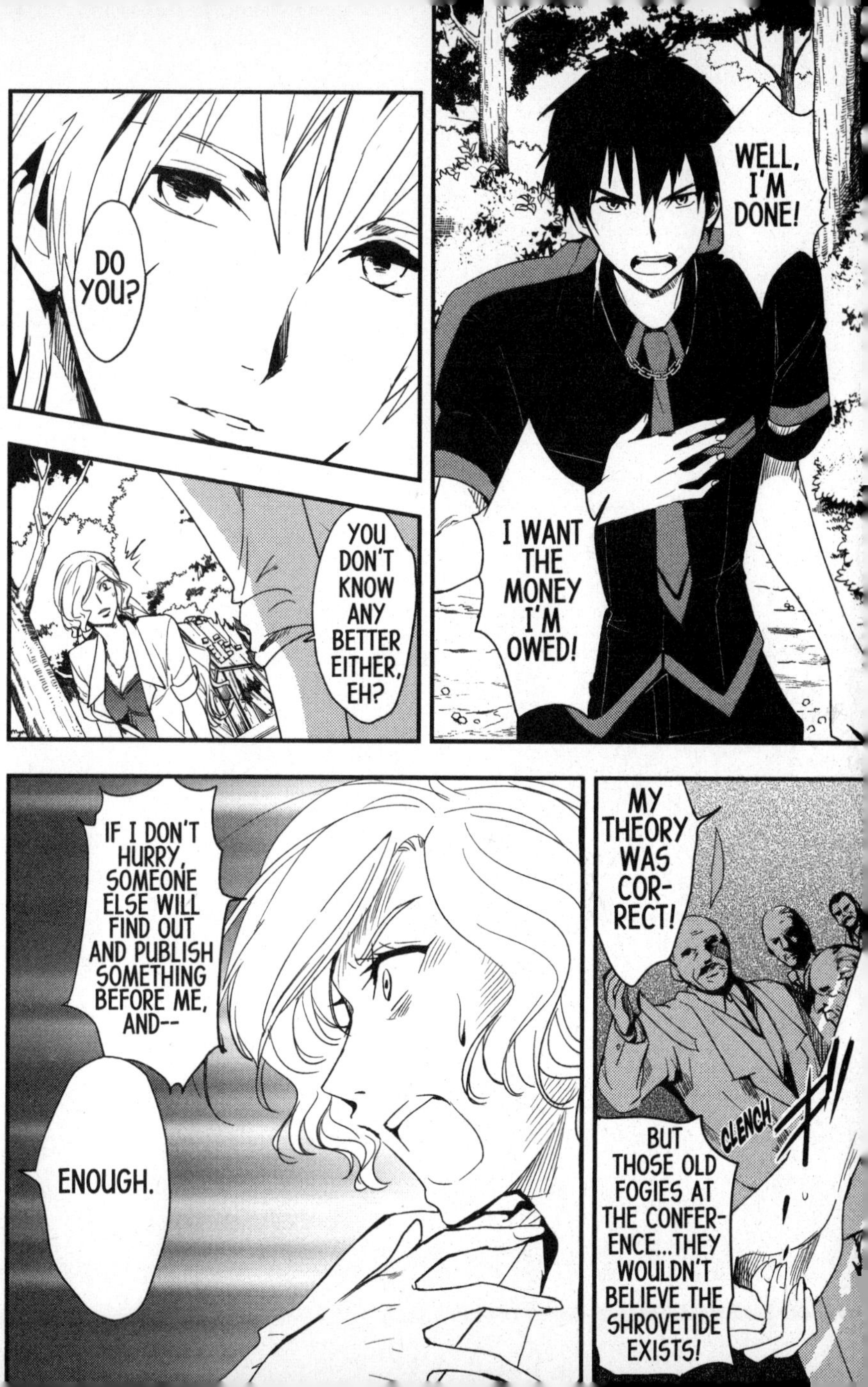

WELL, I'M DONE!
I WANT THE MONEY I'M OWED!
DO YOU?
YOU DON'T KNOW ANY BETTER EITHER, EH?
MY THEORY WAS COR-RECT!
CLENCH
BUT THOSE OLD FOGIES AT THE CONFER-ENCE...THEY WOULDN'T BELIEVE THE SHROVETIDE EXISTS!
IF I DON'T HURRY, SOMEONE ELSE WILL FIND OUT AND PUBLISH SOMETHING BEFORE ME, AND--
ENOUGH.

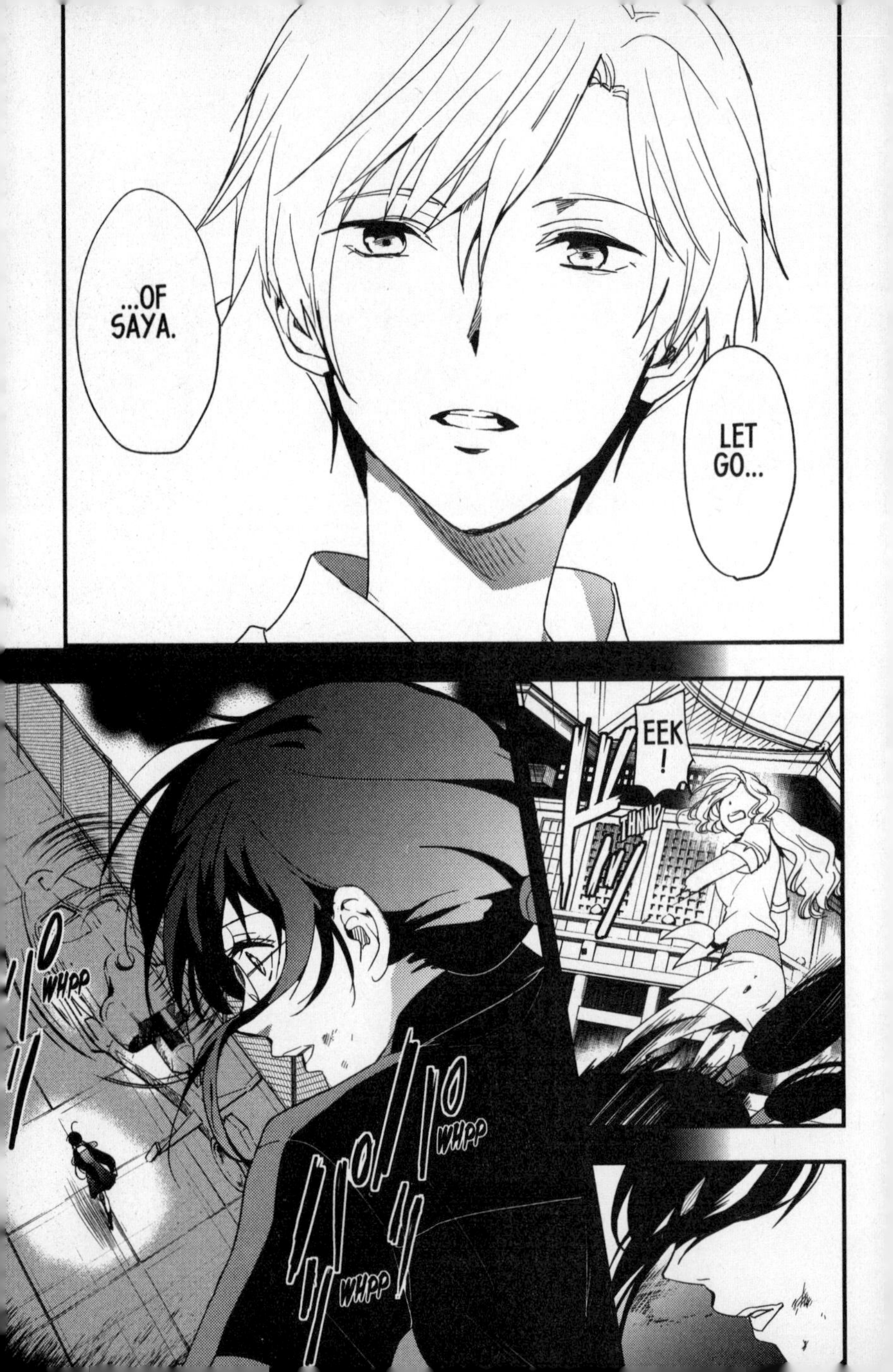
LET GO...
...OF SAYA.
EEK!
THNNP
WHPP
WHPP
WHPP

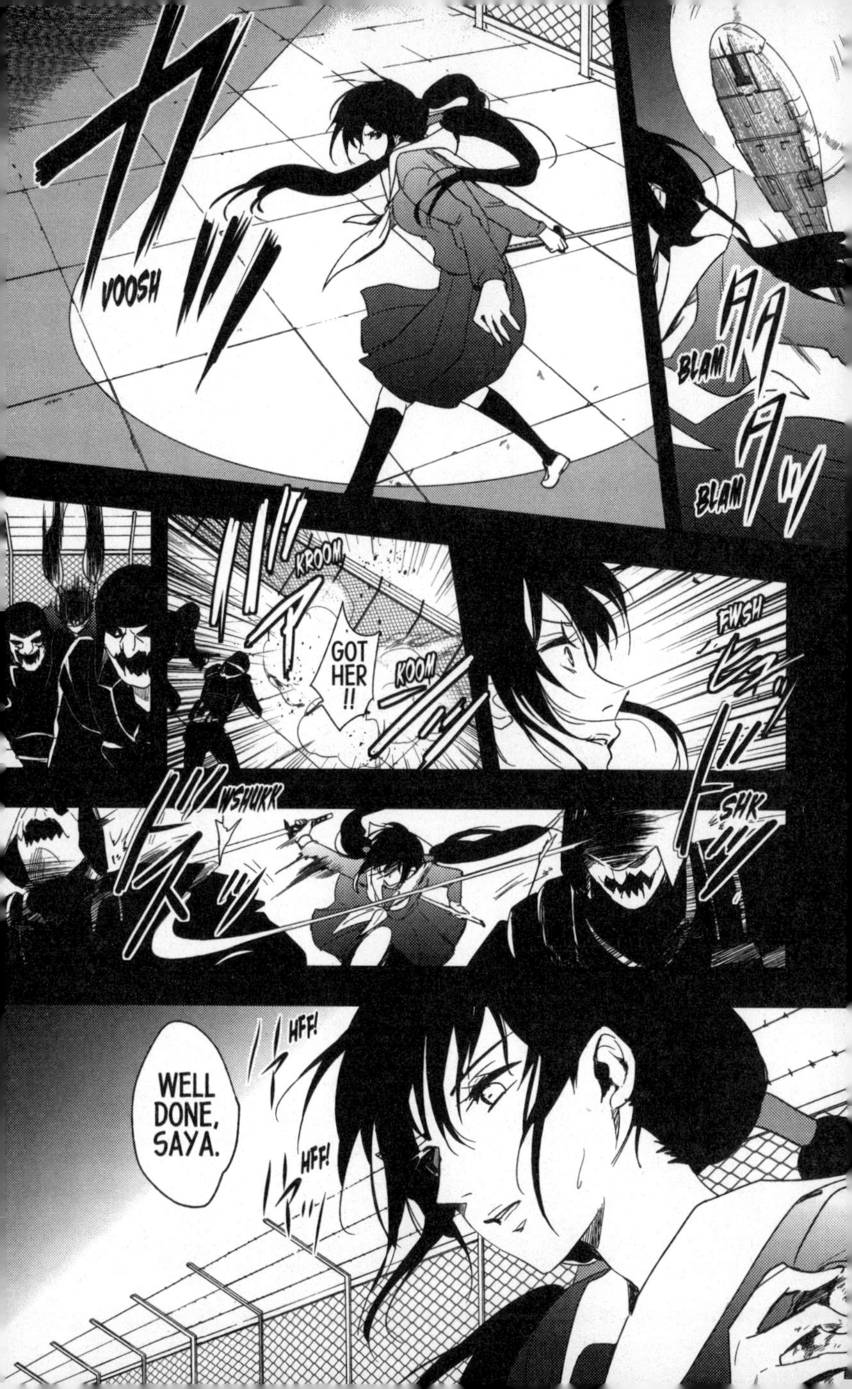
BLAM
BLAM
VOOSH
FWSH
KROOM
GOT HER!!
KOOM
SHK
WSHUKR
HFF!
WELL DONE, SAYA.
HFF!

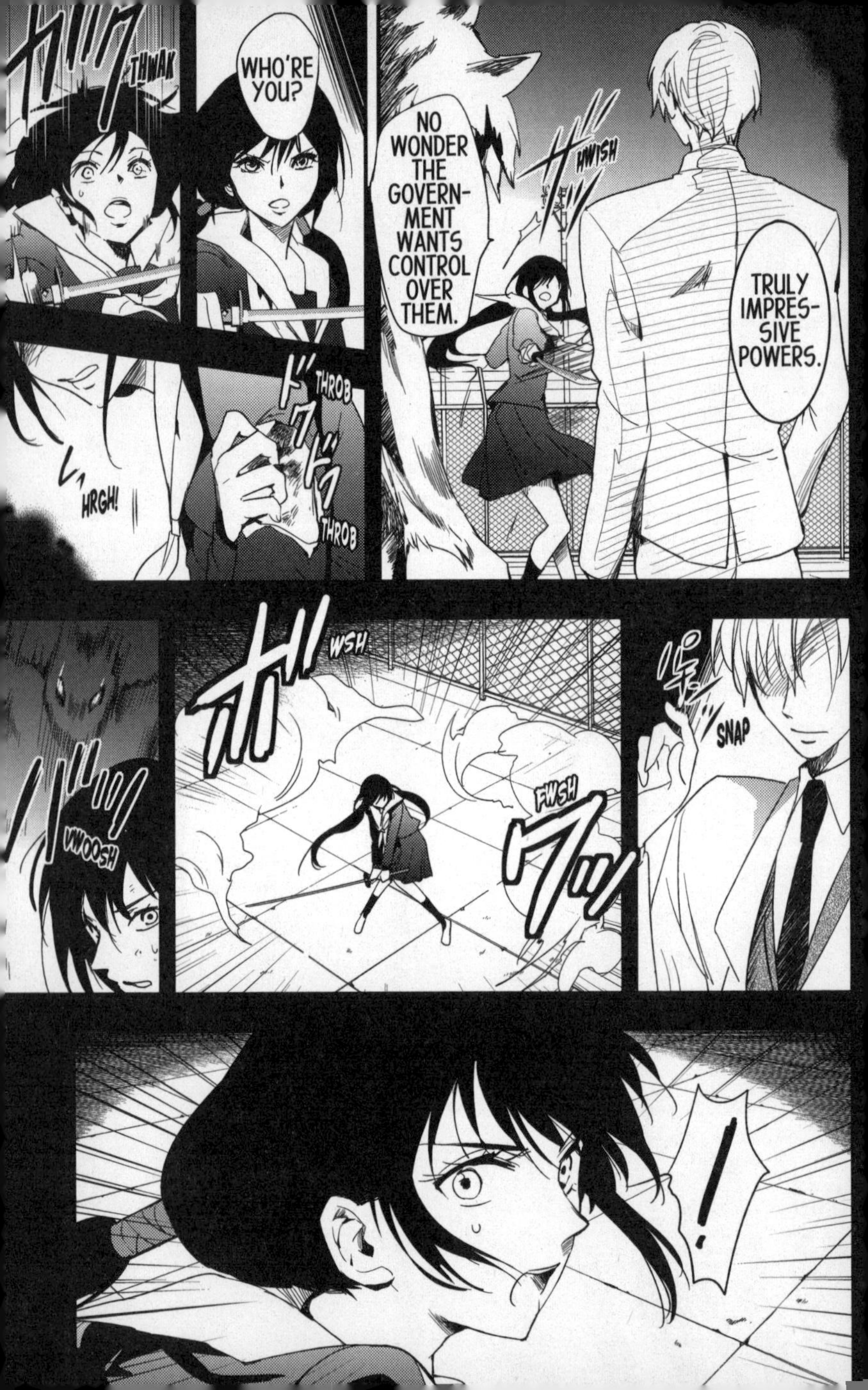
TRULY IMPRESSIVE POWERS.
NO WONDER THE GOVERNMENT WANTS CONTROL OVER THEM.
HWISH
WHO'RE YOU?
THWAK
THROB
THROB
HRGH!
SNAP
WSH
FWSH
VWOOSH
!

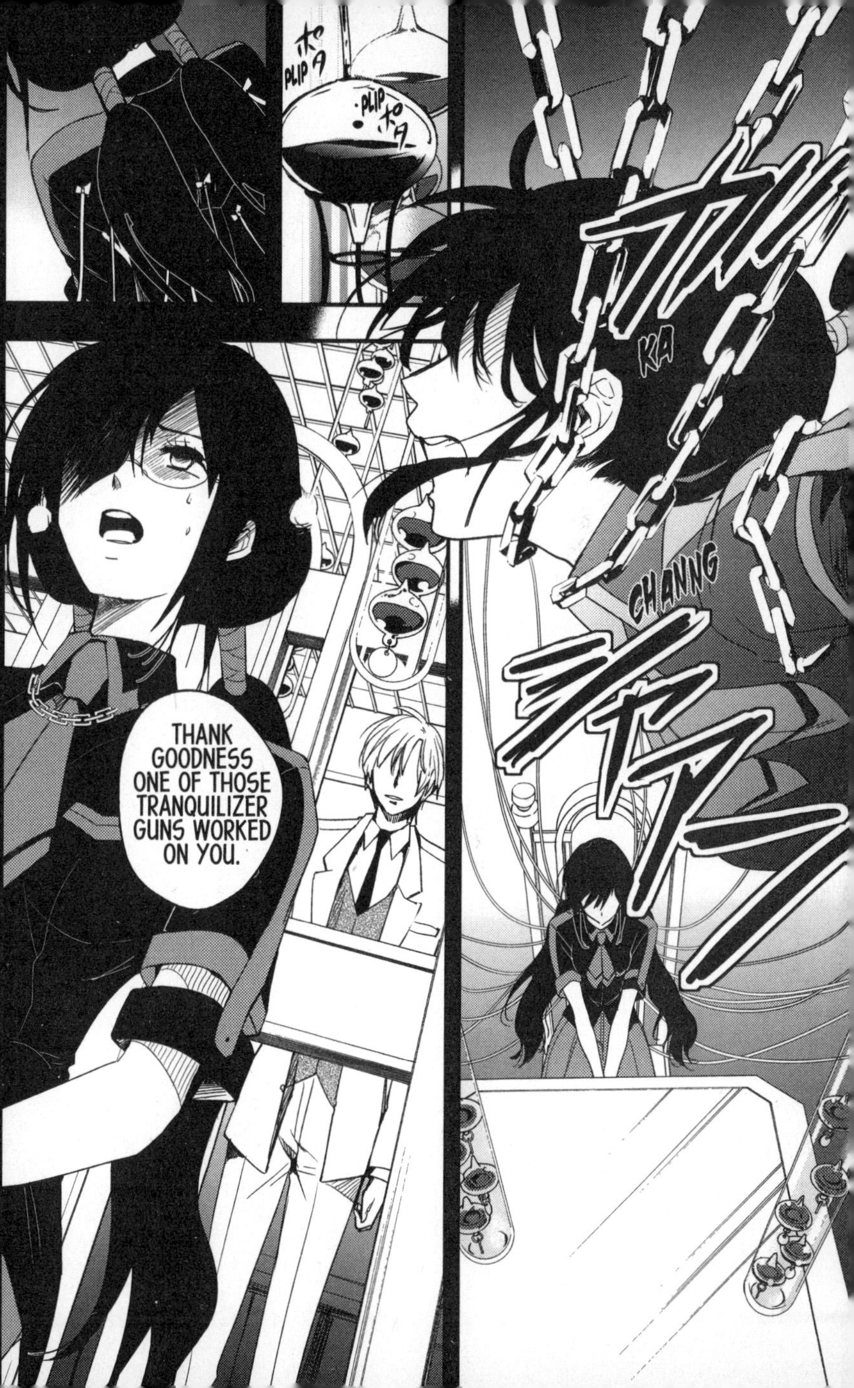
KA
CHANNG
PLIP
ポタ
PLIP
ポタ
THANK GOODNESS ONE OF THOSE TRANQUILIZER GUNS WORKED ON YOU.

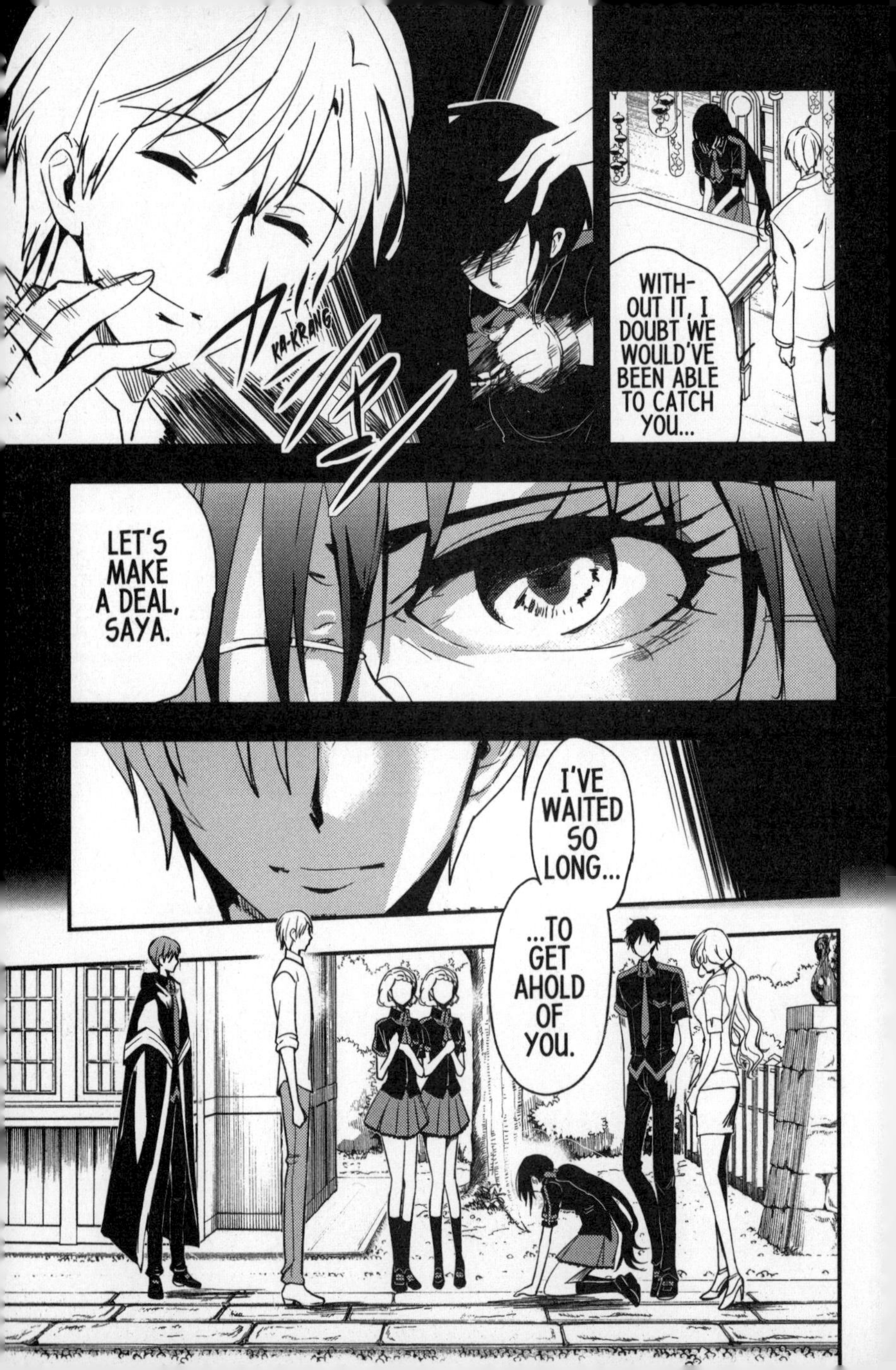
WITH-OUT IT, I DOUBT WE WOULD'VE BEEN ABLE TO CATCH YOU...
KA-KRANG
LET'S MAKE A DEAL, SAYA.
I'VE WAITED SO LONG...
...TO GET AHOLD OF YOU.

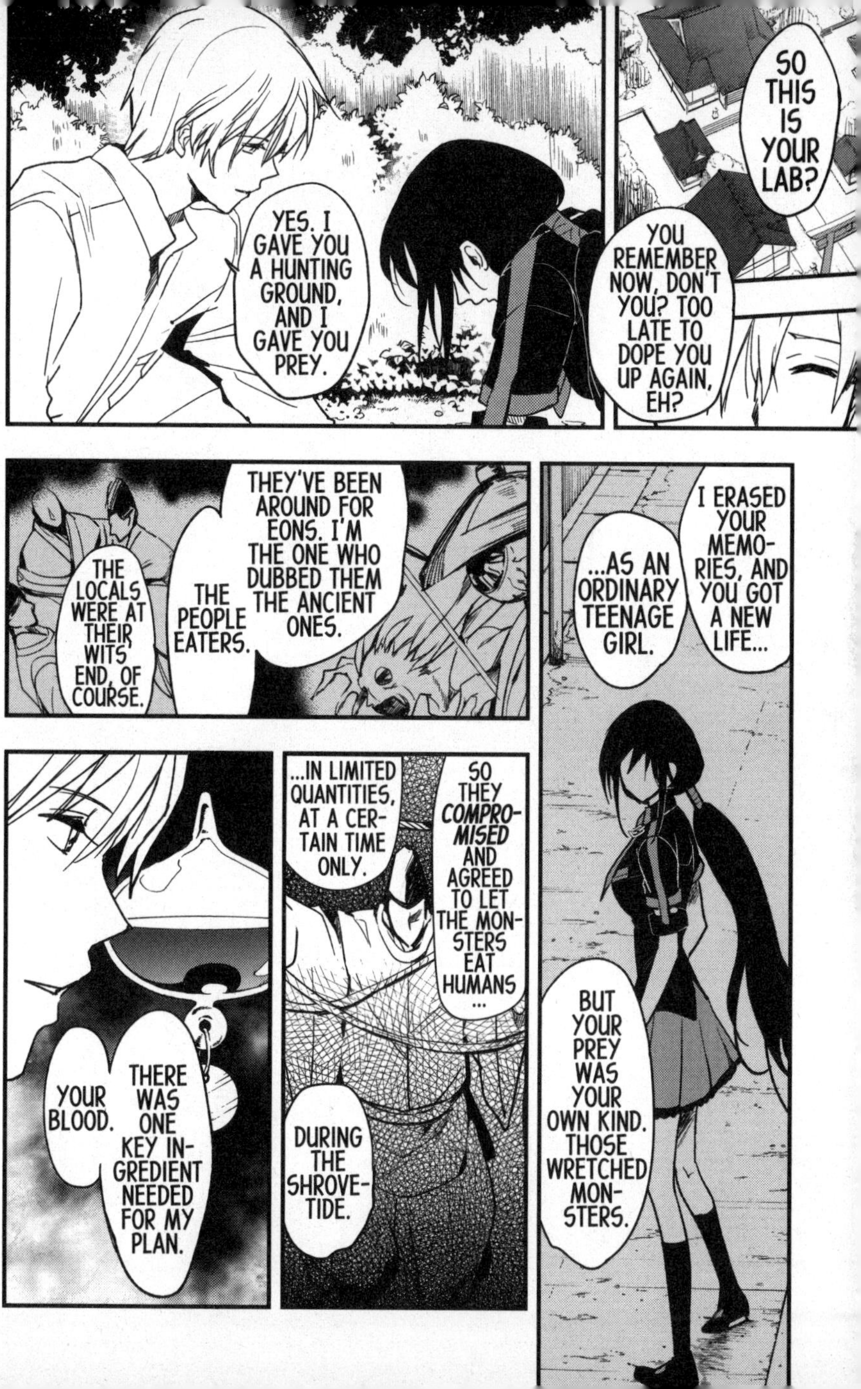
SO THIS IS YOUR LAB?
YOU REMEMBER NOW, DON'T YOU? TOO LATE TO DOPE YOU UP AGAIN, EH?
YES. I GAVE YOU A HUNTING GROUND, AND I GAVE YOU PREY.
I ERASED YOUR MEMO-RIES, AND YOU GOT A NEW LIFE...
...AS AN ORDINARY TEENAGE GIRL.
BUT YOUR PREY WAS YOUR OWN KIND. THOSE WRETCHED MON-STERS.
THEY'VE BEEN AROUND FOR EONS. I'M THE ONE WHO DUBBED THEM THE ANCIENT ONES.
THE PEOPLE EATERS.
THE LOCALS WERE AT THEIR WITS' END, OF COURSE.
SO THEY *COMPRO-MISED* AND AGREED TO LET THE MON-STERS EAT HUMANS ...
...IN LIMITED QUANTITIES, AT A CER-TAIN TIME ONLY.
DURING THE SHROVE-TIDE.
THERE WAS ONE KEY IN-GREDIENT NEEDED FOR MY PLAN.
YOUR BLOOD.

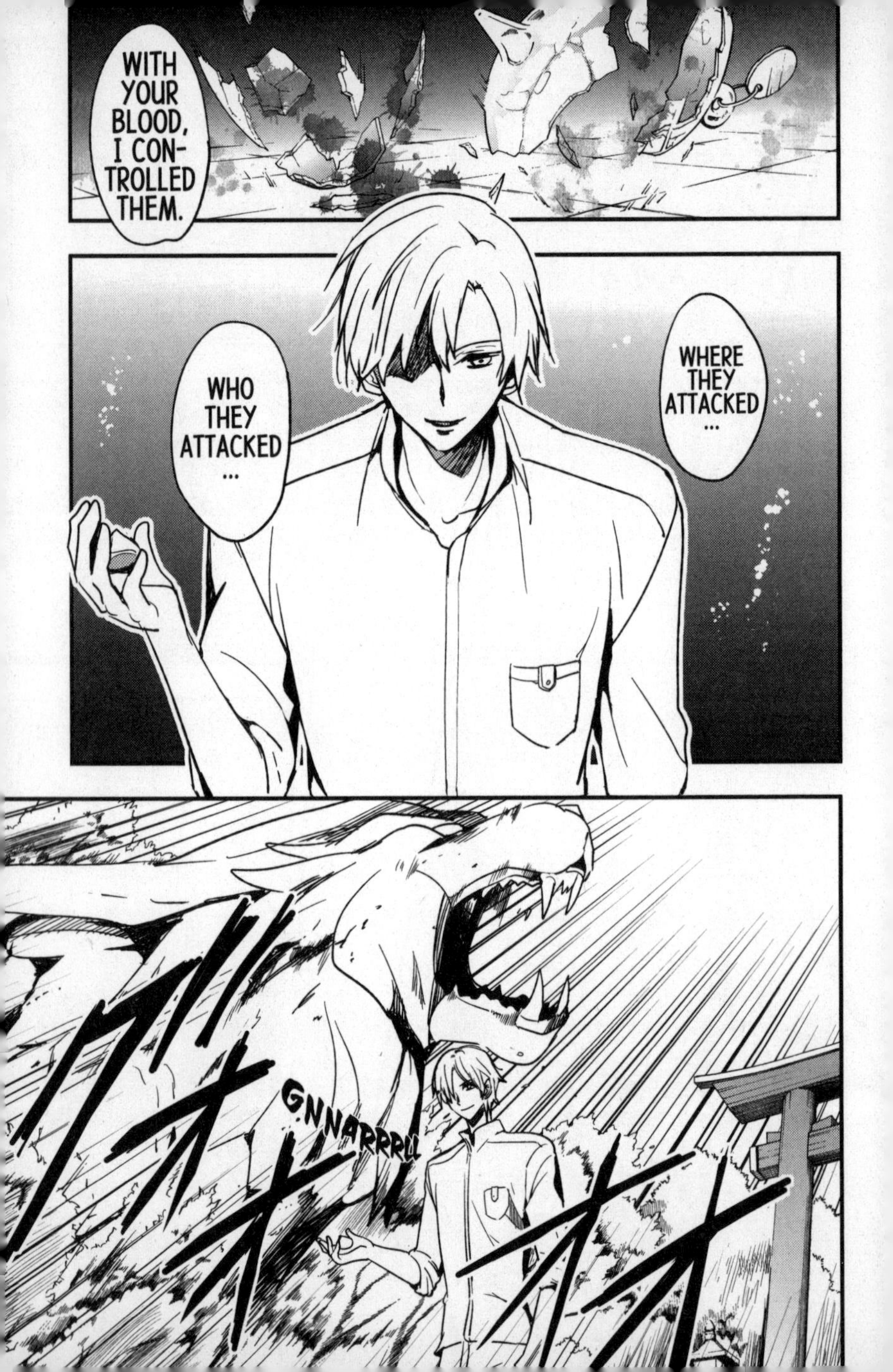
WITH YOUR BLOOD, I CON-TROLLED THEM.
WHERE THEY ATTACKED ...
WHO THEY ATTACKED ...
GNNARRRLL

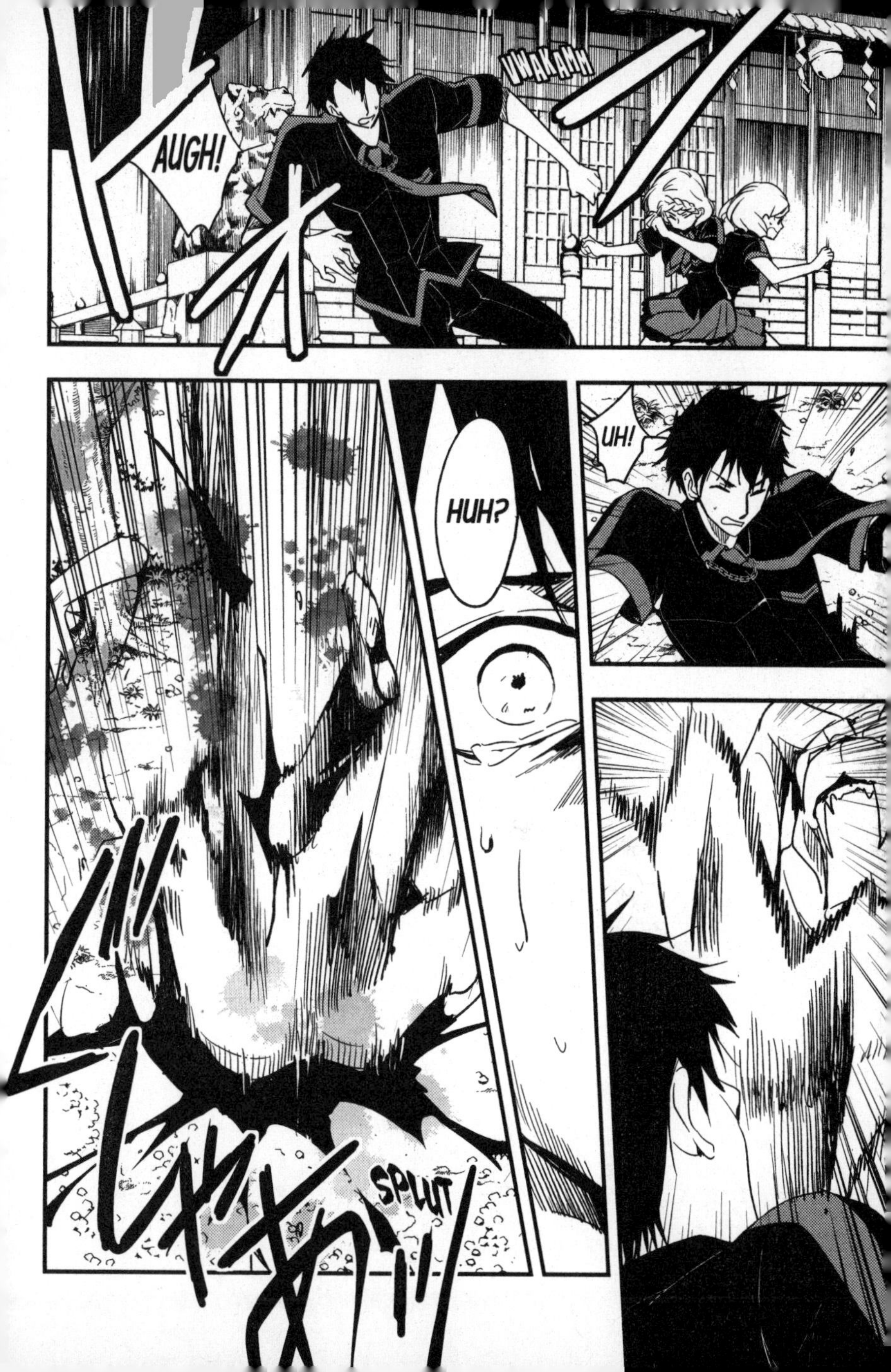
VWAKAMM
AUGH!
UH!
HUH?
SPLUT

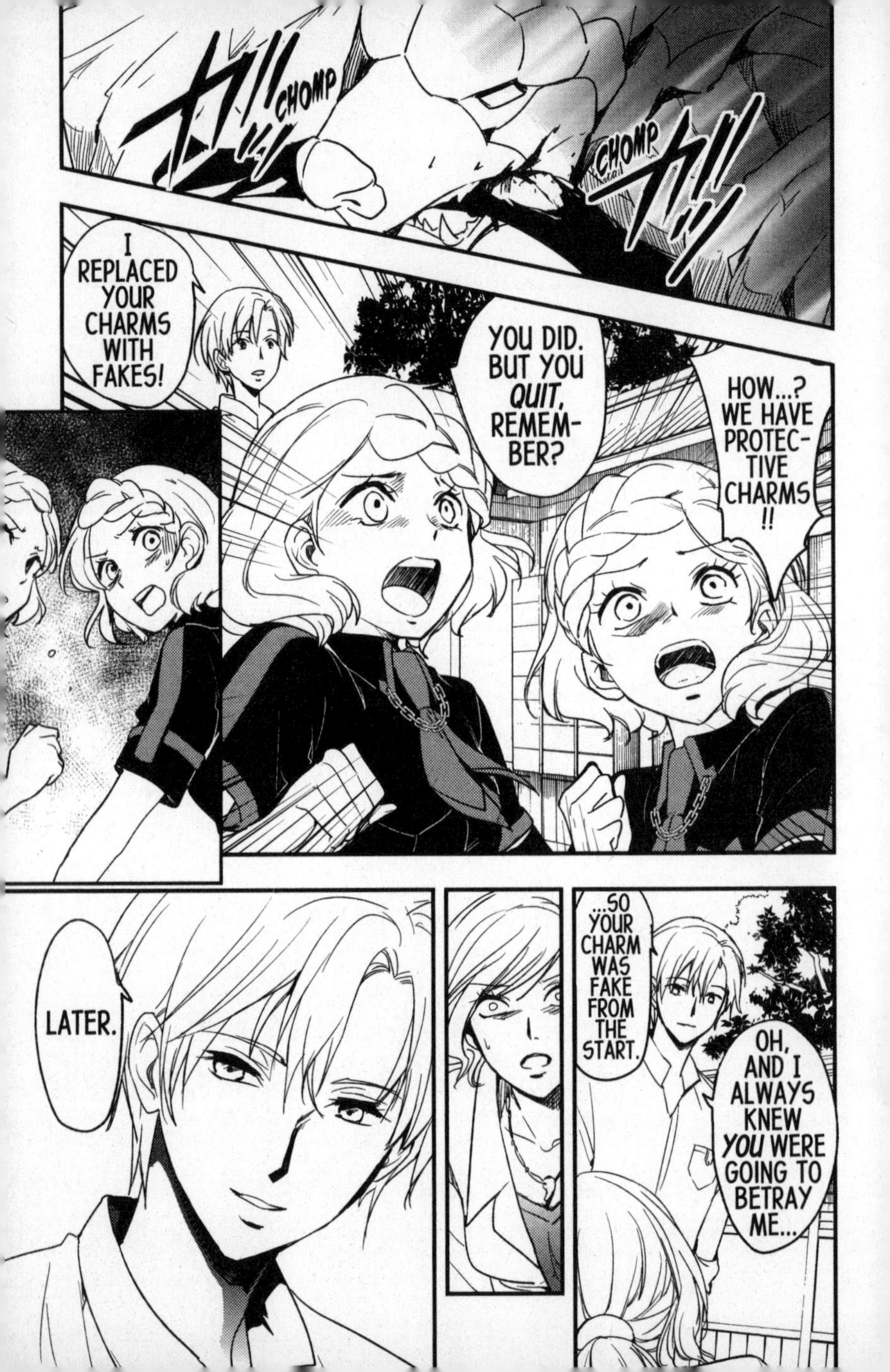
CHOMP
CHOMP
HOW...? WE HAVE PROTECTIVE CHARMS!!
I REPLACED YOUR CHARMS WITH FAKES!
YOU DID. BUT YOU *QUIT*, REMEMBER?
...SO YOUR CHARM WAS FAKE FROM THE START.
OH, AND I ALWAYS KNEW *YOU* WERE GOING TO BETRAY ME...
LATER.

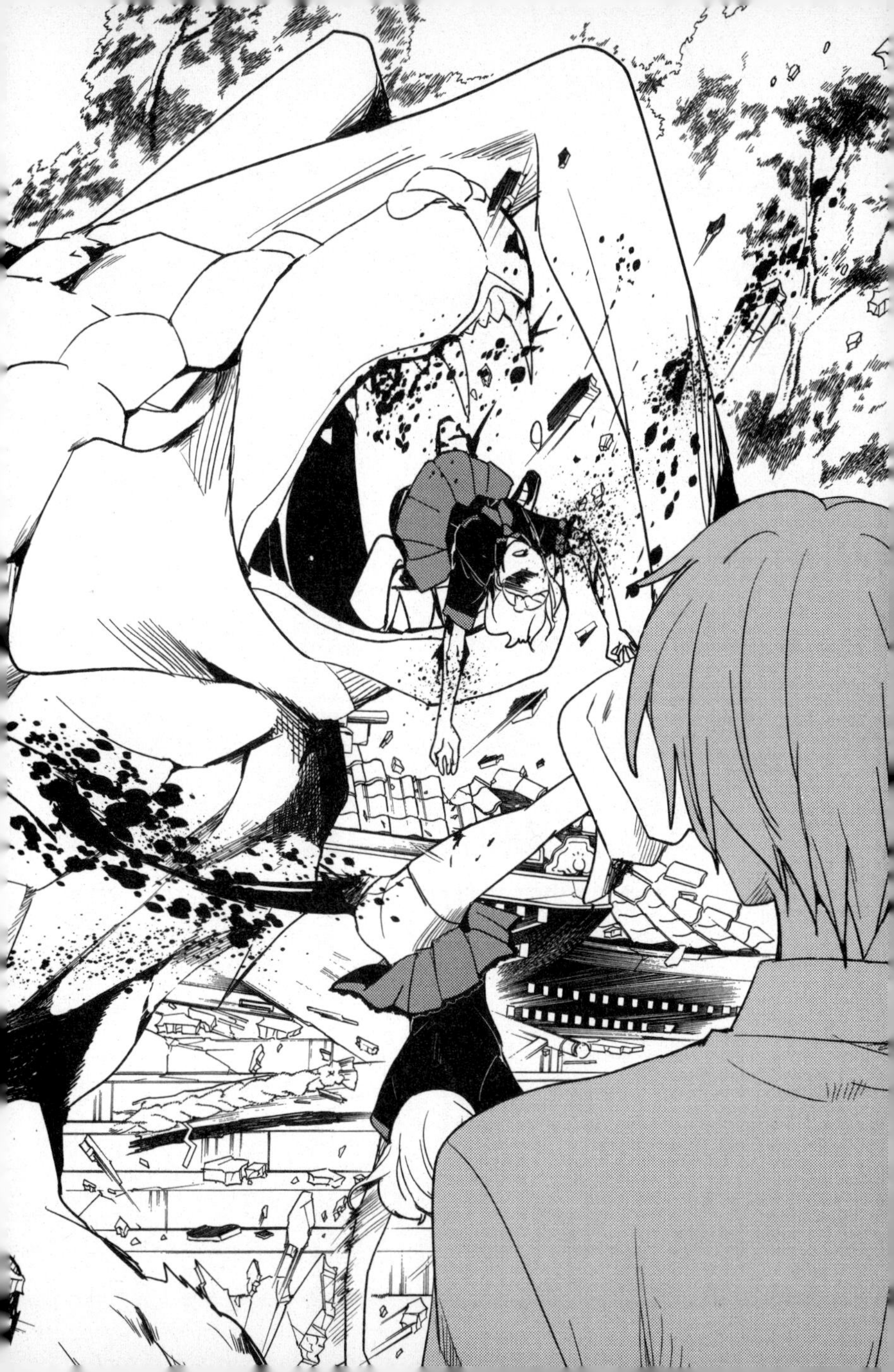

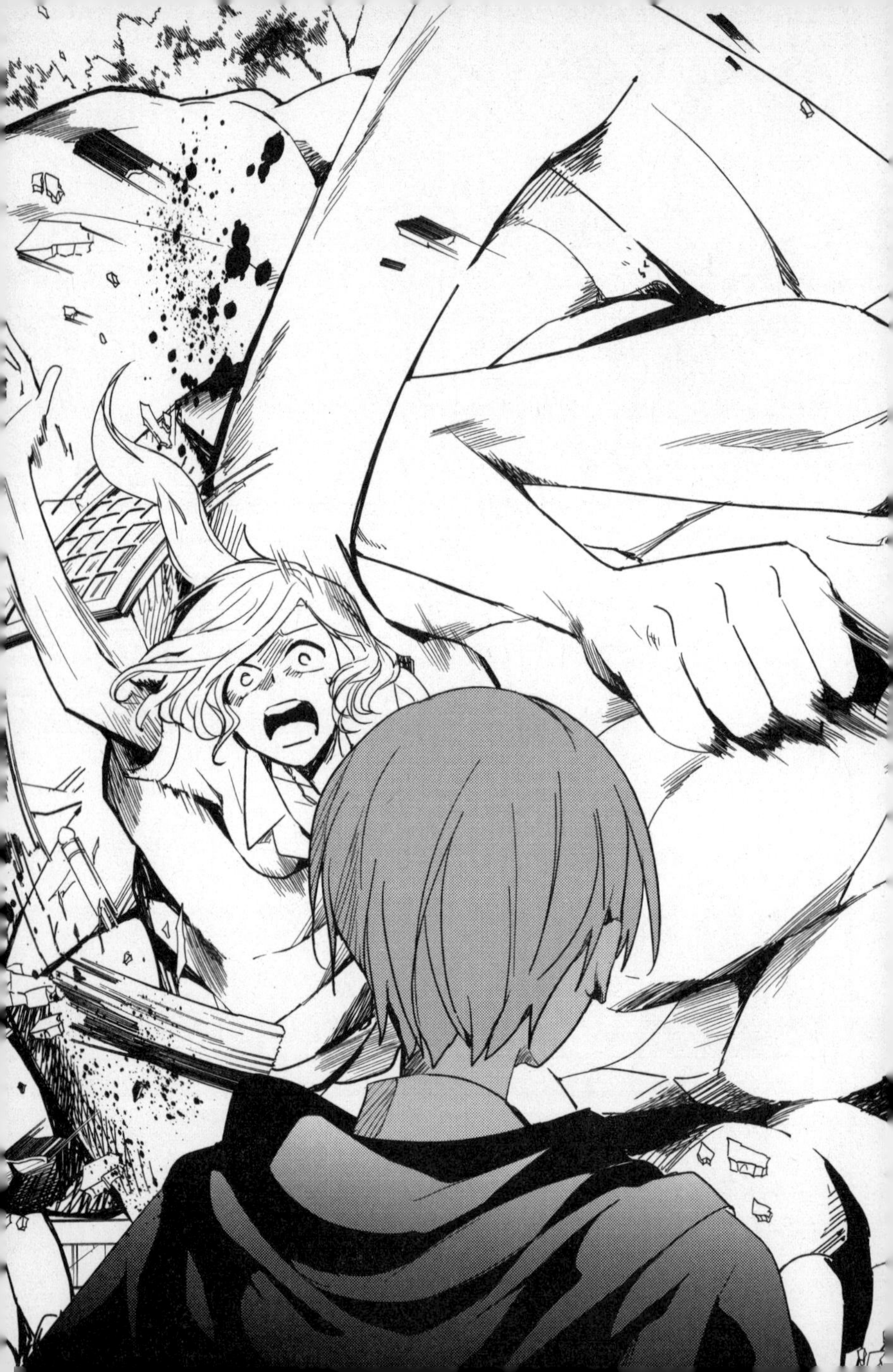

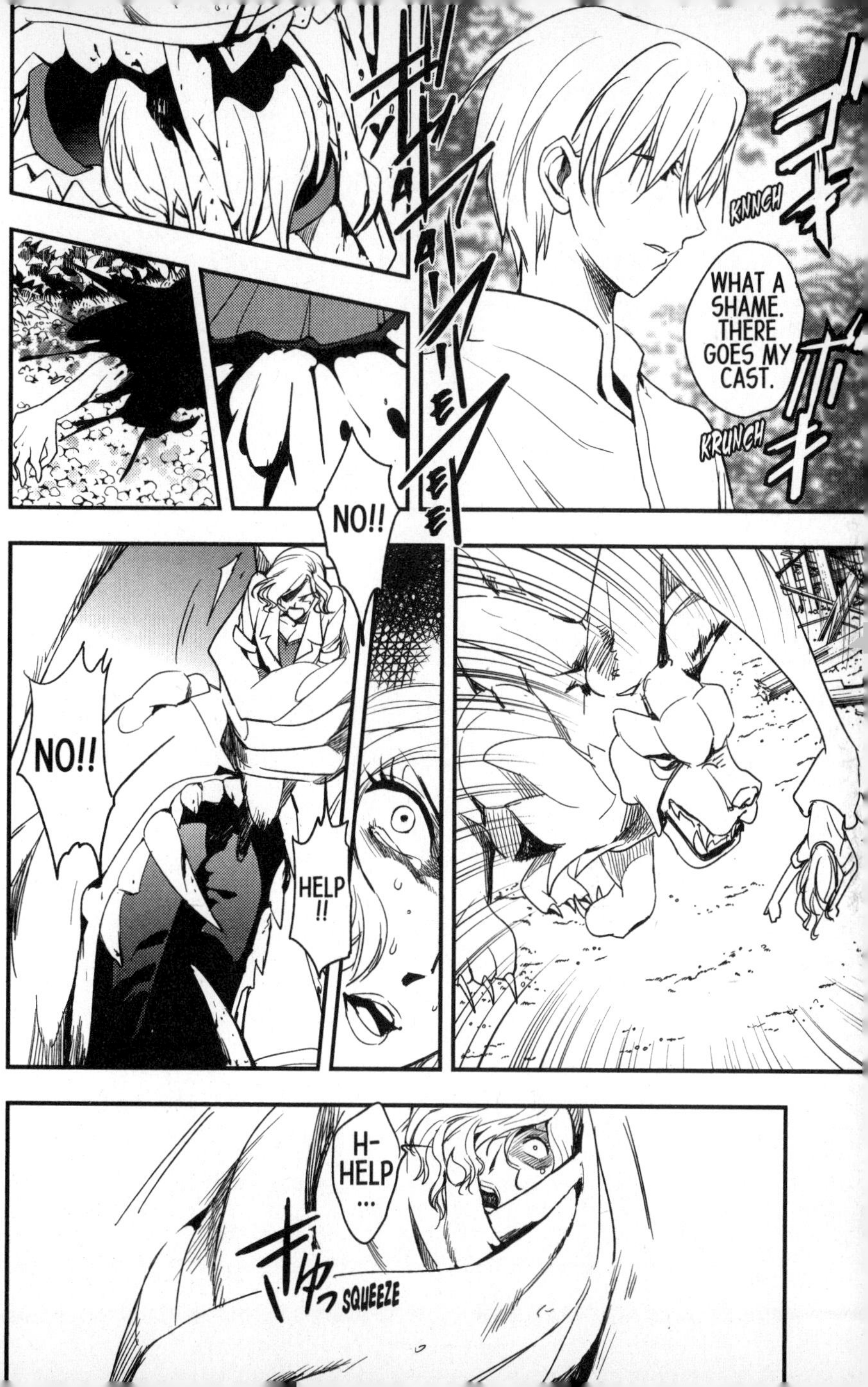
KNNCH
WHAT A SHAME. THERE GOES MY CAST.
KRUNCH
AAIIIEEE
NO!!
NO!!
HELP !!
H-HELP ...
SQUEEZE

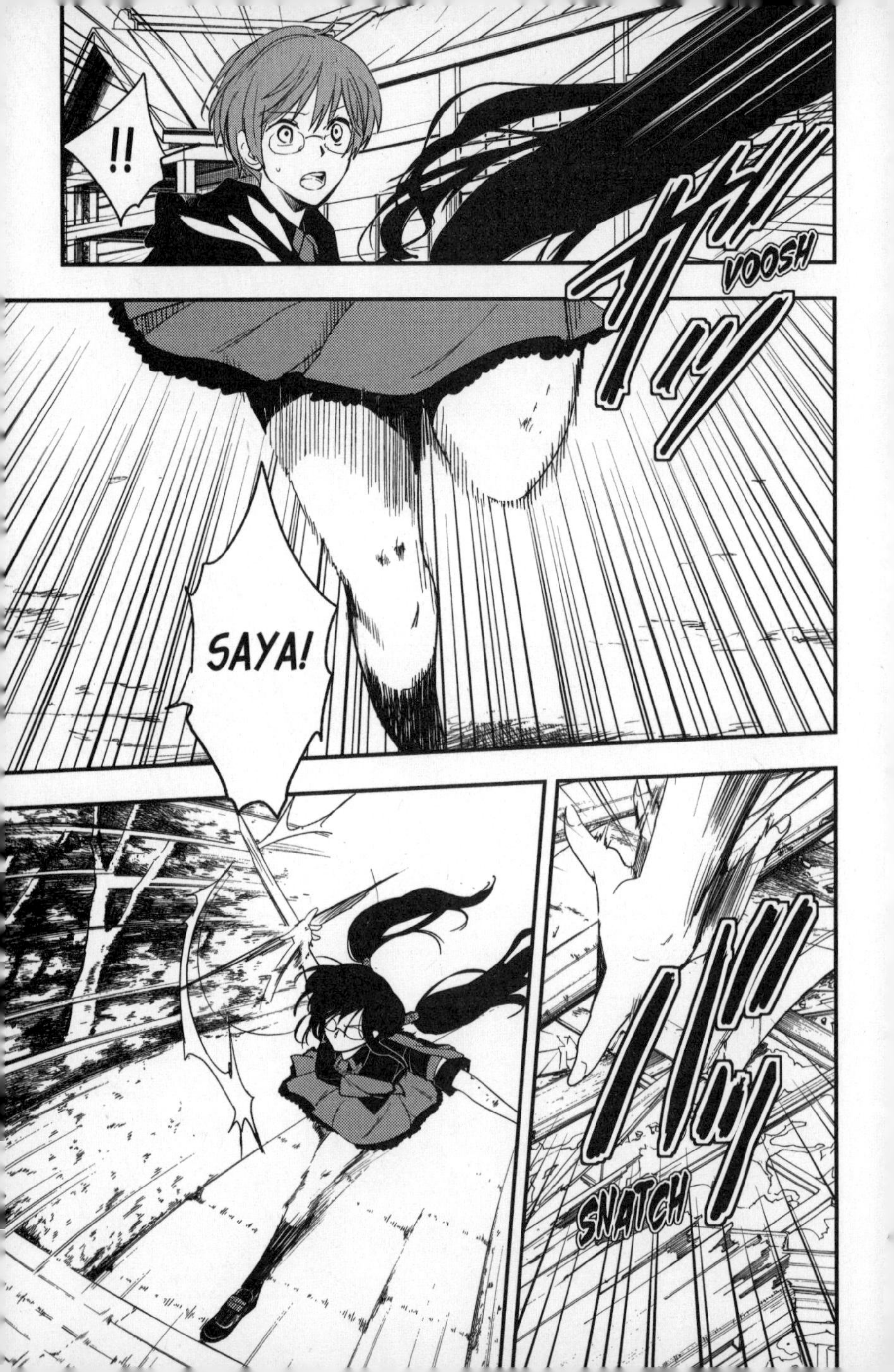

!!
VOOSH
SAYA!
SNATCH

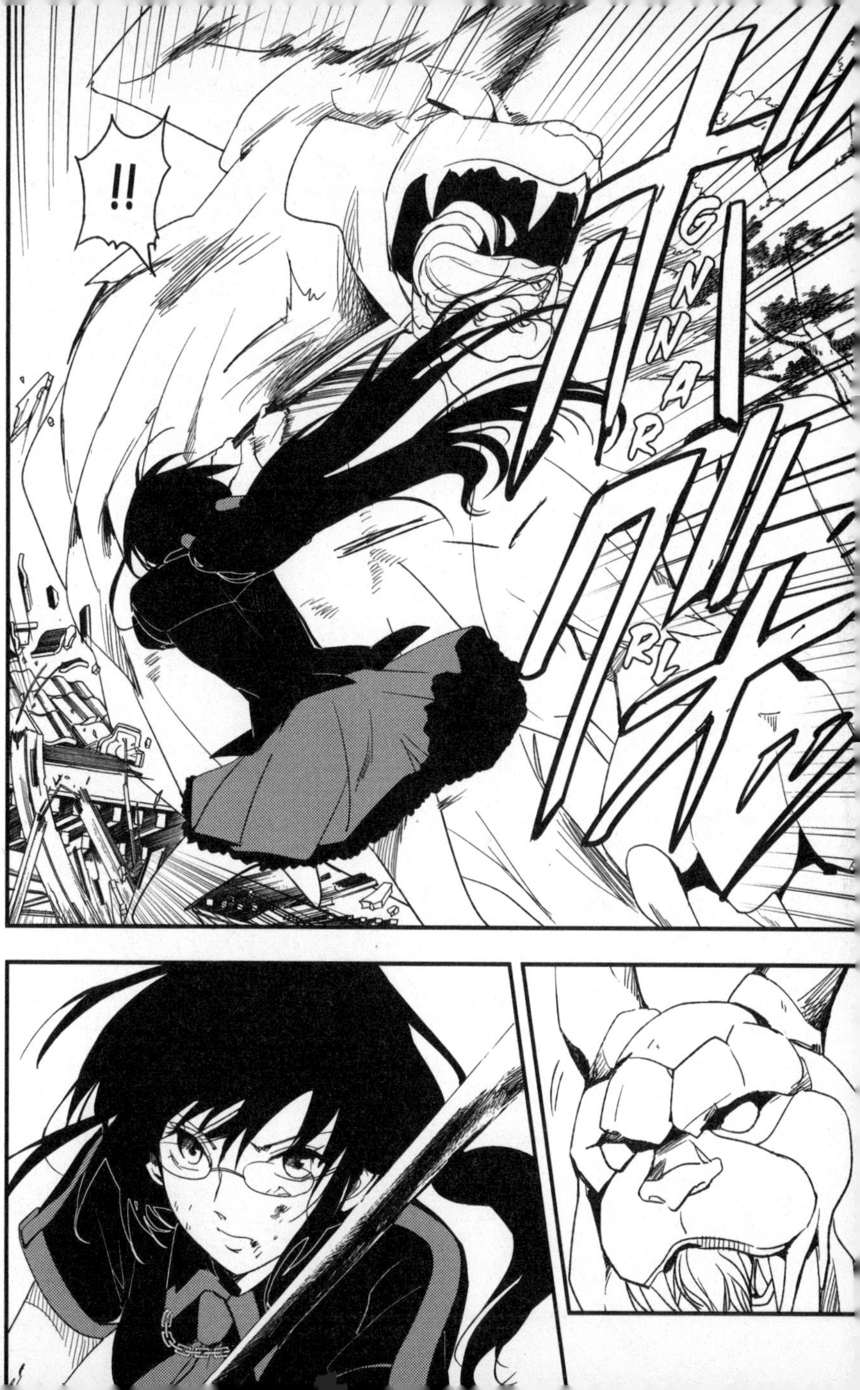
!!
GNNAR
RL

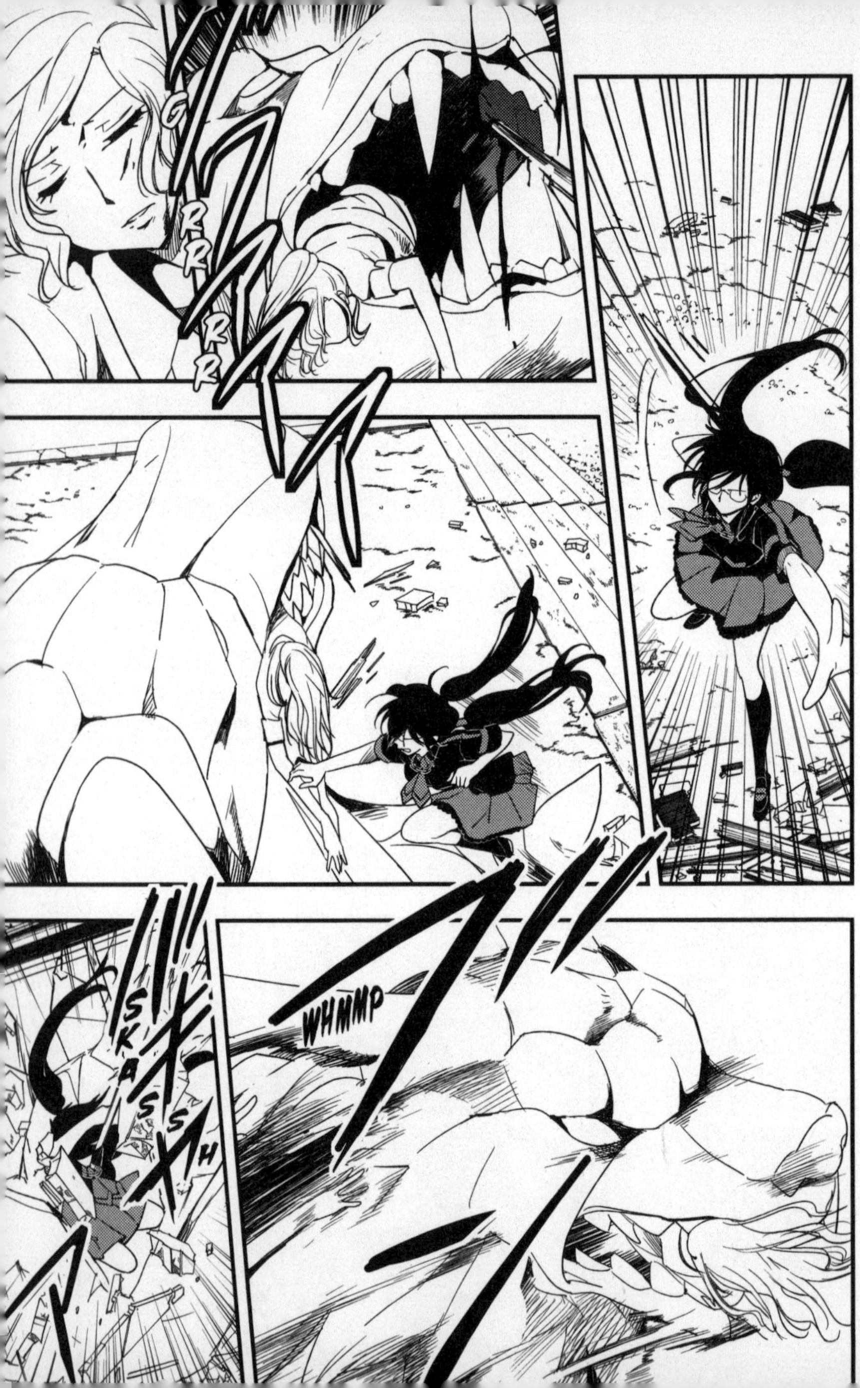
GRRRR
WHMMP
SKASSSH

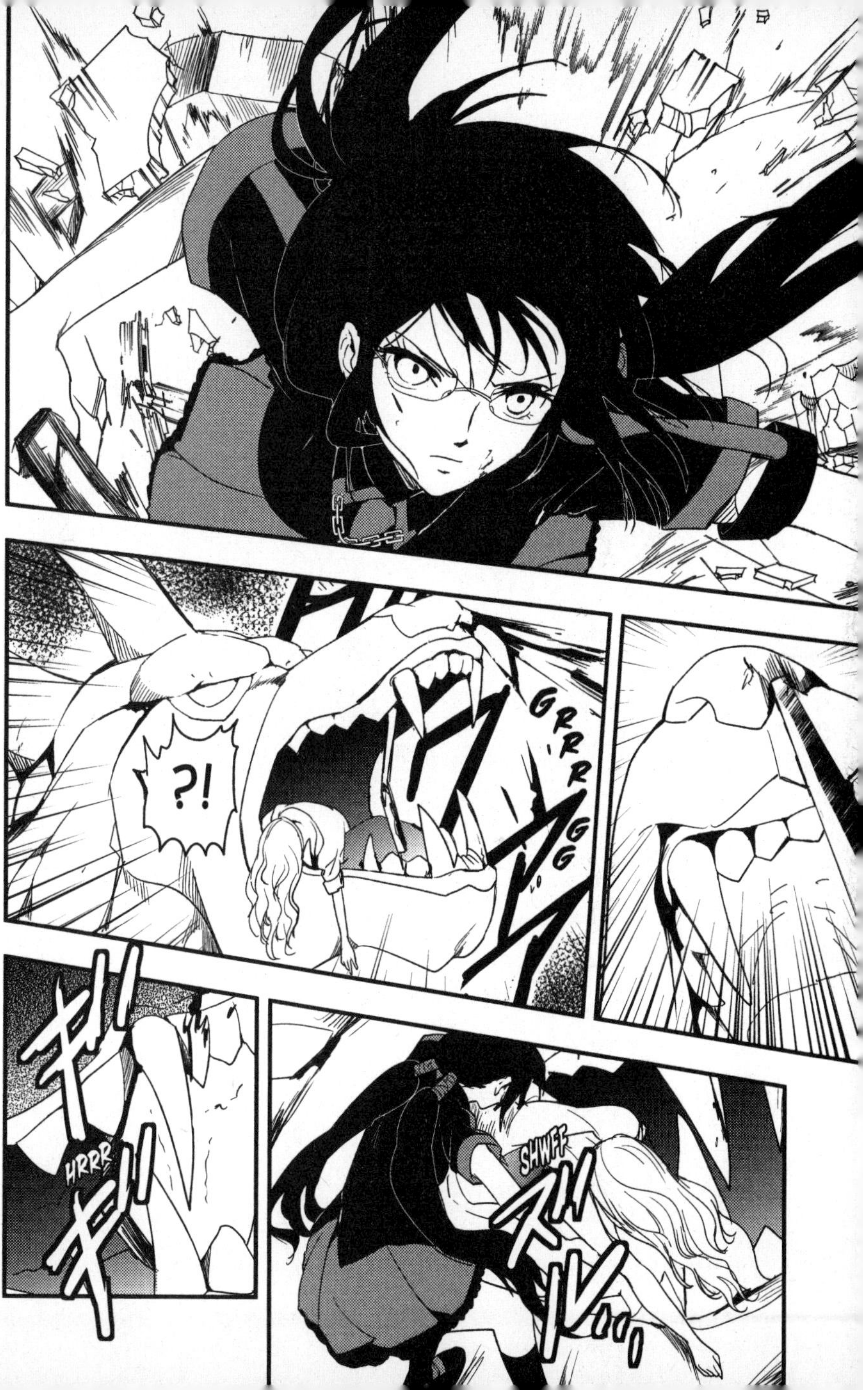
GRRRGGG
?!
SHWFF
HRRR

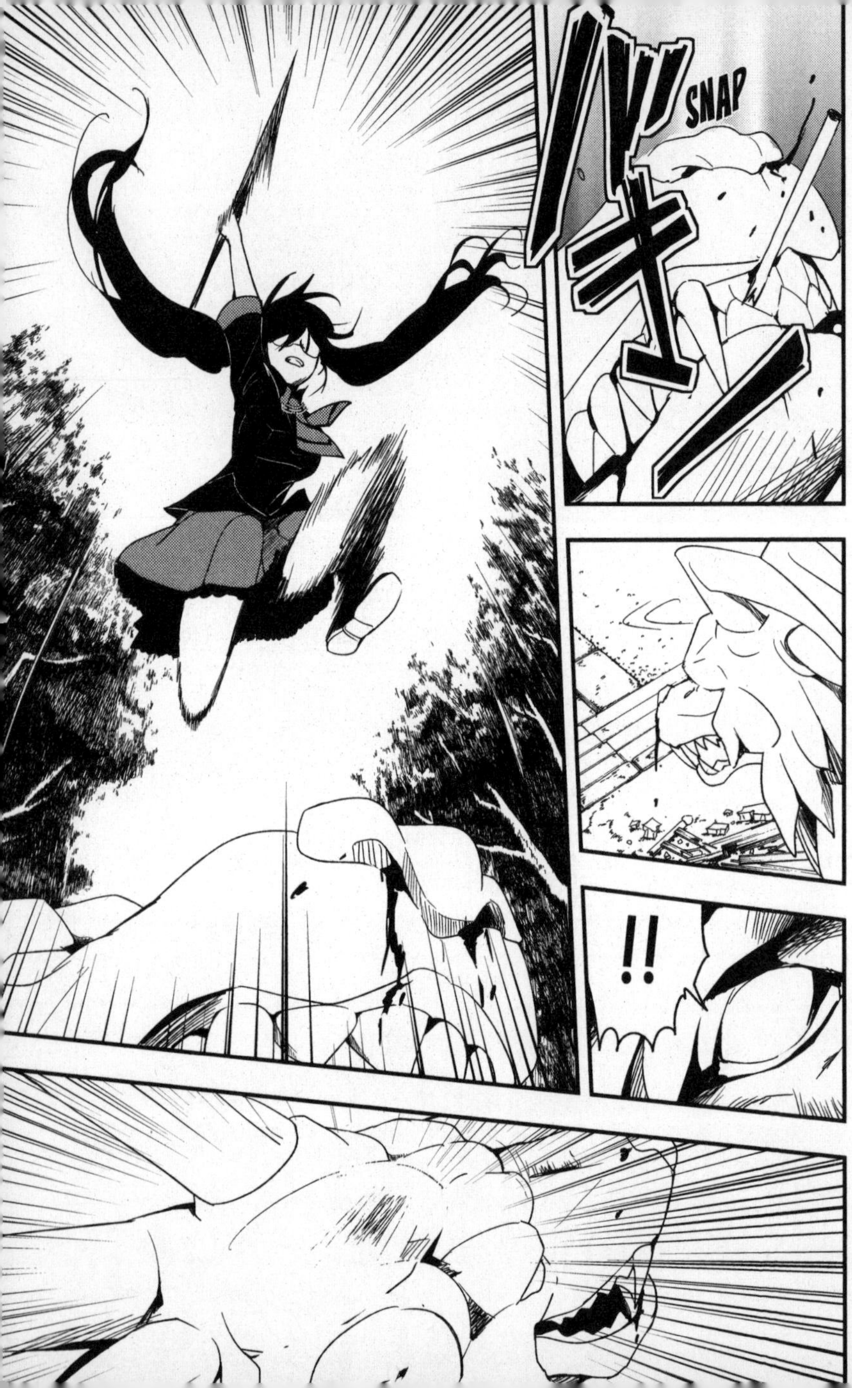
SNAP
!!

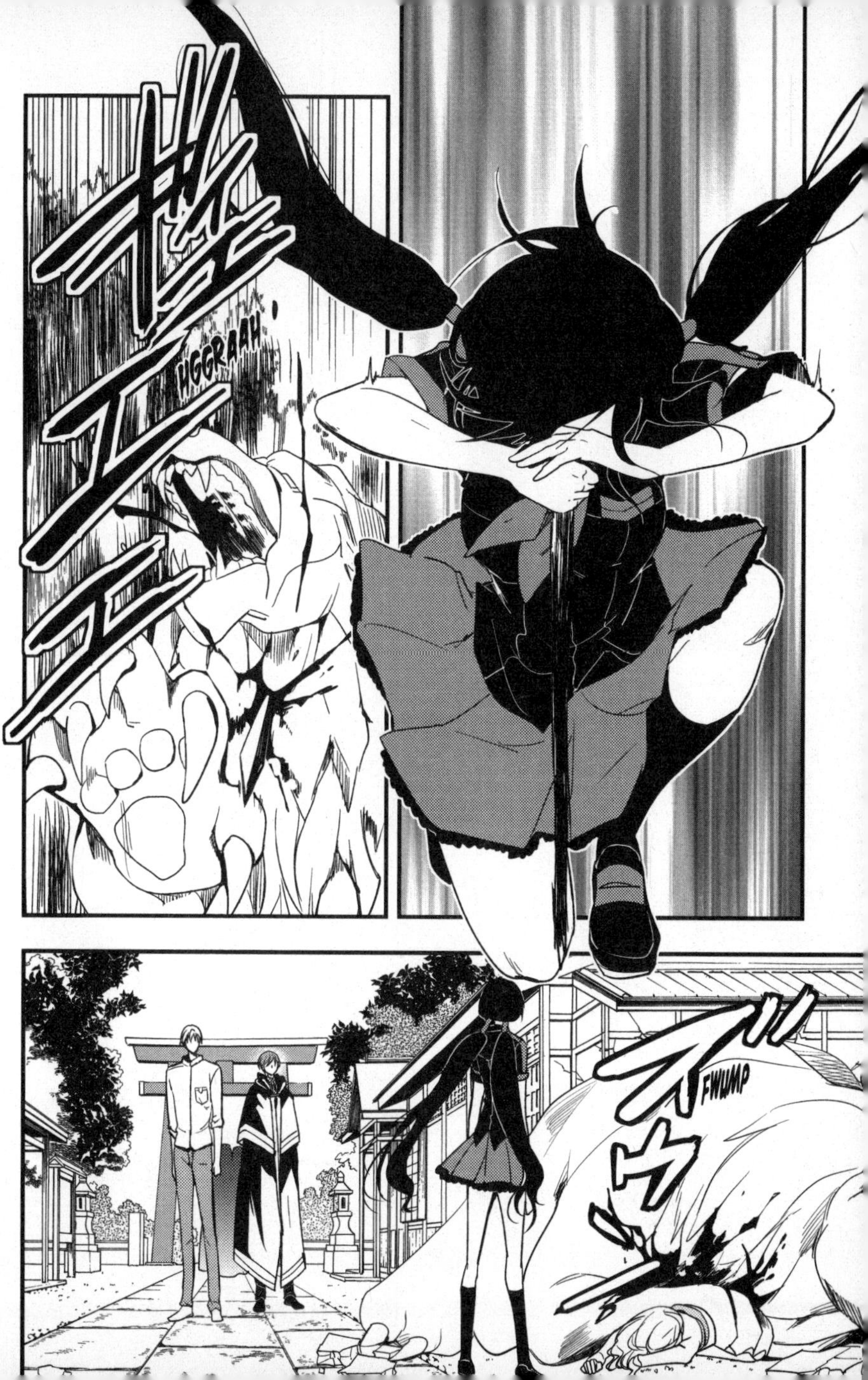
HGGRAAH
FWUMP

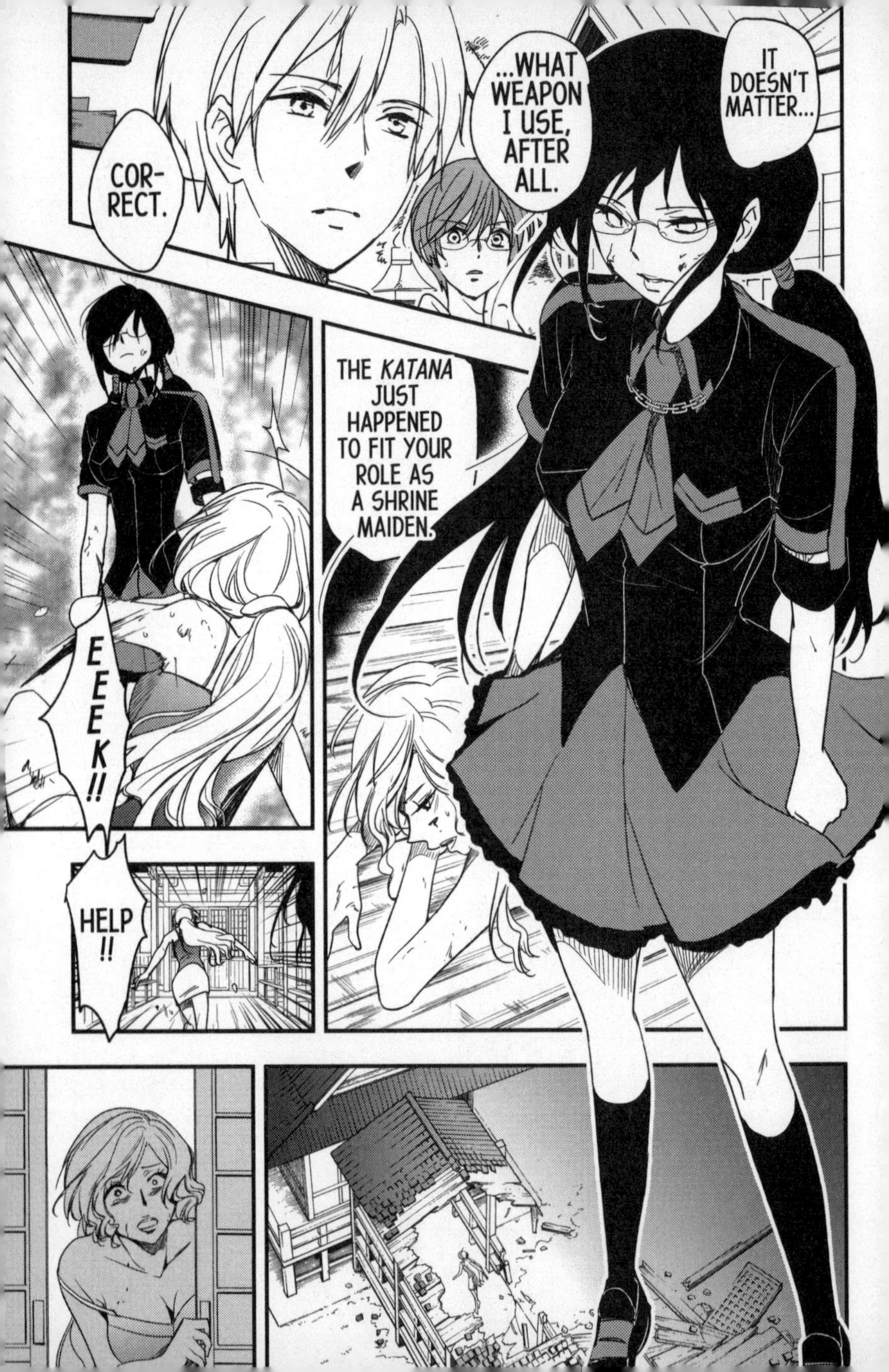
IT DOESN'T MATTER...
...WHAT WEAPON I USE, AFTER ALL.
COR-RECT.
THE *KATANA* JUST HAPPENED TO FIT YOUR ROLE AS A SHRINE MAIDEN.
EEEEK!!
HELP!!

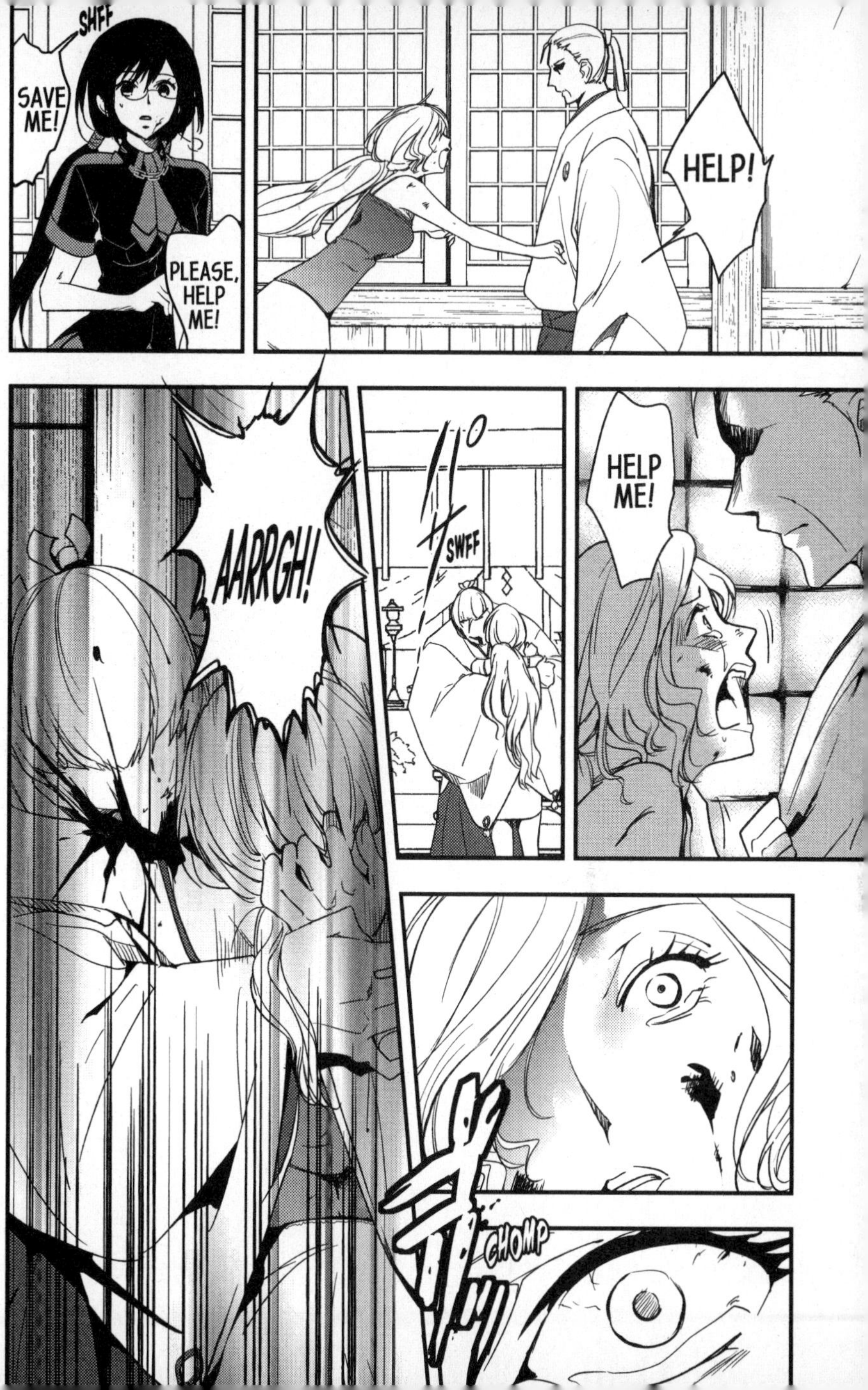
HELP!
SHFF
SAVE ME!
PLEASE, HELP ME!
HELP ME!
SWFF
CHOMP
AARRGH!

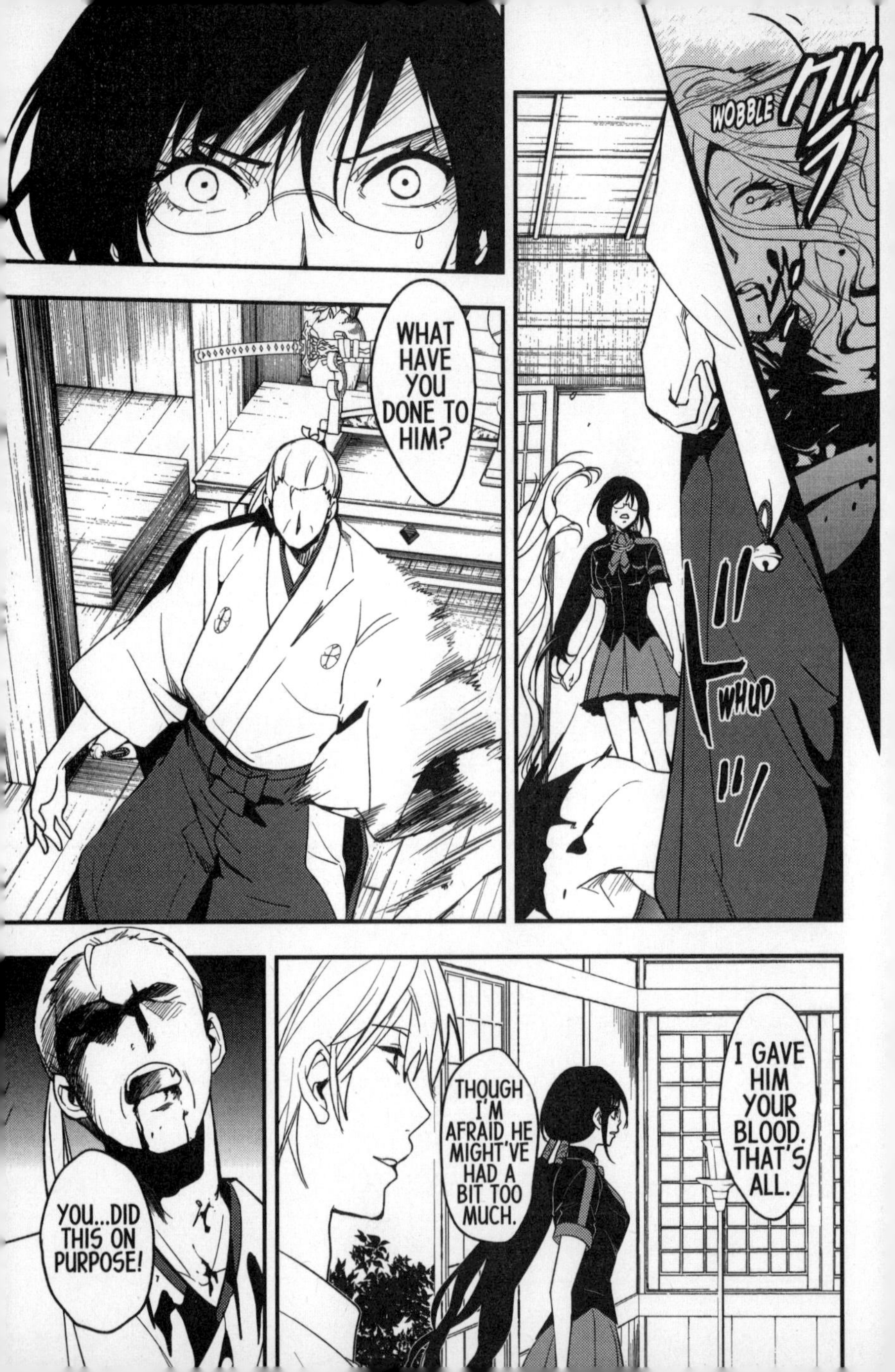
WOBBLE
WHUD
WHAT HAVE YOU DONE TO HIM?
I GAVE HIM YOUR BLOOD. THAT'S ALL.
THOUGH I'M AFRAID HE MIGHT'VE HAD A BIT TOO MUCH.
YOU...DID THIS ON PURPOSE!

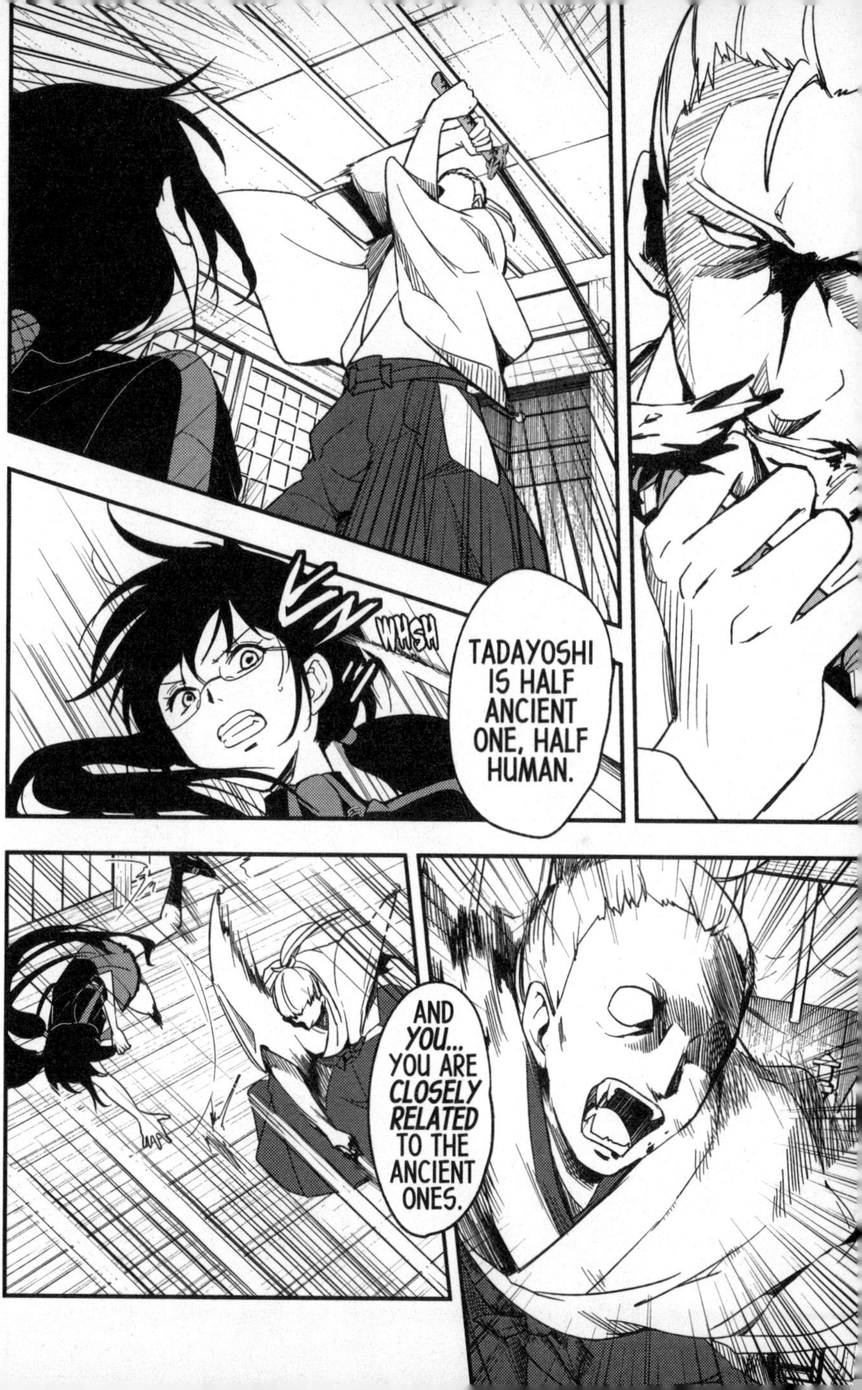
TADAYOSHI IS HALF ANCIENT ONE, HALF HUMAN.
WHSH
AND *YOU*... YOU ARE ***CLOSELY RELATED*** TO THE ANCIENT ONES.

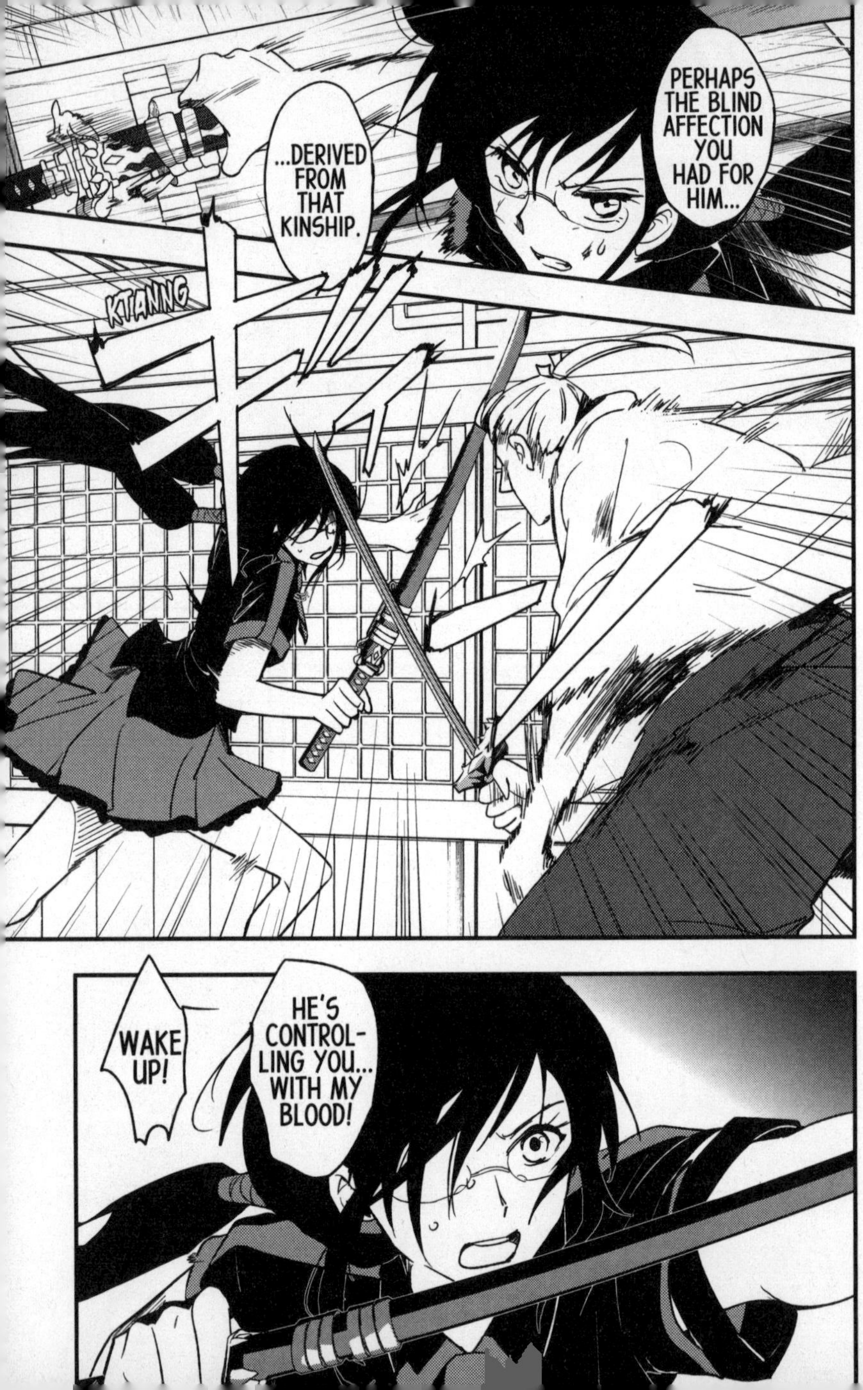
PERHAPS THE BLIND AFFECTION YOU HAD FOR HIM...
...DERIVED FROM THAT KINSHIP.
KTANNG
HE'S CONTROL-LING YOU... WITH MY BLOOD!
WAKE UP!

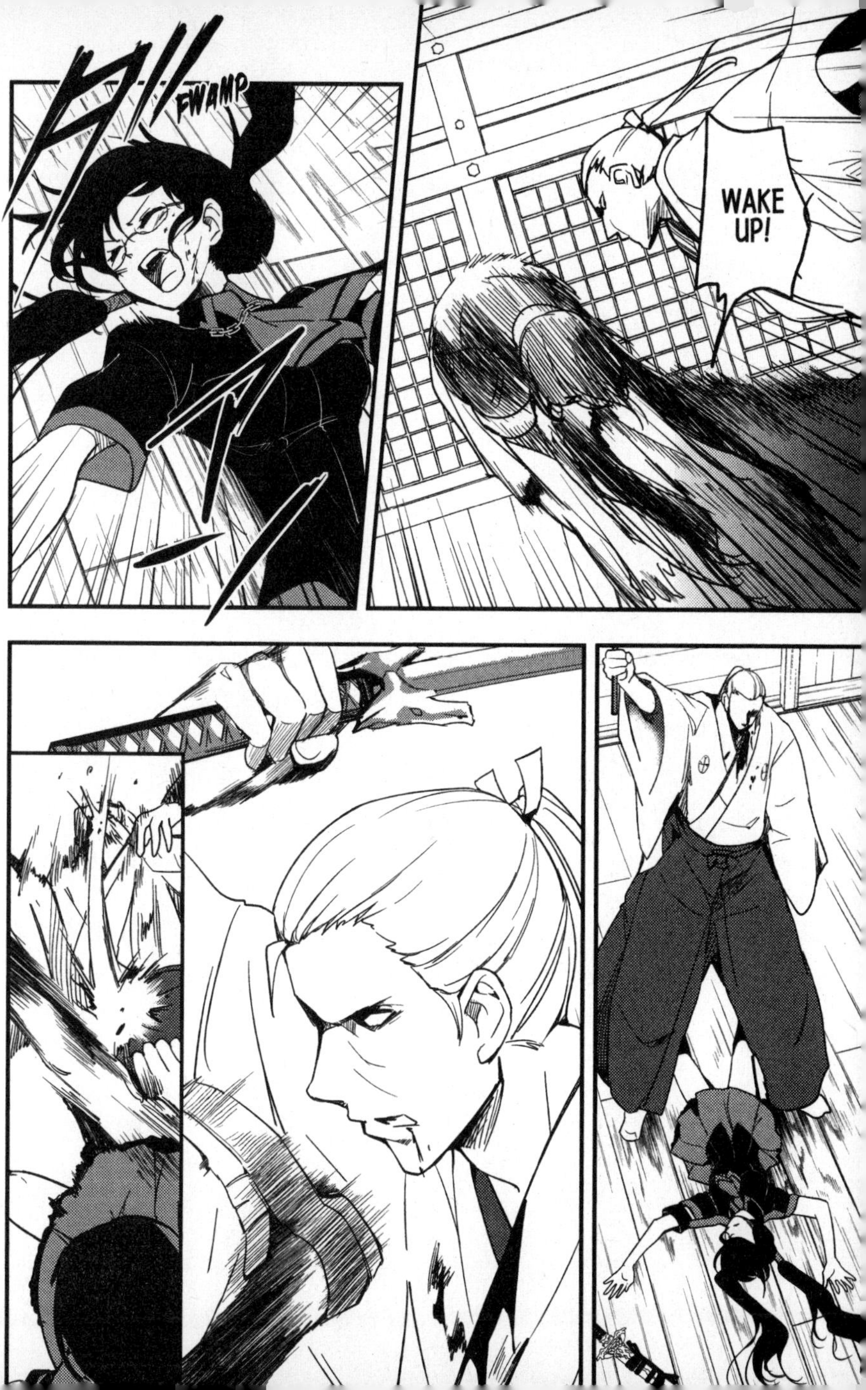
WAKE UP!
FWAMP

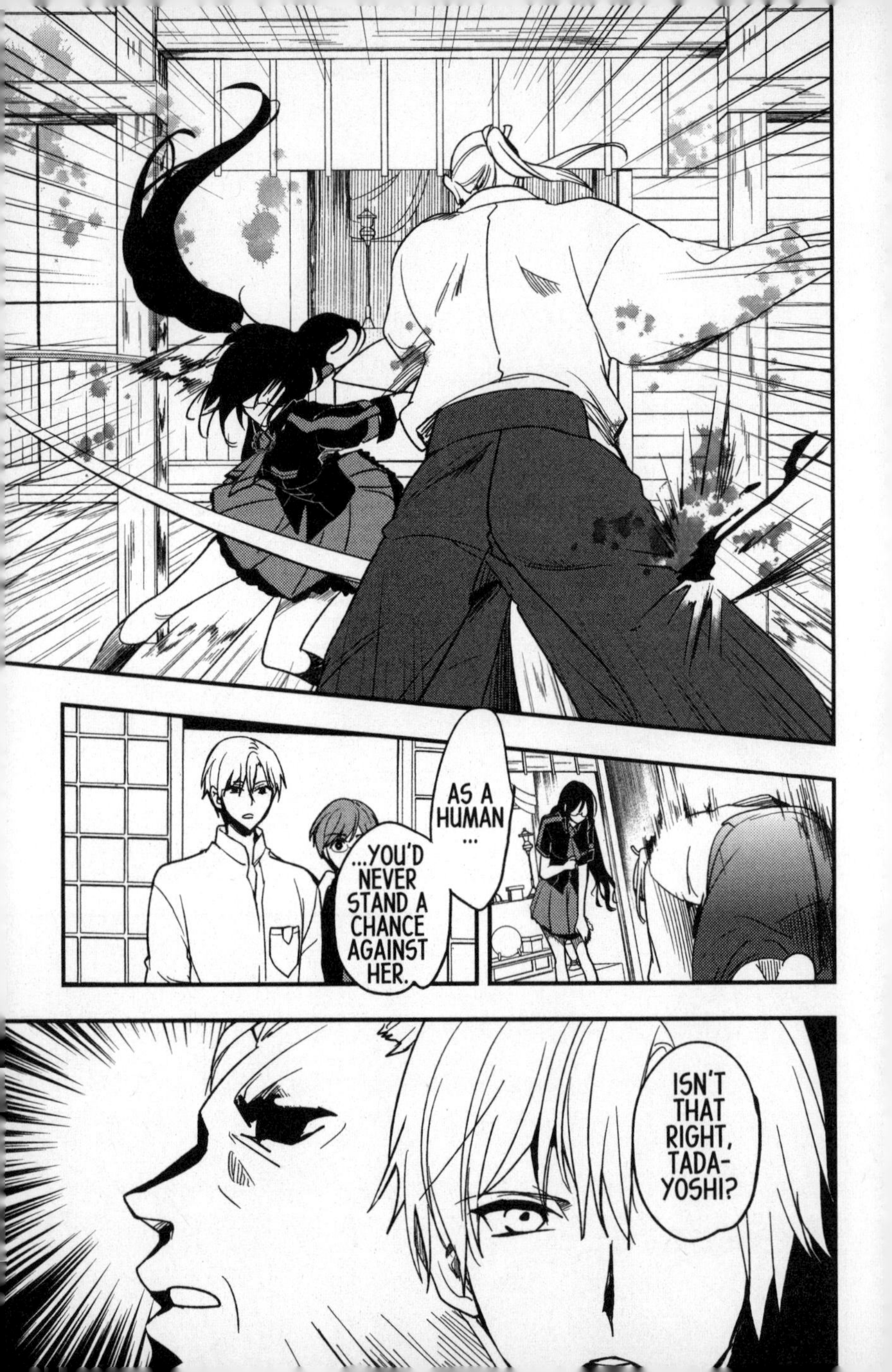
AS A HUMAN ...
...YOU'D NEVER STAND A CHANCE AGAINST HER.
ISN'T THAT RIGHT, TADA-YOSHI?

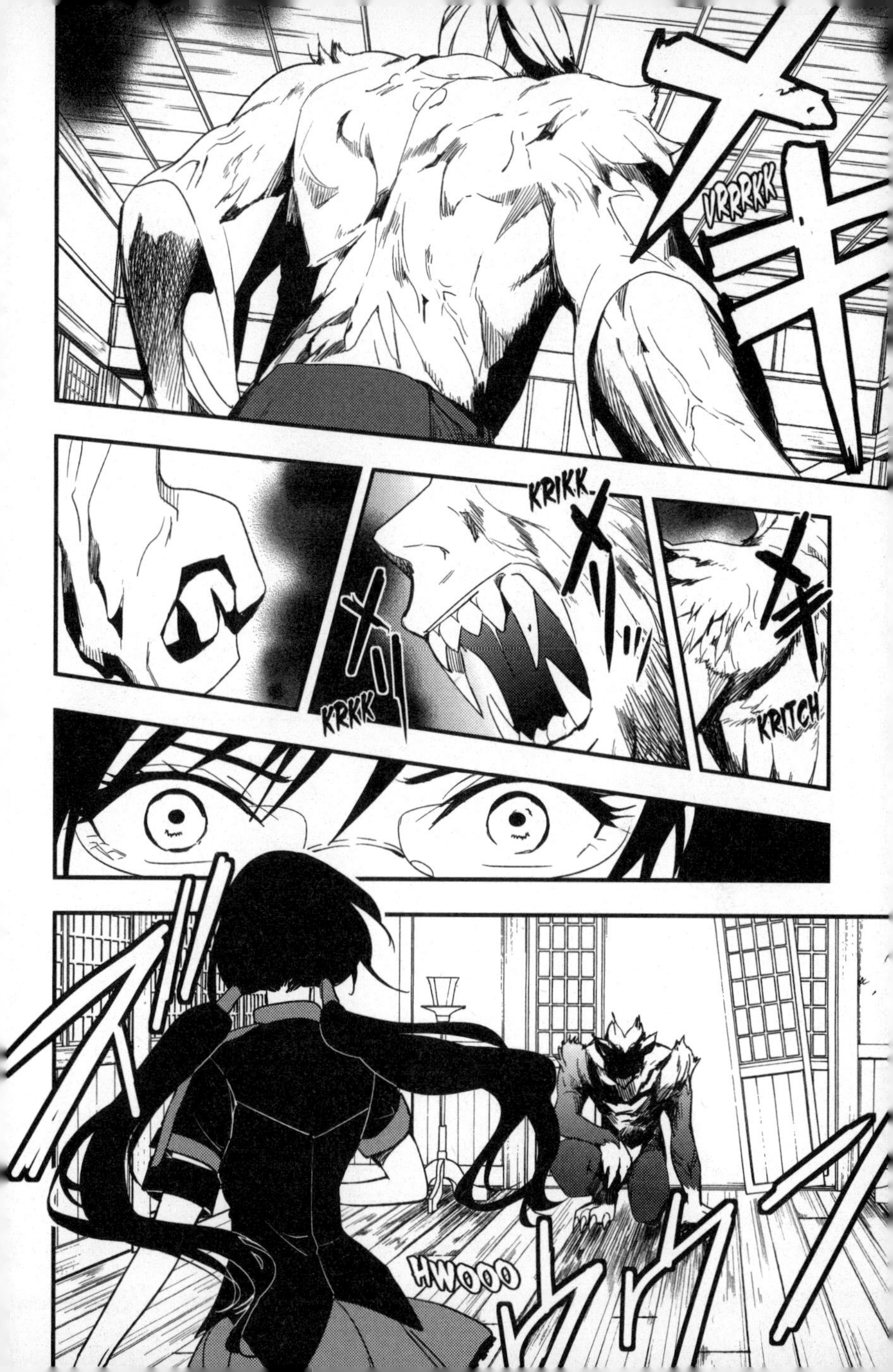
VRRRKK
KRITCH
KRIKK
KRKK
HWOOO

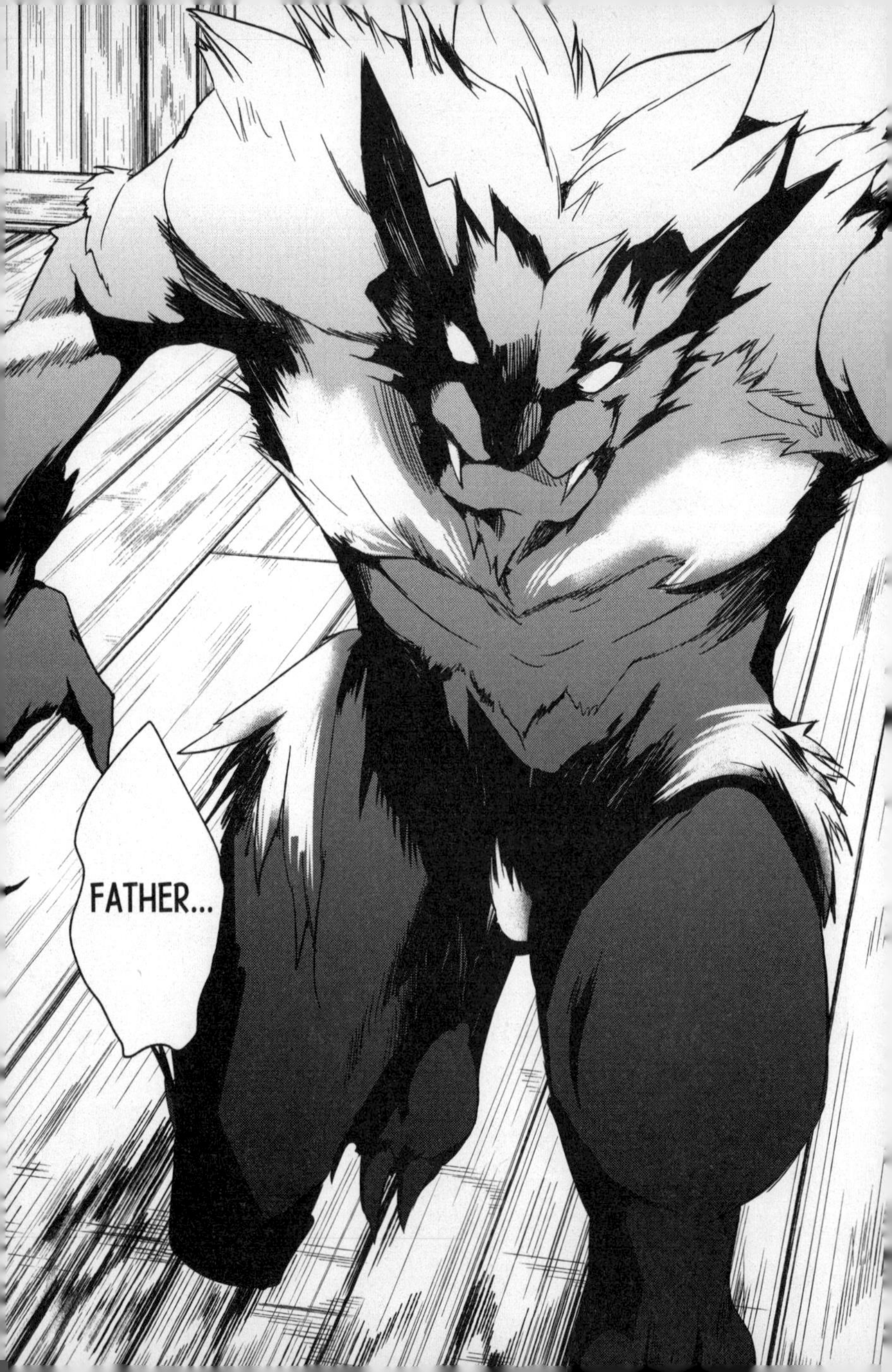
FATHER...

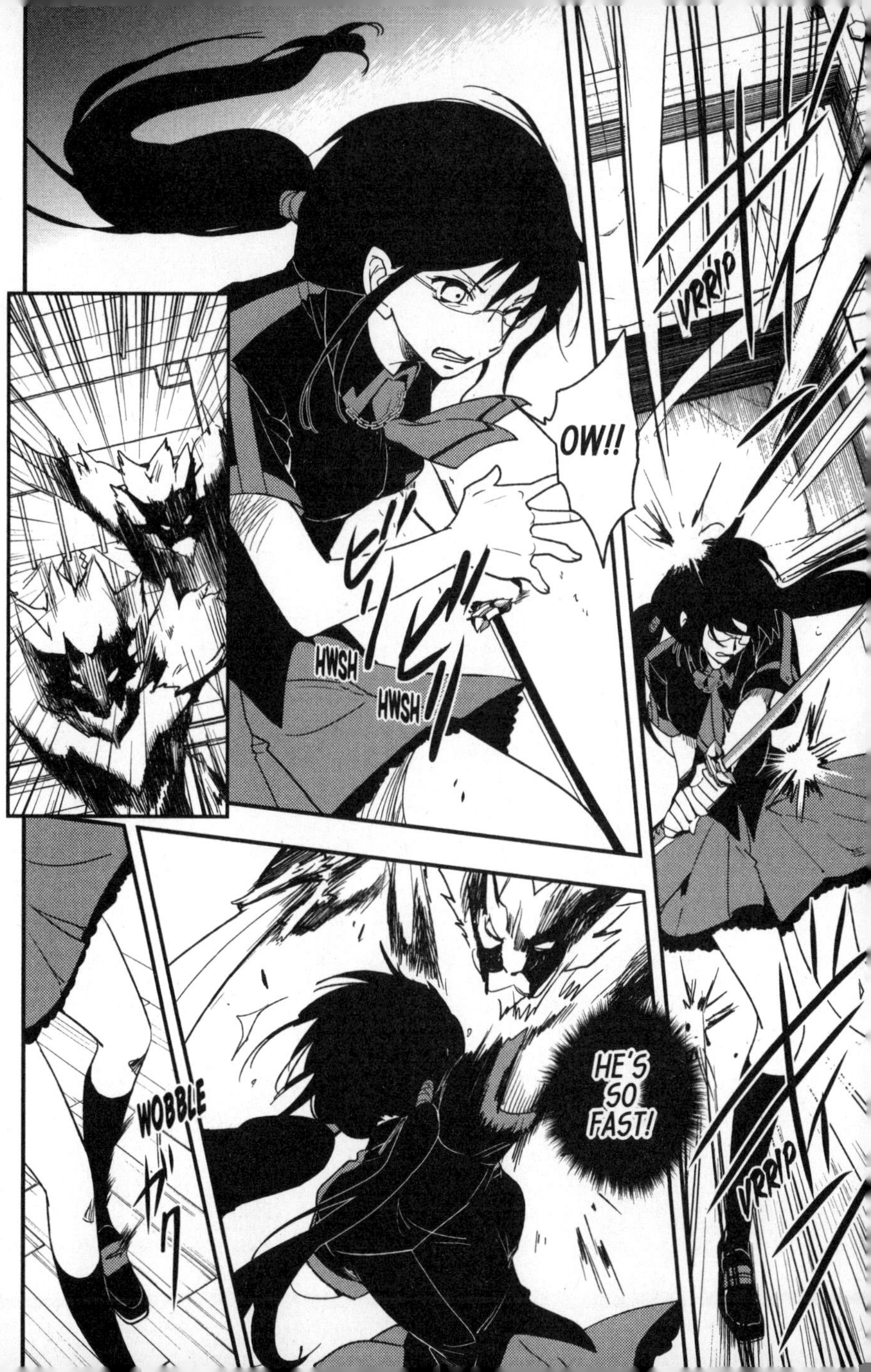
VRRIP
OW!!
HWSH
HWSH
VRRIP
HE'S SO FAST!
WOBBLE
ガク

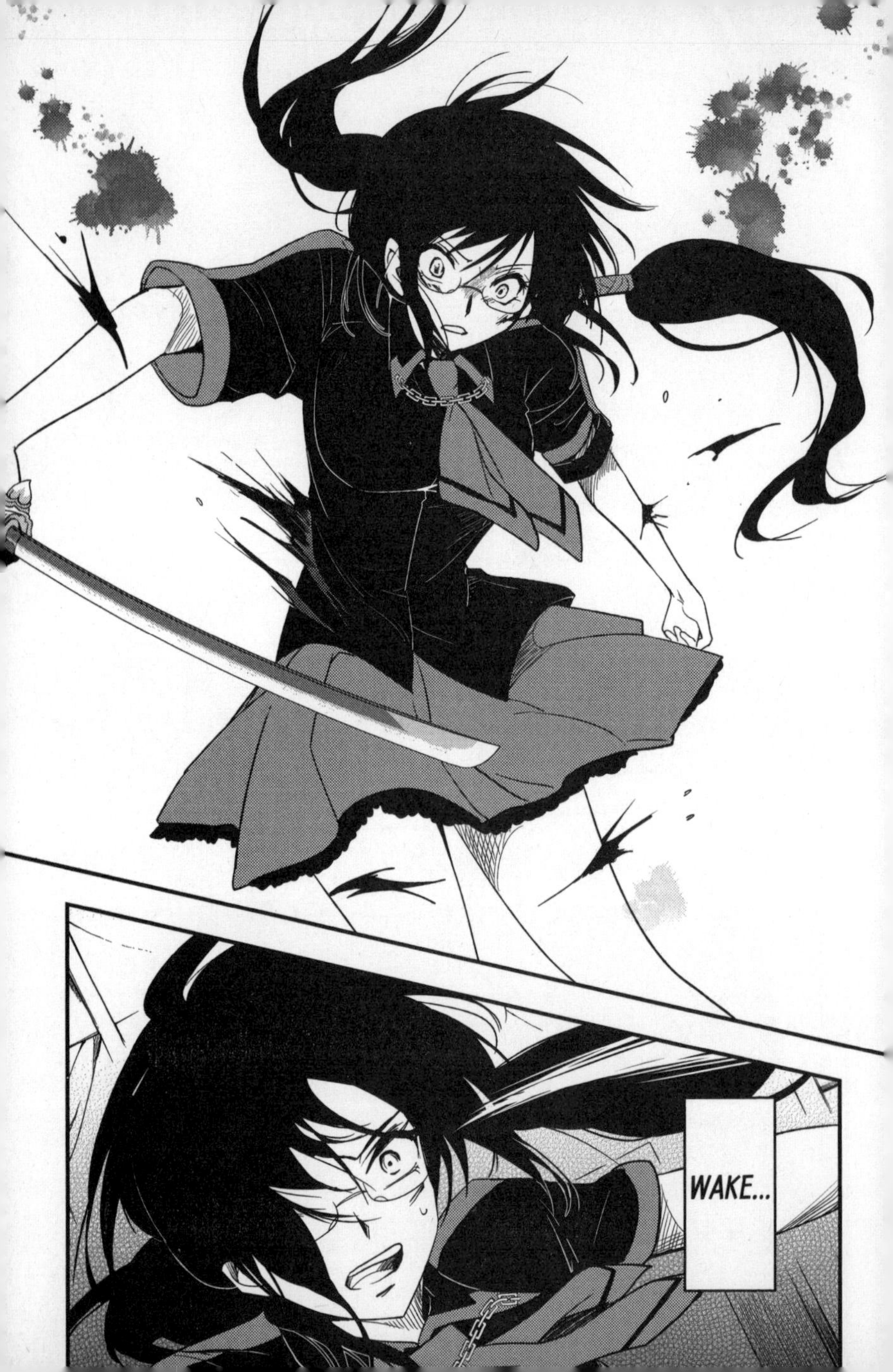
WAKE...

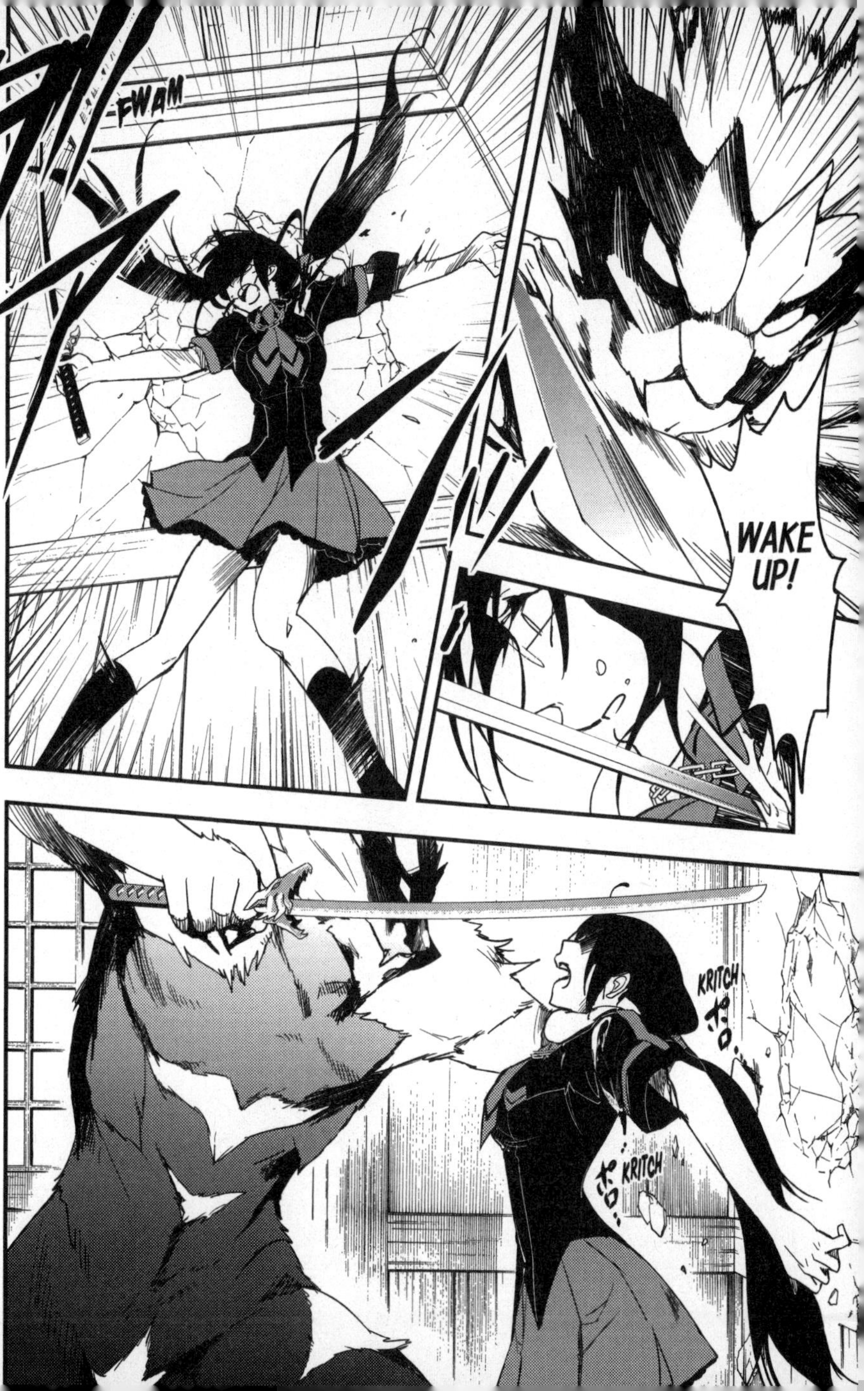
WAKE UP!
FWAM
KRITCH
KRITCH

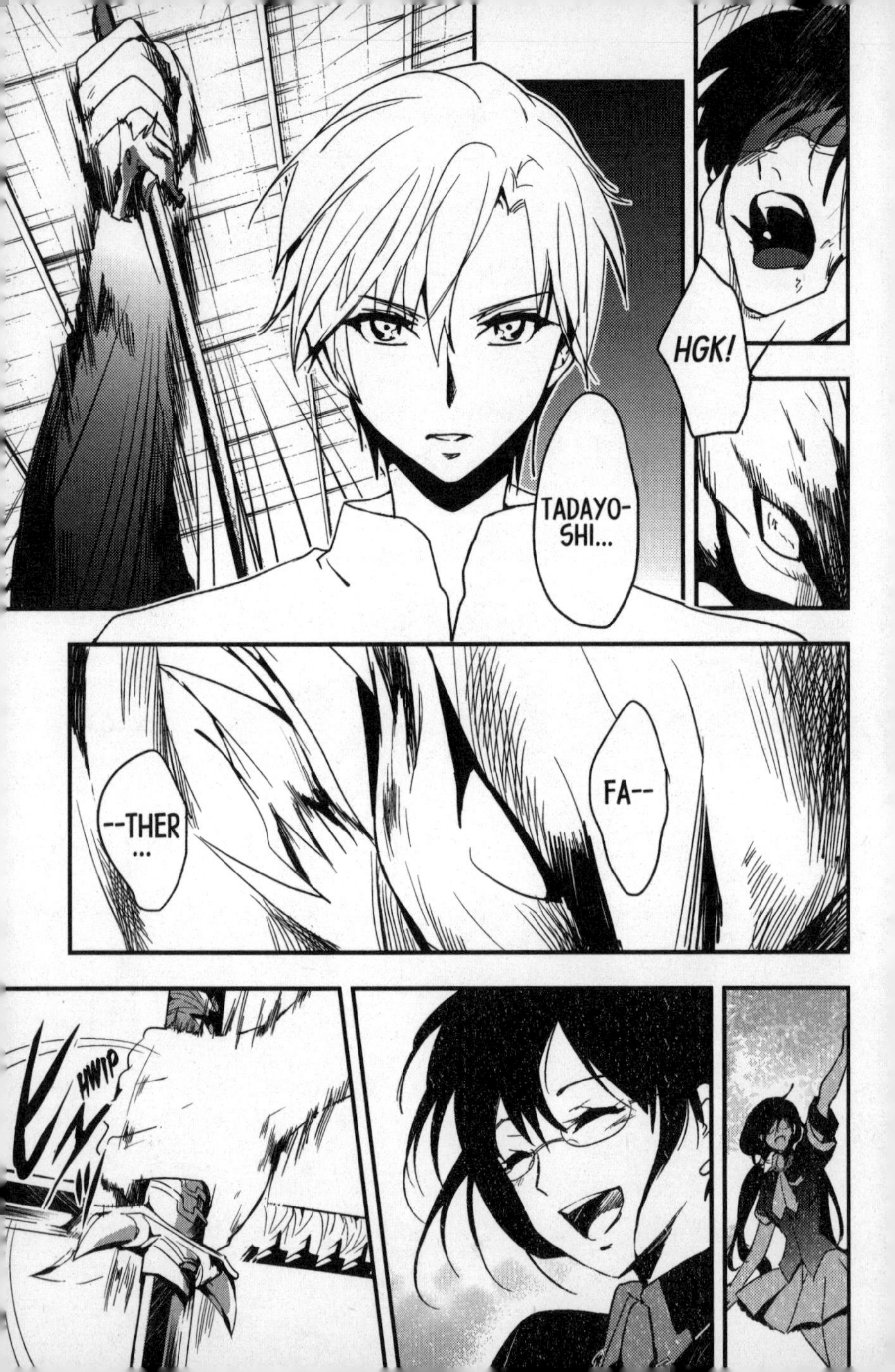
HGK!
TADAYO-SHI...
FA--
--THER ...
HWIP

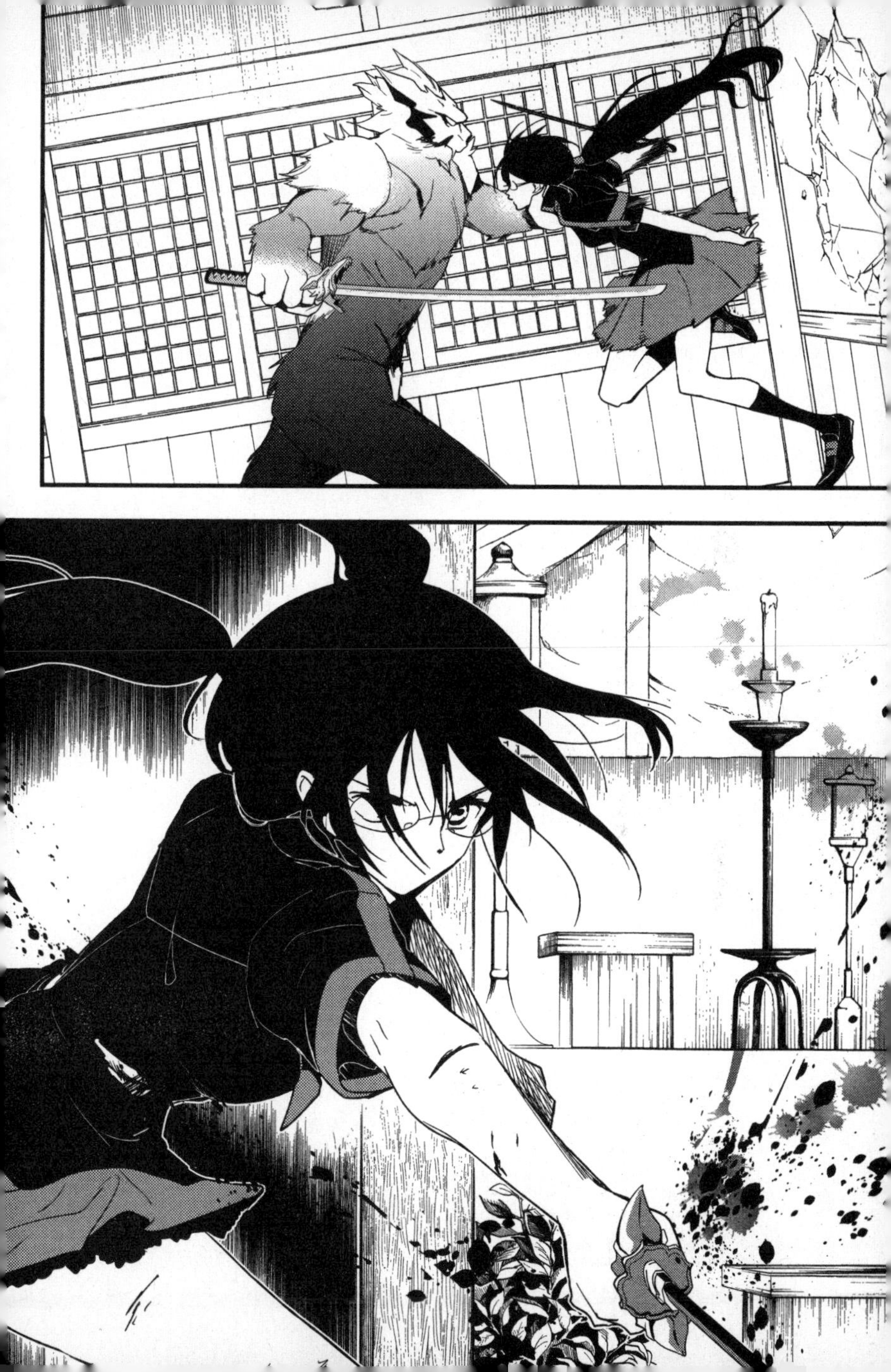

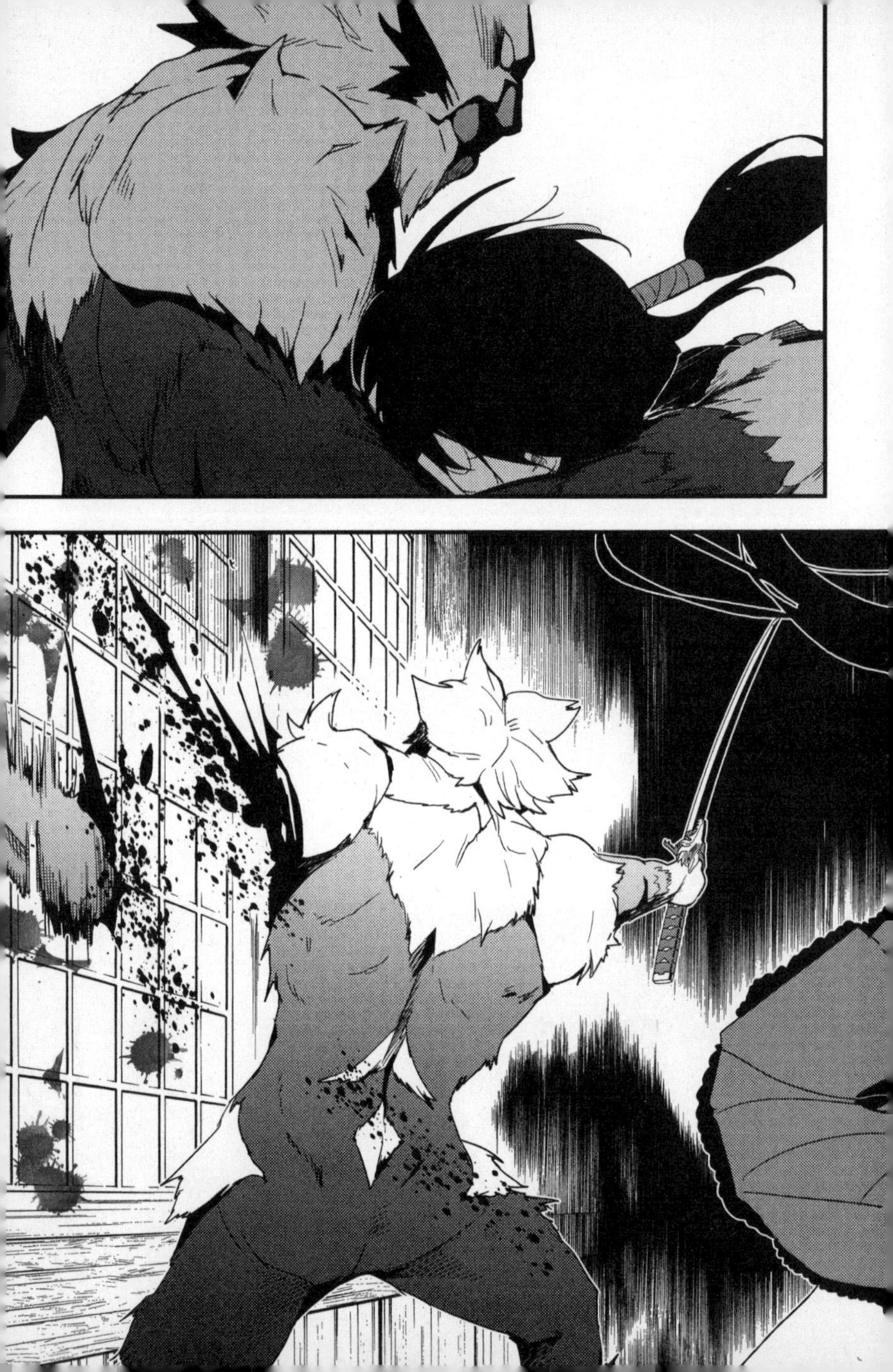

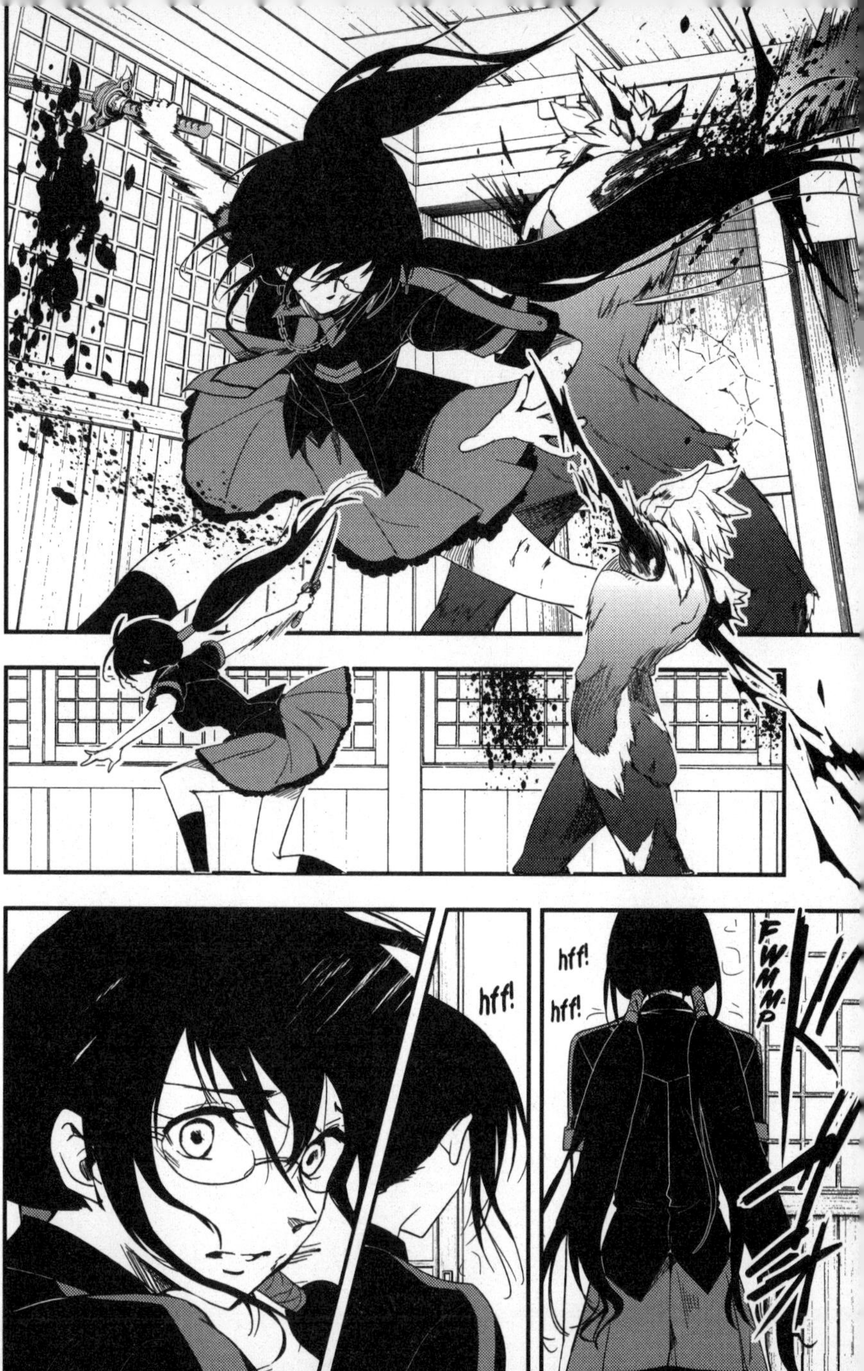
FWMMP
hff!
hff!
hff!

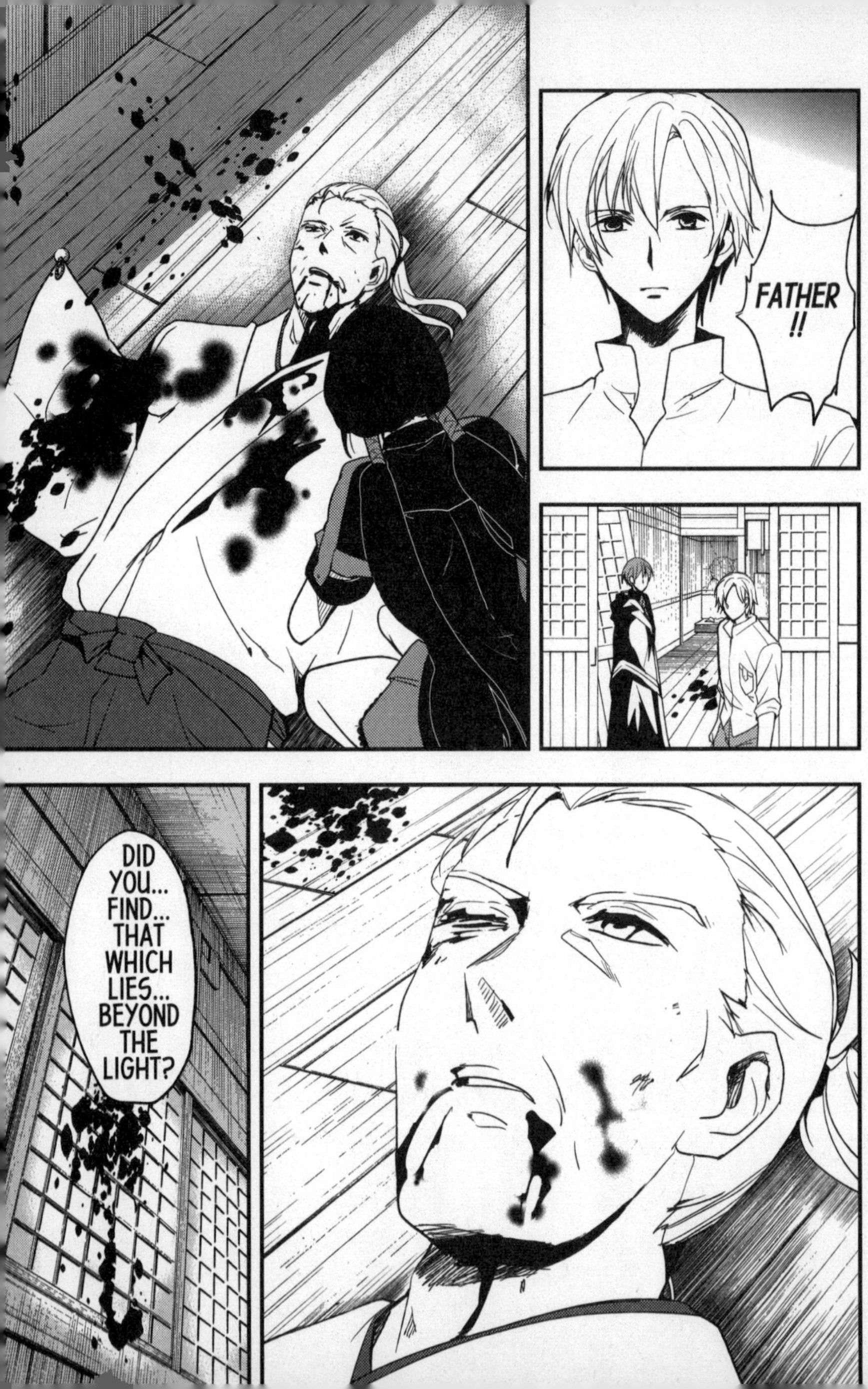
FATHER !!
DID YOU... FIND... THAT WHICH LIES... BEYOND THE LIGHT?

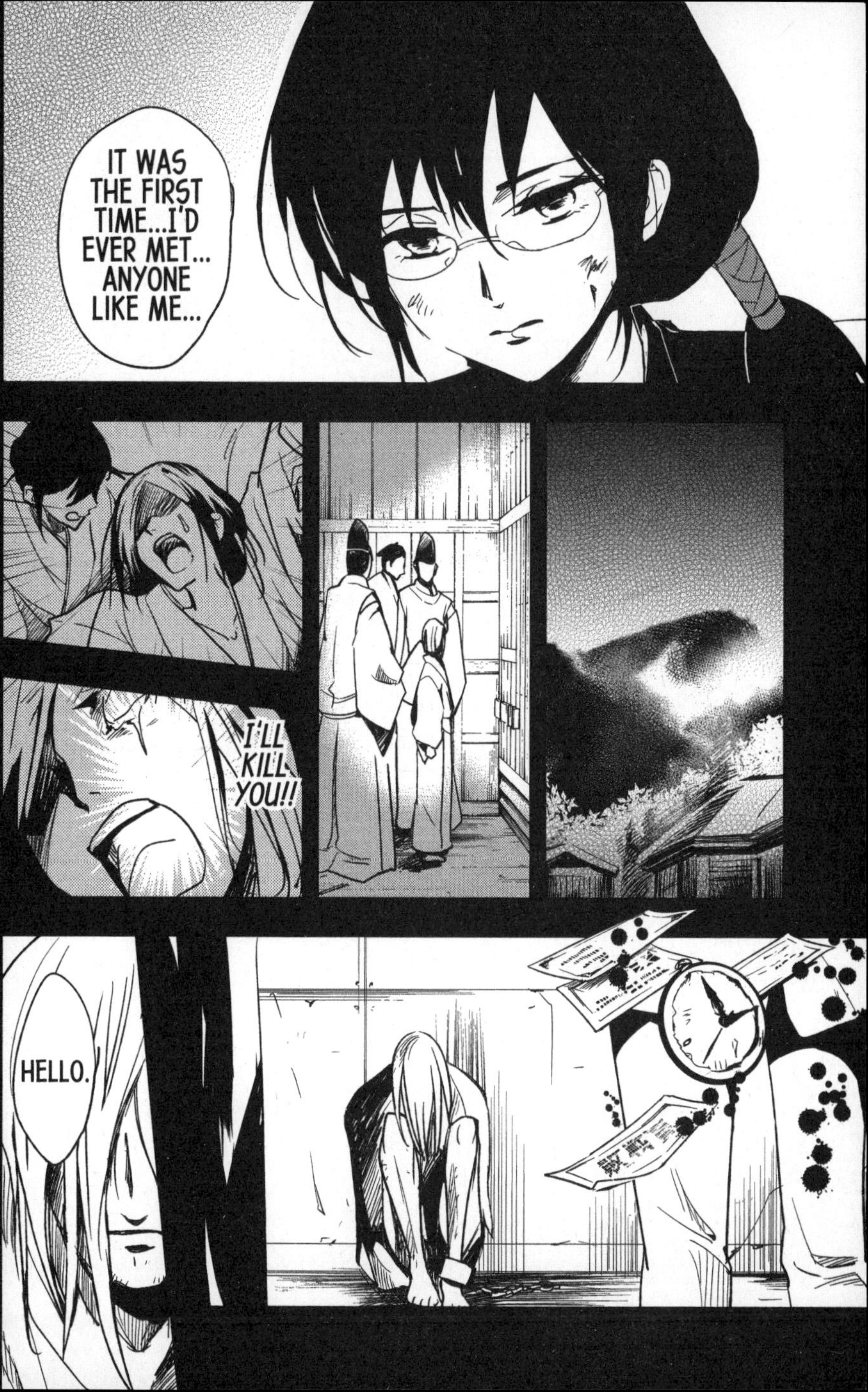
IT WAS THE FIRST TIME...I'D EVER MET... ANYONE LIKE ME...
I'LL KILL YOU!!
HELLO.

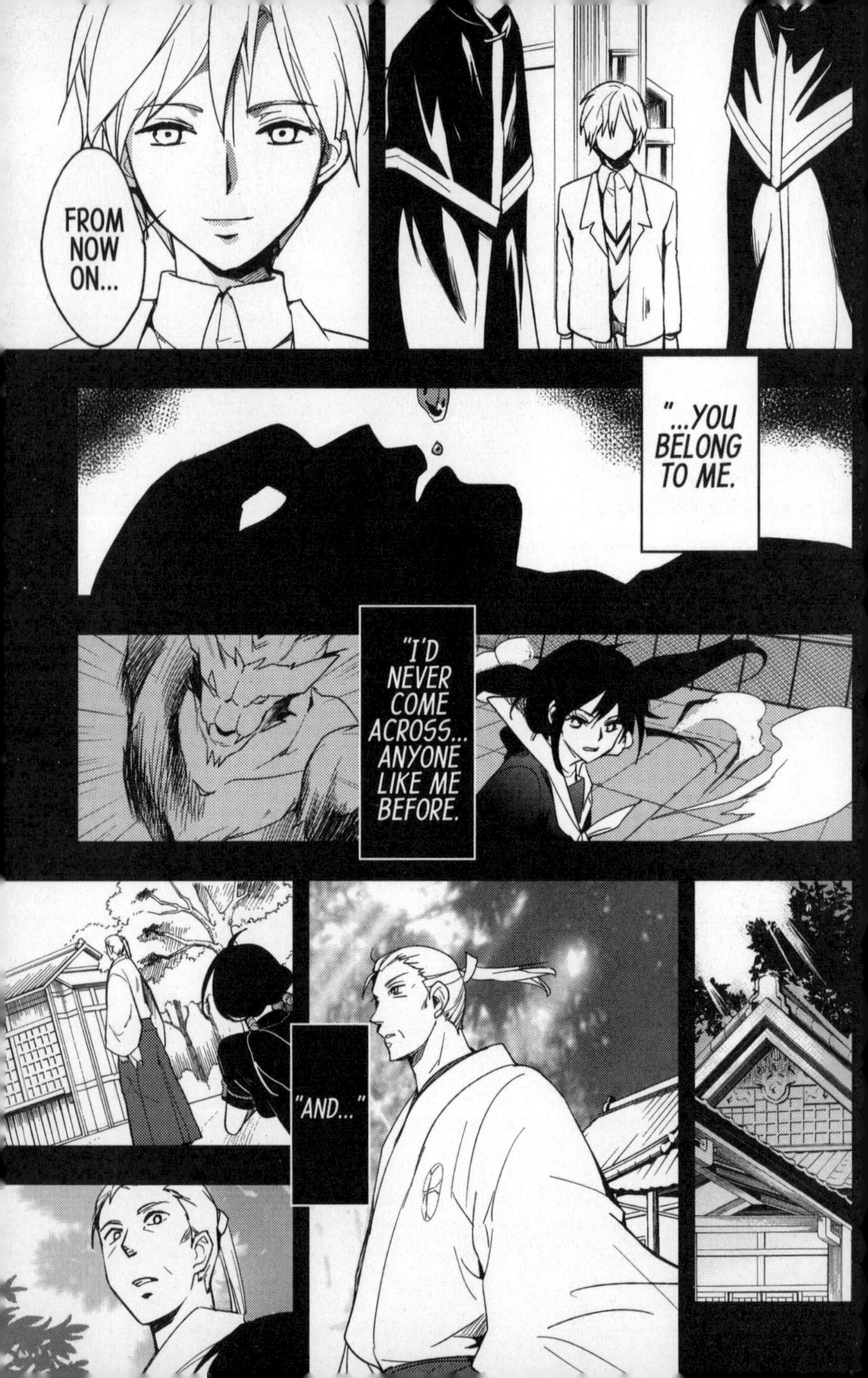
FROM NOW ON...
"...YOU BELONG TO ME.
"I'D NEVER COME ACROSS... ANYONE LIKE ME BEFORE.
"AND..."

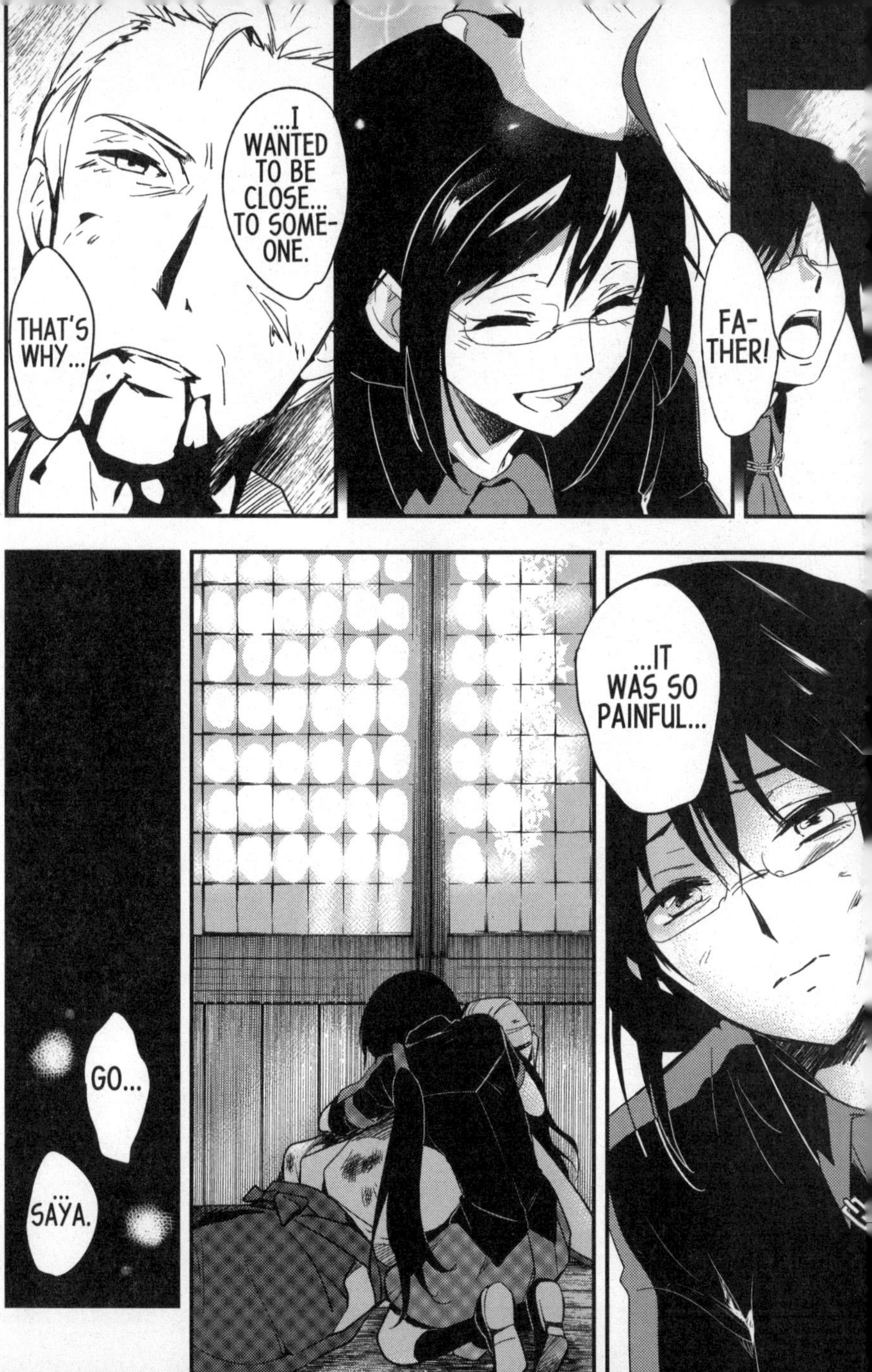
FA-THER!
...I WANTED TO BE CLOSE... TO SOME-ONE.
THAT'S WHY...
...IT WAS SO PAINFUL...
GO...
...SAYA.

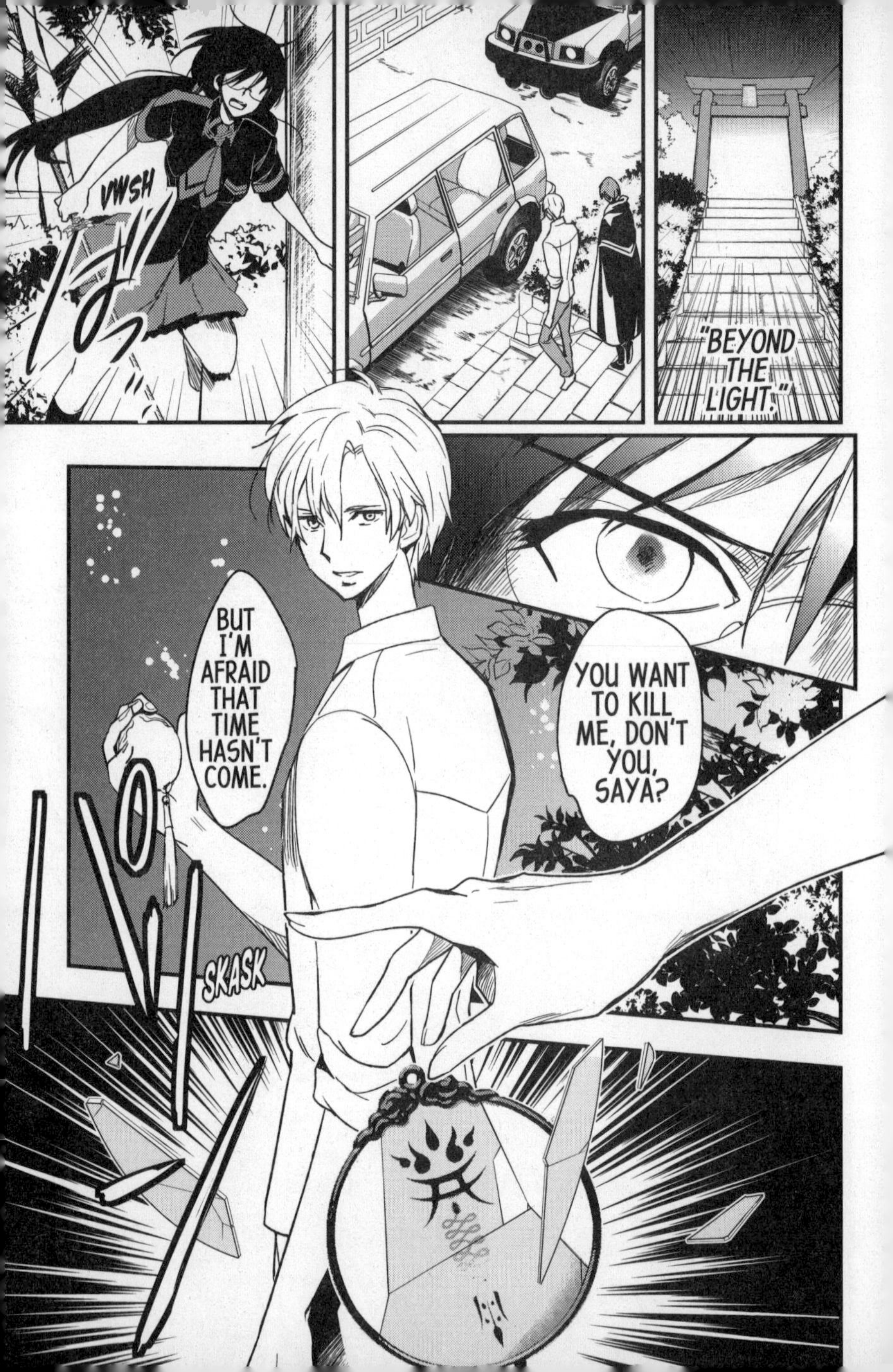
"BEYOND THE LIGHT."
VWSH
YOU WANT TO KILL ME, DON'T YOU, SAYA?
BUT I'M AFRAID THAT TIME HASN'T COME.
SKASK

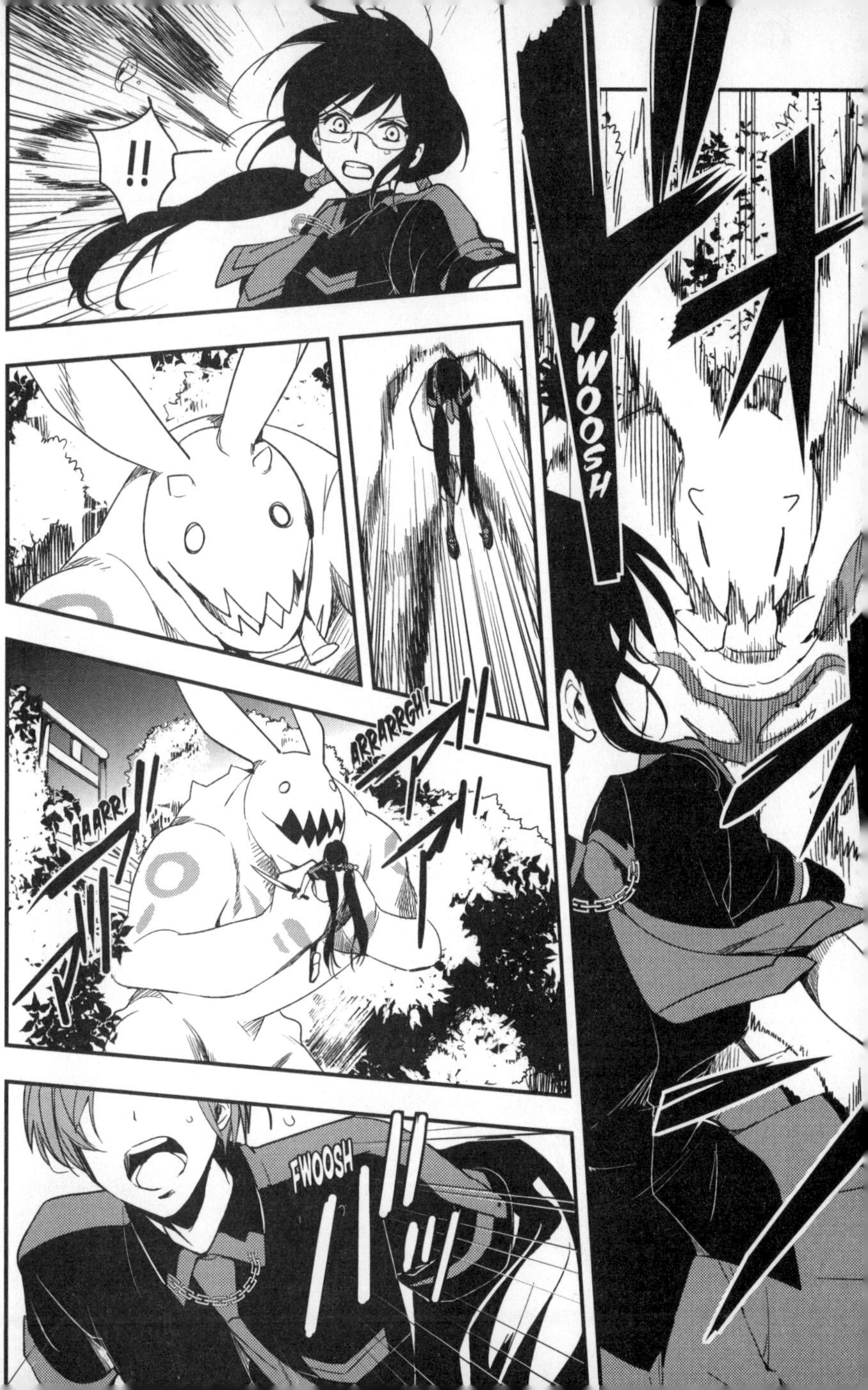
VWOOSH
!!
ARRARRGH!
AAARR!
FWOOSH

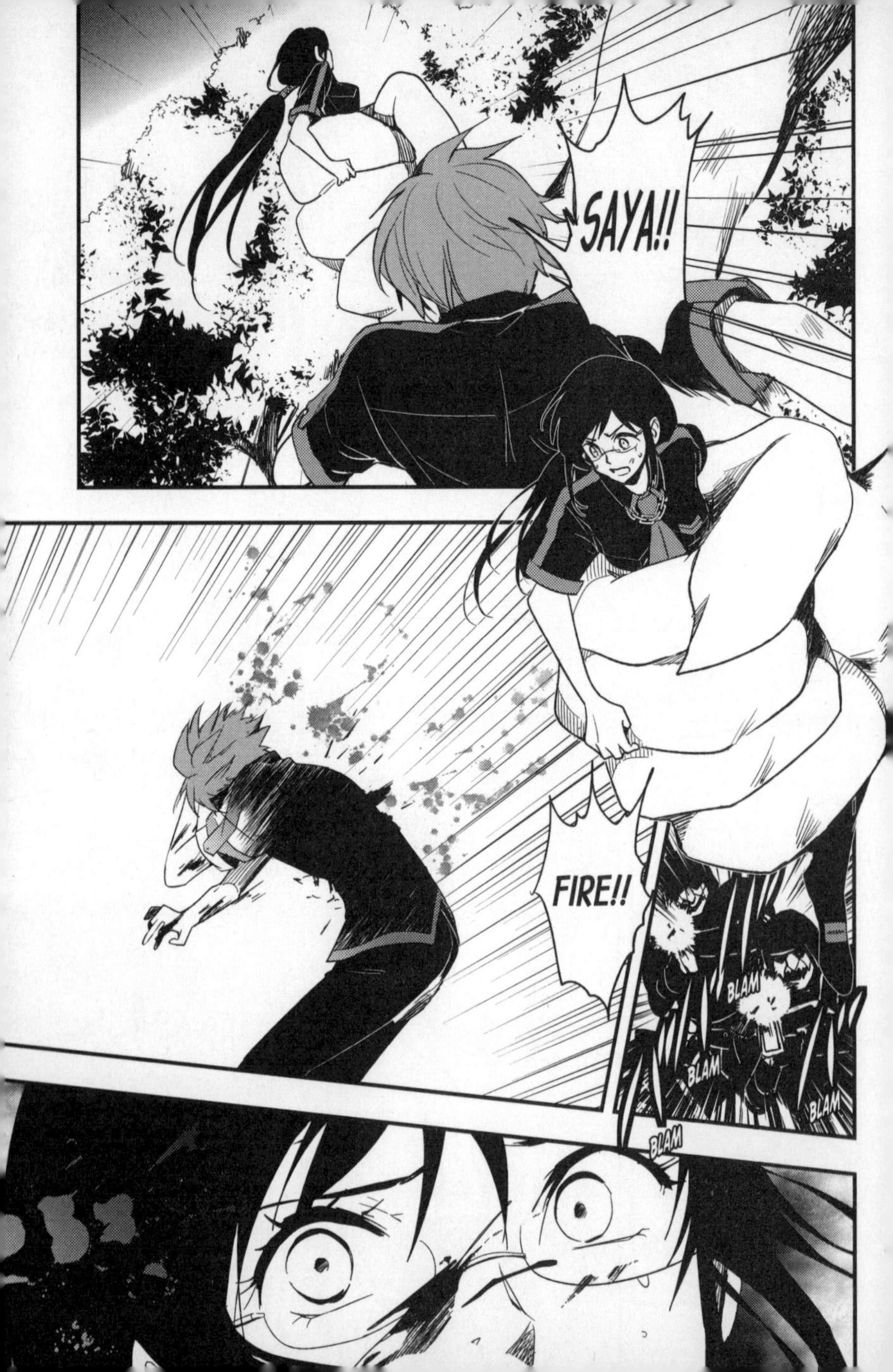
SAYA!!
FIRE!!
BLAM
BLAM
BLAM
BLAM

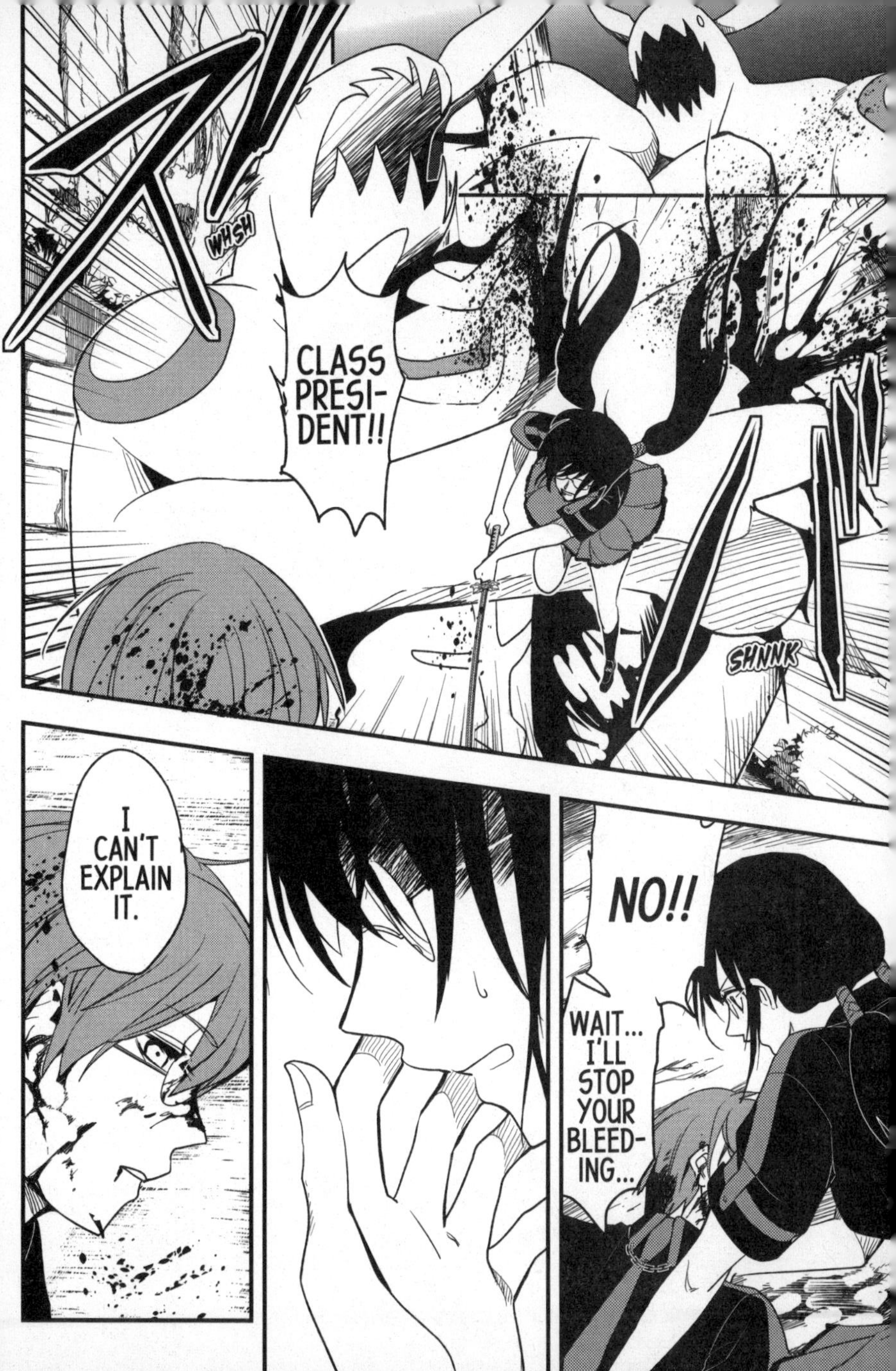
CLASS PRESIDENT!!
SHNNK
WHSH
NO!!
WAIT... I'LL STOP YOUR BLEEDING...
I CAN'T EXPLAIN IT.

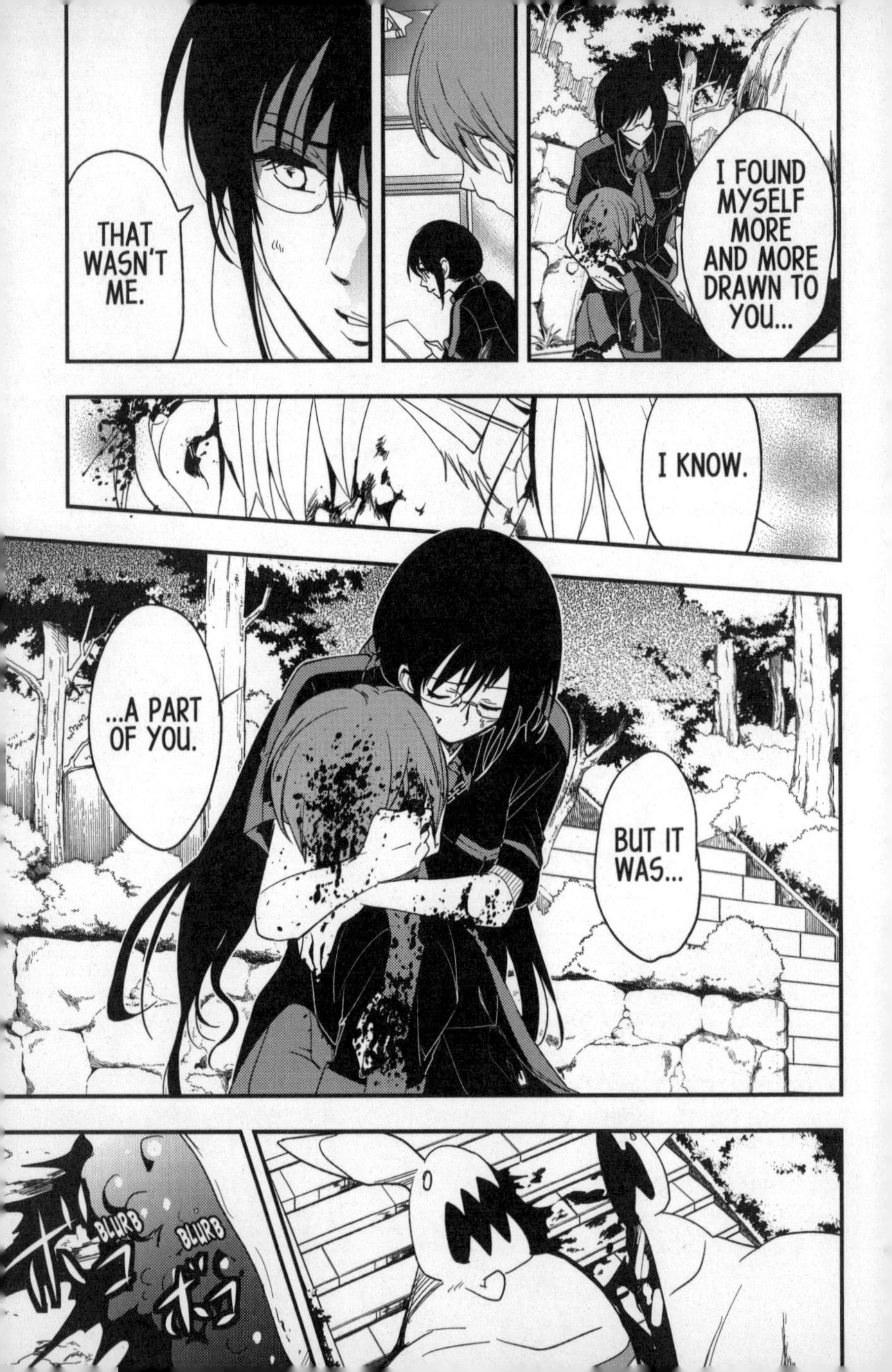
I FOUND MYSELF MORE AND MORE DRAWN TO YOU...
THAT WASN'T ME.
I KNOW.
BUT IT WAS...
...A PART OF YOU.
BLURB
BLURB

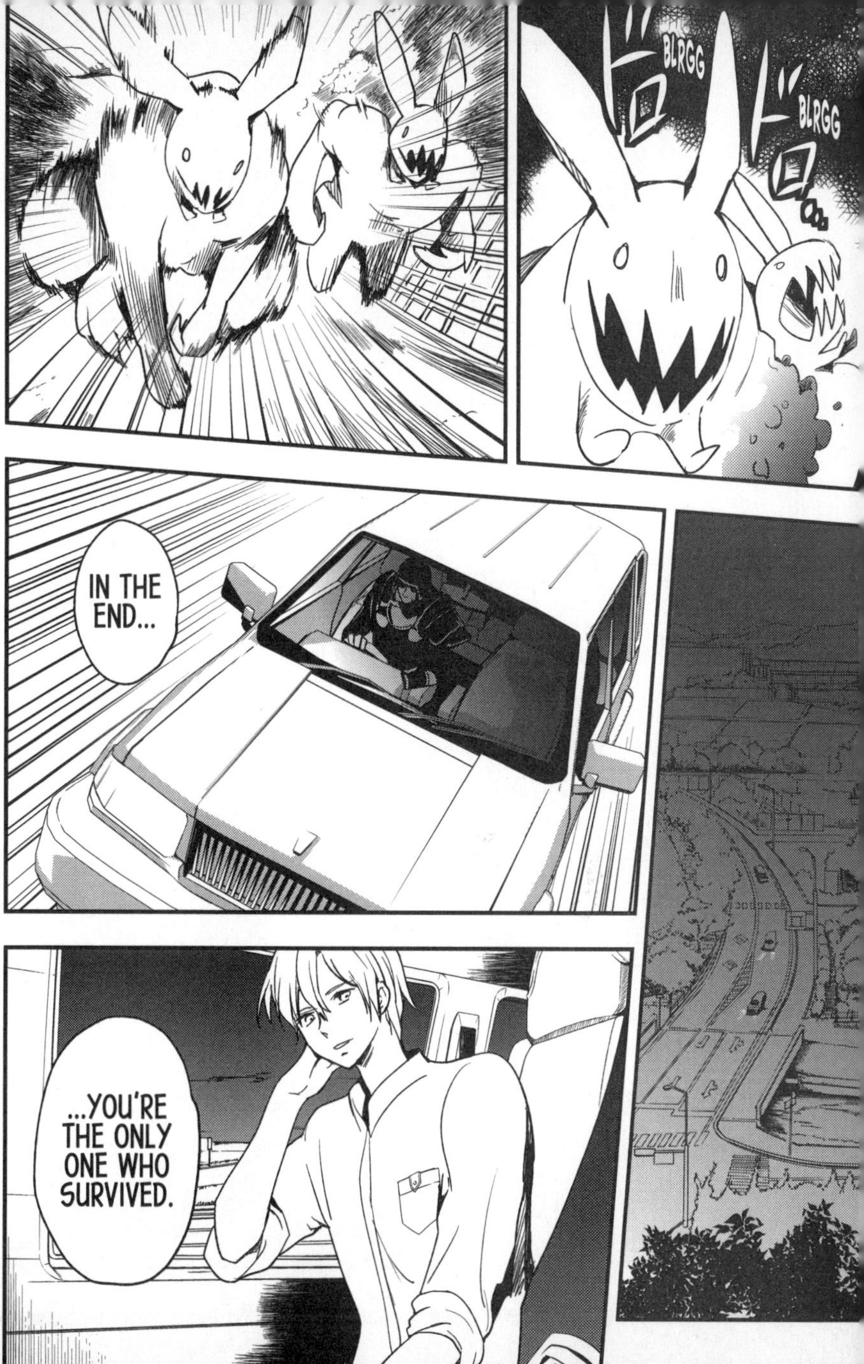
BLRGG
BLRGG
IN THE END...
...YOU'RE THE ONLY ONE WHO SURVIVED.

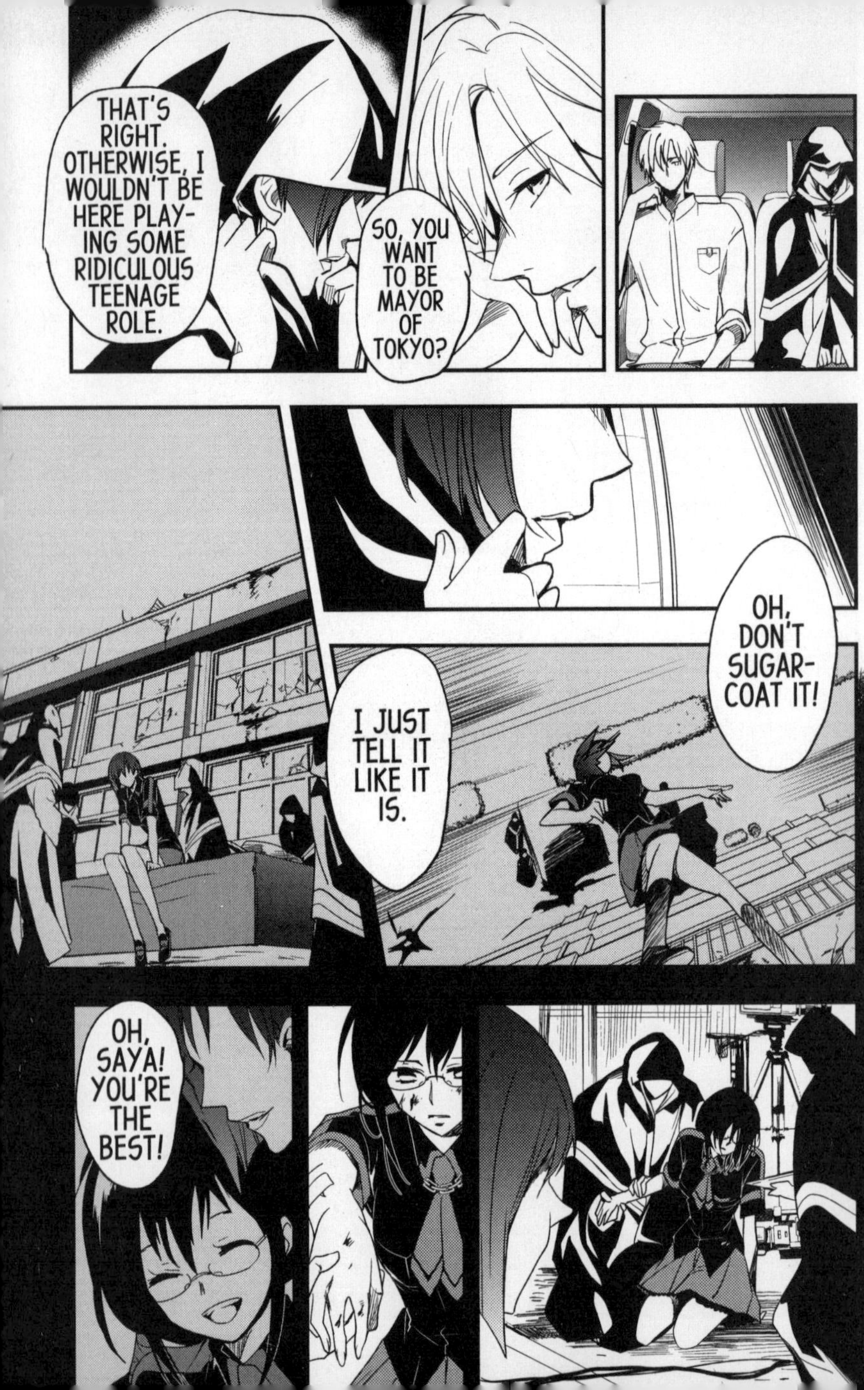
SO, YOU WANT TO BE MAYOR OF TOKYO?
THAT'S RIGHT. OTHERWISE, I WOULDN'T BE HERE PLAY-ING SOME RIDICULOUS TEENAGE ROLE.
OH, DON'T SUGAR-COAT IT!
I JUST TELL IT LIKE IT IS.
OH, SAYA! YOU'RE THE BEST!

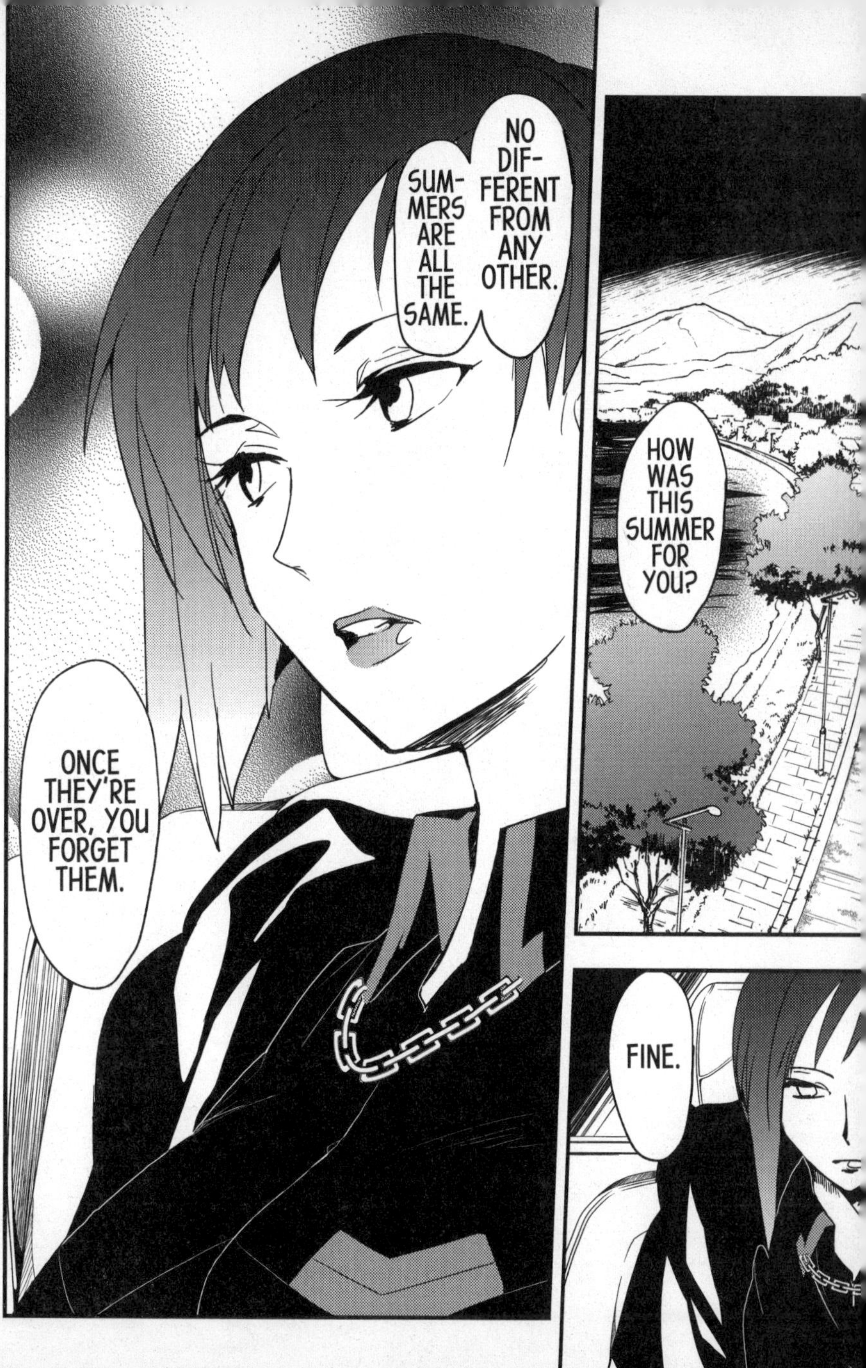
HOW WAS THIS SUMMER FOR YOU?
FINE.
NO DIFFERENT FROM ANY OTHER.
SUMMERS ARE ALL THE SAME.
ONCE THEY'RE OVER, YOU FORGET THEM.

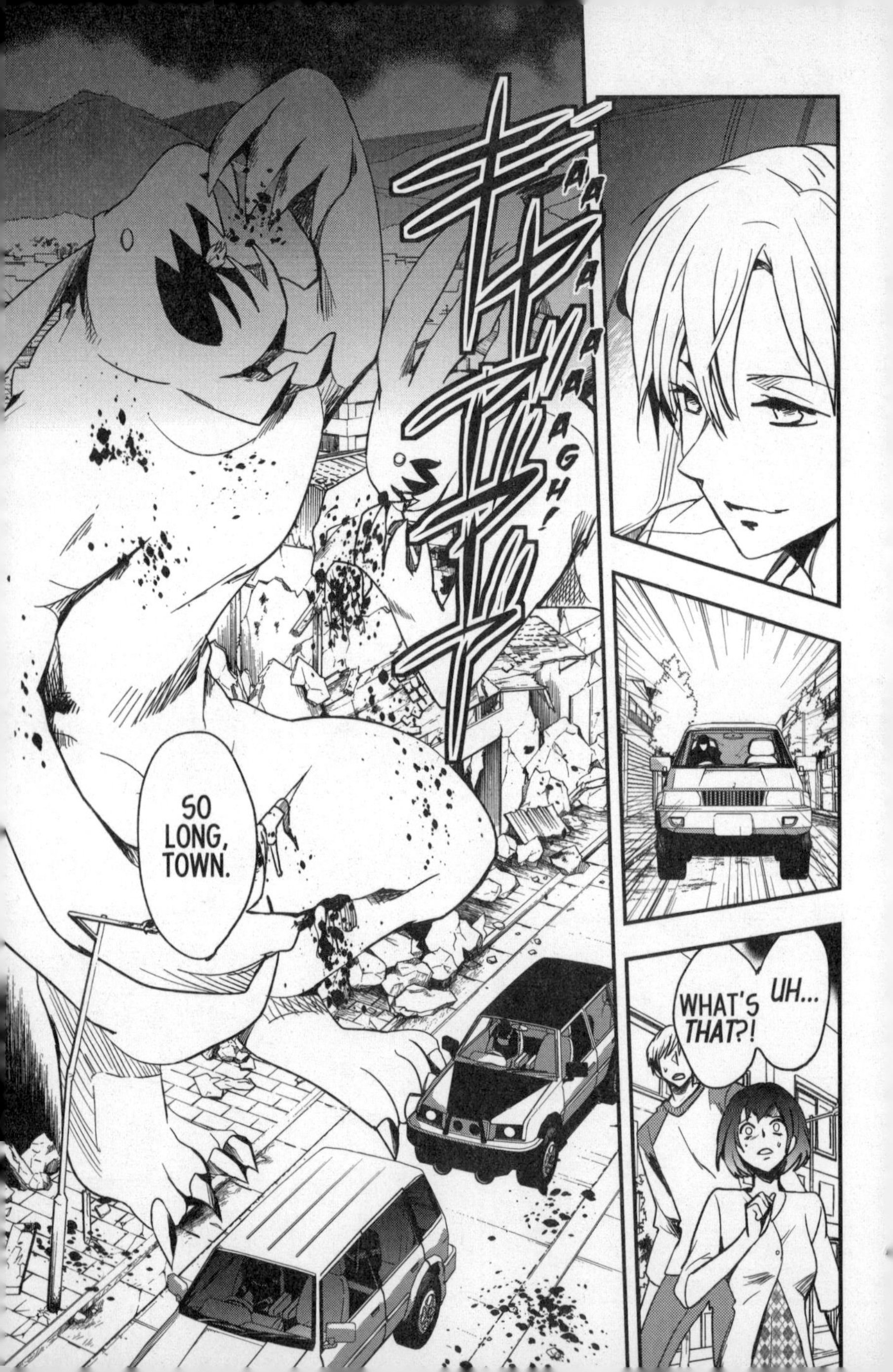
UH... WHAT'S THAT?!
AAAAAAAGH!
SO LONG, TOWN.

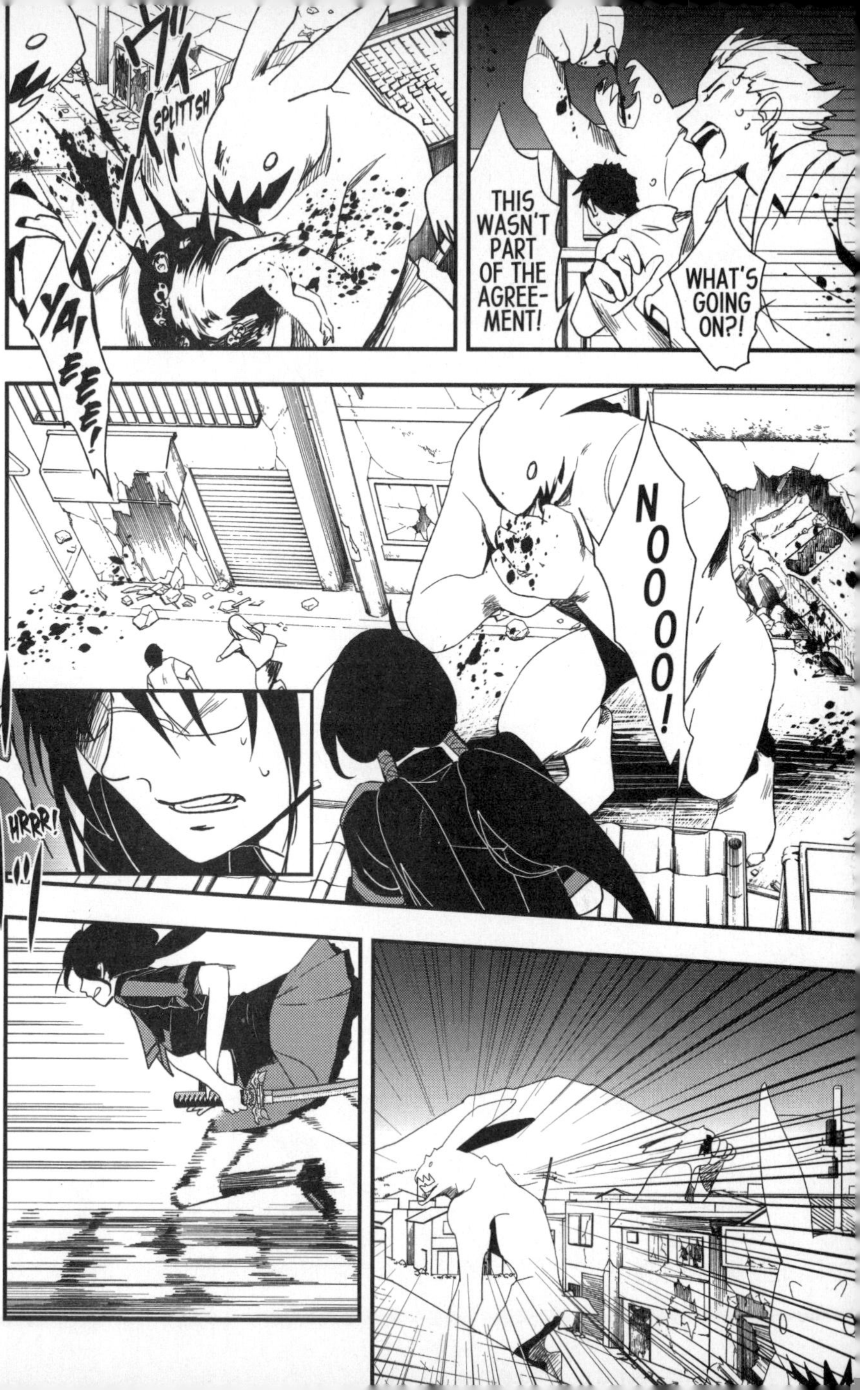
WHAT'S GOING ON?!
THIS WASN'T PART OF THE AGREEMENT!
SPLITTSH
YAIEEEE!
NOOOOO!
HRRR!

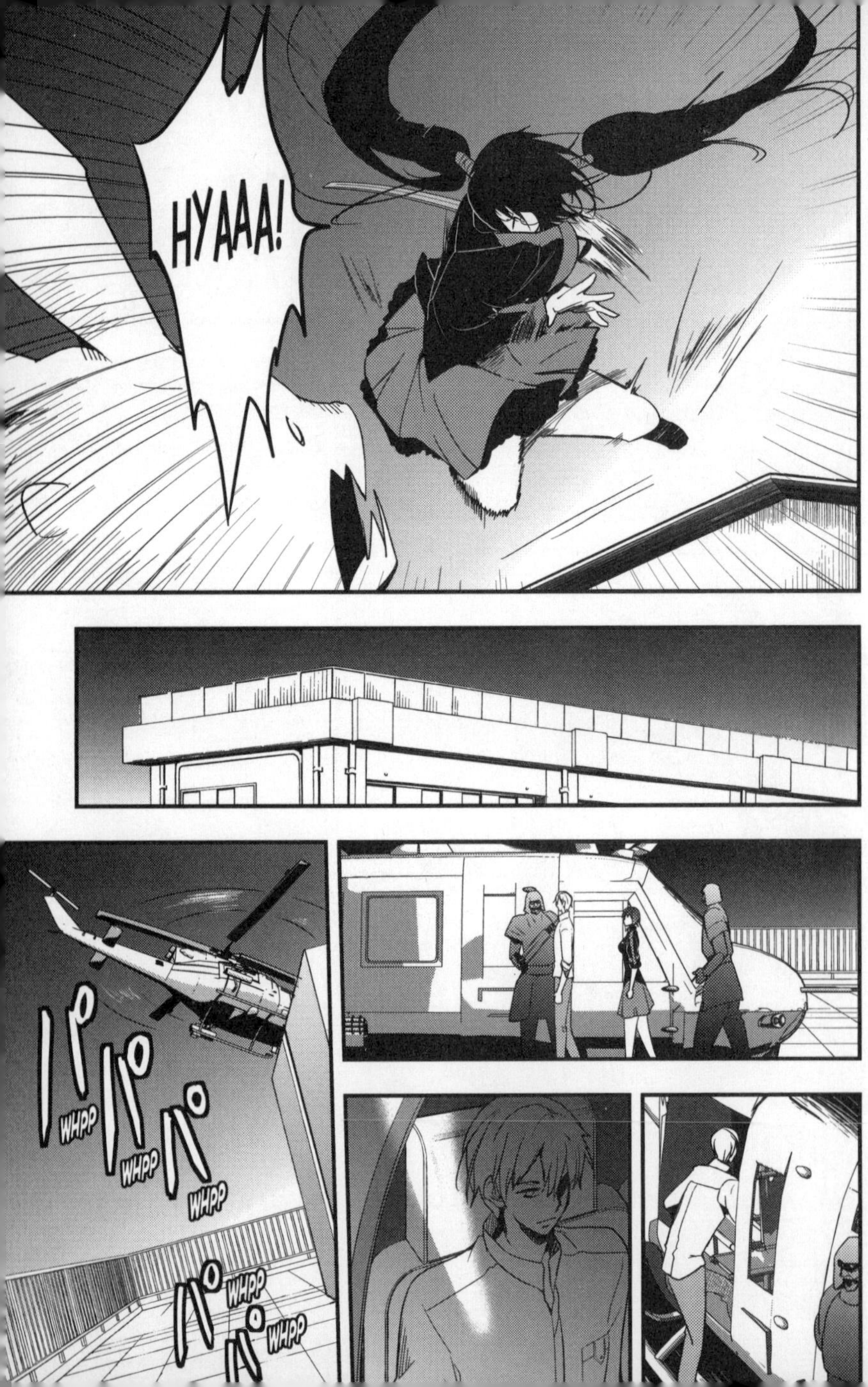
HYAAA!
パ
WHPP
パ
WHPP
パ
WHPP
パ
WHPP
パ
WHPP

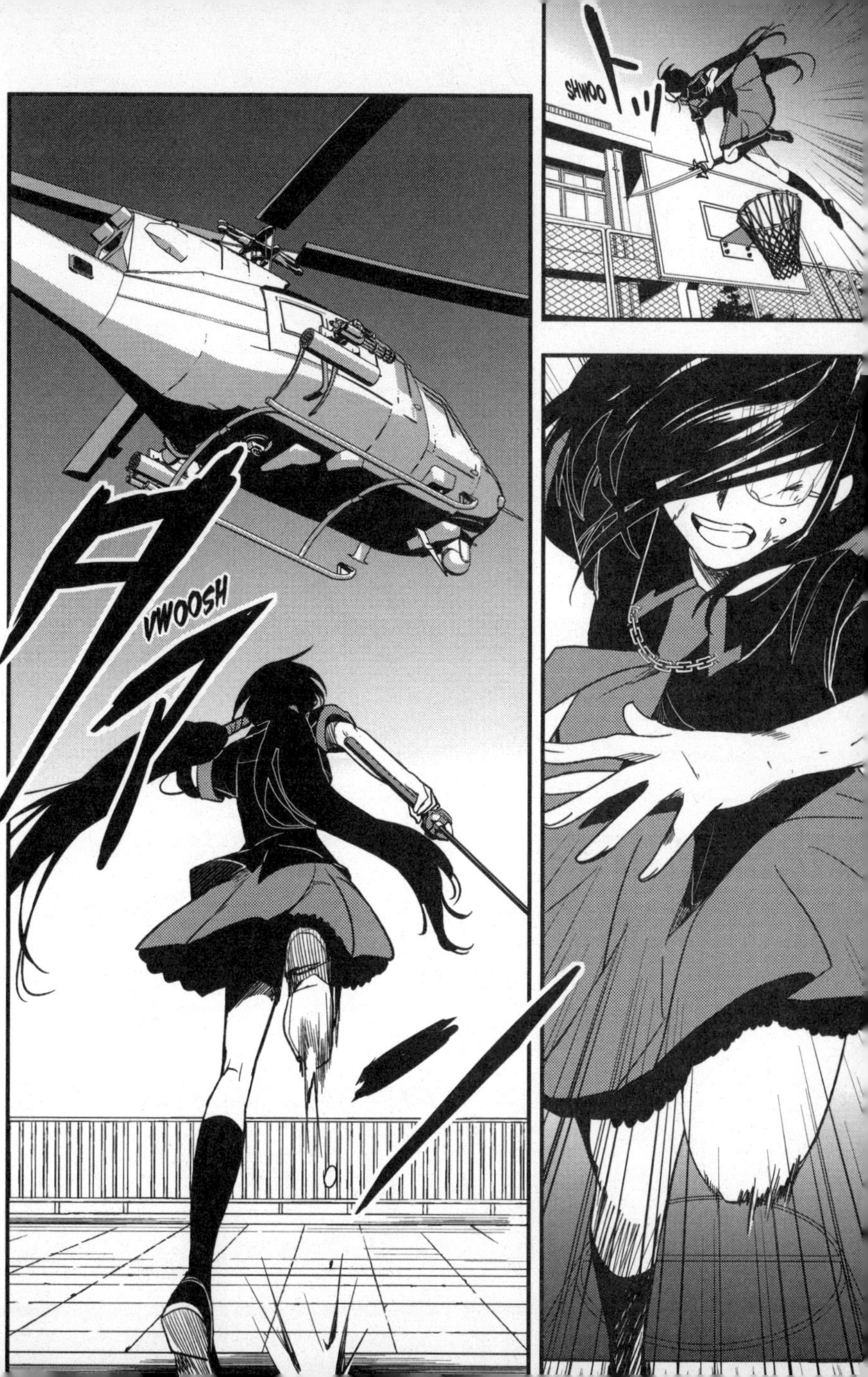
SHWOO
VWOOSH

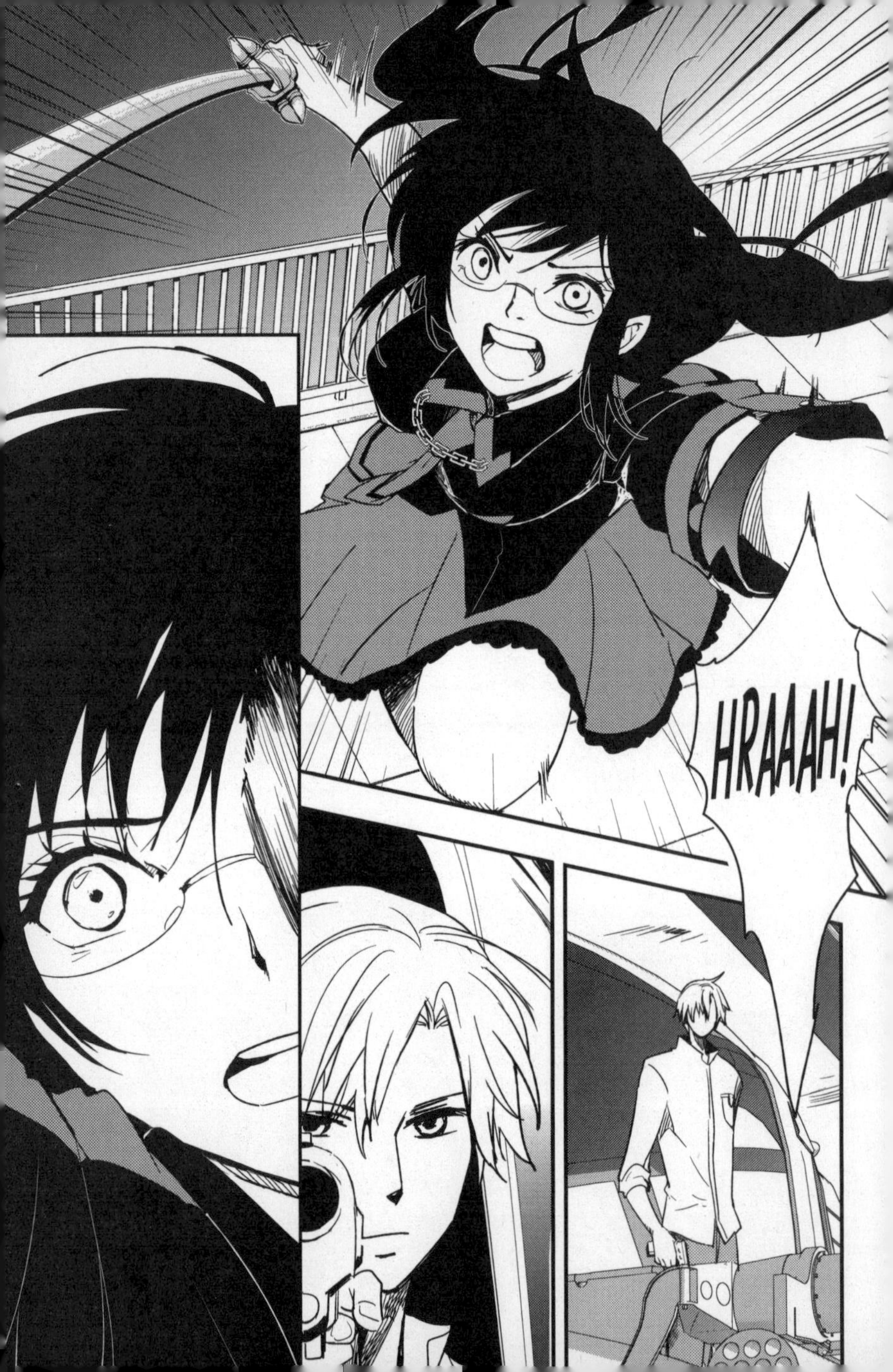
HRAAAH!

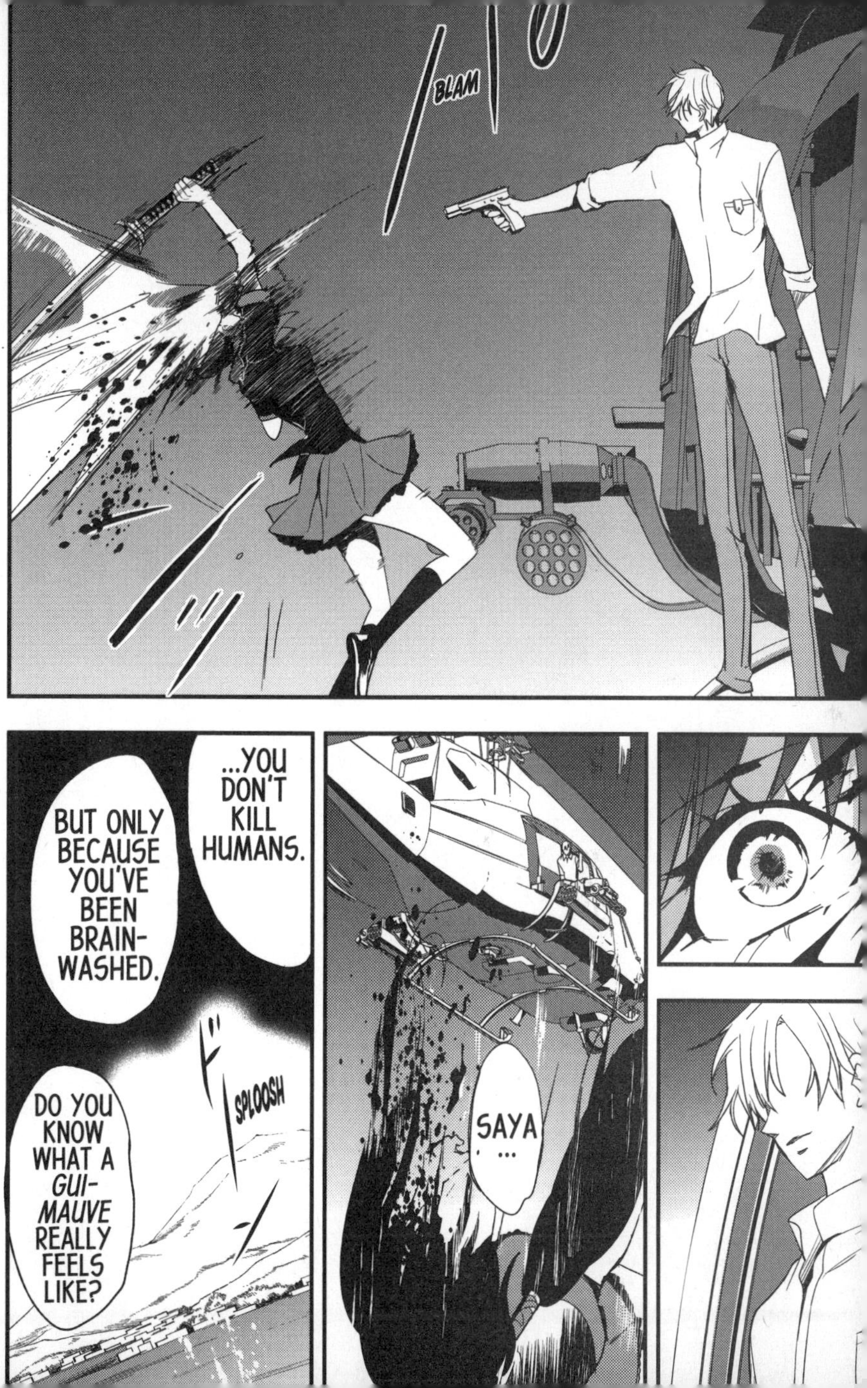
BLAM
SAYA ...
...YOU DON'T KILL HUMANS.
BUT ONLY BECAUSE YOU'VE BEEN BRAIN-WASHED.
ド
SPLOOSH
DO YOU KNOW WHAT A *GUI-MAUVE* REALLY FEELS LIKE?

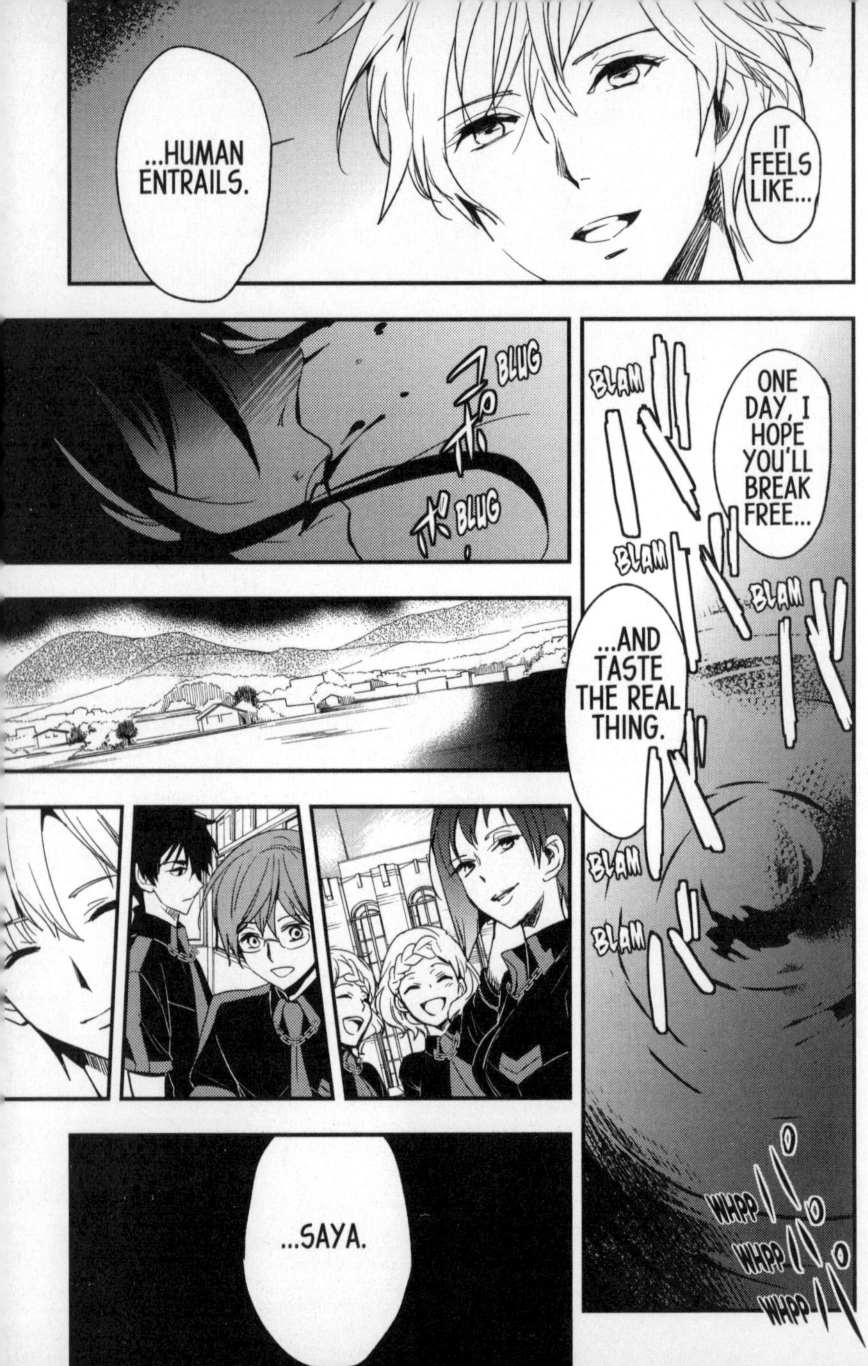
IT FEELS LIKE...
...HUMAN ENTRAILS.
BLAM
ONE DAY, I HOPE YOU'LL BREAK FREE...
BLAM
BLAM
...AND TASTE THE REAL THING.
BLAM
BLAM
WHPP
WHPP
WHPP
BLUG
BLUG
...SAYA.

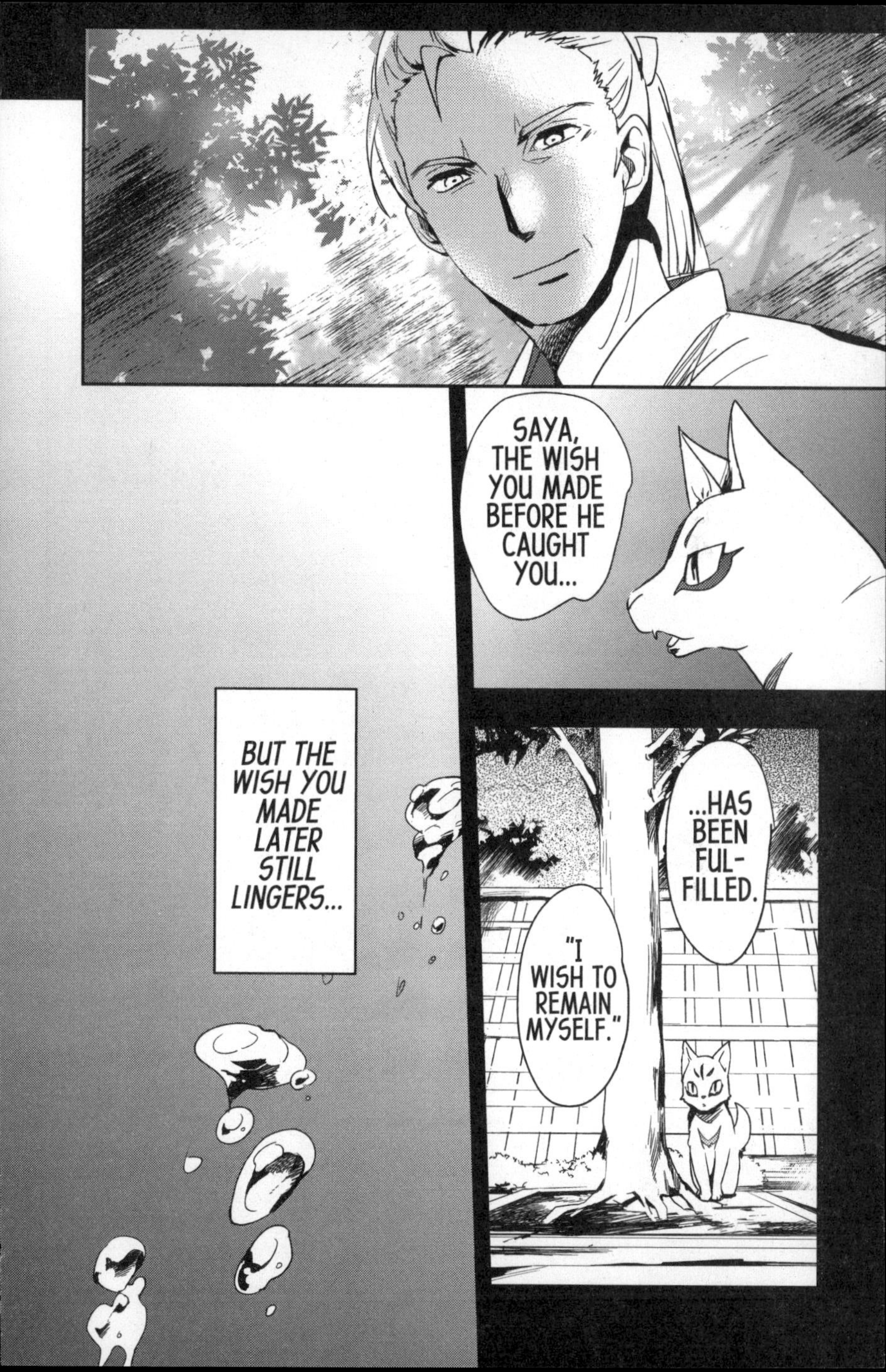
SAYA, THE WISH YOU MADE BEFORE HE CAUGHT YOU...
...HAS BEEN FUL-FILLED.
"I WISH TO REMAIN MYSELF."
BUT THE WISH YOU MADE LATER STILL LINGERS...

CAST

Lead Character (Saya Kisaragi)
Saya

Saya's Father , Tadayoshi Kisaragi
(A half-breed, deceased)

Café Owner
Fumito Nanahara

Classmate (Friend 1)
Yuka Amino

Classmates (Friends 2 and 3)
Nono Motoe and Nene Motoe (deceased)

Classmate (Class President, Saya's admirer)
Itsuki Tomofusa (deceased)

Classmate (Saya's love interest and confidant)
Shinichiro Tokizane (deceased)

Homeroom and Science Teacher
Kanako Tsutsutori (deceased)

STAFF

Project Head
Fumito Nanahara

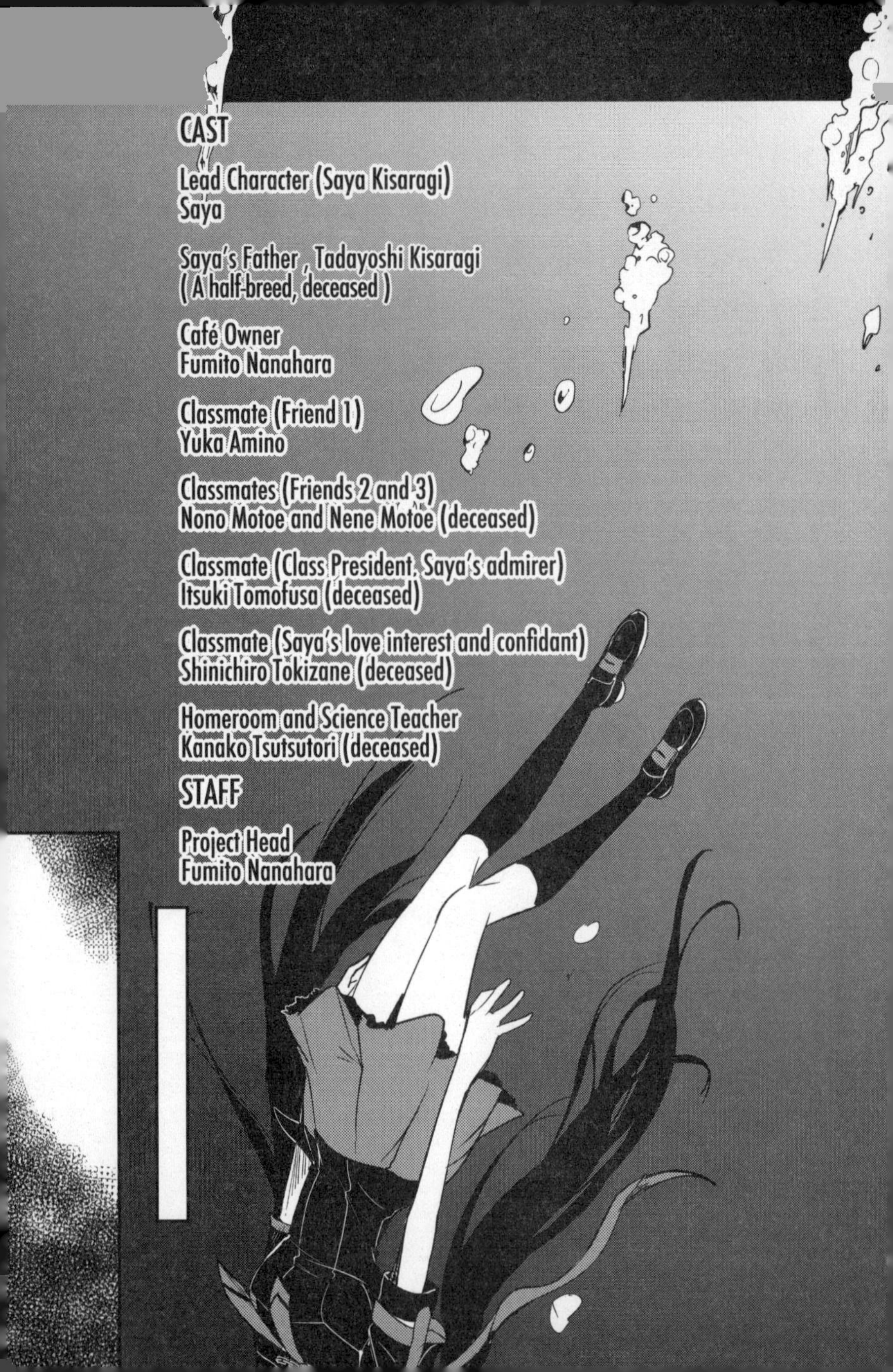

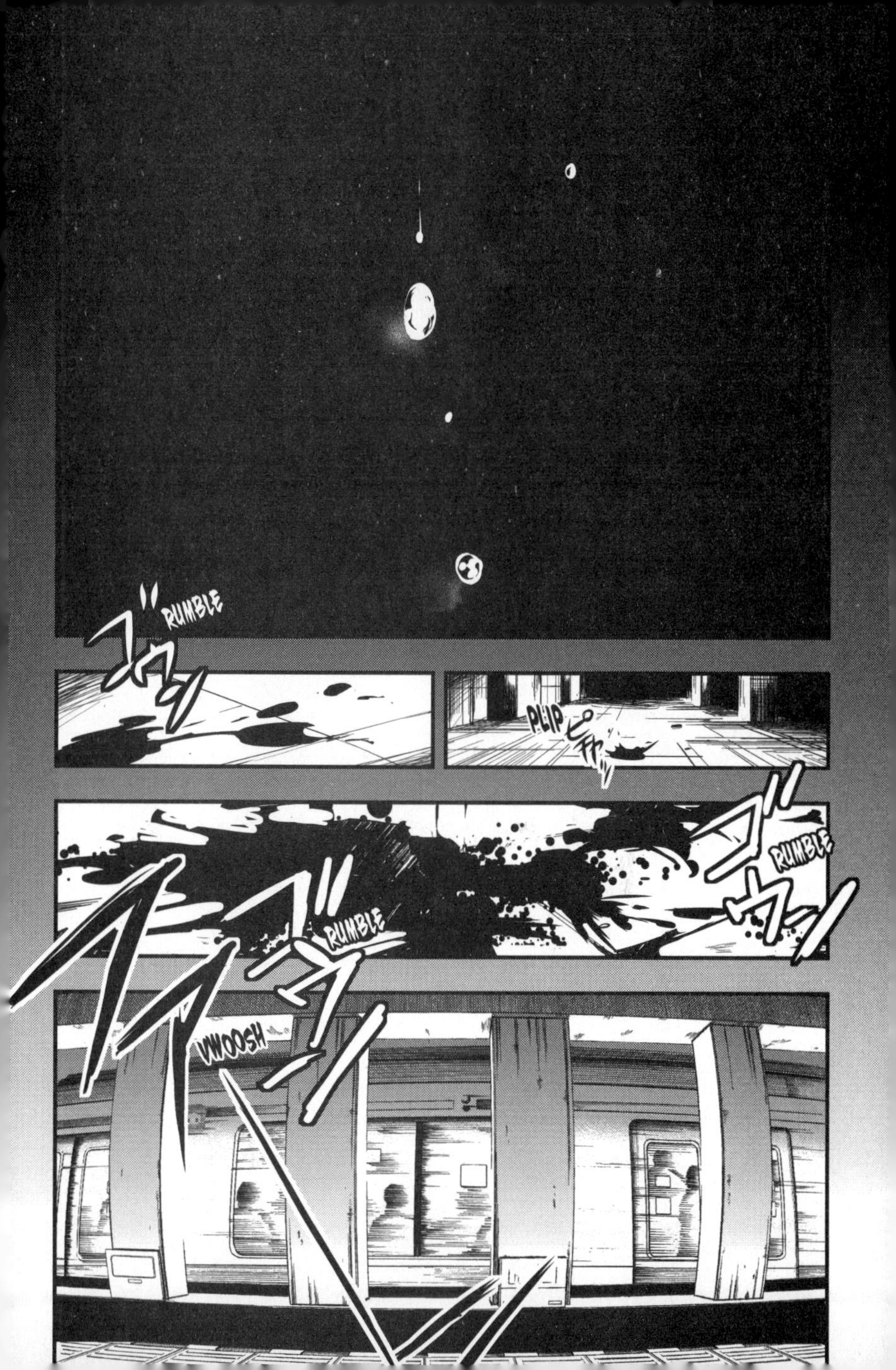
PLIP
RUMBLE
RUMBLE
RUMBLE
VWOOSH

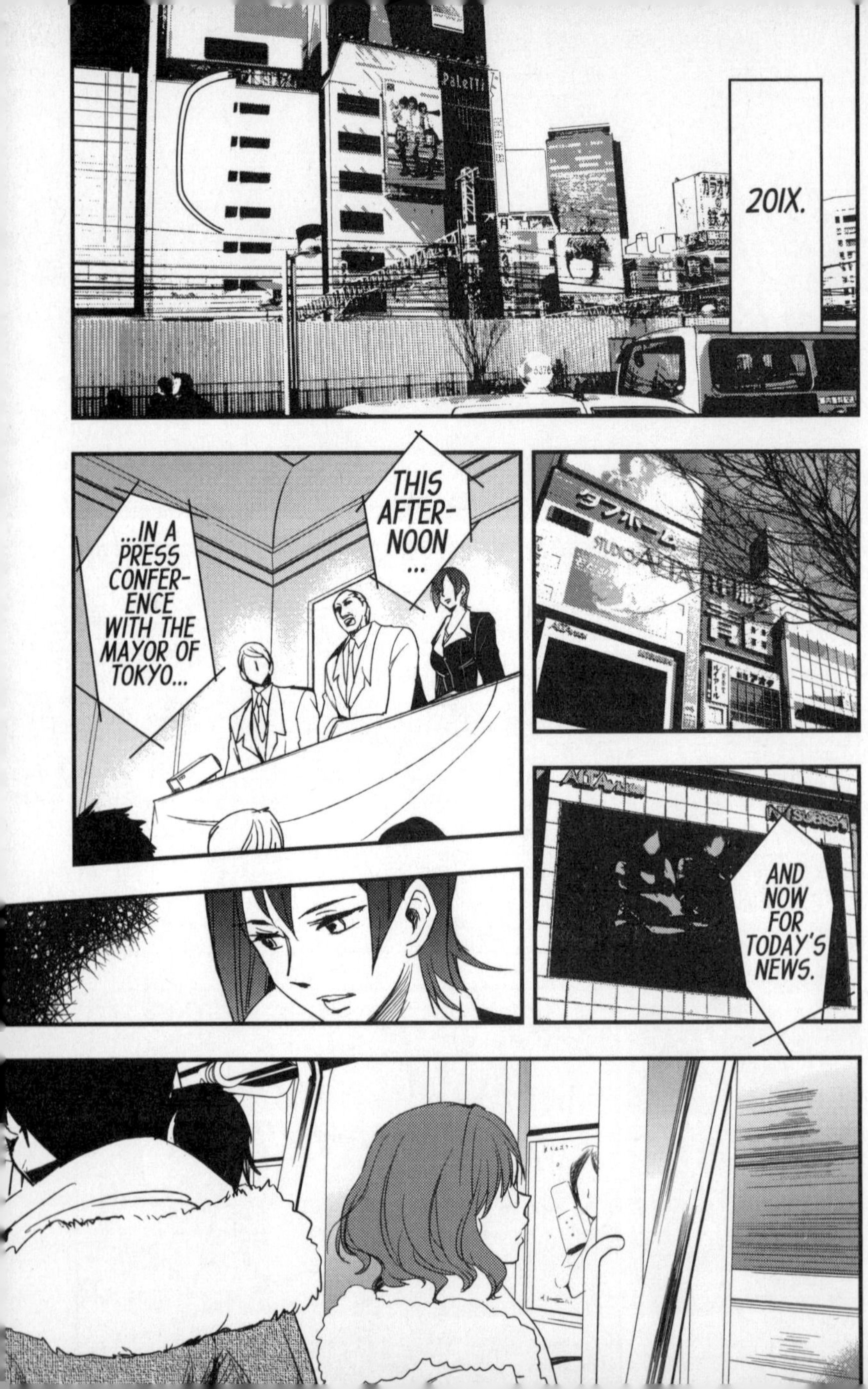
201X.
AND NOW FOR TODAY'S NEWS.
THIS AFTERNOON...
...IN A PRESS CONFERENCE WITH THE MAYOR OF TOKYO...

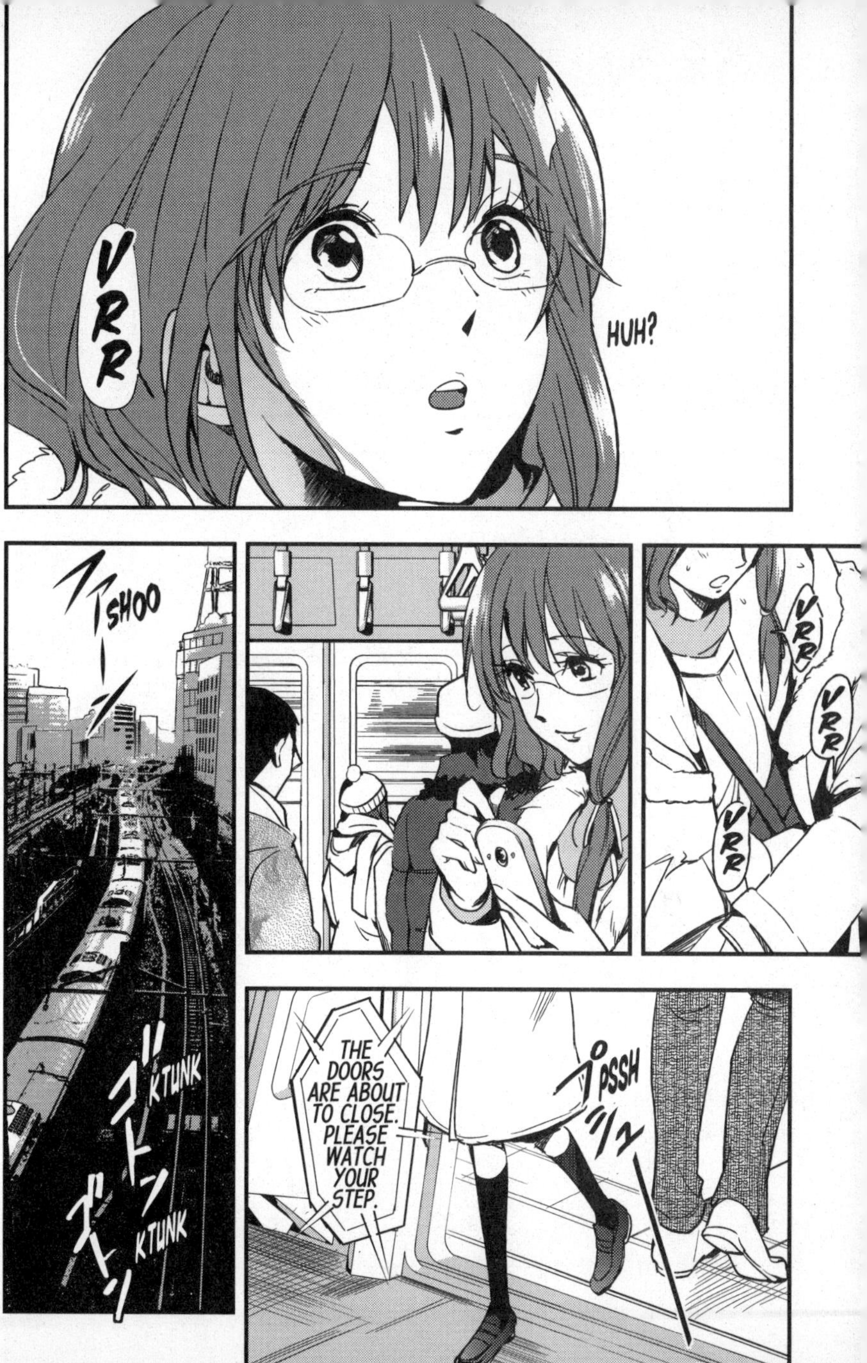

VRR
HUH?
VRR
VRR
VRR
PSSH
THE DOORS ARE ABOUT TO CLOSE. PLEASE WATCH YOUR STEP.
SHOO
KTUNK
KTUNK

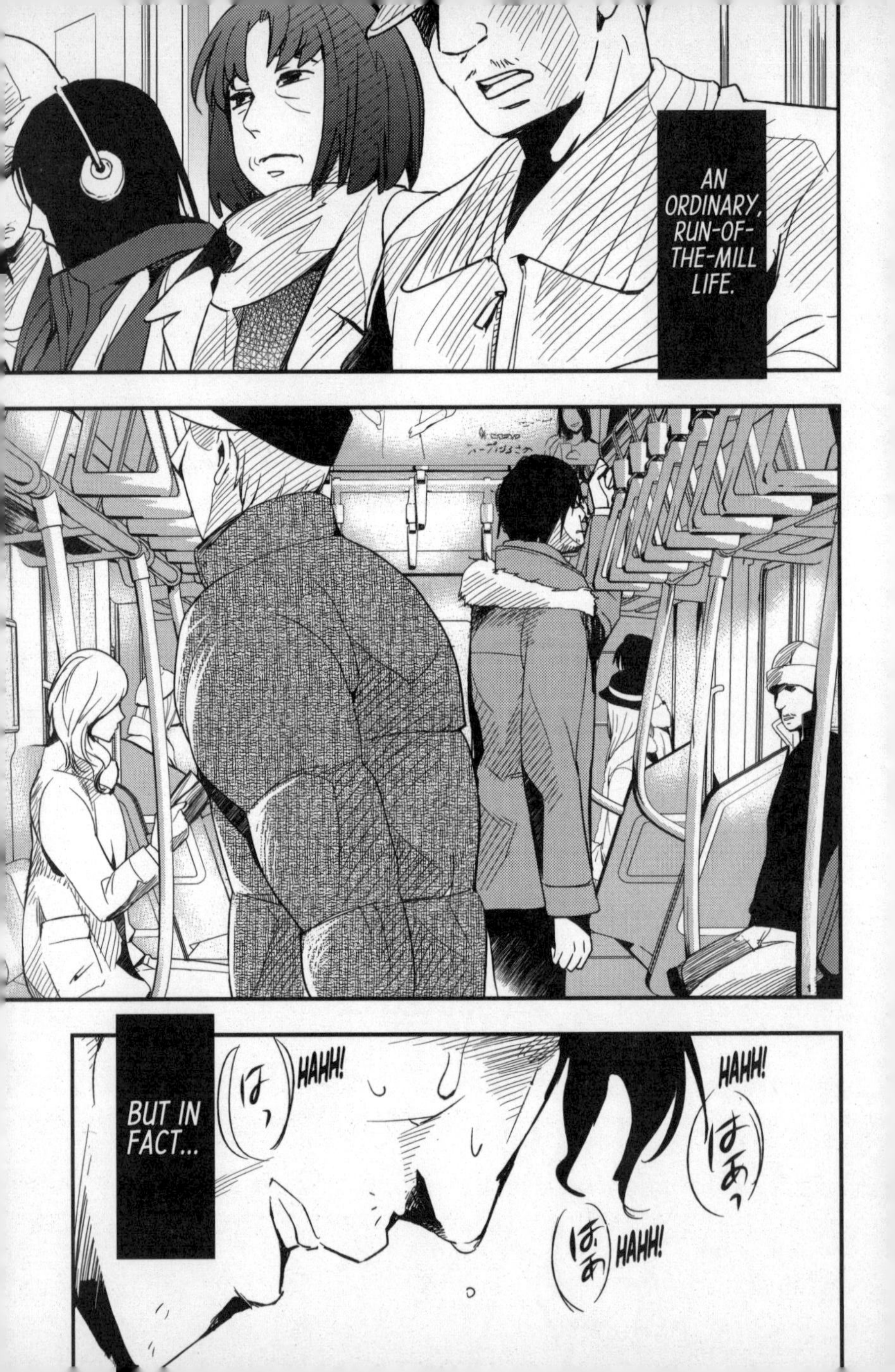
AN ORDINARY, RUN-OF-THE-MILL LIFE.
HAHH!
はあっ
はあ
HAHH!
BUT IN FACT...
はっ
HAHH!

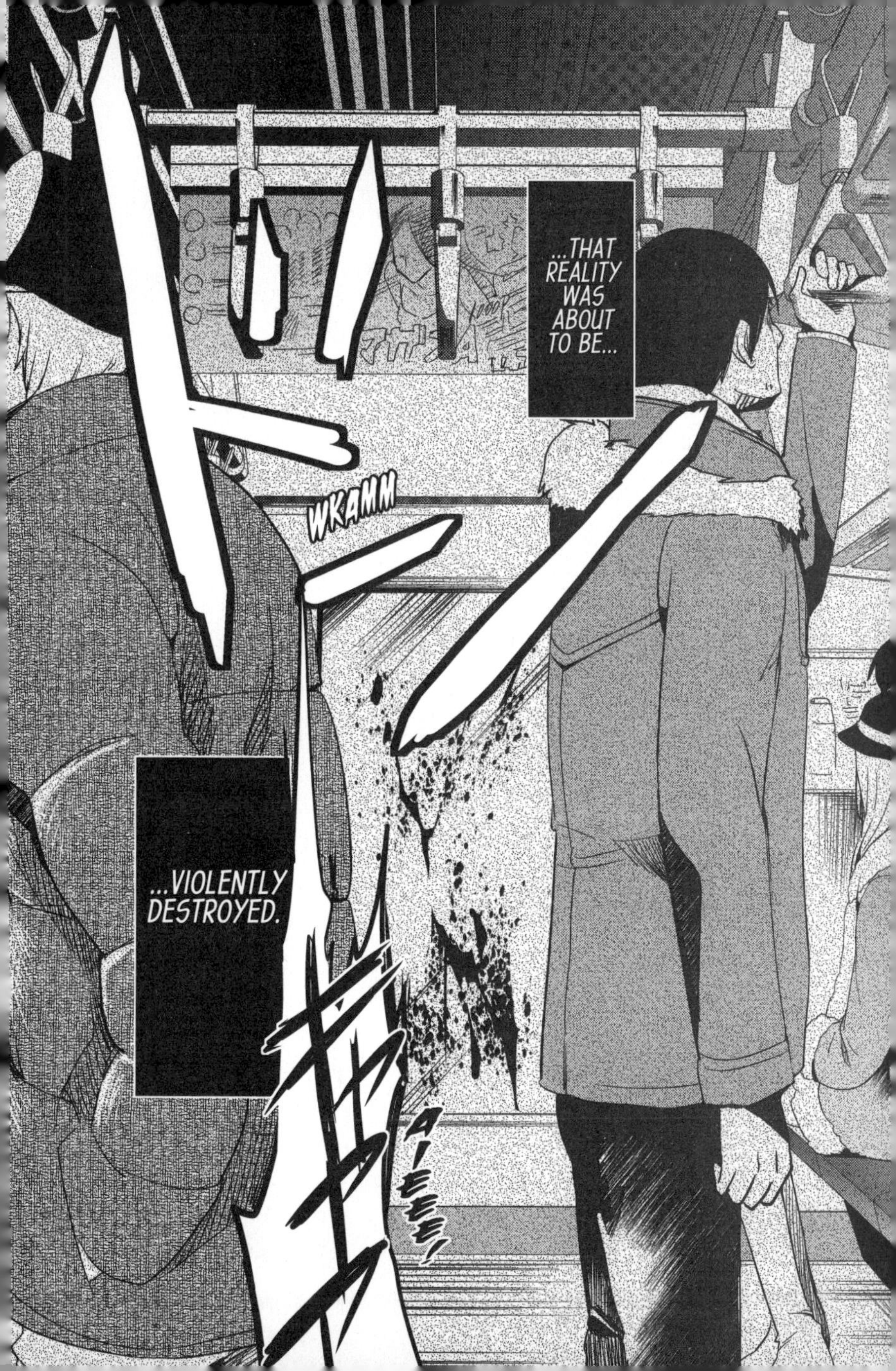
...THAT REALITY WAS ABOUT TO BE...
WKAMM
...VIOLENTLY DESTROYED.
AIEEE!

BLOOD-C

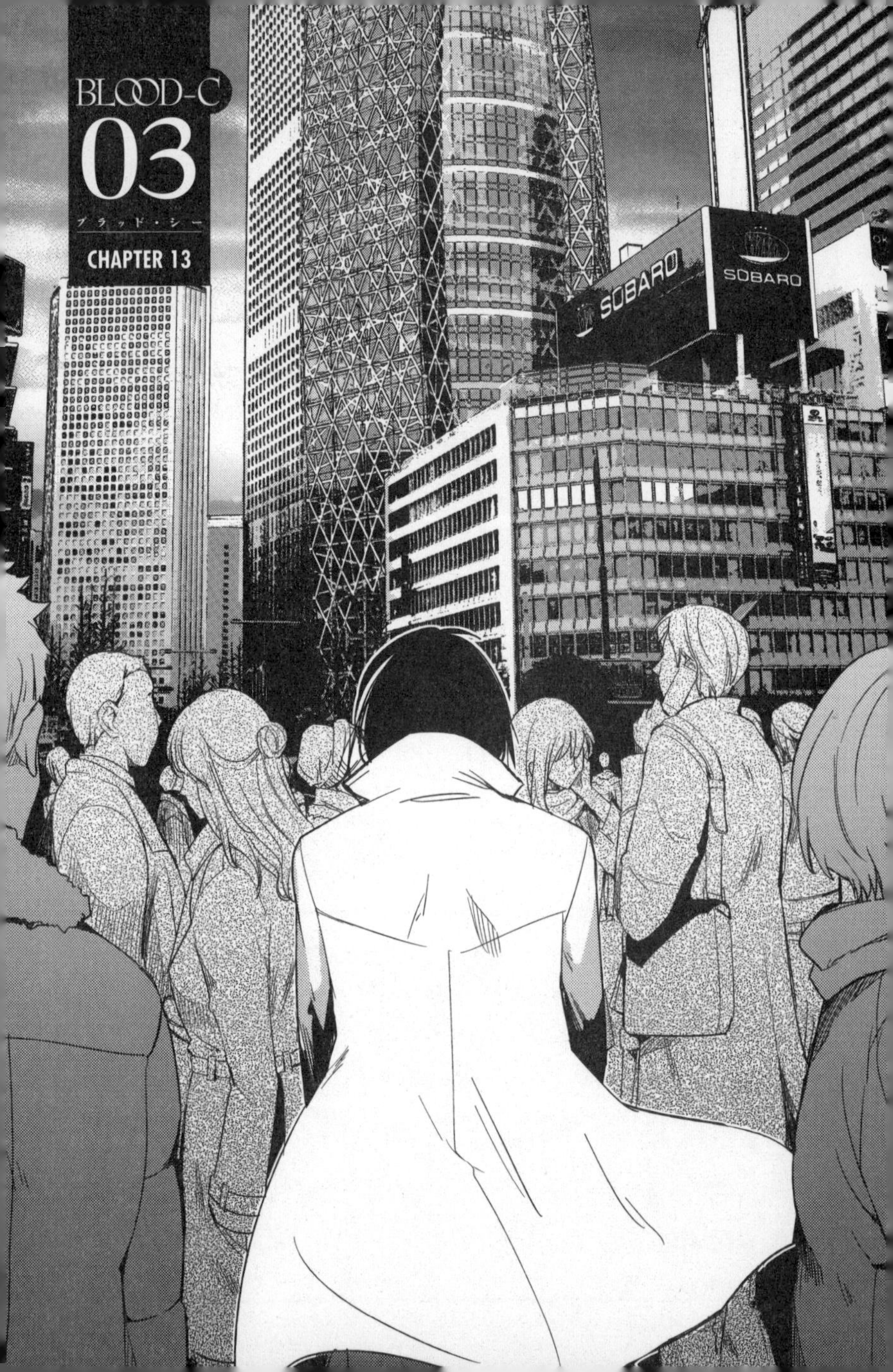
BLOOD-C
03
ブラッド・シー
CHAPTER 13
SOBARO
SOBARO
SOBARO

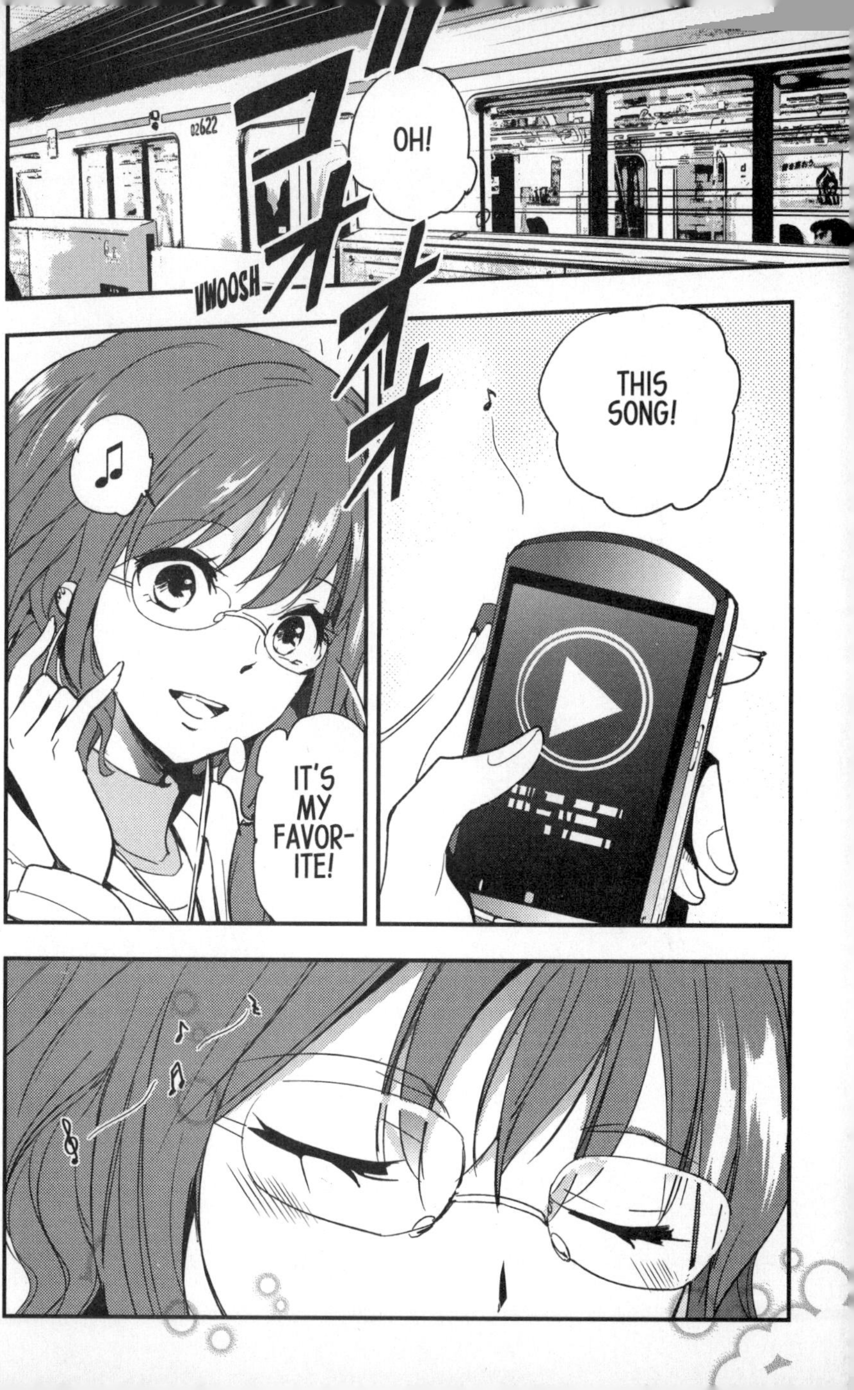
OH!
VWOOSH
THIS SONG!
IT'S MY FAVOR-ITE!

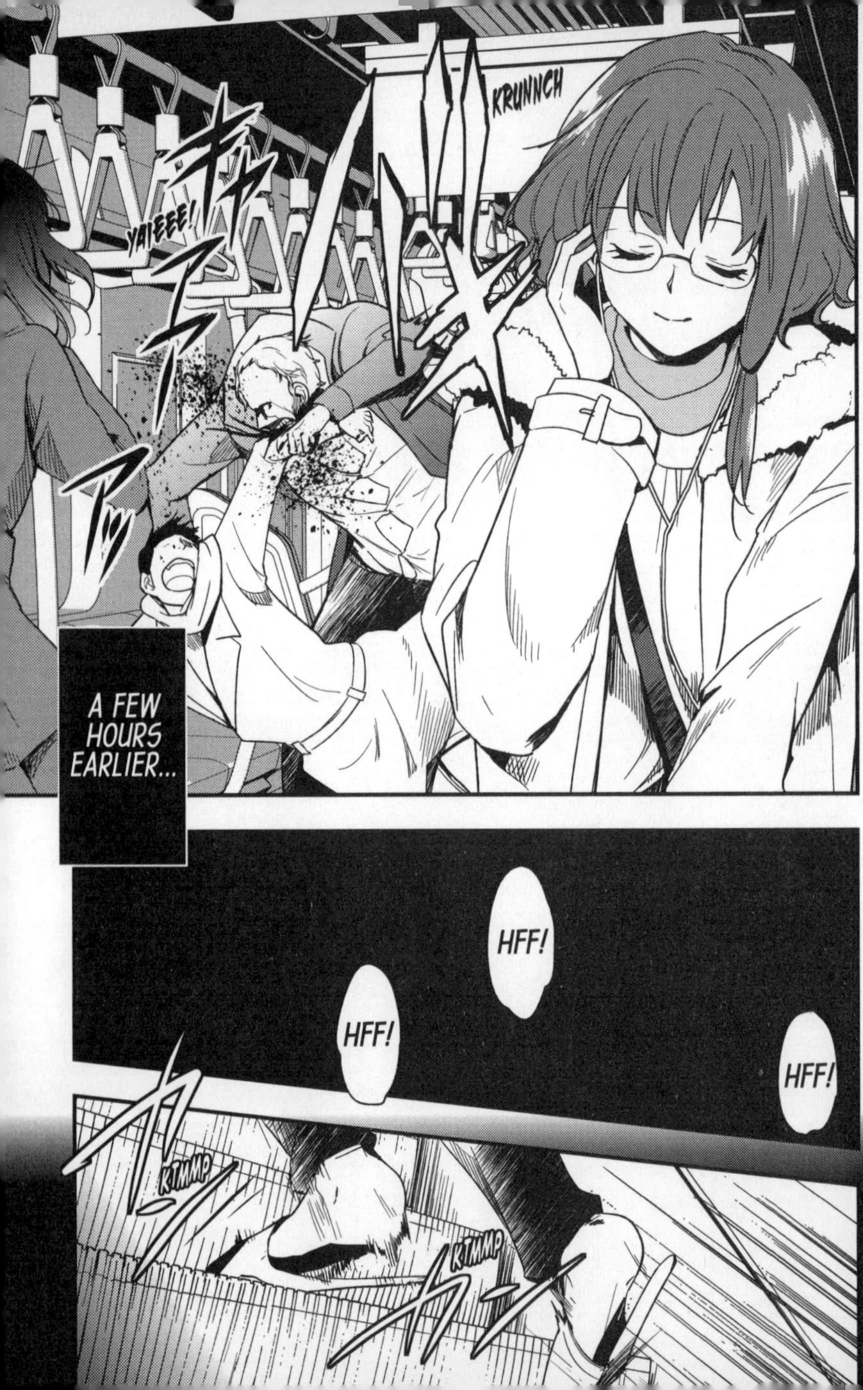
KRUNNCH
YAIEEE!
A FEW HOURS EARLIER...
HFF!
HFF!
HFF!
KTMMP
KTMMP

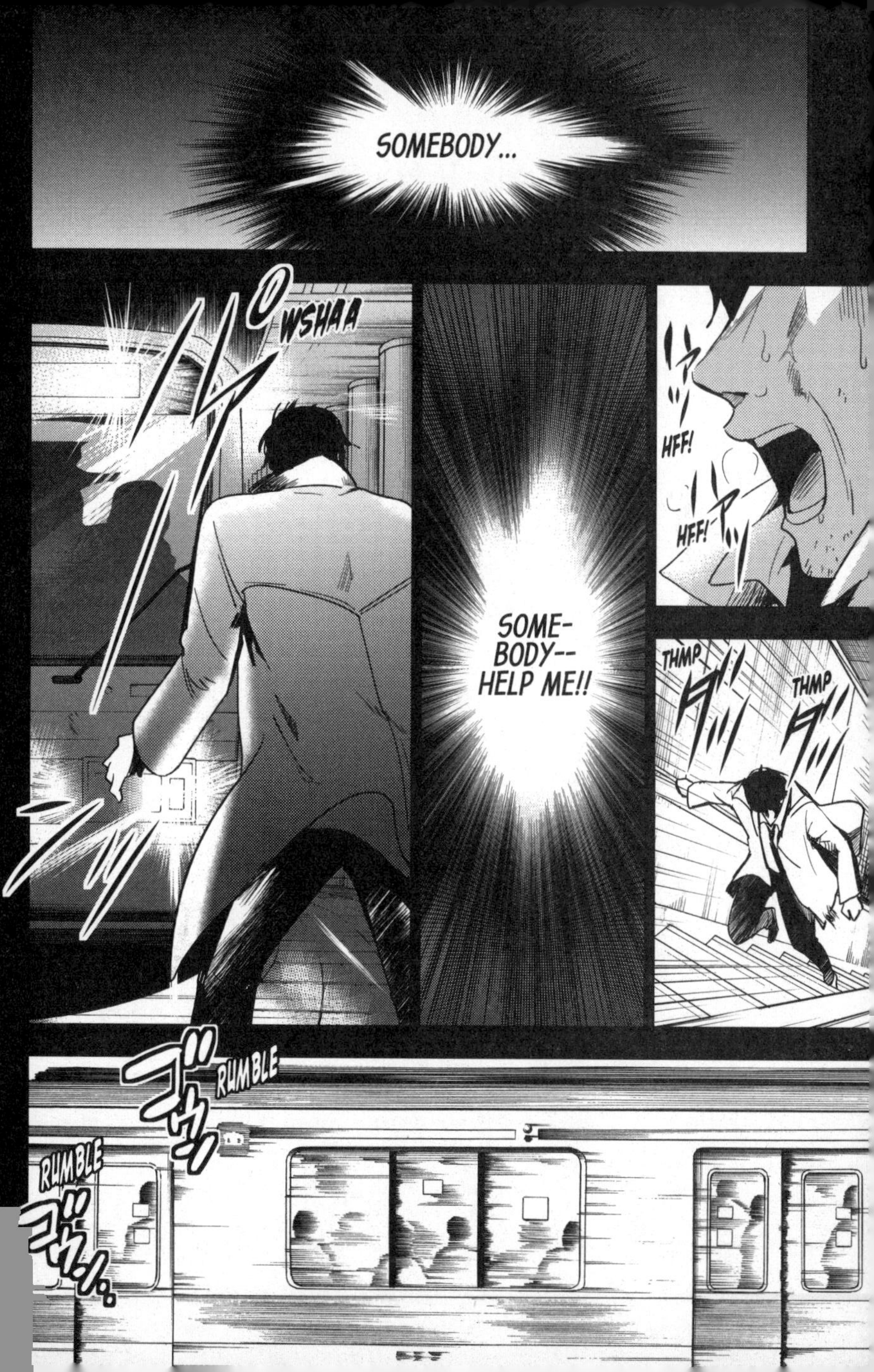
SOMEBODY...
HFF!
HFF!
THMP
THMP
SOME-
BODY--
HELP ME!!
WSHAA
RUMBLE
RUMBLE

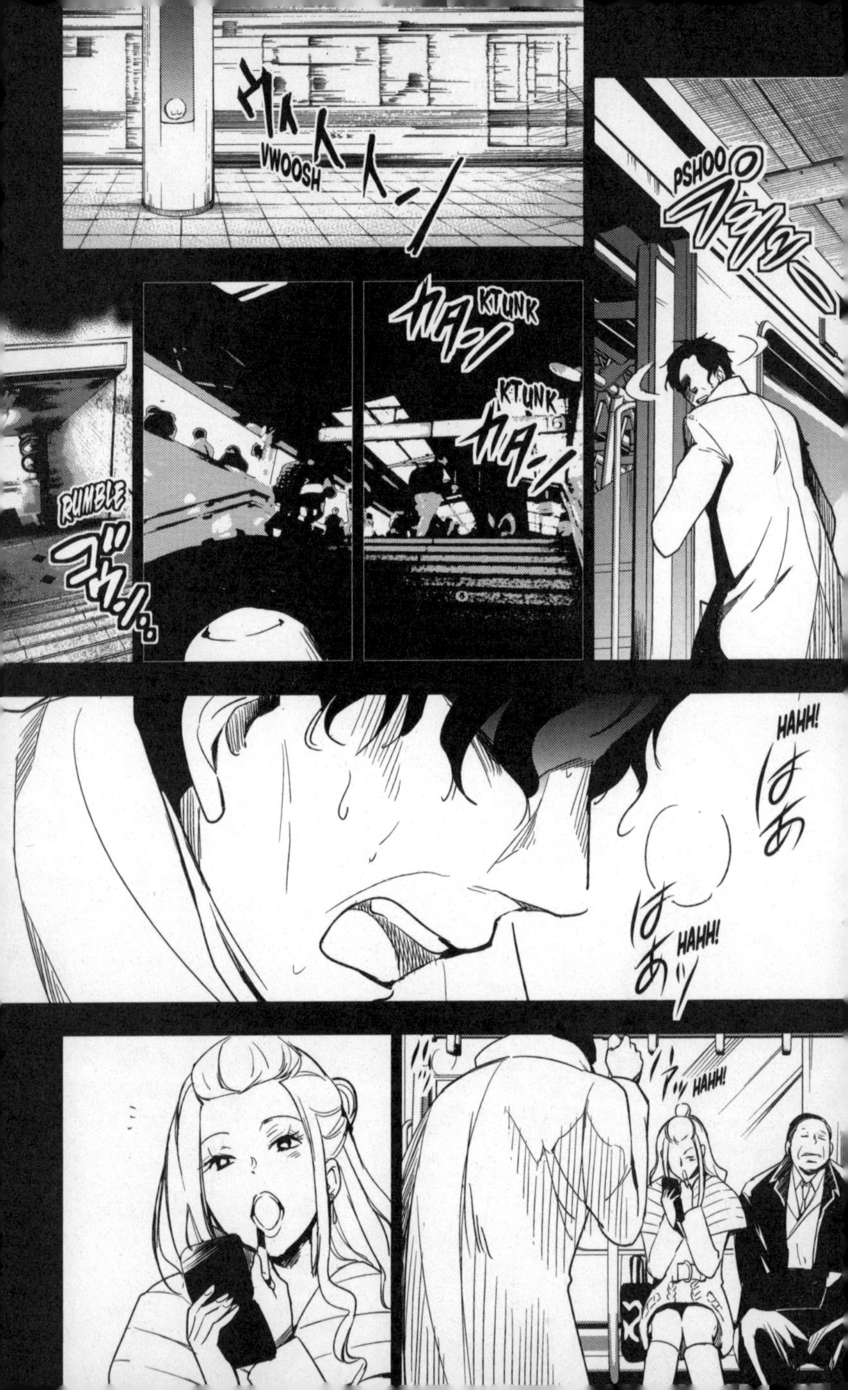
PSHOO
VWOOSH
KTUNK
KTUNK
RUMBLE
HAHH!
はあ
HAHH!
はあッ
HAHH!

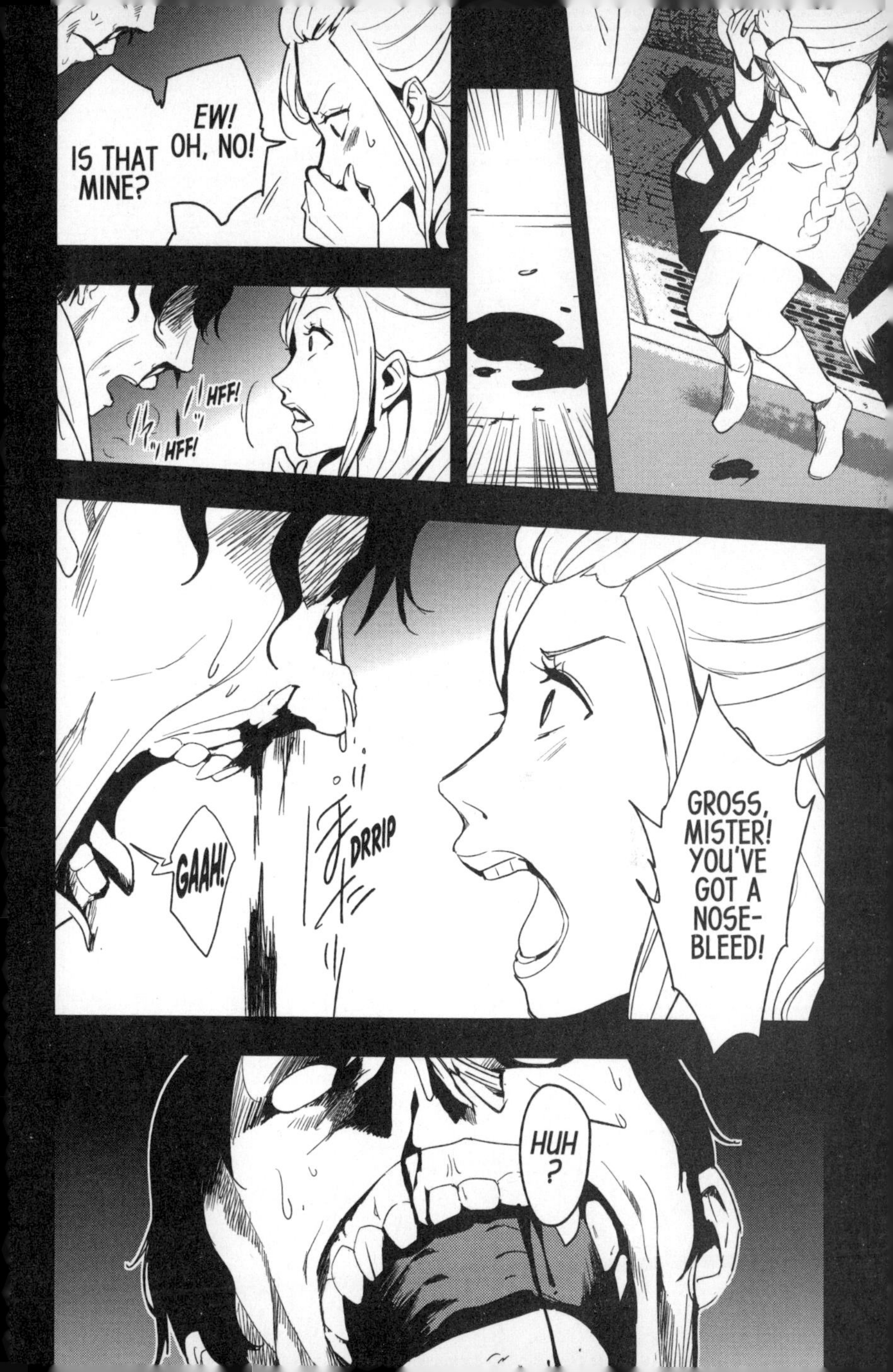
EW! OH, NO!
IS THAT MINE?
HFF! HFF!
GROSS, MISTER! YOU'VE GOT A NOSE-BLEED!
DRRIP
GAAH!
HUH?

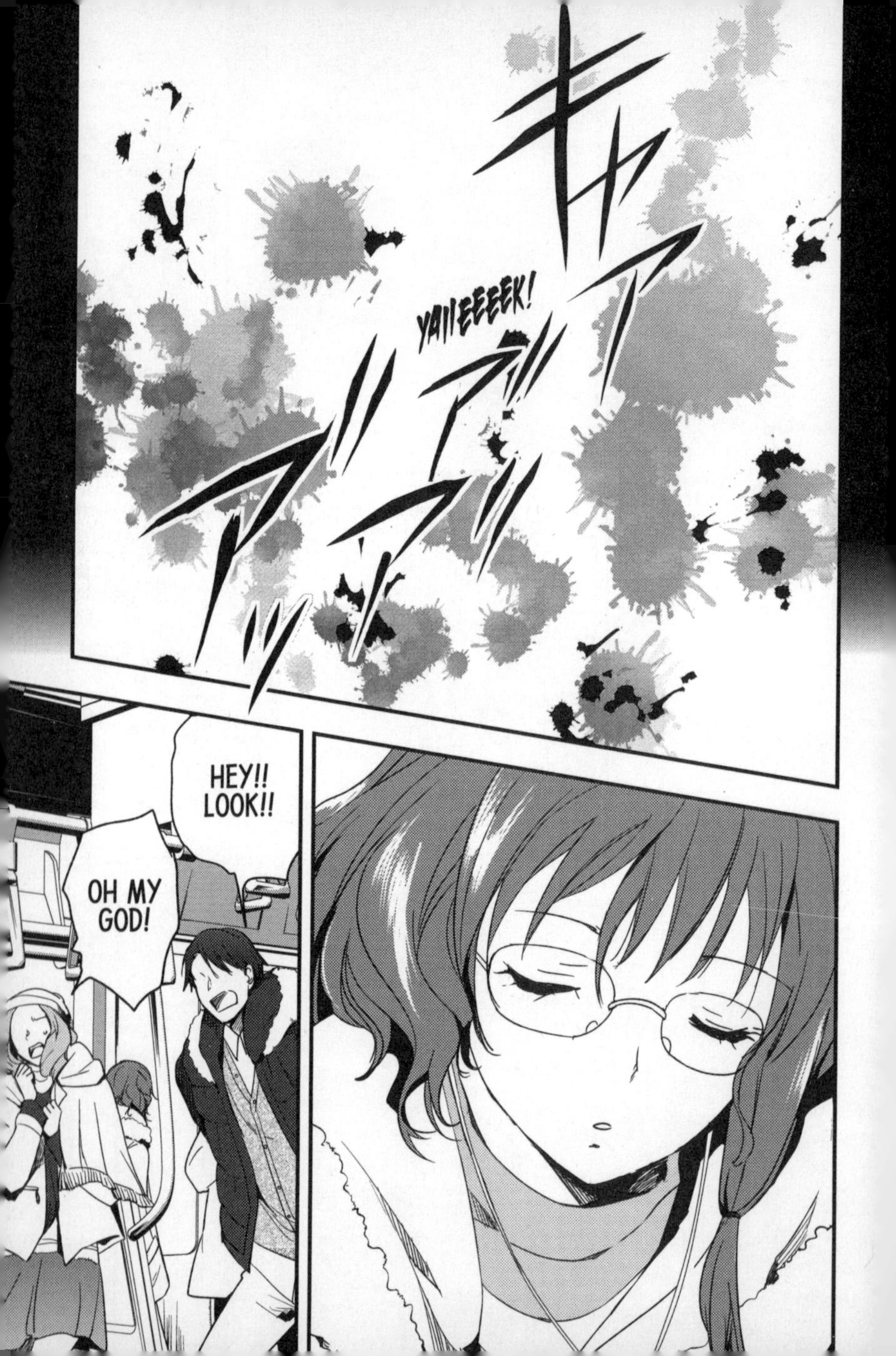
YAIIEEEK!
HEY!! LOOK!!
OH MY GOD!

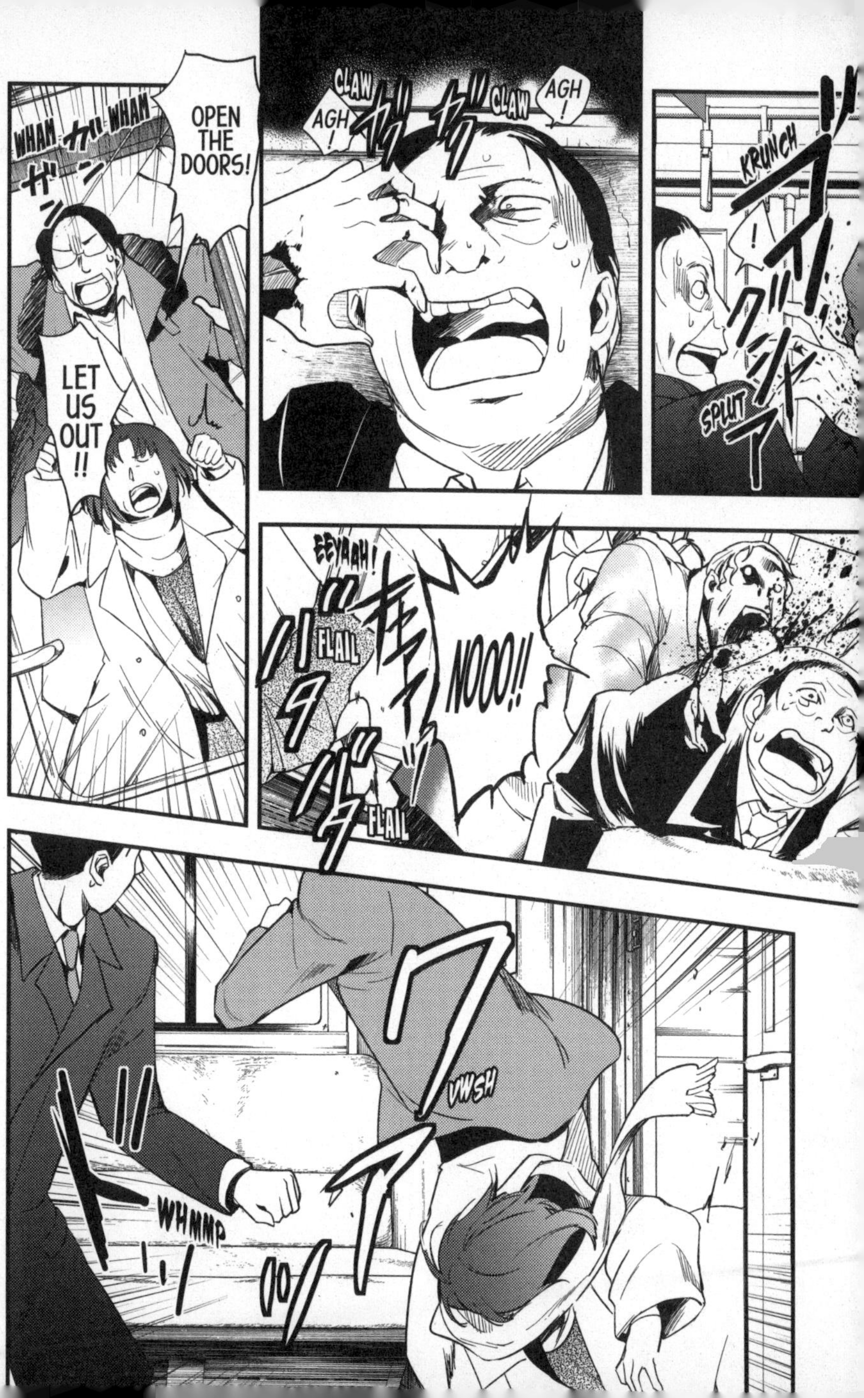
KRUNCH
SPLUT
CLAW
AGH!
CLAW
AGH!
EEYAAH!
FLAIL
NOOO!!
FLAIL
OPEN THE DOORS!
WHAM
WHAM
LET US OUT!!
VWSH
WHMMP

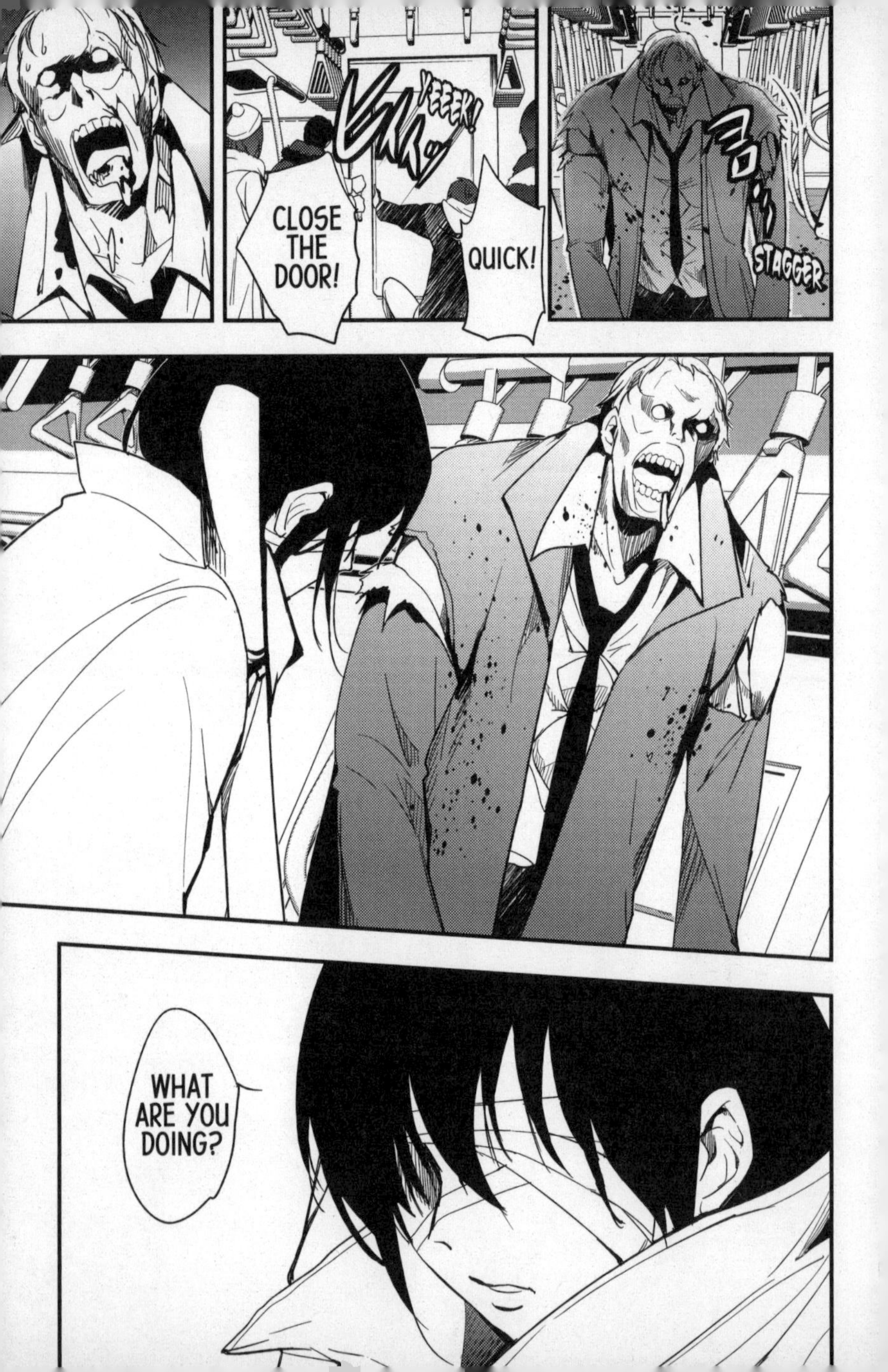
STAGGER
YEEEK!
QUICK!
CLOSE THE DOOR!
WHAT ARE YOU DOING?

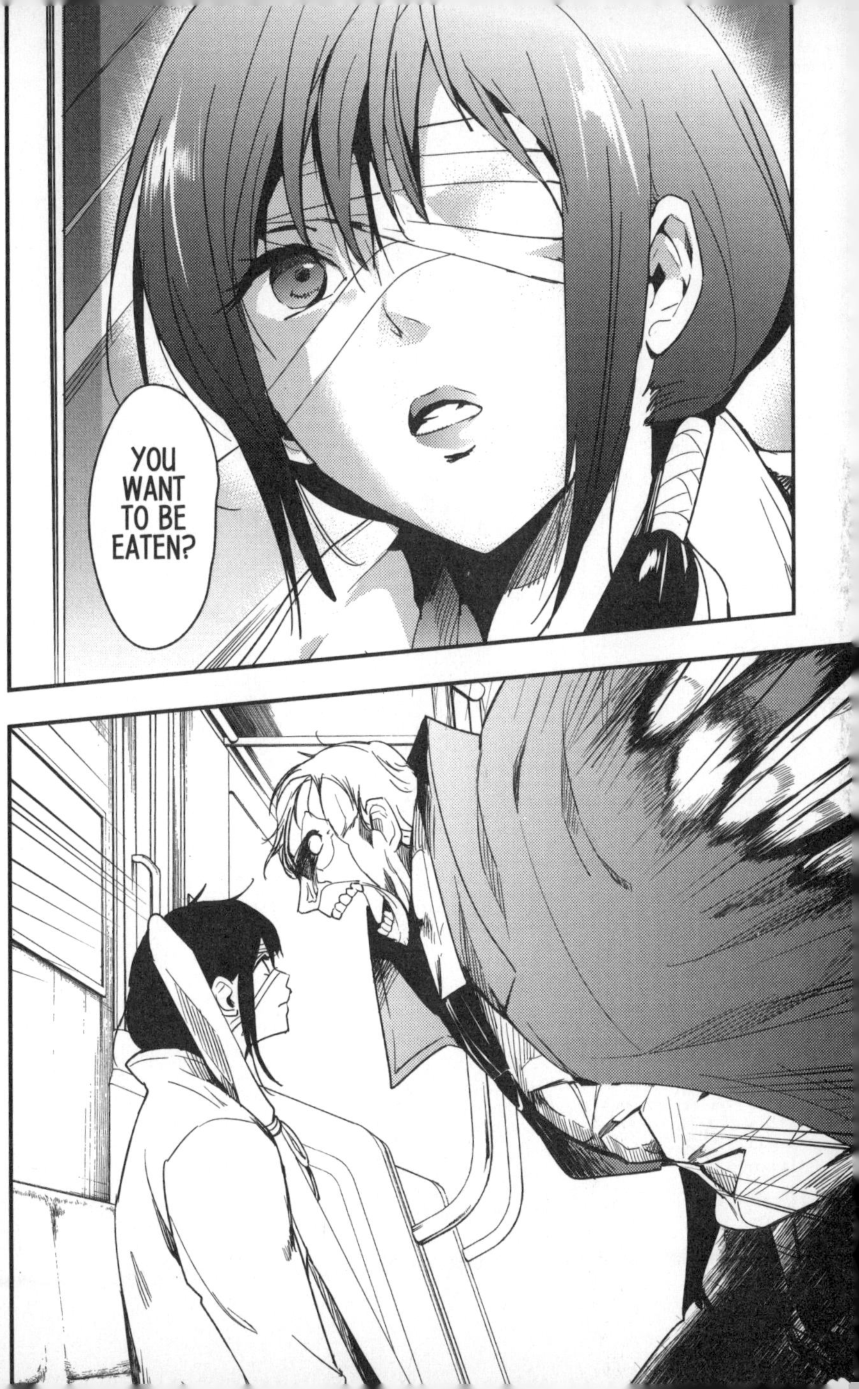
YOU WANT TO BE EATEN?

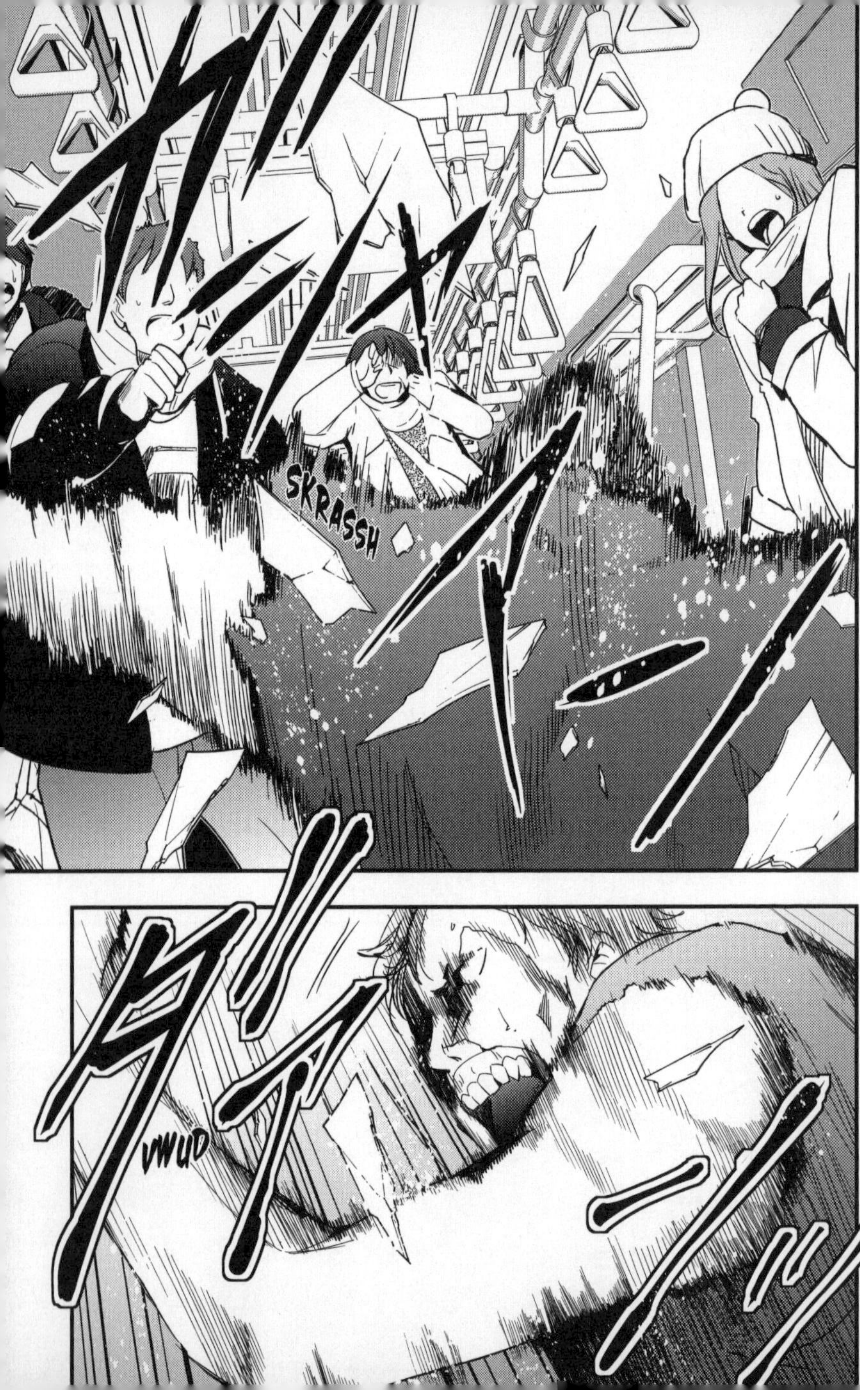
SKRASSH
VWUD

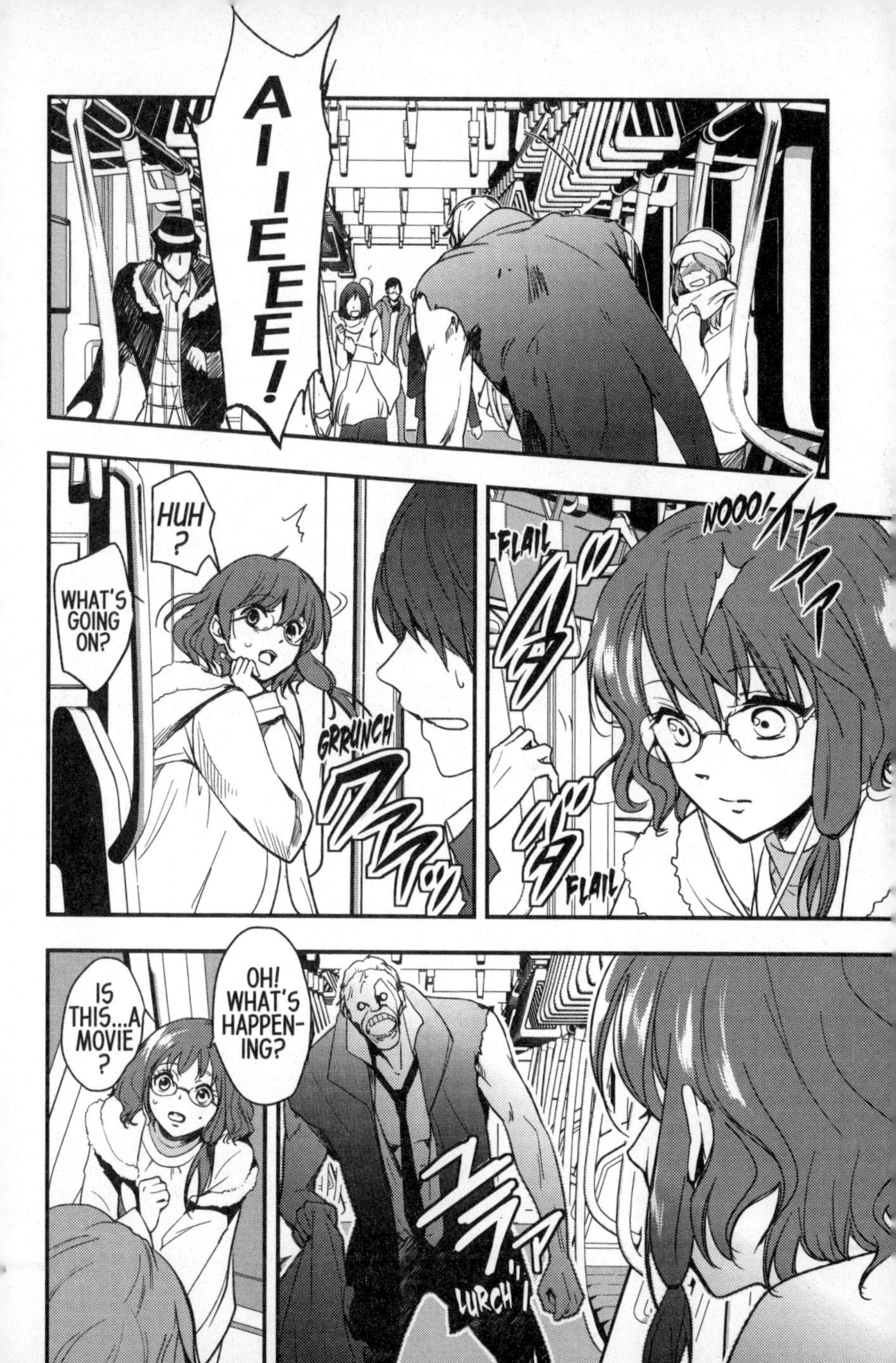
AIIEEEE!
NOOO!
FLAIL
FLAIL
HUH?
WHAT'S GOING ON?
GRRUNCH
OH! WHAT'S HAPPEN-ING?
IS THIS...A MOVIE?
LURCH!

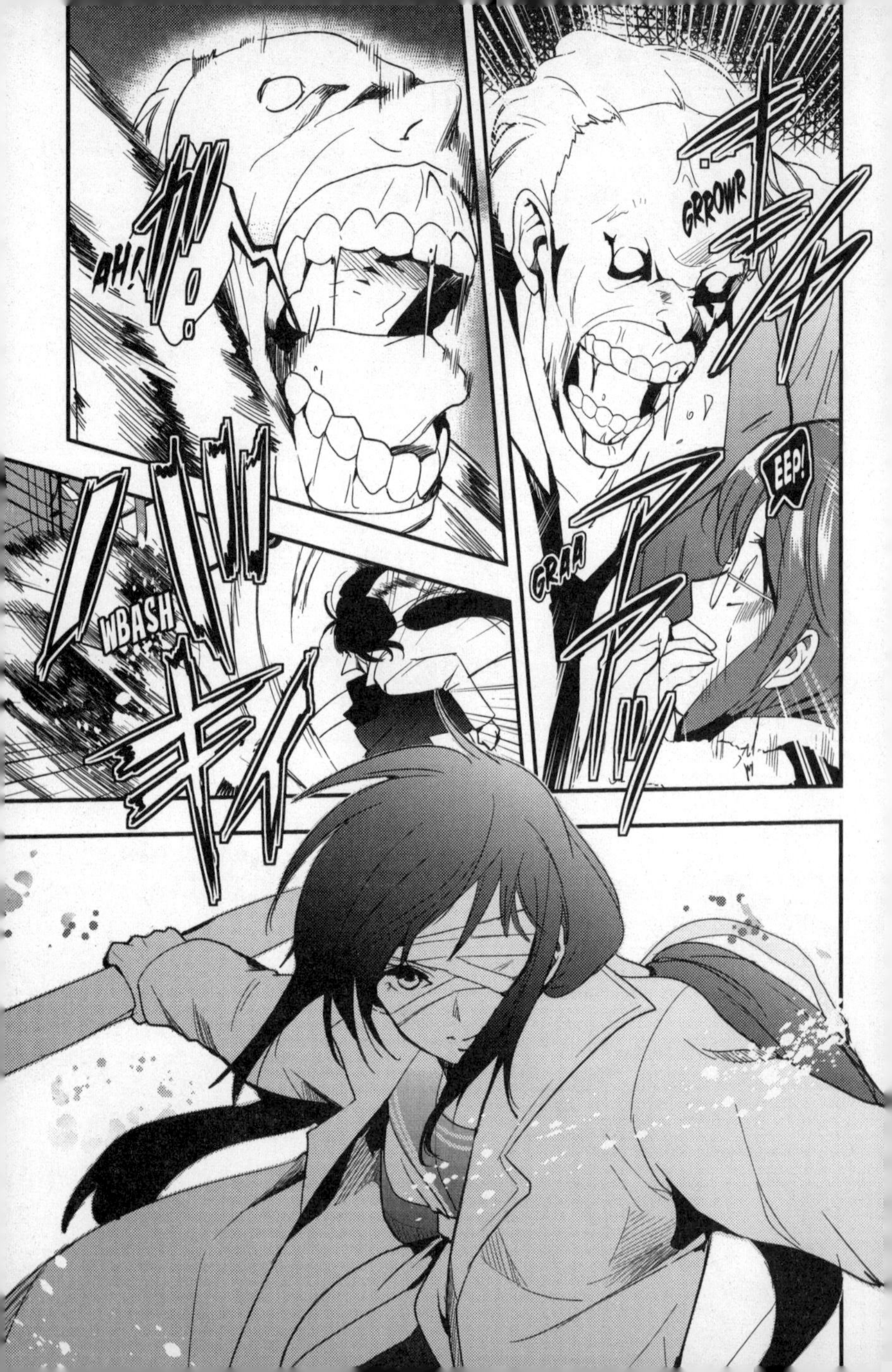
GRROWR
EEP!
GRAA
AH!
WBASH

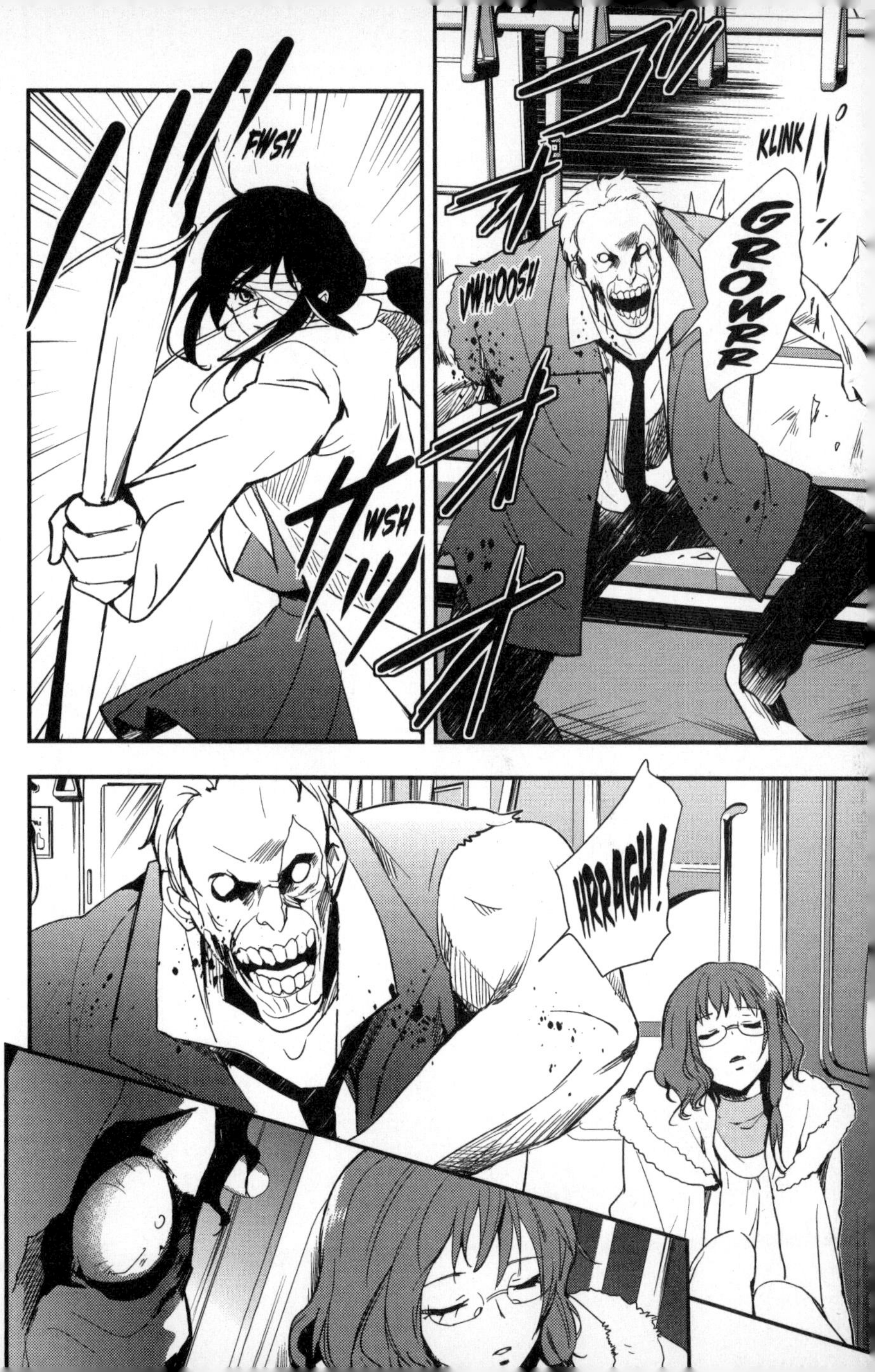
KLINK
GROWRR
VWHOOSH
FWSH
WSH
HRRAGH!

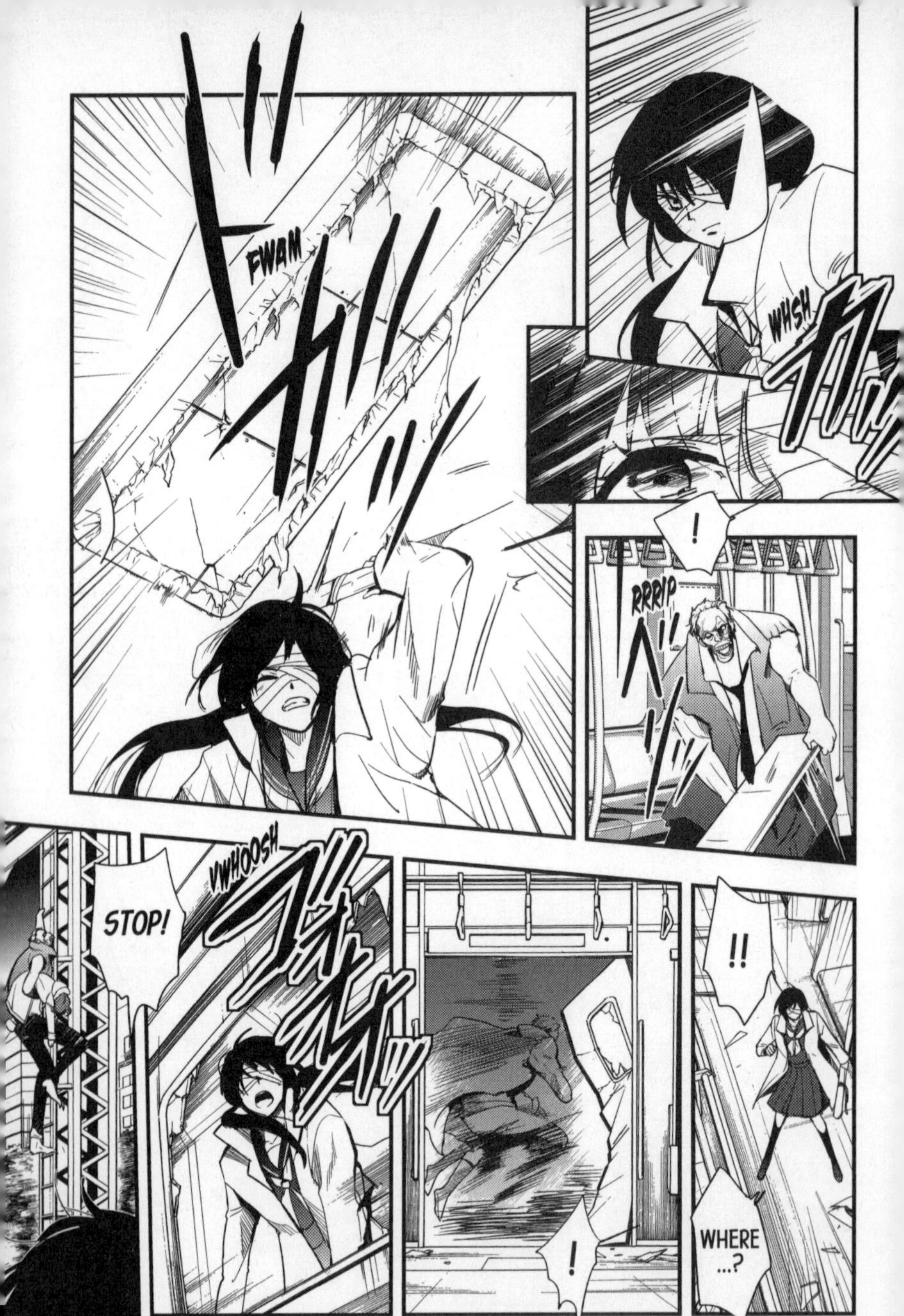
WHSH
!
RRRIP
FWAM
!!
WHERE ...?
!
VWHOOSH
STOP!

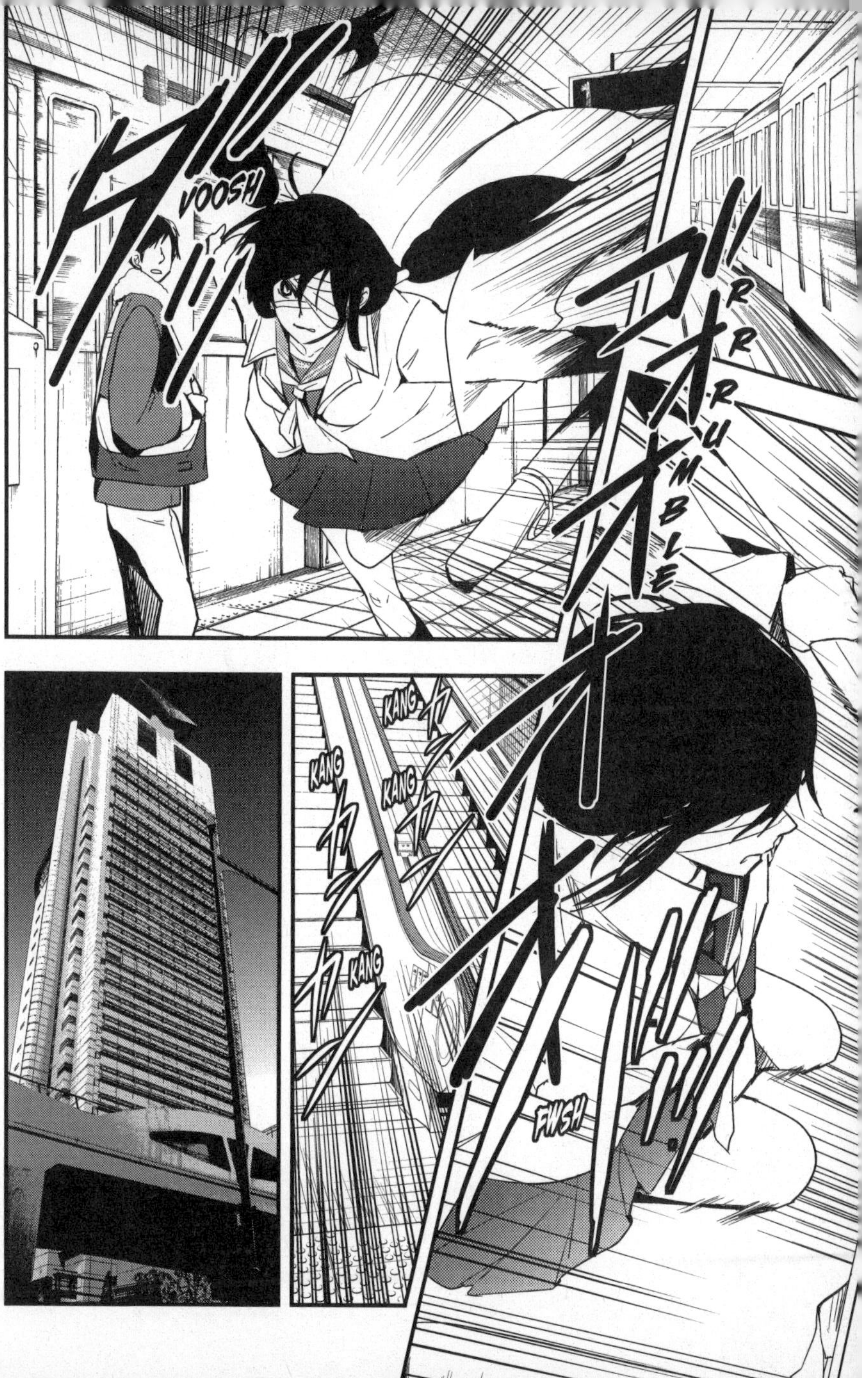
VOOSH
RRRUMBLE
KANG
KANG
KANG
KANG
FWSH

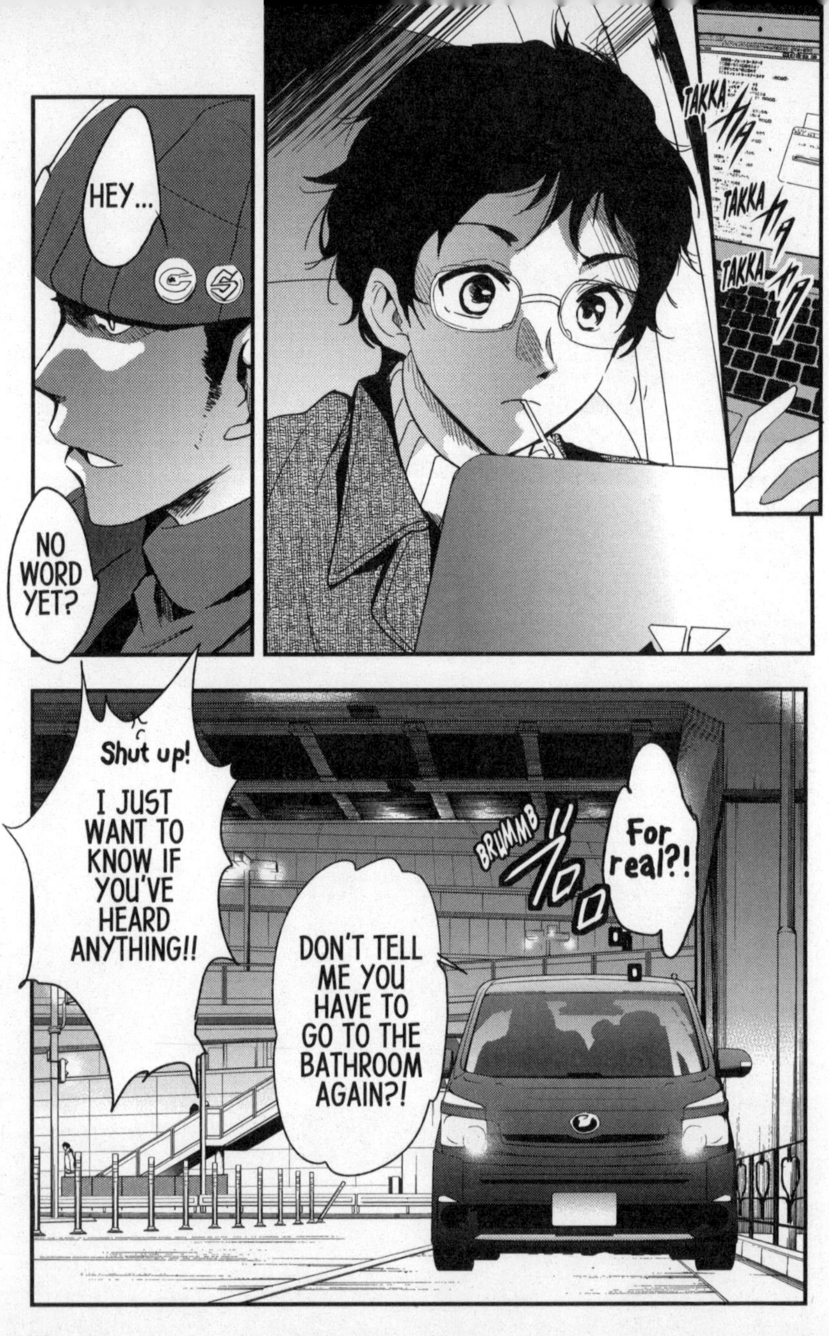
TAKKA
TAKKA
TAKKA
HEY...
NO WORD YET?
For real?!
BRUMMB
DON'T TELL ME YOU HAVE TO GO TO THE BATHROOM AGAIN?!
Shut up!
I JUST WANT TO KNOW IF YOU'VE HEARD ANYTHING!!

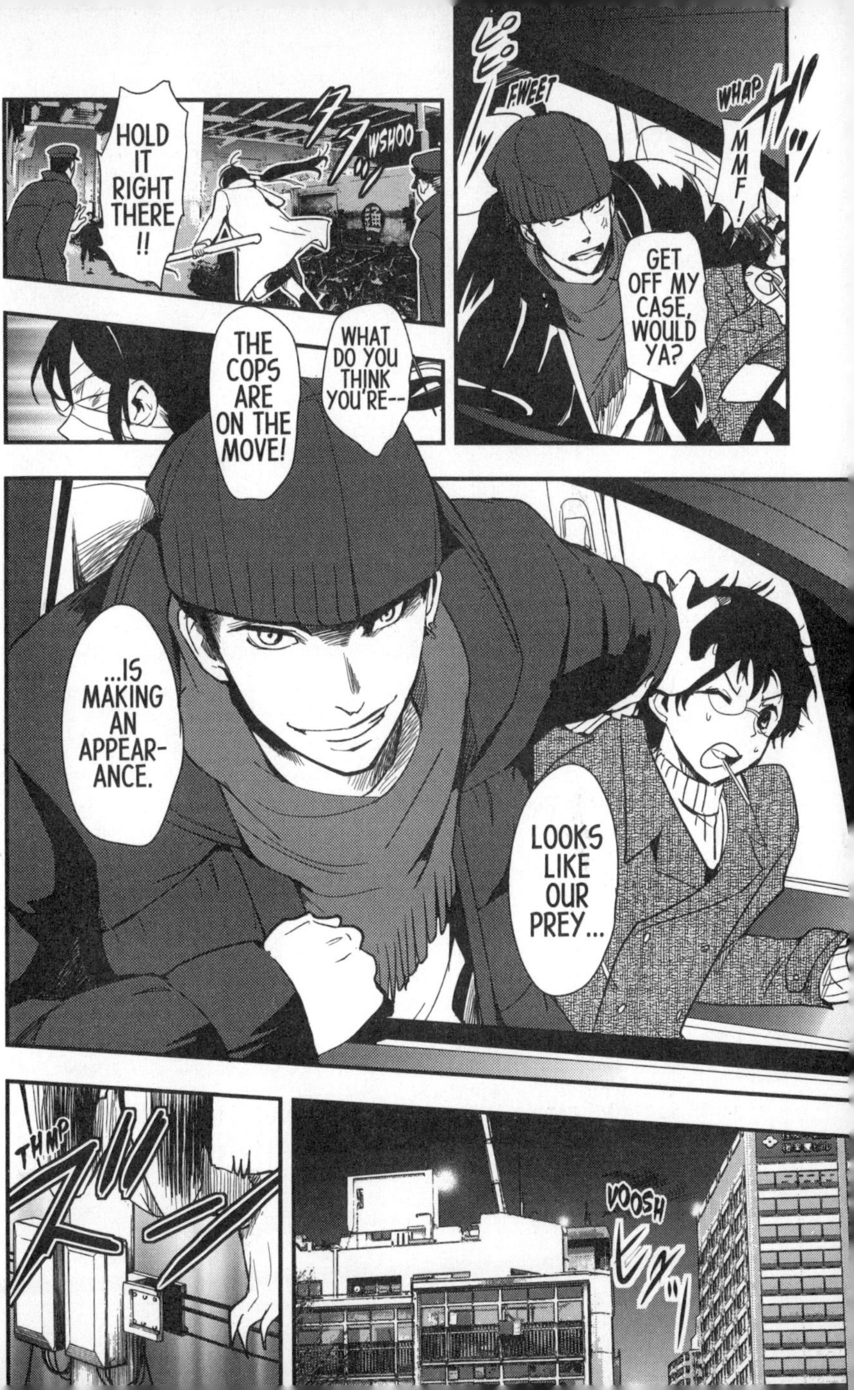
FWEET
WHAP
MMF!
GET OFF MY CASE, WOULD YA?
HOLD IT RIGHT THERE!!
WSHOO
WHAT DO YOU THINK YOU'RE--
THE COPS ARE ON THE MOVE!
LOOKS LIKE OUR PREY...
...IS MAKING AN APPEARANCE.
VOOSH
THMP

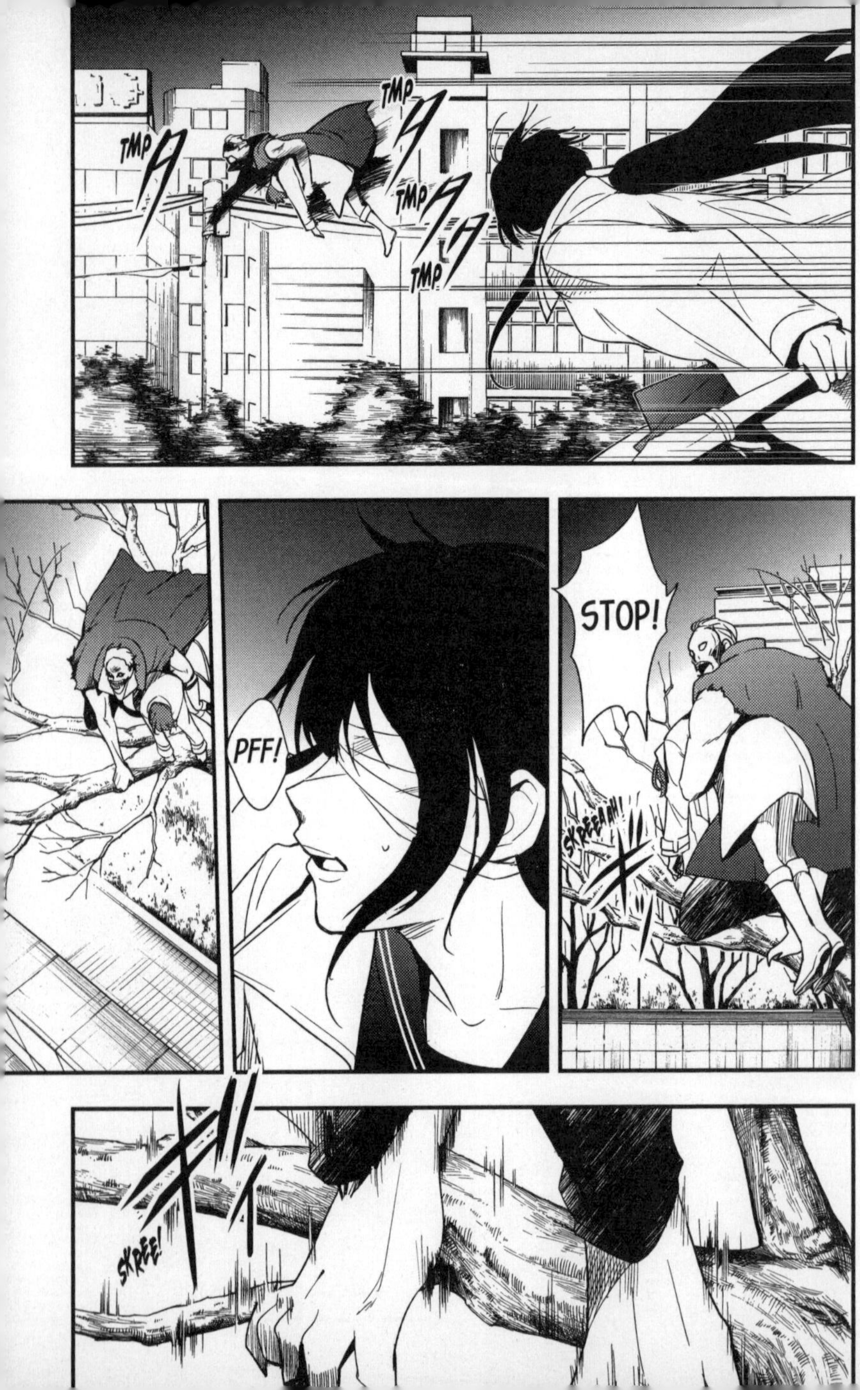
TMP
TMP
TMP
TMP
STOP!
SKREEAAH!
PFF!
SKREE!

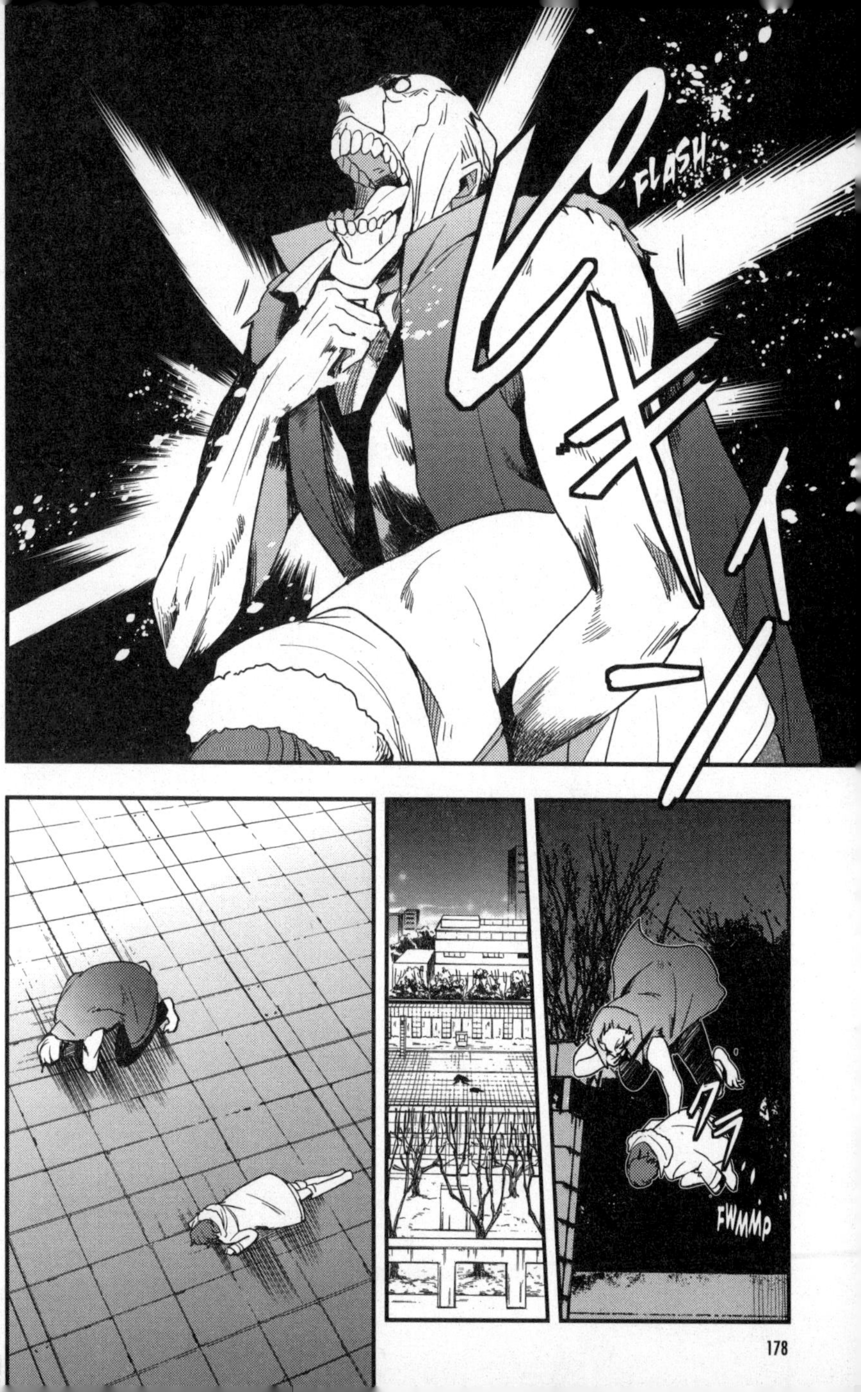
FLASH
FWMMP

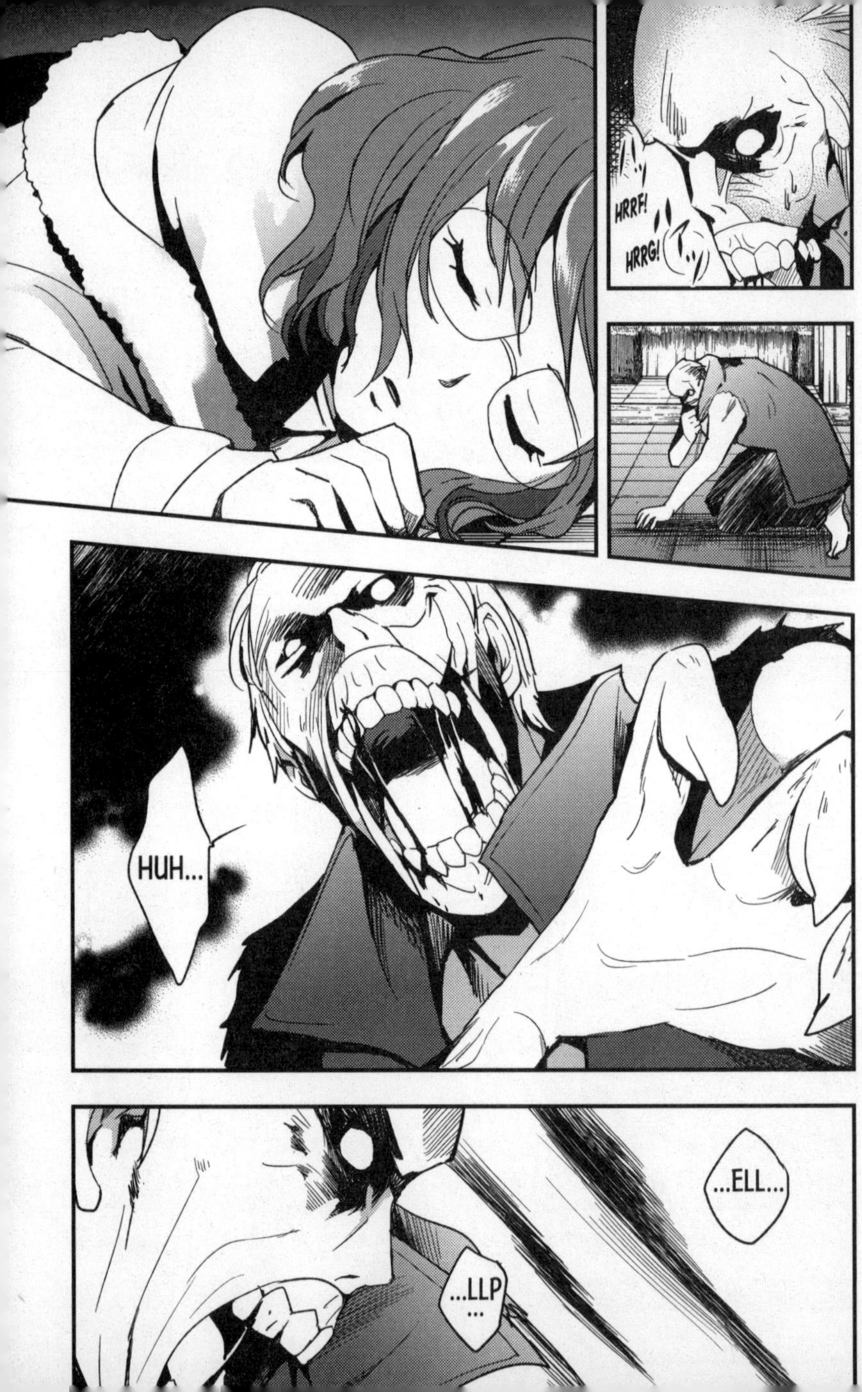
HRRF!
HRRG!
HUH...
...ELL...
...LLP
...

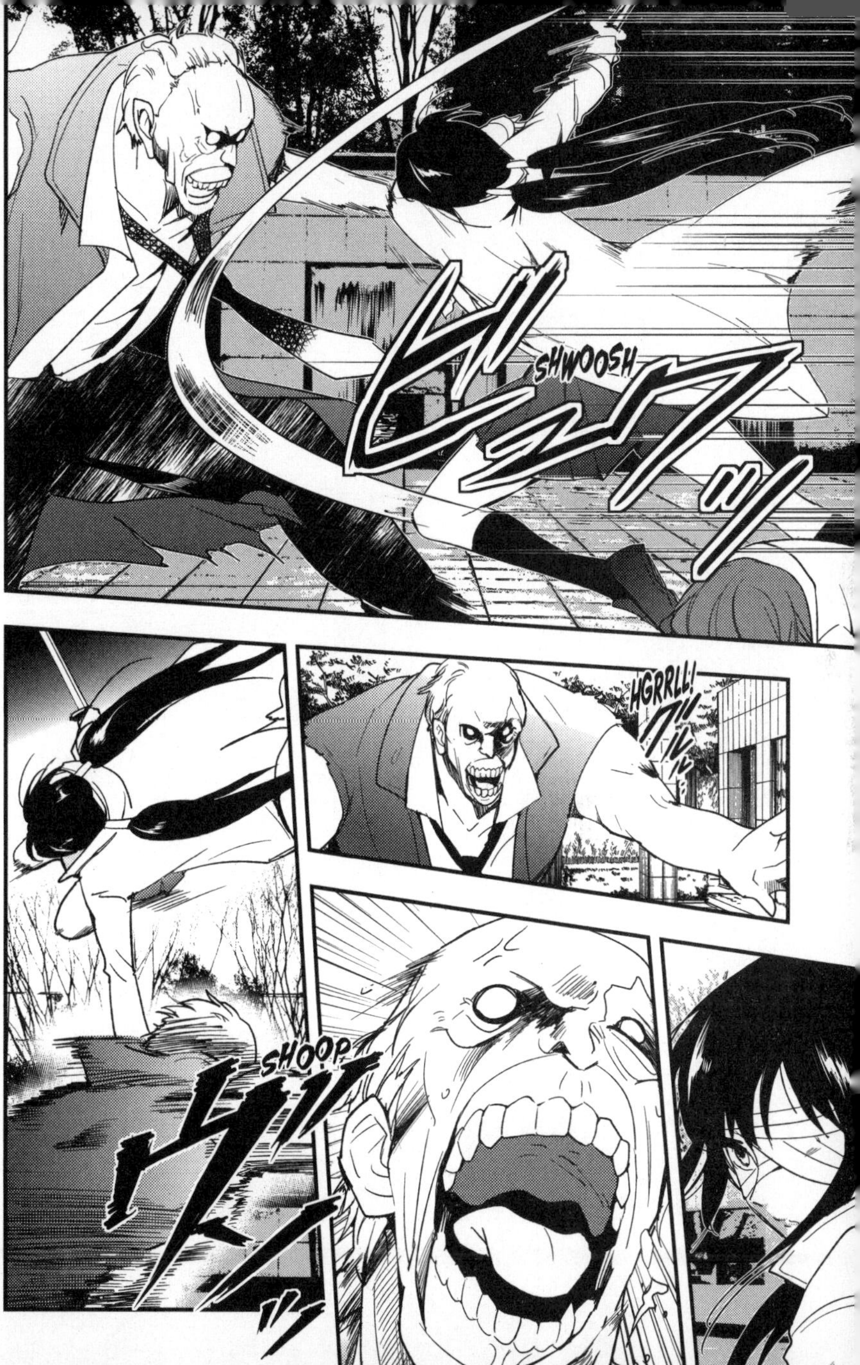
SHWOOSH
HGRRLL!
SHOOP

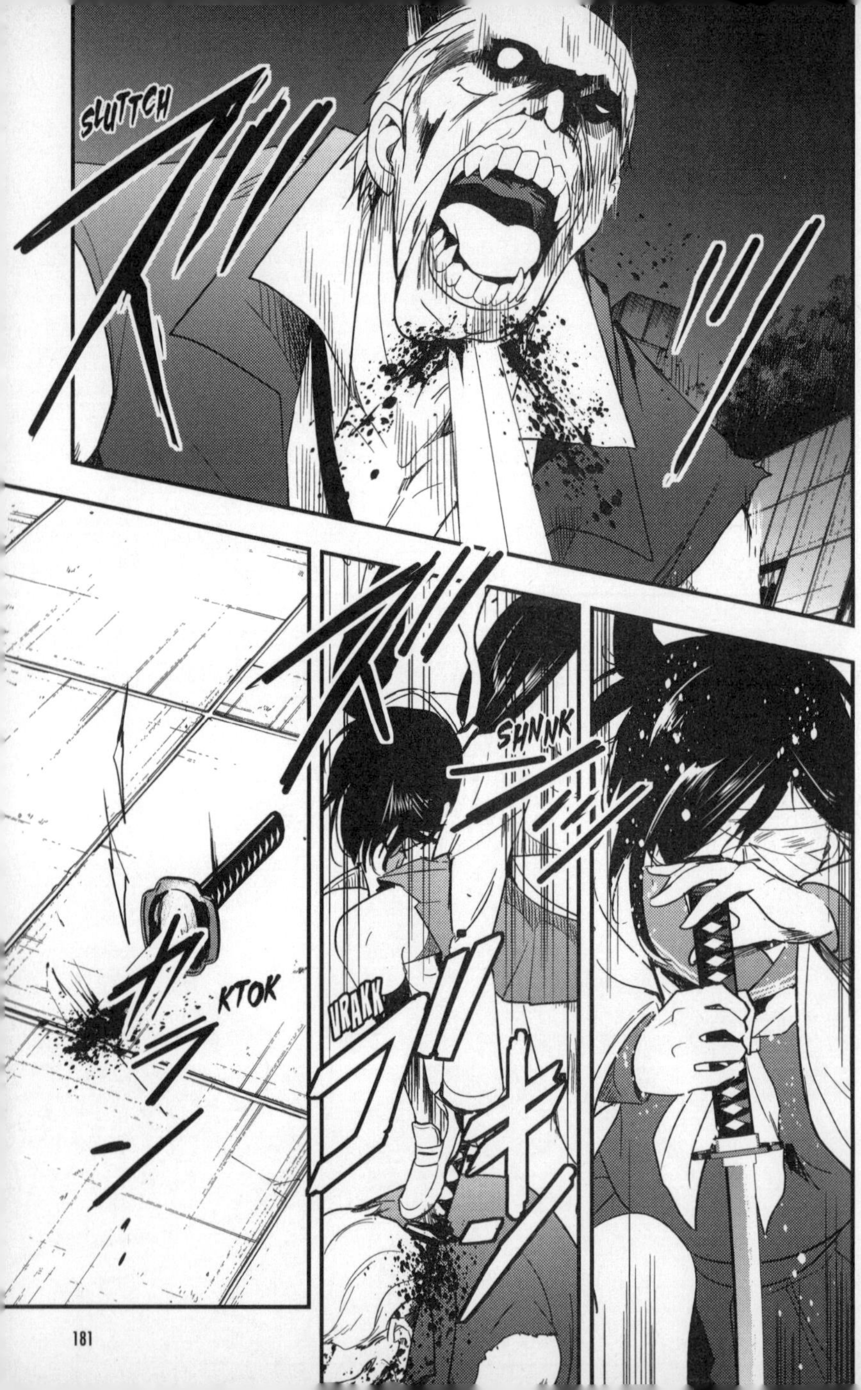
SLUTTCH
SHNNK
URAKK
KTOK

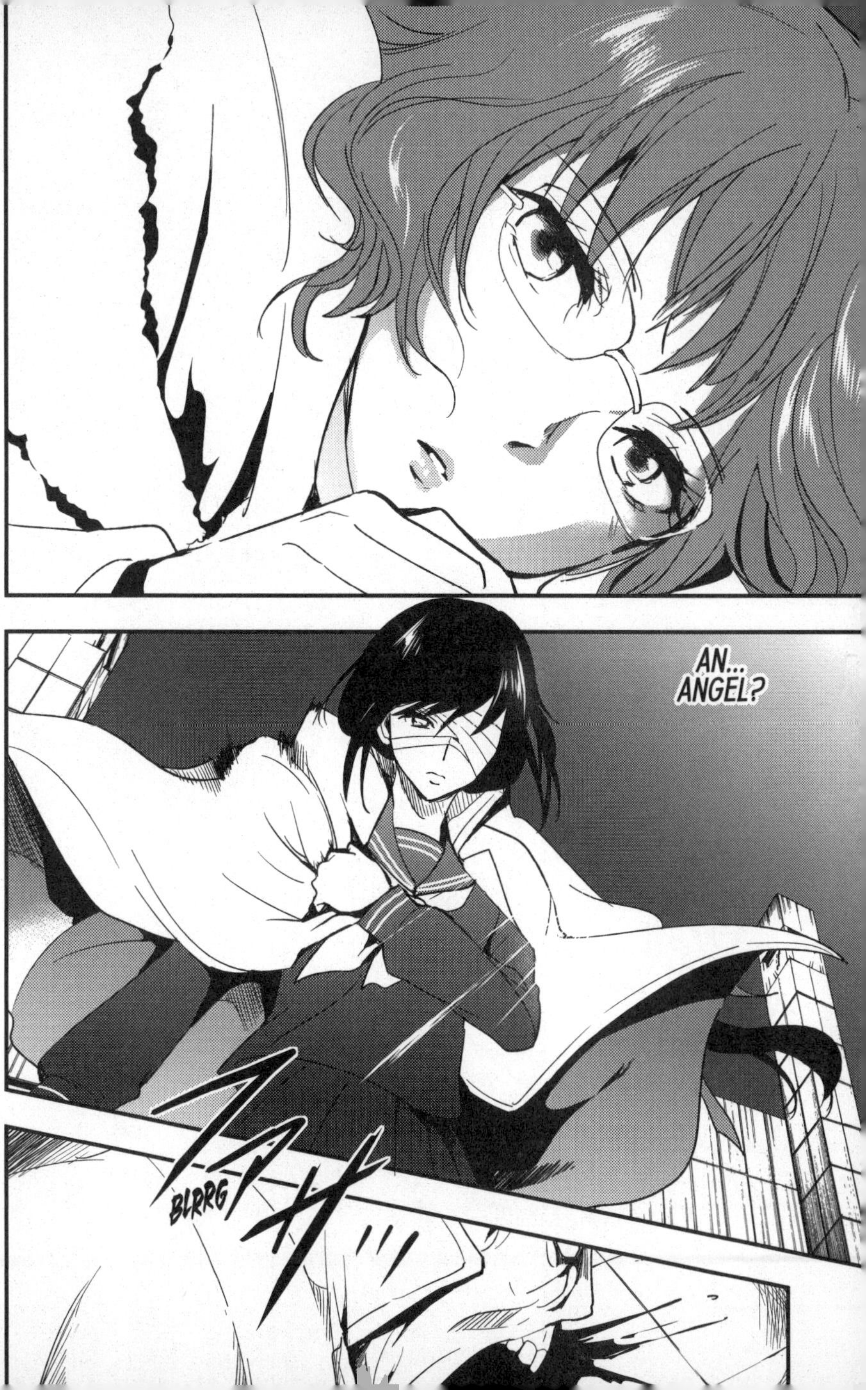
AN... ANGEL?
BLRRG

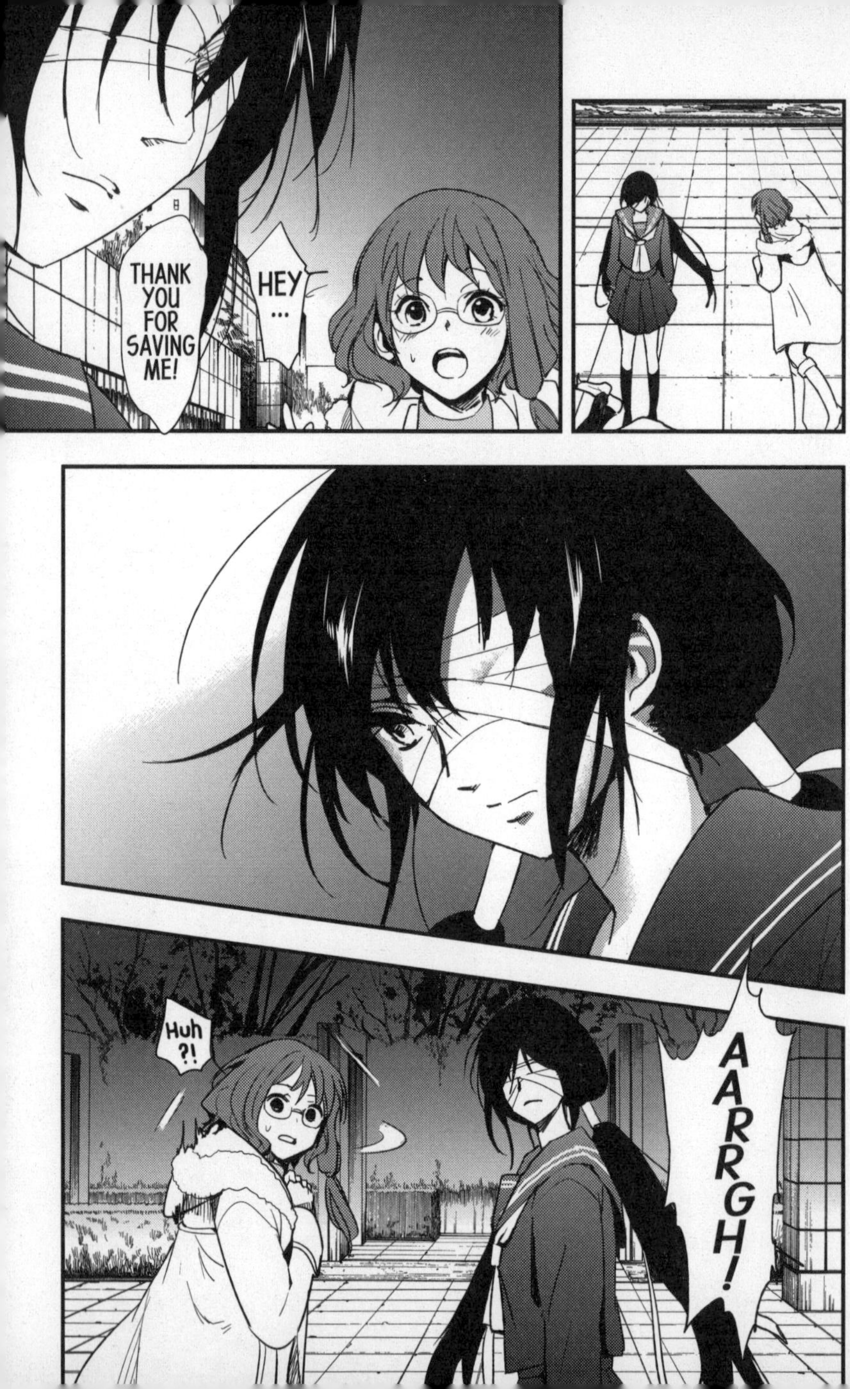
HEY ...
THANK YOU FOR SAVING ME!
AARRGH!
Huh ?!

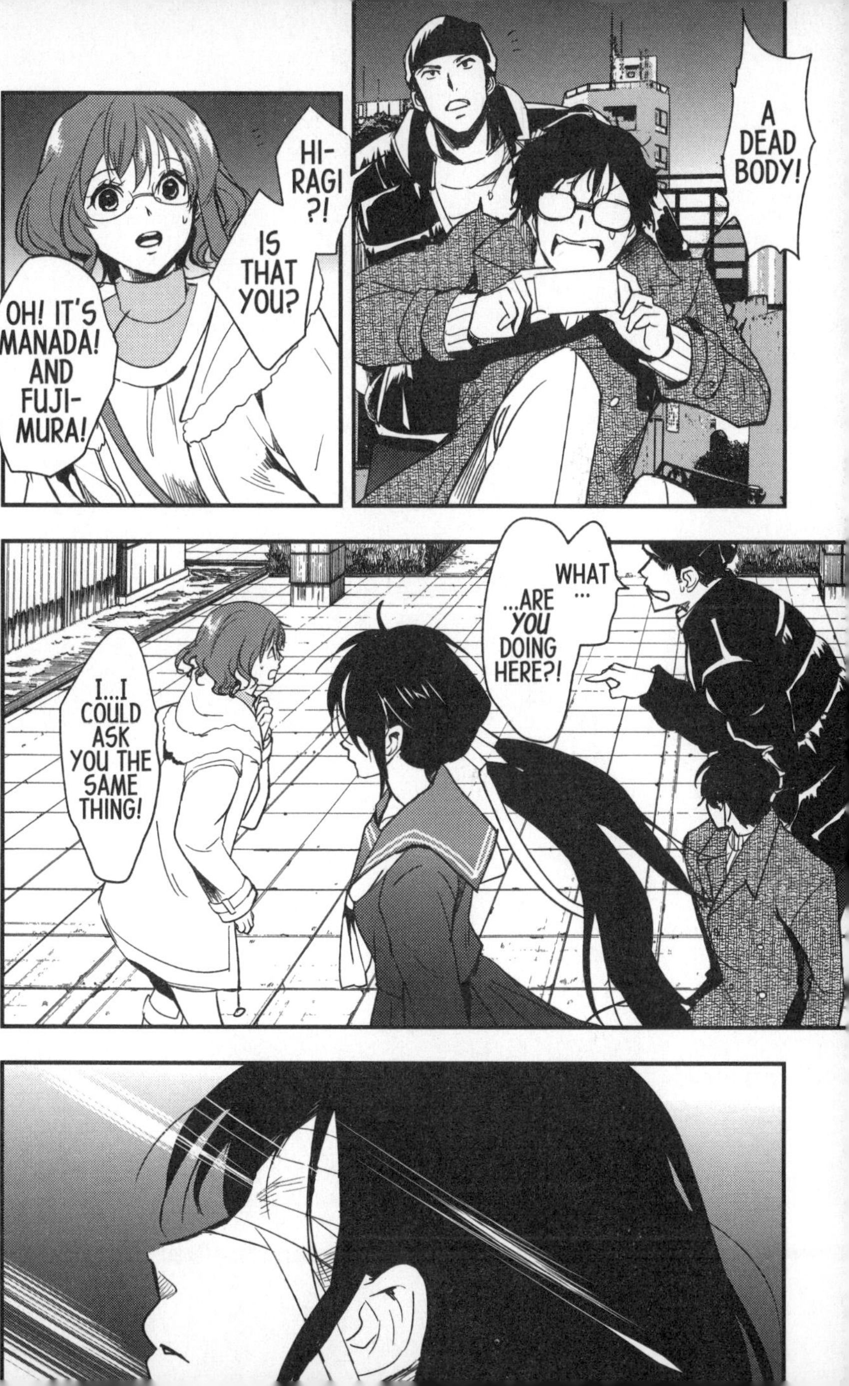
A DEAD BODY!
HI-RAGI?!
IS THAT YOU?
OH! IT'S MANADA! AND FUJI-MURA!
WHAT ...
...ARE *YOU* DOING HERE?!
I...I COULD ASK YOU THE SAME THING!

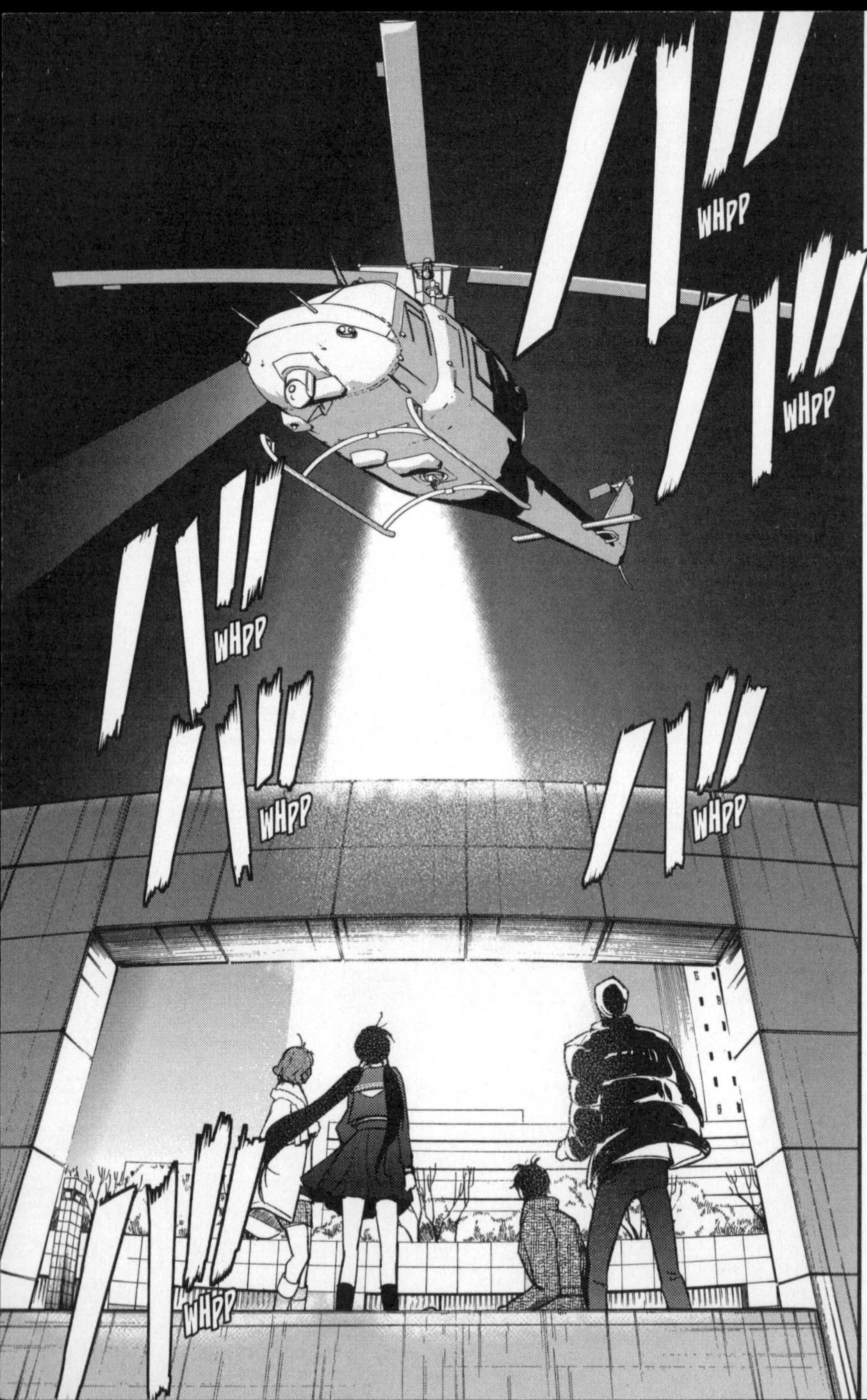
WHPP
WHPP
WHPP
WHPP
WHPP
WHPP

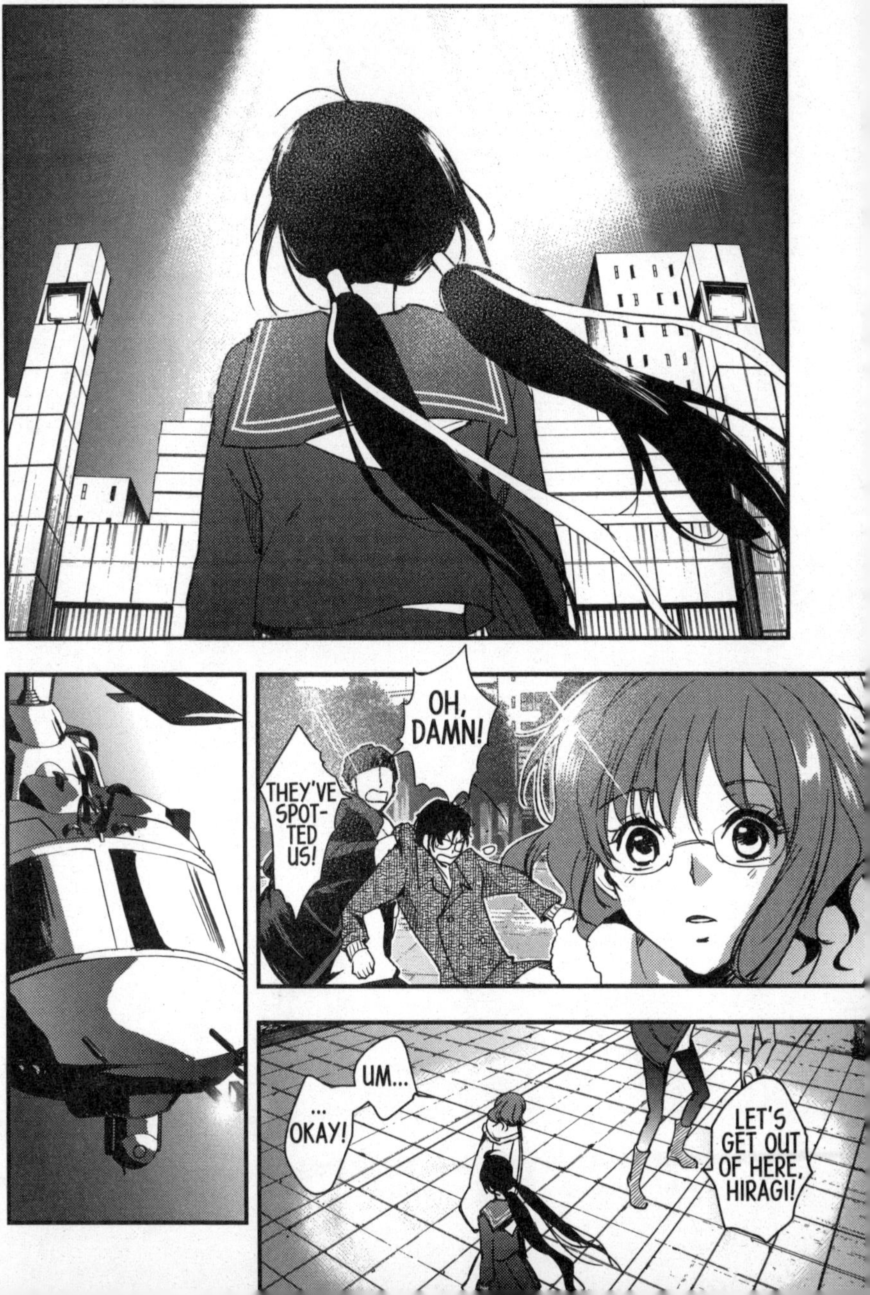
OH, DAMN!
THEY'VE SPOTTED US!
LET'S GET OUT OF HERE, HIRAGI!
UM...
...OKAY!

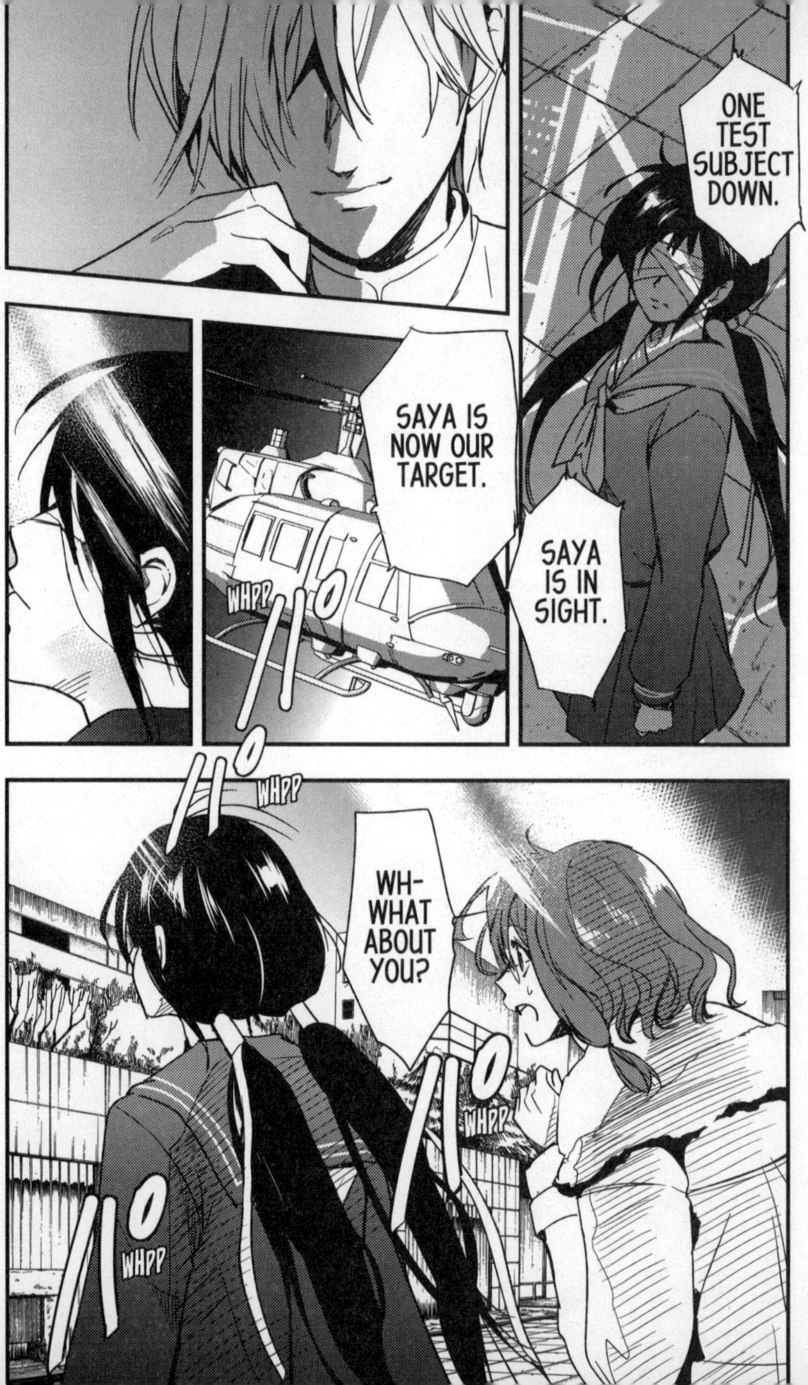
ONE TEST SUBJECT DOWN.
SAYA IS IN SIGHT.
SAYA IS NOW OUR TARGET.
WHPP
WHPP
WH- WHAT ABOUT YOU?
WHPP
WHPP

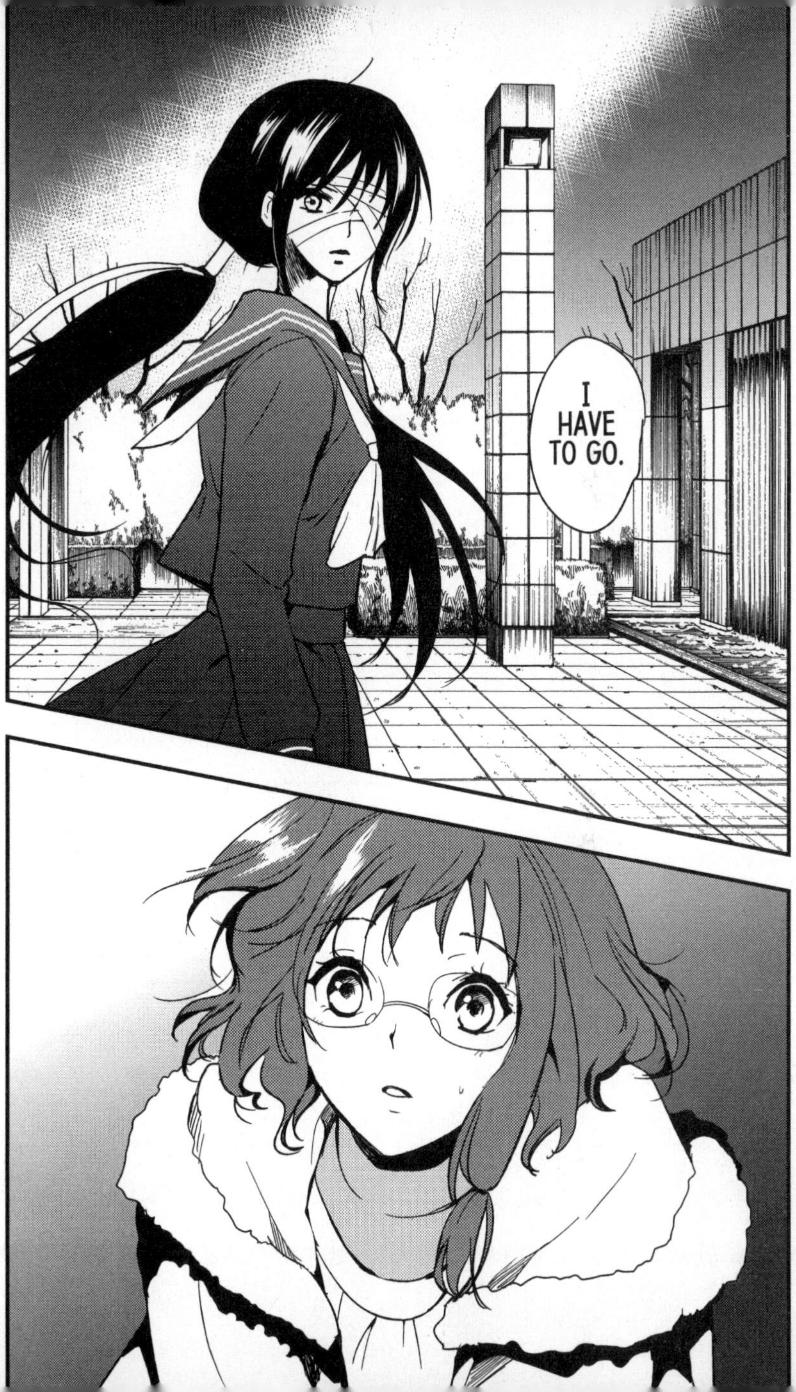
I HAVE TO GO.

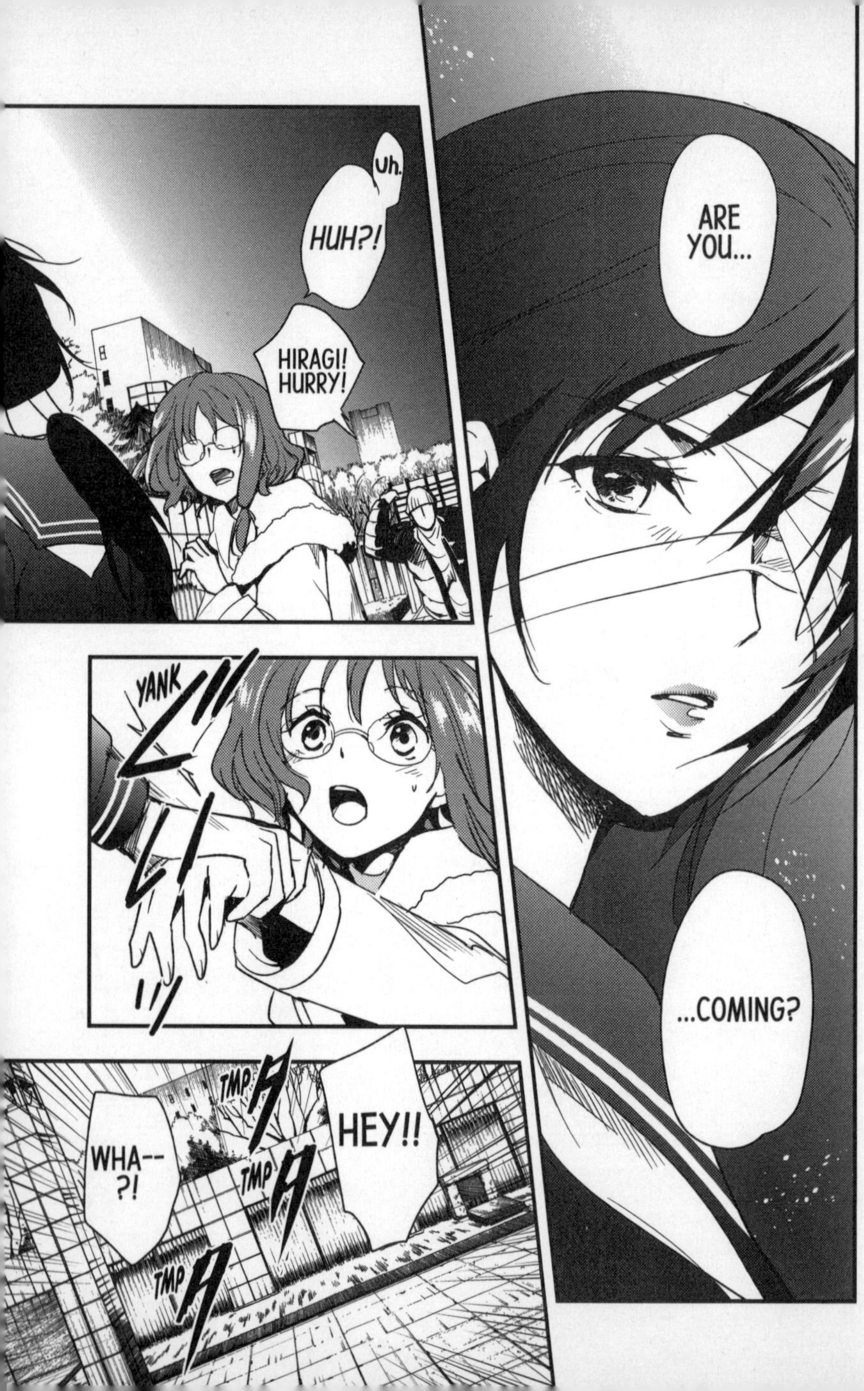
ARE YOU...
...COMING?
Uh.
HUH?!
HIRAGI! HURRY!
YANK
HEY!!
TMP
TMP
TMP
WHA-- ?!

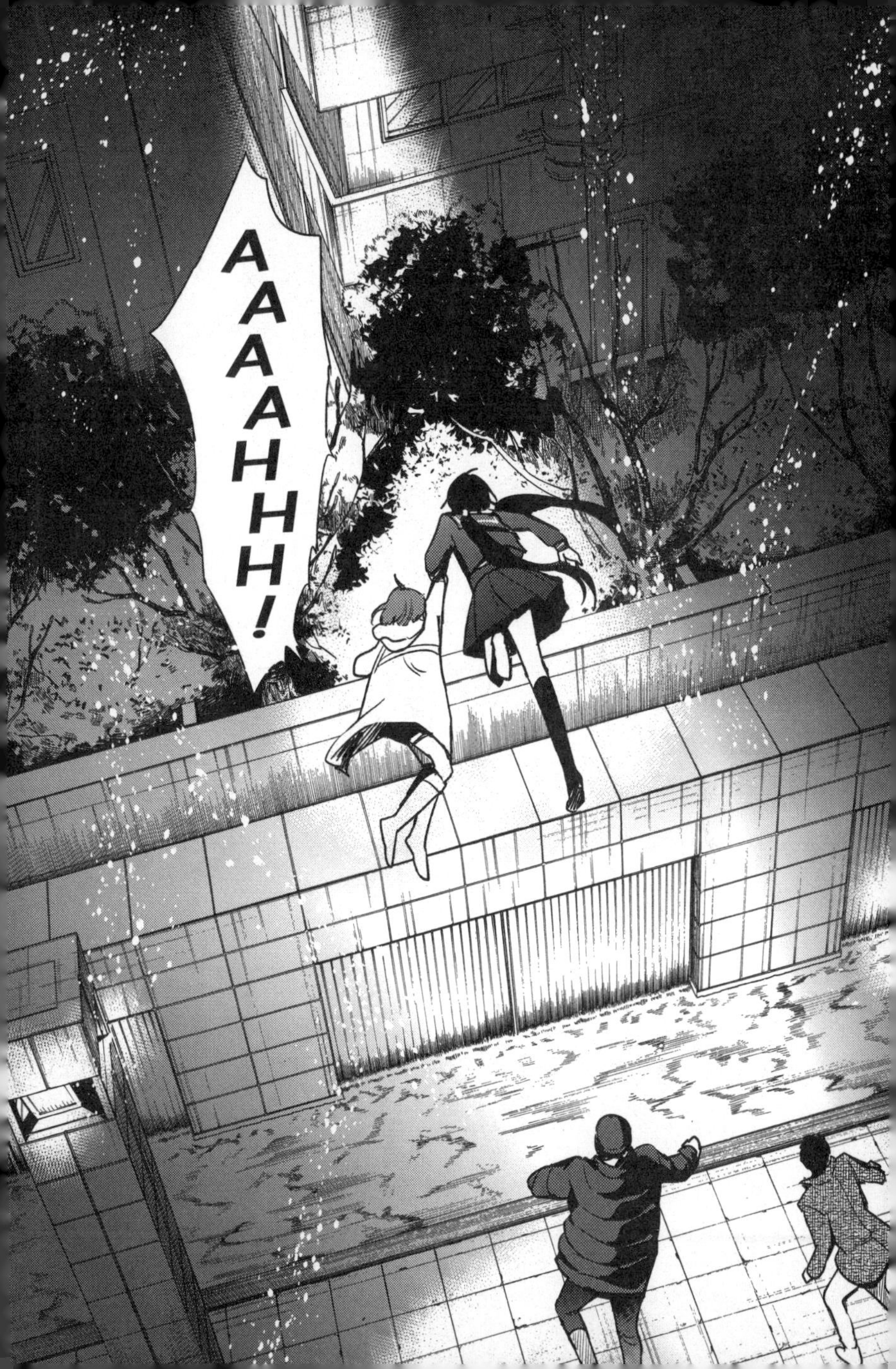
AAAAHHH!

BLOOD·C

publisher
MIKE RICHARDSON

editor
PHILIP R. SIMON

assistant editor
EVERETT PATTERSON

collection designer
ADAM GRANO

digital production
CHRIS HORN

Special thanks to Michael Gombos, Annie Gullion, and Carl Gustav Horn.

BLOOD-C Volume 3
© Ranmaru Kotone 2012
© 2011 Production I.G, CLAMP/Project BLOOD-C TV/MBS
Edited by Kadokawa Shoten
First published in Japan in 2012 by KADOKAWA CORPORATION, Tokyo. English translation rights arranged with
KADOKAWA CORPORATION, Tokyo, through TOHAN CORPORATION, Tokyo. Dark Horse Manga™ is a trademark of Dark
Horse Comics, Inc. All rights reserved. This English-language edition © 2014 by Dark Horse Comics, Inc. All other material
© 2014 by Dark Horse Comics, Inc. All rights reserved. No portion of this publication may be reproduced or transmitted,
in any form or by any means, without the express written permission of the copyright holders. Names, characters, places,
and incidents featured in this publication either are the product of the author's imagination or are used fictitiously. Any
resemblance to actual persons (living or dead), events, institutions, or locales, without satiric intent, is coincidental.

Dark Horse Manga, a division of Dark Horse Comics, Inc.
10956 SE Main Street, Milwaukie, OR 97222
DarkHorse.com

To find a comics shop in your area, call the Comic Shop Locator Service toll-free at 1-888-266-4226.

First edition: February 2014
ISBN 978-1-61655-314-2

1 3 5 7 9 10 8 6 4 2

Printed in the United States of America

GATE 7
ゲート セブン

BRAND NEW FROM CLAMP—COMING TO THE U.S. JUST MONTHS AFTER JAPAN!

An innocent sightseeing trip to a legendary shrine opens up a magical realm to shy high schooler Chikahito Takamoto! Chikahito finds himself in the mystical world of Hana and her comrades, and his immunity to their powers leads them to believe he's no ordinary, awkward teenager! Protecting our world from violent elemental beasts, Hana and her team welcome the confused and cautious Chikahito—who isn't quite sure that he wants to be caught in the middle of their war!

Volume One
ISBN 978-1-59582-806-4

Volume Two
ISBN 978-1-59582-807-1

Volume Three
ISBN 978-1-59582-902-3
Coming in June

$10.99 each

written by RYO IKEHATA | illustrations by CHIZU HASHII

BLOOD+

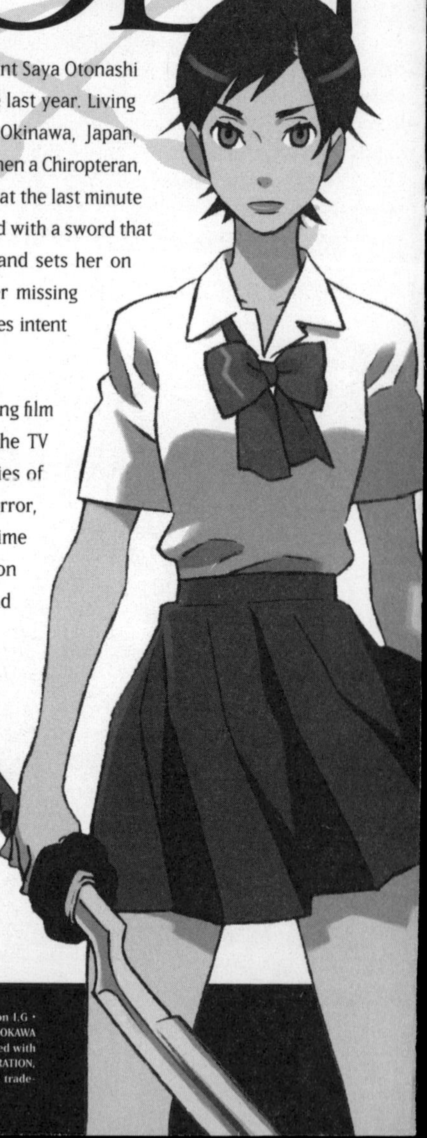

Suffering from extreme amnesia, high school student Saya Otonashi can't remember anything from her life beyond the last year. Living with a foster family outside a military base in Okinawa, Japan, Saya's attempts to live a normal life are shattered when a Chiropteran, a horrific vampire-like monster, attacks her. Saved at the last minute by a mysterious man named Hagi, Saya is presented with a sword that awakens in her a warrior's skills and bloodlust, and sets her on a course that will lead her to the answers of her missing memories, and into battle against a race of creatures intent on destroying the world.

The epic adventure that began in the groundbreaking film *Blood: the Last Vampire* and continues through the TV series *Blood+* is brought to life in this all-new series of novels adapting the hit show. Saya's journey of horror, magic, romance, and mystery will stretch across time and around the globe, expanding on the television series with new characters, new adventures, and breathtaking action.

Each novel features all new exclusive illustrations by animated series character designer Chizu Hashii!

VOLUME 1: FIRST KISS
ISBN 978-1-59307-898-0

VOLUME 2: CHEVALIER
ISBN 978-1-59307-931-4

VOLUME 3: BOY MEETS GIRL
ISBN 978-1-59307-932-1

VOLUME 4: NANKURUNAISA
ISBN 978-1-59307-933-8

$8.99 EACH

DARK HORSE BOOKS

ASUKA KAT

BL

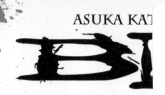

A companion series to the popular *Blood+* anime hit, Asuka Katsura's official, five-volume manga adaptation delivers moments of jarring violence and nonstop action in a tale that spans several centuries. Kumiko Suekane's two-volume *Blood+ Adagio* manga series explores Saya's struggles at the eve of the Russian Revolution, and Hirotaka Kisaragi's *Blood+ Kowloon Nights* one-shot finds Hagi on a solo adventure in modern-day Hong Kong! These eight manga volumes overflow with mystery, bloodletting, Chiropterans, unique heroes, and tenacious villains! Look for *Blood* and *Blood+* novels—also released by Dark Horse!

MANGA VOLUME 1
ISBN 978-1-59307-880-5
$10.99

MANGA VOLUME 2
ISBN 978-1-59307-935-2
$10.99

MANGA VOLUME 3
ISBN 978-1-59307-936-9
$10.99

MANGA VOLUME 4
ISBN 978-1-59582-194-2
$10.99

MANGA VOLUME 5
ISBN 978-1-59582-241-3
$10.99

BLOOD+ ADAGIO
VOLUME ONE
ISBN 978-1-59582-276-5
$10.99
VOLUME TWO
ISBN 978-1-59582-277-2
$10.99

BLOOD+ KOWLOON NIGHTS
ISBN 978-1-59582-444-8
$9.99

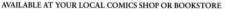

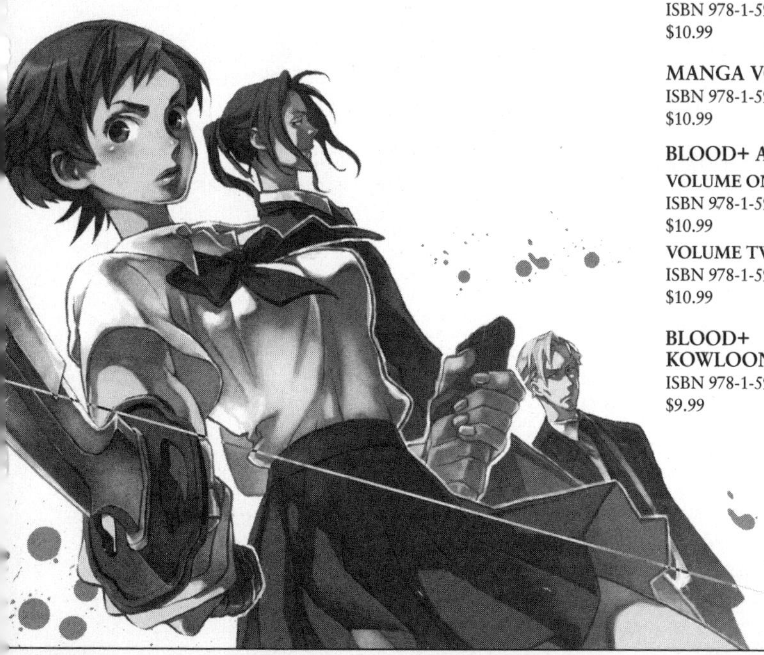

AVAILABLE AT YOUR LOCAL COMICS SHOP OR BOOKSTORE
To find a comics shop in your area, call 1.888.266.4226. For more information or to order direct: •On the web: darkhorse.com •E-mail: mailorder@darkhorse.com •Phone: 1.800.862.0052 Mon.–Fri. 9 AM to 5 PM Pacific Time.

DARK HORSE MANGA
darkhorse.com